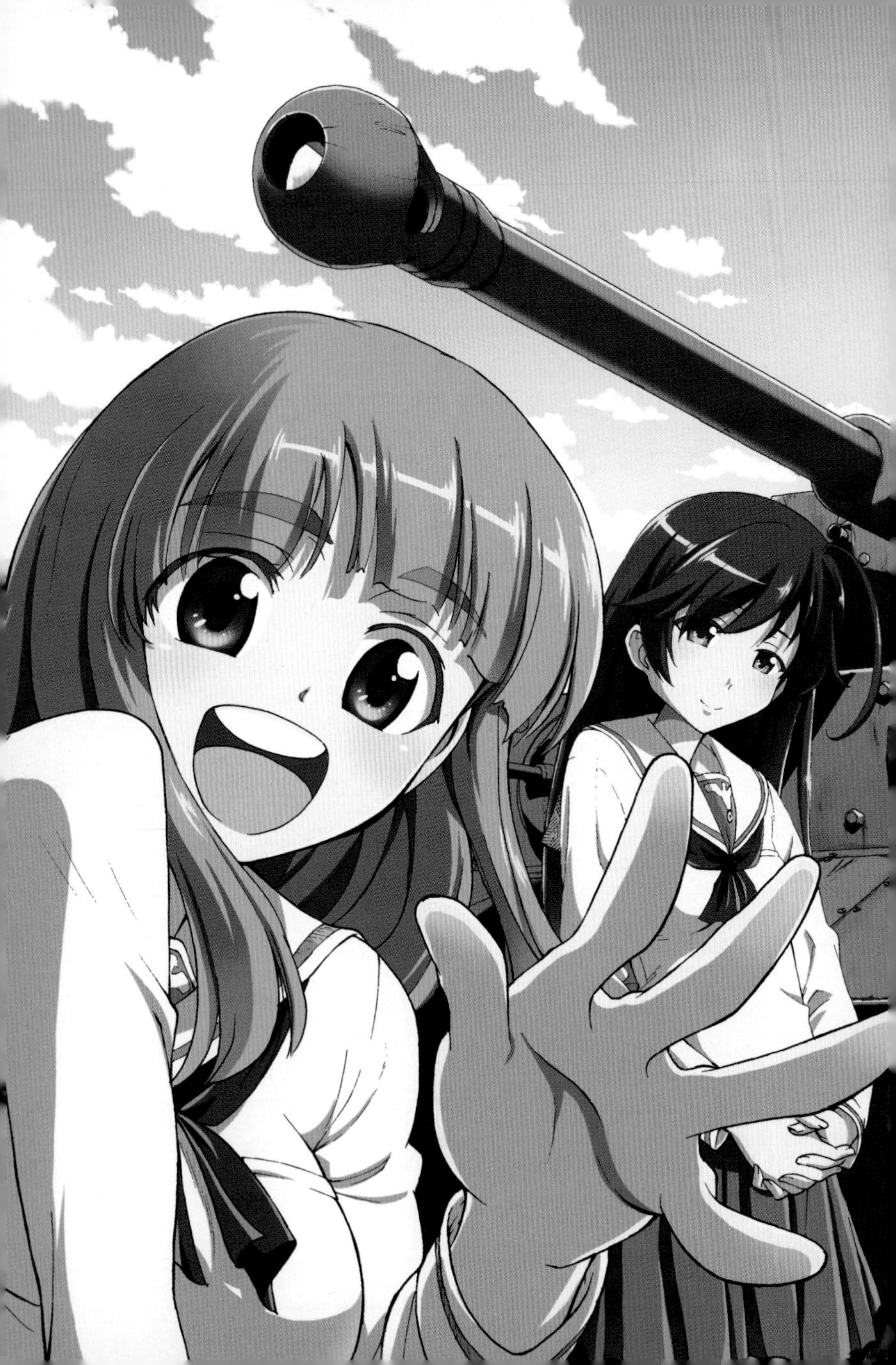

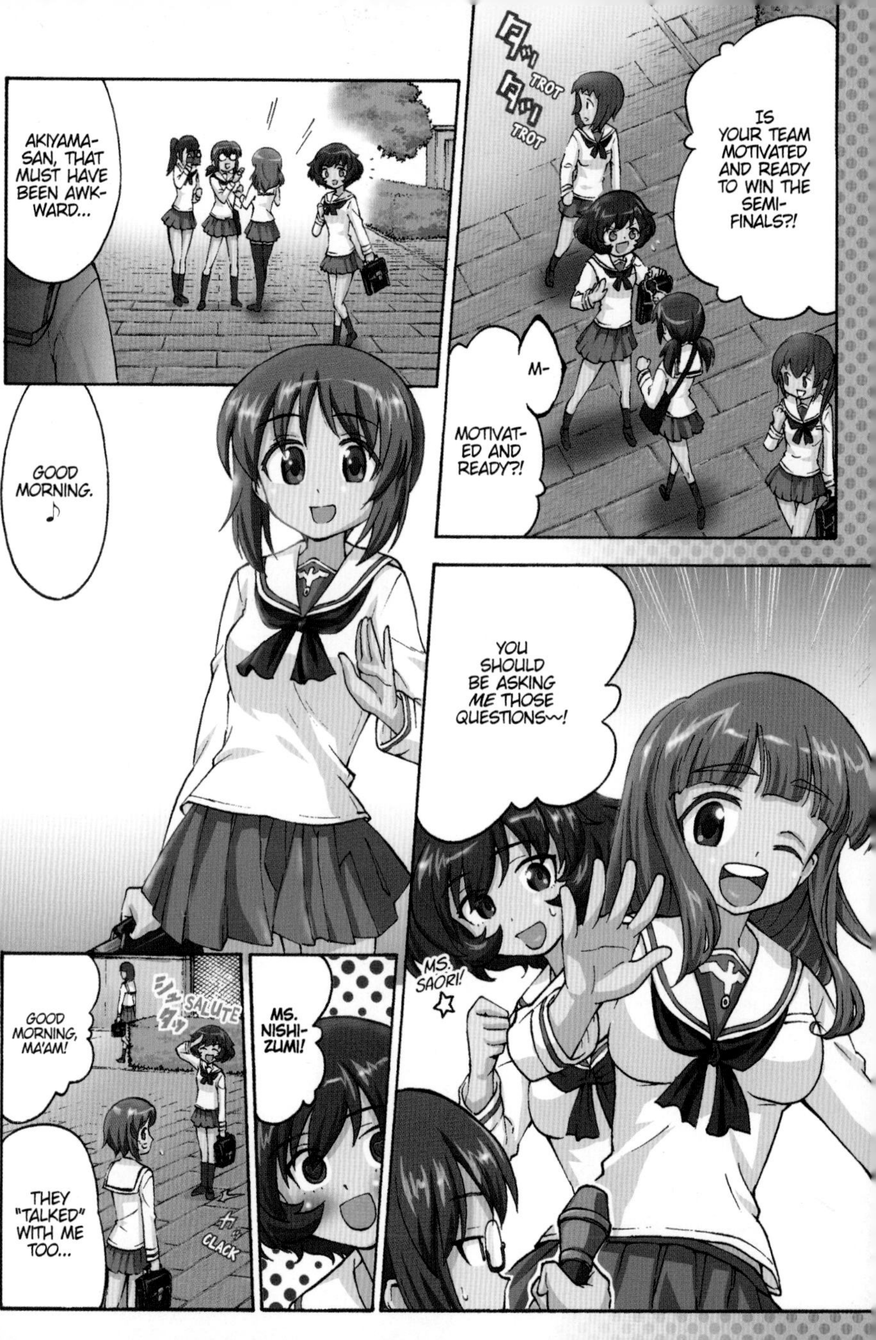
TROT
TROT
IS YOUR TEAM MOTIVATED AND READY TO WIN THE SEMI-FINALS?!
M-
MOTIVAT-ED AND READY?!
AKIYAMA-SAN, THAT MUST HAVE BEEN AWK-WARD...
YOU SHOULD BE ASKING *ME* THOSE QUESTIONS~!
MS. SAORI!
GOOD MORNING. ♪
MS. NISHI-ZUMI!
SALUTE
GOOD MORNING, MA'AM!
CLACK
THEY "TALKED" WITH ME TOO...

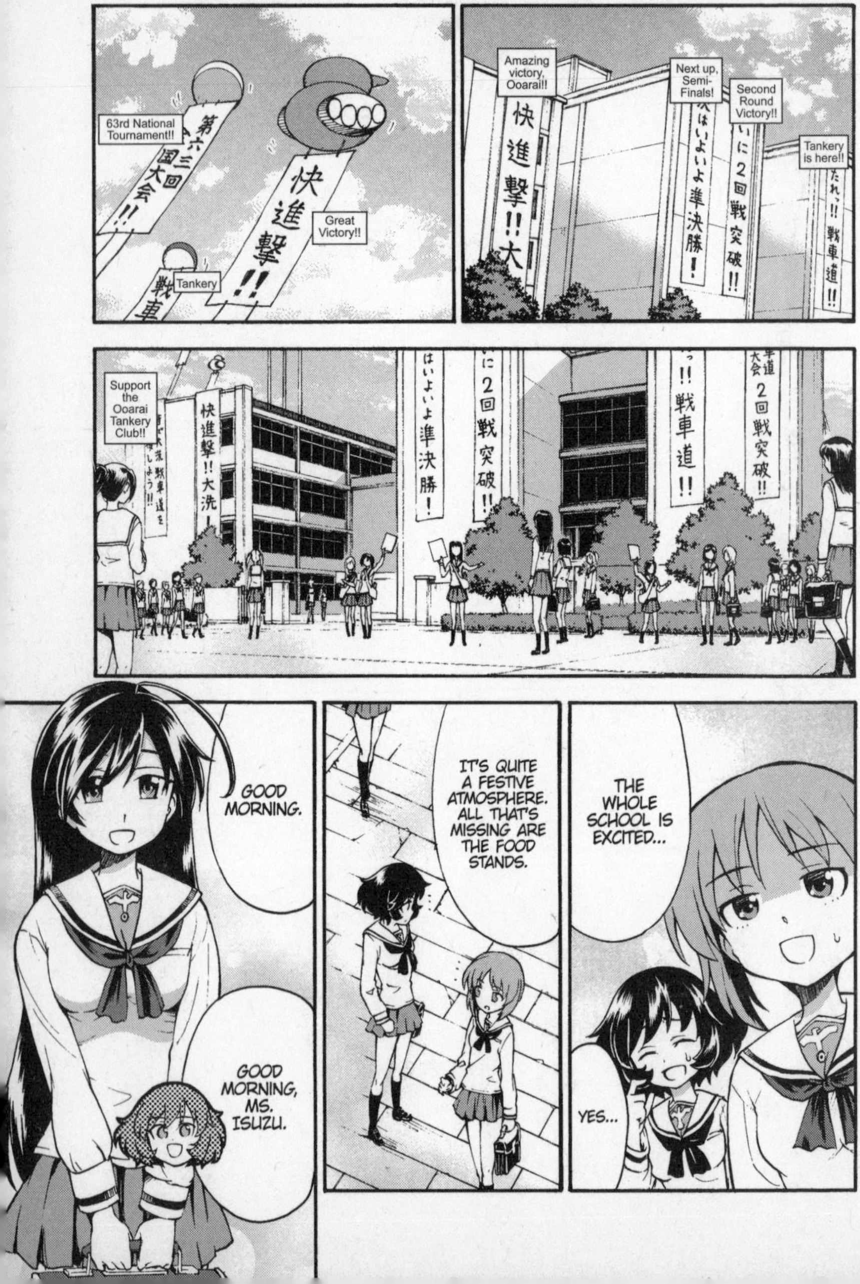

Tankery is here!!
Second Round Victory!!
Next up, Semi-Finals!
Amazing victory, Ooarai!!
快進撃!!
Great Victory!!
63rd National Tournament!!
Tankery
Support the Ooarai Tankery Club!!
THE WHOLE SCHOOL IS EXCITED...
YES...
IT'S QUITE A FESTIVE ATMOSPHERE. ALL THAT'S MISSING ARE THE FOOD STANDS.
GOOD MORNING.
GOOD MORNING, MS. ISUZU.

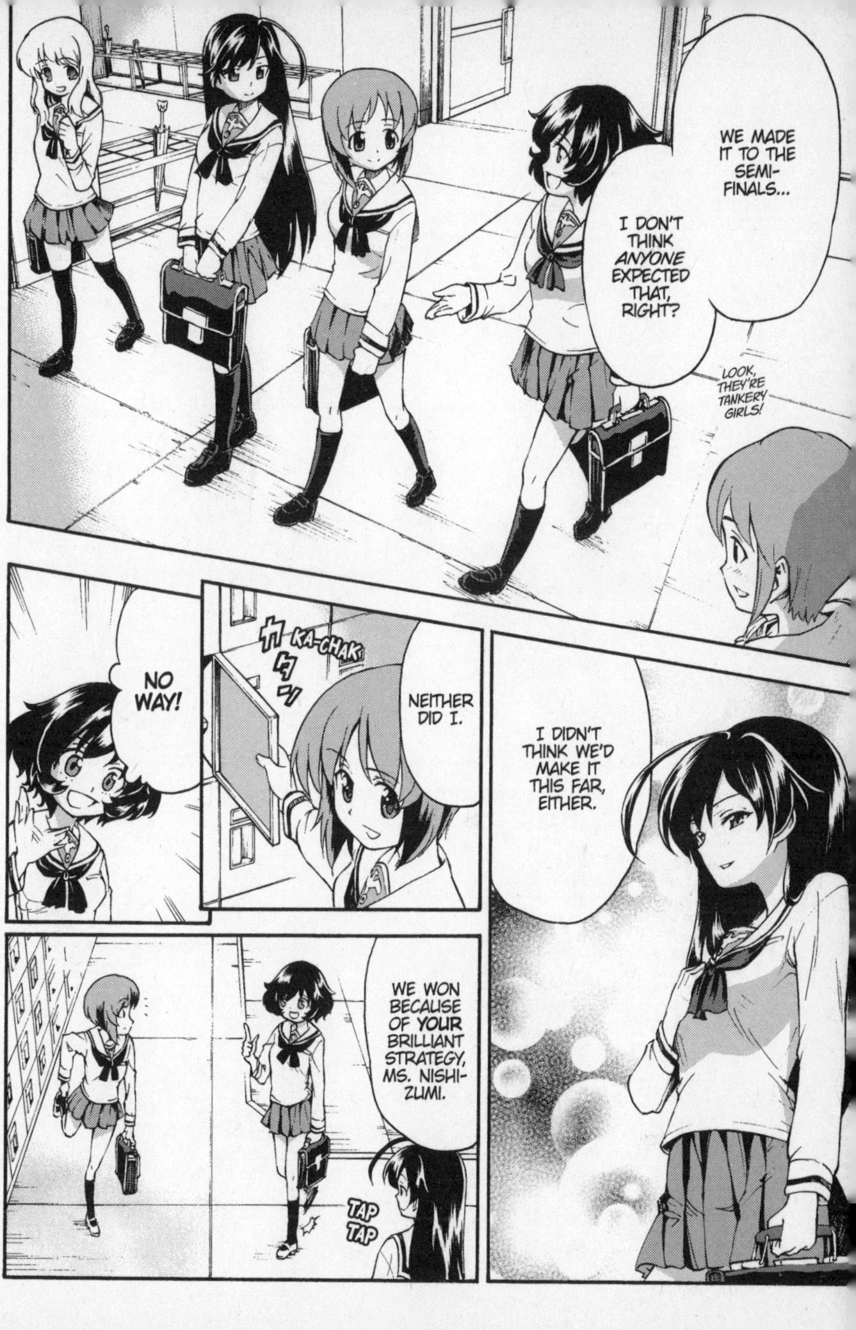
WE MADE IT TO THE SEMI-FINALS...
I DON'T THINK *ANYONE* EXPECTED THAT, RIGHT?
LOOK, THEY'RE TANKERY GIRLS!
I DIDN'T THINK WE'D MAKE IT THIS FAR, EITHER.
NEITHER DID I.
KA-CHAK
NO WAY!
WE WON BECAUSE OF **YOUR** BRILLIANT STRATEGY, MS. NISHIZUMI.
TAP TAP

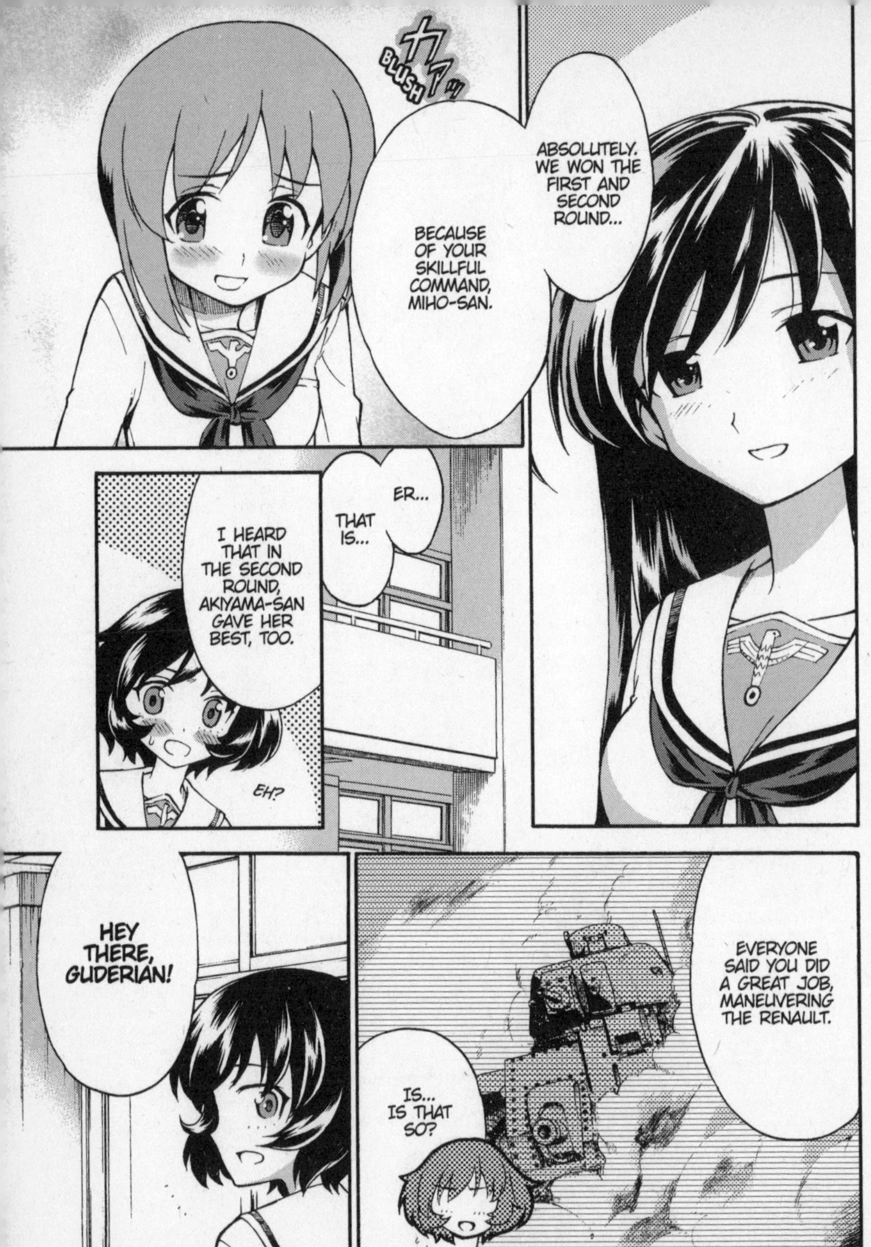
ABSOLUTELY. WE WON THE FIRST AND SECOND ROUND...
BECAUSE OF YOUR SKILLFUL COMMAND, MIHO-SAN.
BLUSH
ER... THAT IS...
I HEARD THAT IN THE SECOND ROUND, AKIYAMA-SAN GAVE HER BEST, TOO.
EH?
EVERYONE SAID YOU DID A GREAT JOB, MANEUVERING THE RENAULT.
IS... IS THAT SO?
HEY THERE, GUDERIAN!

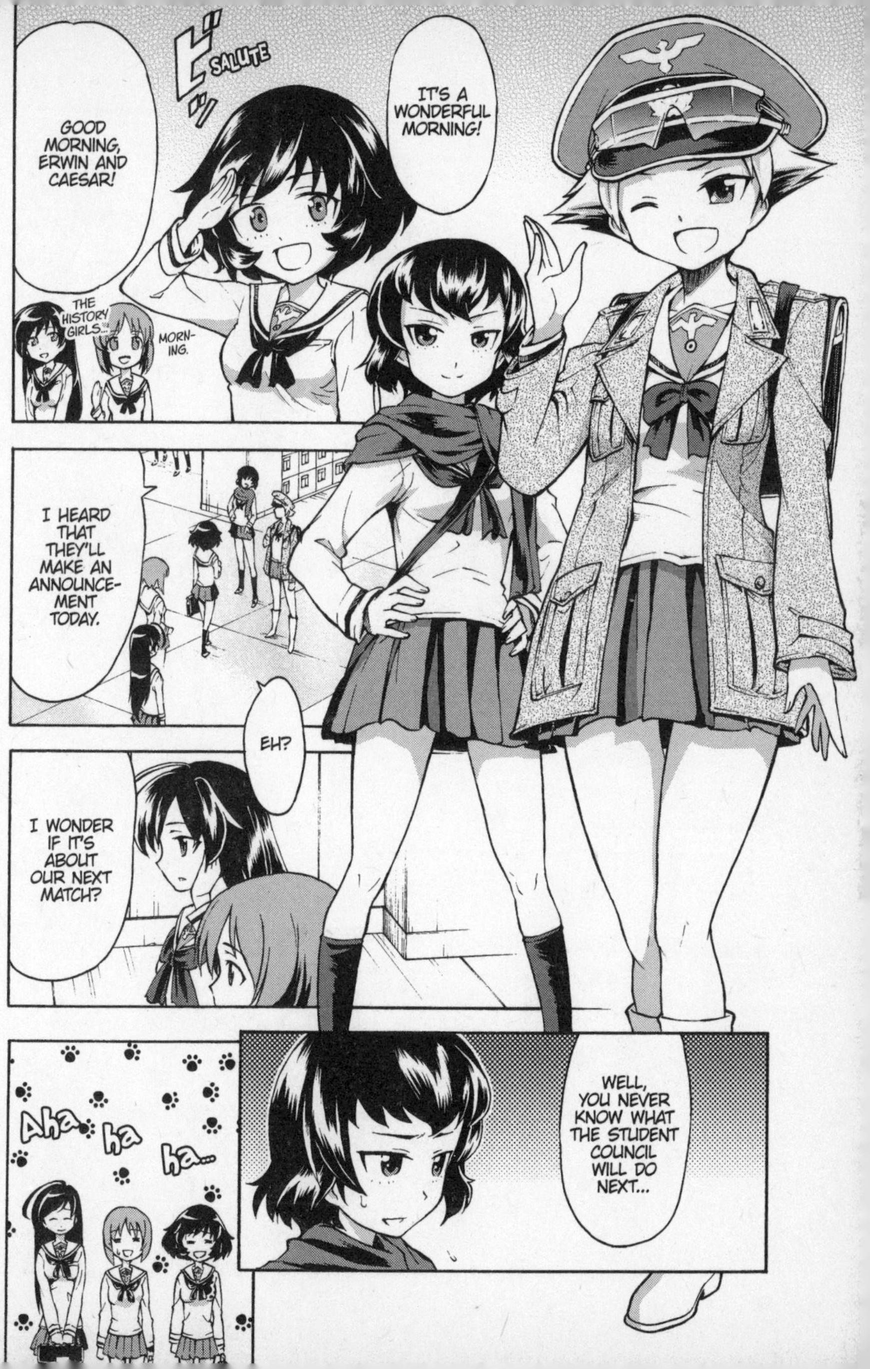
IT'S A WONDERFUL MORNING!
SALUTE
GOOD MORNING, ERWIN AND CAESAR!
THE HISTORY GIRLS...
MORNING.
I HEARD THAT THEY'LL MAKE AN ANNOUNCEMENT TODAY.
EH?
I WONDER IF IT'S ABOUT OUR NEXT MATCH?
WELL, YOU NEVER KNOW WHAT THE STUDENT COUNCIL WILL DO NEXT...
Aha ha ha...

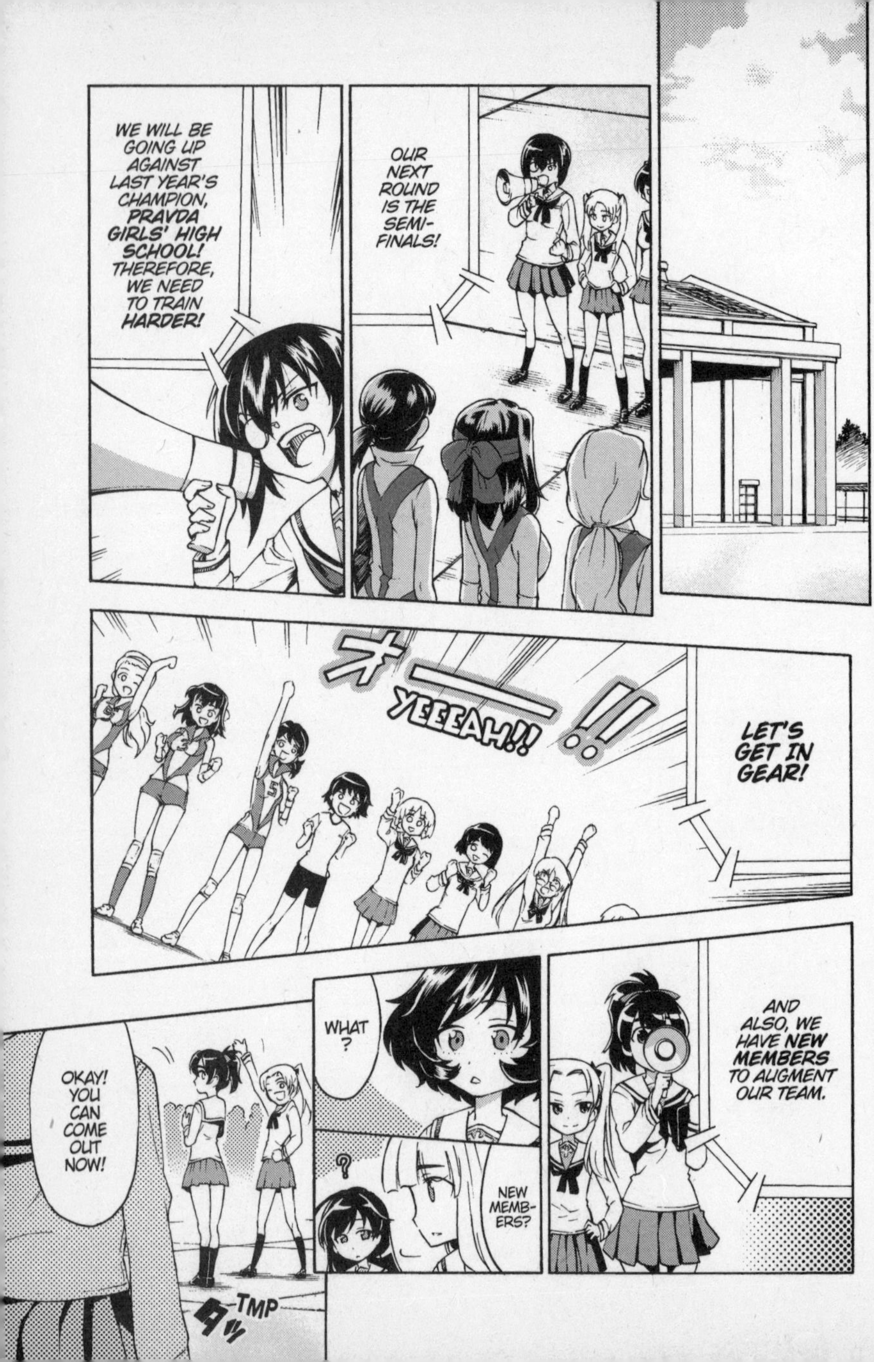
OUR NEXT ROUND IS THE SEMI-FINALS!
WE WILL BE GOING UP AGAINST LAST YEAR'S CHAMPION, PRAVDA GIRLS' HIGH SCHOOL! THEREFORE, WE NEED TO TRAIN HARDER!
LET'S GET IN GEAR!
オー!!
YEEEAH!!
AND ALSO, WE HAVE NEW MEMBERS TO AUGMENT OUR TEAM.
WHAT?
NEW MEMBERS?
OKAY! YOU CAN COME OUT NOW!
タッ
TMP

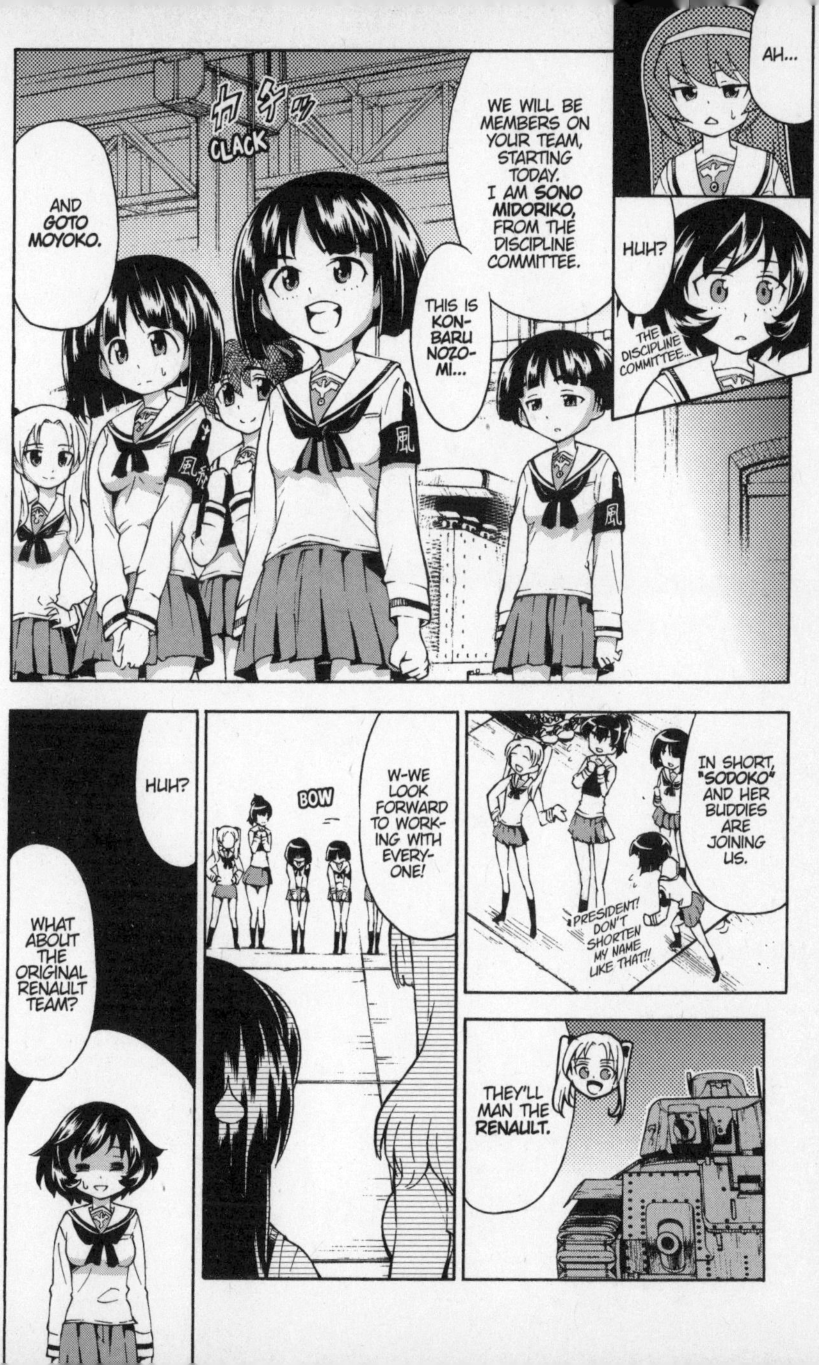
AH...
HUH?
THE DISCIPLINE COMMITTEE...
WE WILL BE MEMBERS ON YOUR TEAM, STARTING TODAY. I AM SONO MIDORIKO, FROM THE DISCIPLINE COMMITTEE.
THIS IS KONBARU NOZOMI...
カチッ
CLACK
AND GOTO MOYOKO.
IN SHORT, "SODOKO" AND HER BUDDIES ARE JOINING US.
PRESIDENT! DON'T SHORTEN MY NAME LIKE THAT!!
THEY'LL MAN THE RENAULT.
W-WE LOOK FORWARD TO WORKING WITH EVERYONE!
BOW
HUH?
WHAT ABOUT THE ORIGINAL RENAULT TEAM?

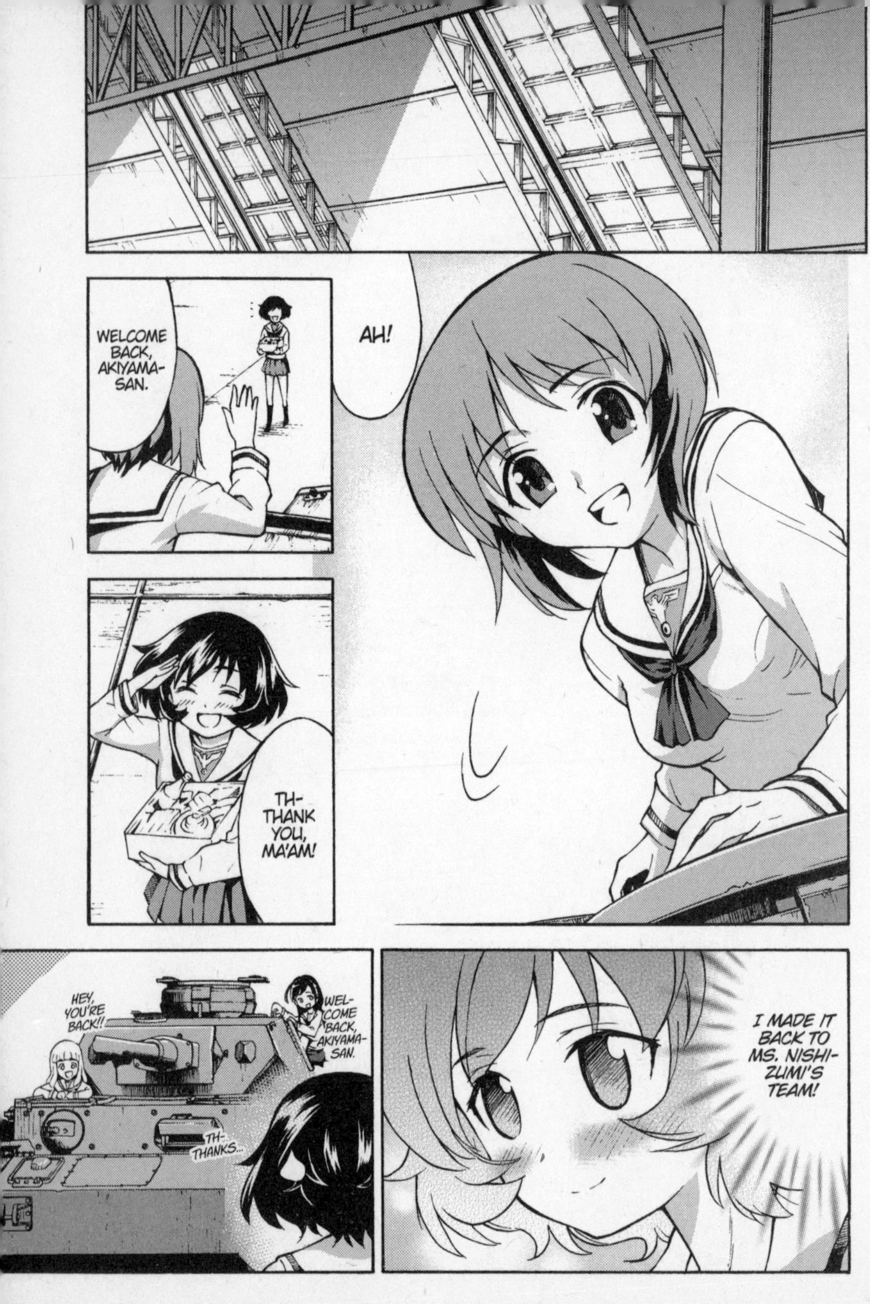
AH!
WELCOME BACK, AKIYAMA-SAN.
TH-THANK YOU, MA'AM!
I MADE IT BACK TO MS. NISHI-ZUMI'S TEAM!
WEL-COME BACK, AKIYAMA-SAN.
HEY, YOU'RE BACK!!
TH-THANKS...

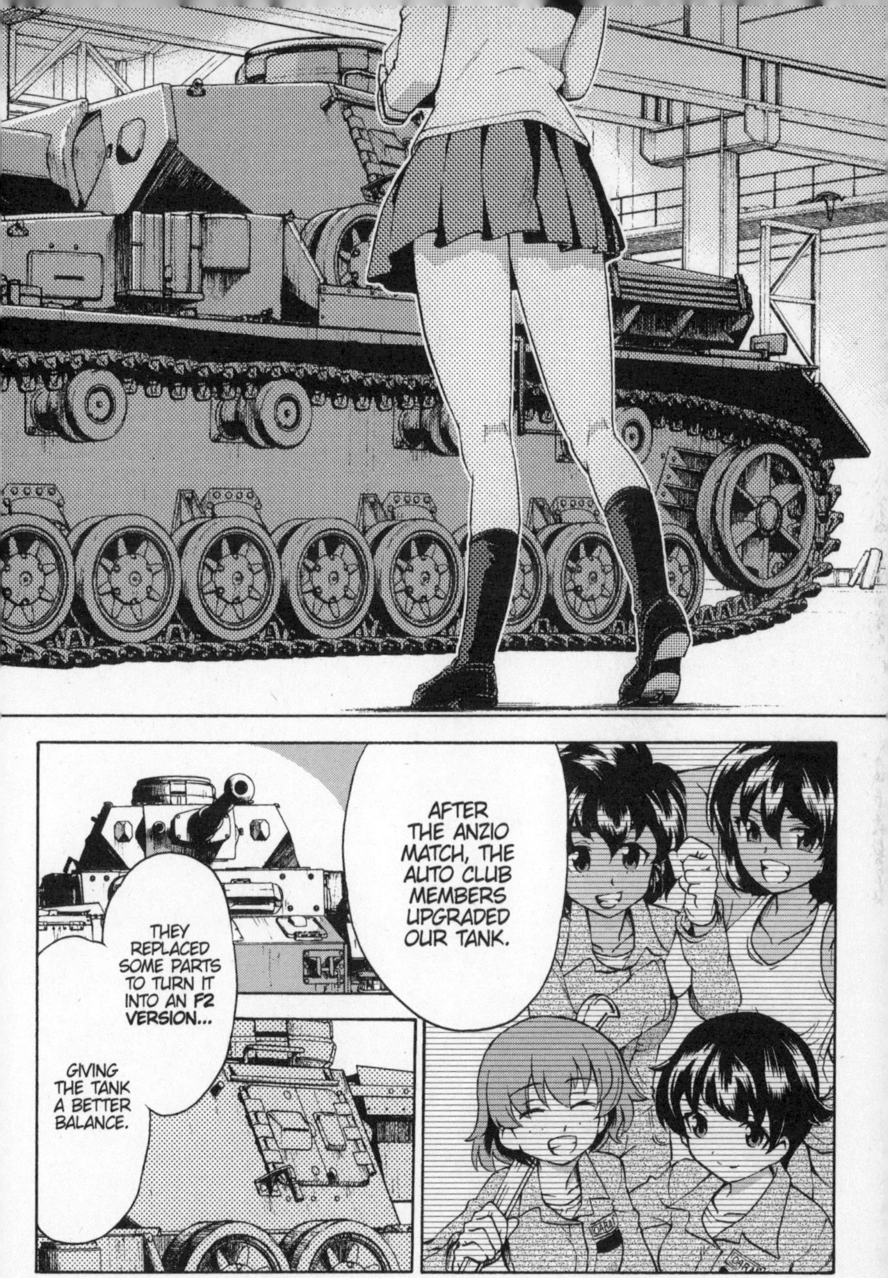
AFTER THE ANZIO MATCH, THE AUTO CLUB MEMBERS UPGRADED OUR TANK.
THEY REPLACED SOME PARTS TO TURN IT INTO AN F2 VERSION...
GIVING THE TANK A BETTER BALANCE.

AH...

AKIYAMA-SAN, YOU NOTICED?

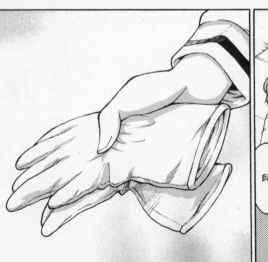

AND THIS IS FOR YOU, AKIYAMA-SAN.

EH?

THOSE ARE THE GLOVES...

OF A LOADER.

WE'RE GLAD TO HAVE YOU BACK.

OH...

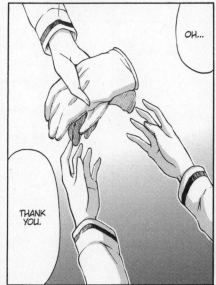

THANK YOU.

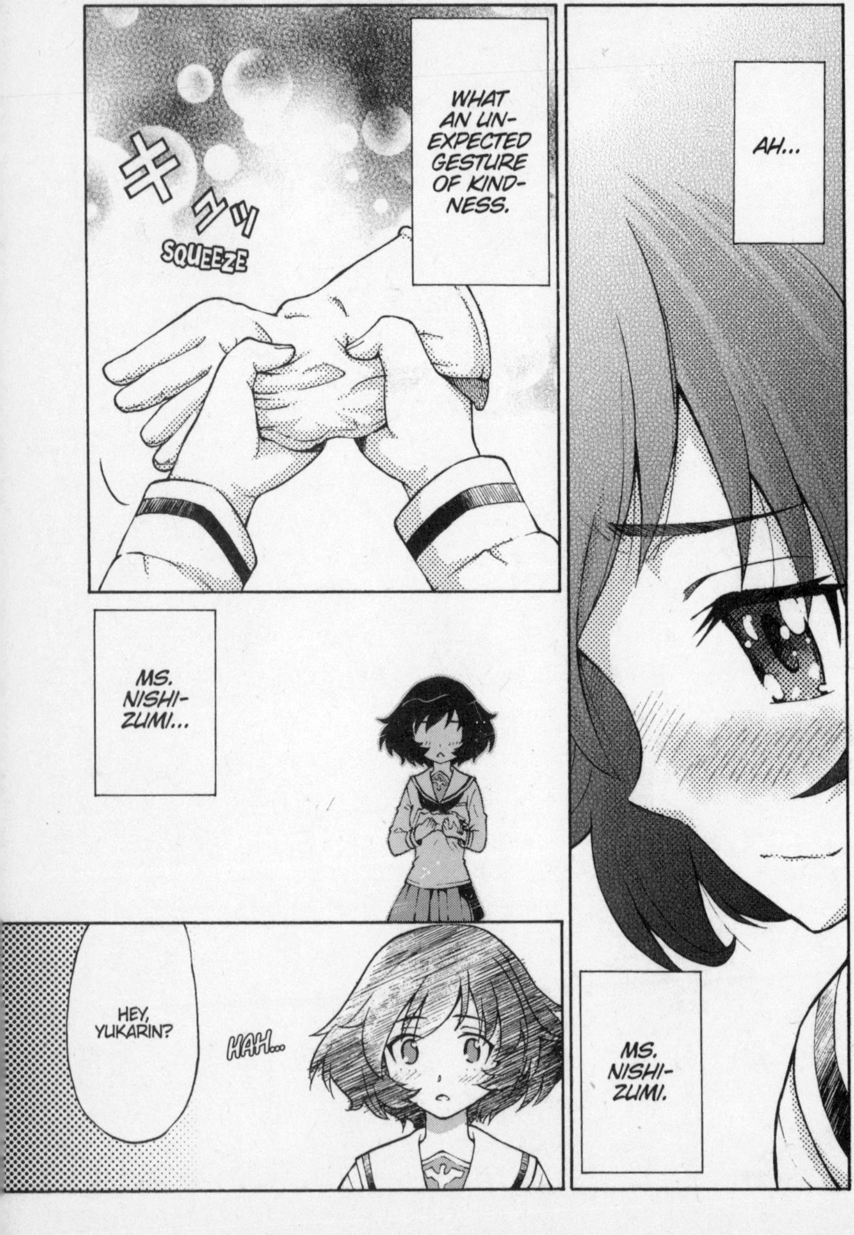
AH...
MS. NISHI-ZUMI.
WHAT AN UN-EXPECTED GESTURE OF KIND-NESS.
キュッ
SQUEEZE
MS. NISHI-ZUMI...
HAH...
HEY, YUKARIN?

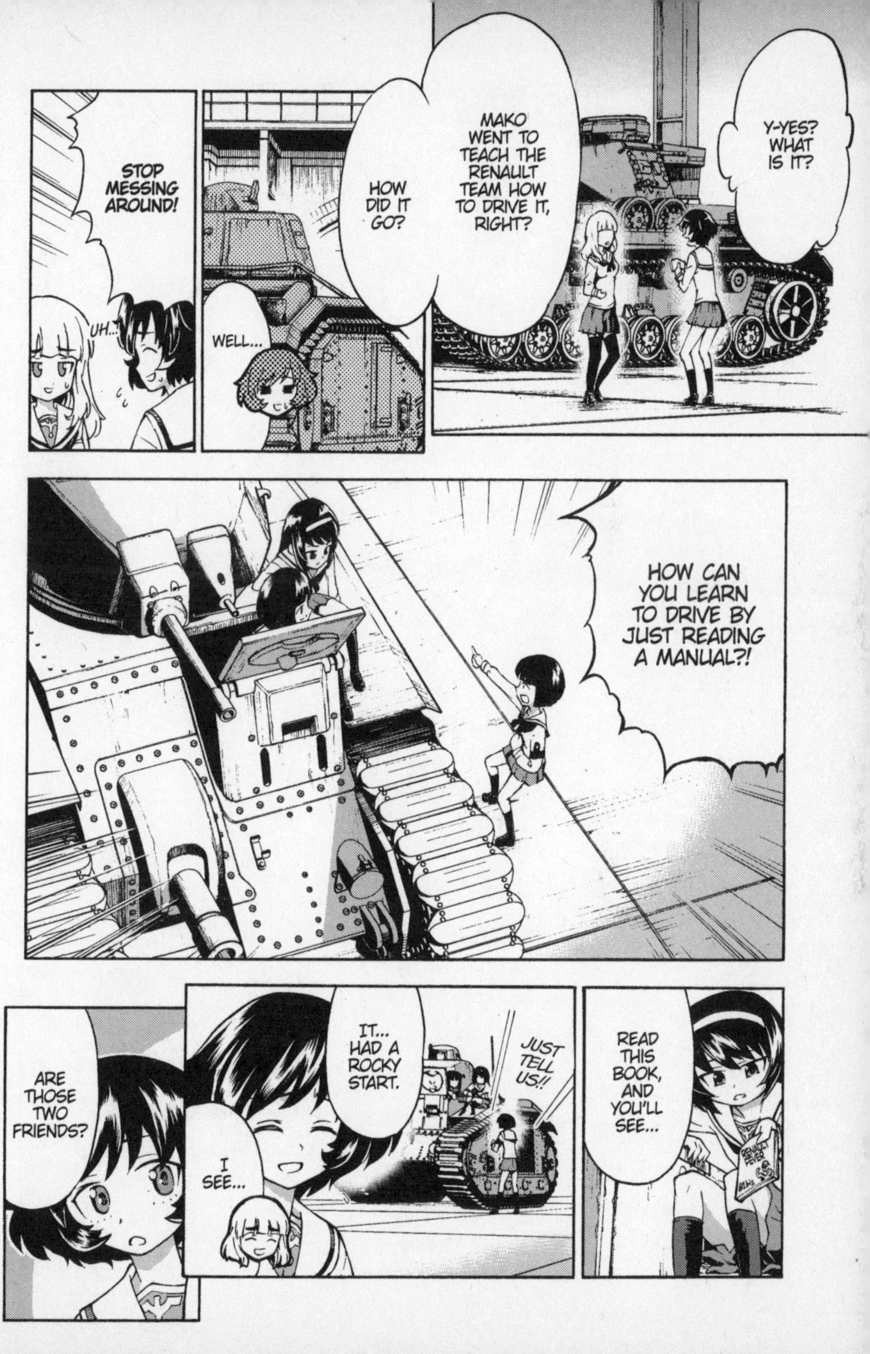
Y-YES? WHAT IS IT?
MAKO WENT TO TEACH THE RENAULT TEAM HOW TO DRIVE IT, RIGHT?
HOW DID IT GO?
WELL...
STOP MESSING AROUND!
UH...
HOW CAN YOU LEARN TO DRIVE BY JUST READING A MANUAL?!
READ THIS BOOK, AND YOU'LL SEE...
RENAULT FEVER
JUST TELL US!!
IT... HAD A ROCKY START.
I SEE...
ARE THOSE TWO FRIENDS?

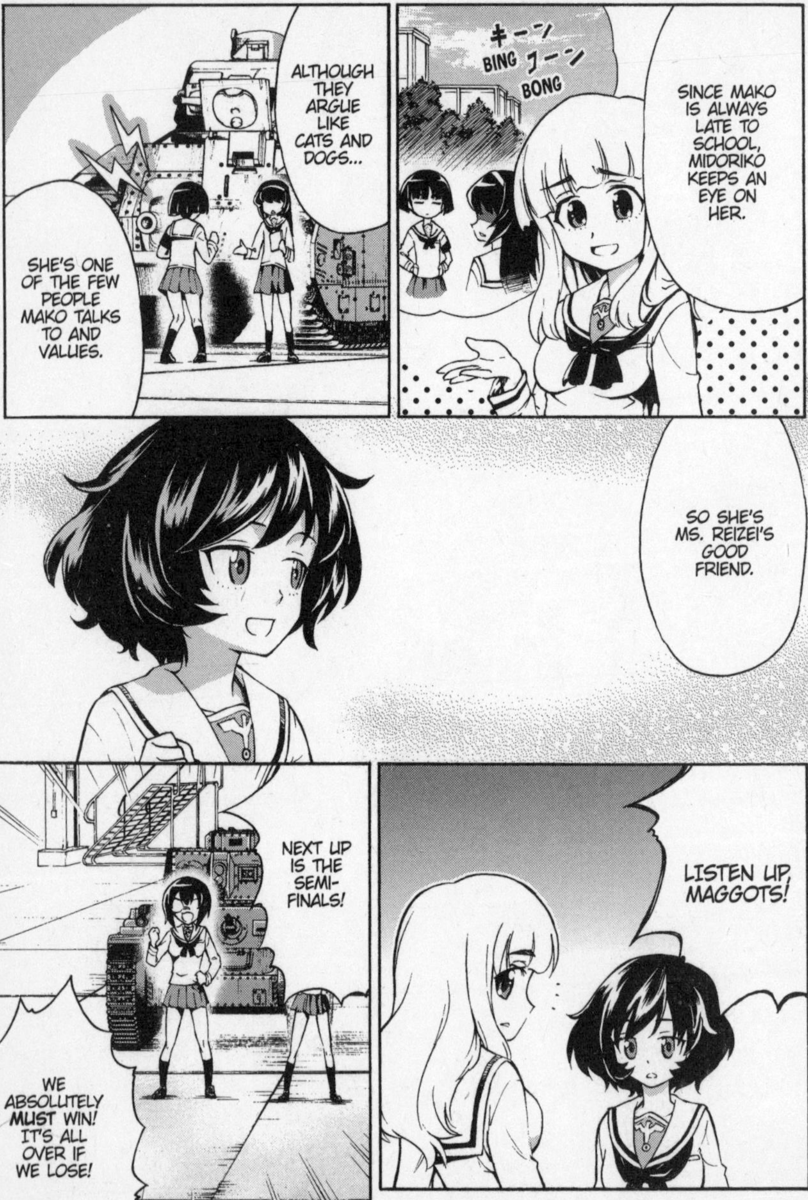
キーン
BING
コーン
BONG
SINCE MAKO IS ALWAYS LATE TO SCHOOL, MIDORIKO KEEPS AN EYE ON HER.
ALTHOUGH THEY ARGUE LIKE CATS AND DOGS...
SHE'S ONE OF THE FEW PEOPLE MAKO TALKS TO AND VALUES.
SO SHE'S MS. REIZEI'S GOOD FRIEND.
LISTEN UP, MAGGOTS!
NEXT UP IS THE SEMI-FINALS!
WE ABSOLUTELY **MUST** WIN! IT'S ALL OVER IF WE LOSE!

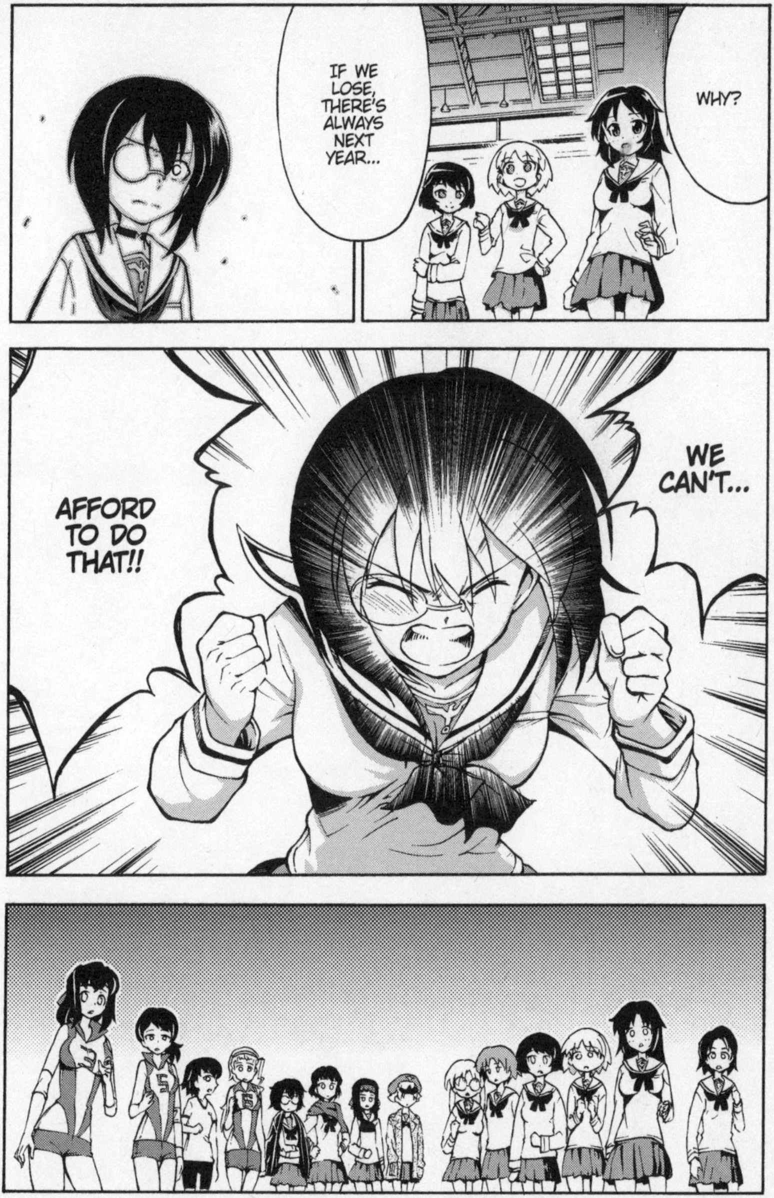
WHY?
IF WE LOSE, THERE'S ALWAYS NEXT YEAR...
WE CAN'T...
AFFORD TO DO THAT!!

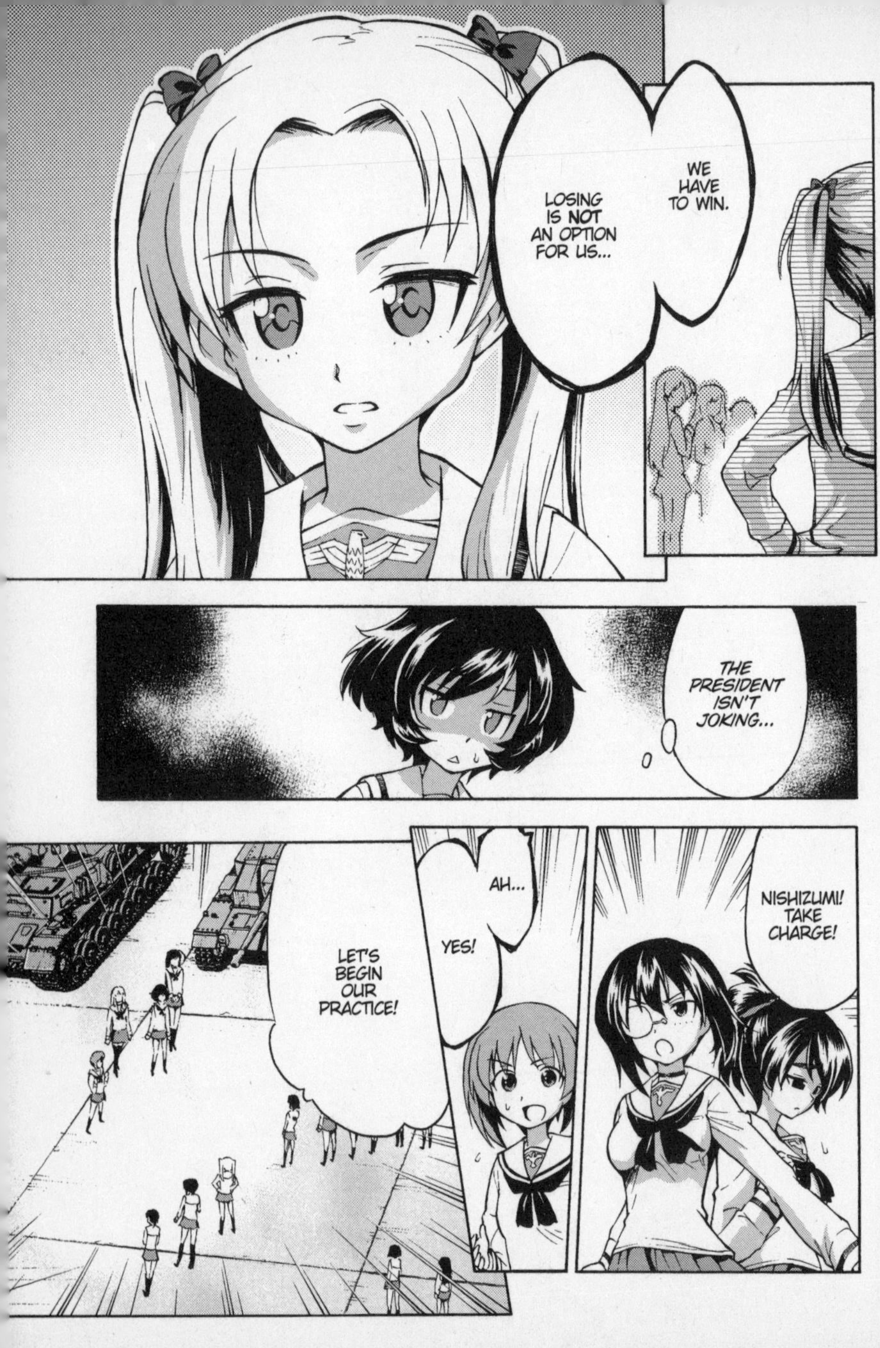
WE HAVE TO WIN.
LOSING IS NOT AN OPTION FOR US...
THE PRESIDENT ISN'T JOKING...
NISHIZUMI! TAKE CHARGE!
AH...
YES!
LET'S BEGIN OUR PRACTICE!

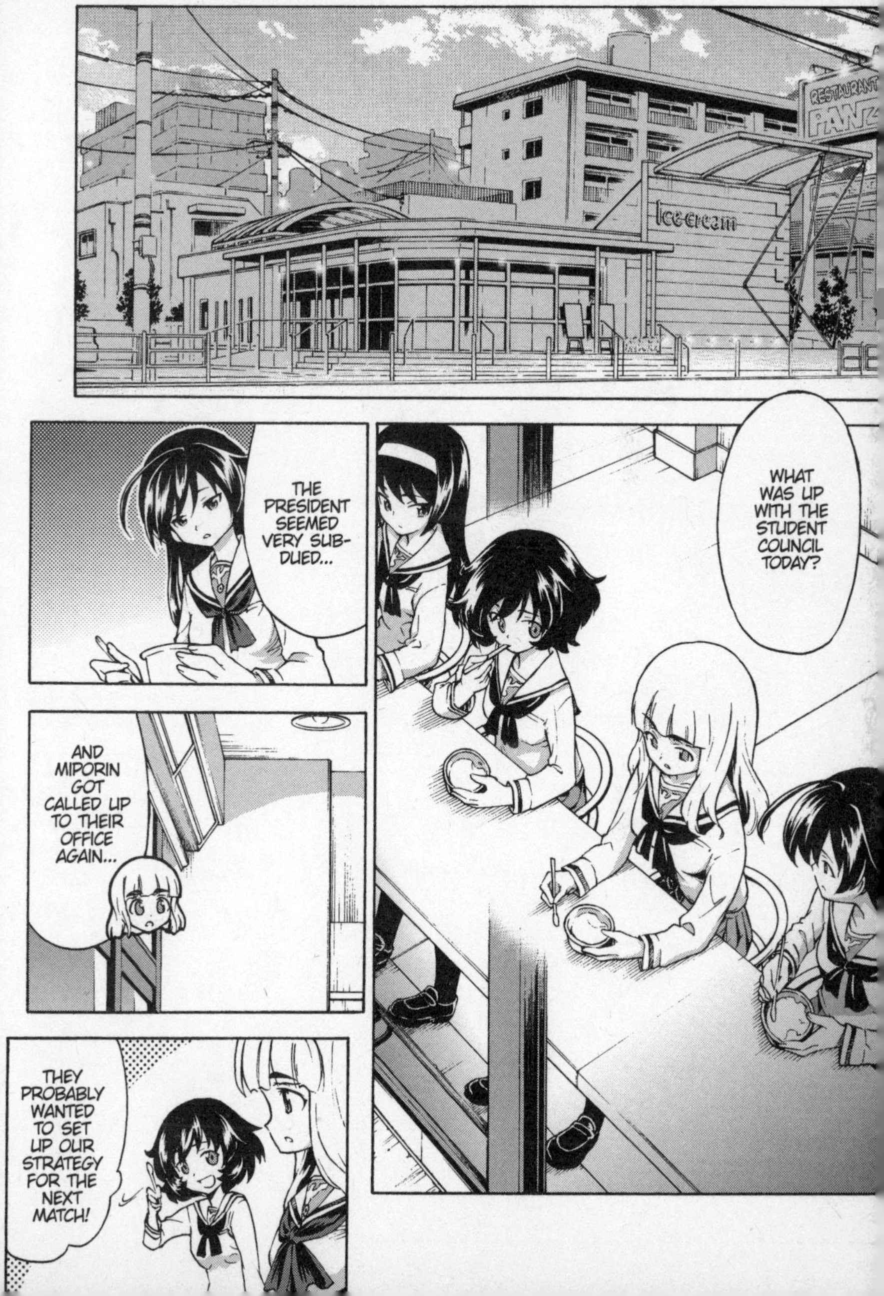
RESTAURANT
Ice cream
WHAT WAS UP WITH THE STUDENT COUNCIL TODAY?
THE PRESIDENT SEEMED VERY SUB-DUED...
AND MIPORIN GOT CALLED UP TO THEIR OFFICE AGAIN...
THEY PROBABLY WANTED TO SET UP OUR STRATEGY FOR THE NEXT MATCH!

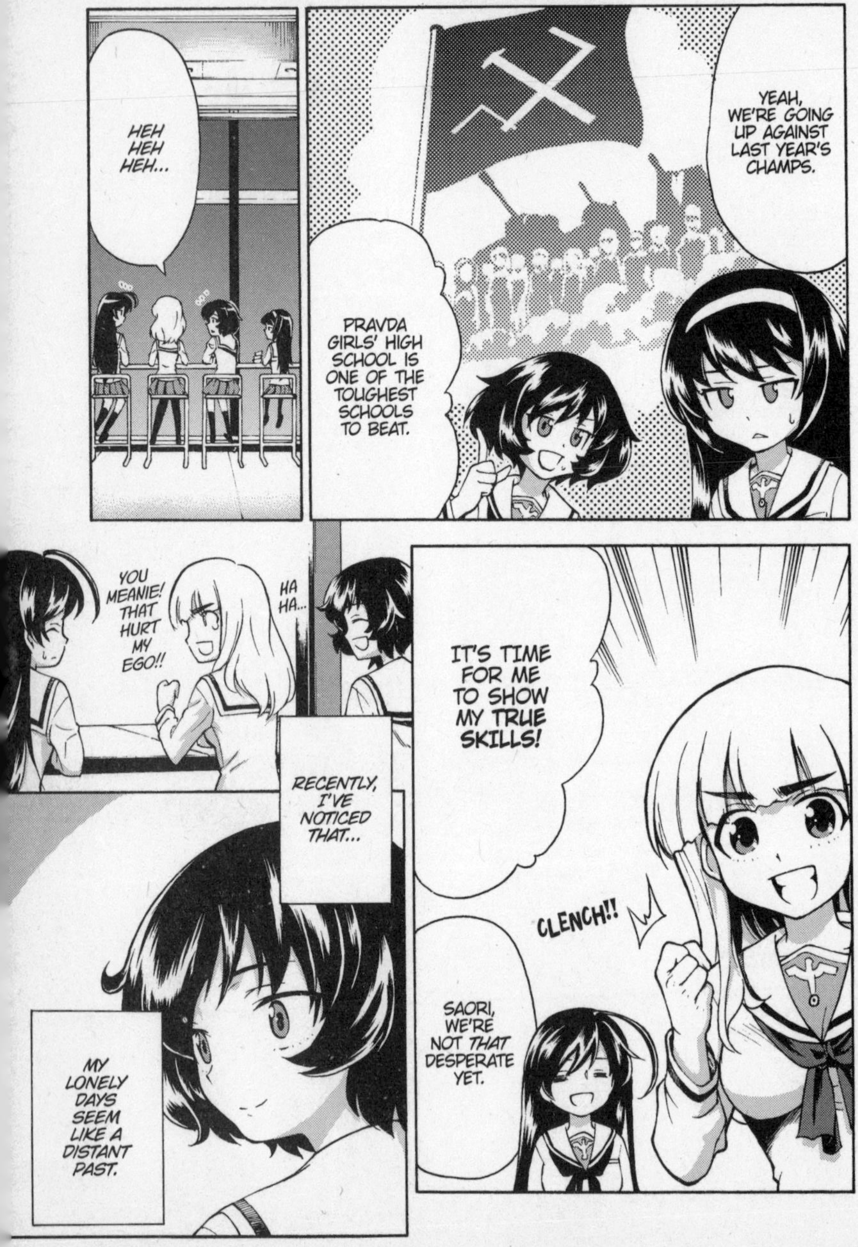
YEAH, WE'RE GOING UP AGAINST LAST YEAR'S CHAMPS.
PRAVDA GIRLS' HIGH SCHOOL IS ONE OF THE TOUGHEST SCHOOLS TO BEAT.
HEH HEH HEH...
IT'S TIME FOR ME TO SHOW MY TRUE SKILLS!
CLENCH!!
SAORI, WE'RE NOT *THAT* DESPERATE YET.
HA HA...
YOU MEANIE! THAT HURT MY EGO!!
RECENTLY, I'VE NOTICED THAT...
MY LONELY DAYS SEEM LIKE A DISTANT PAST.

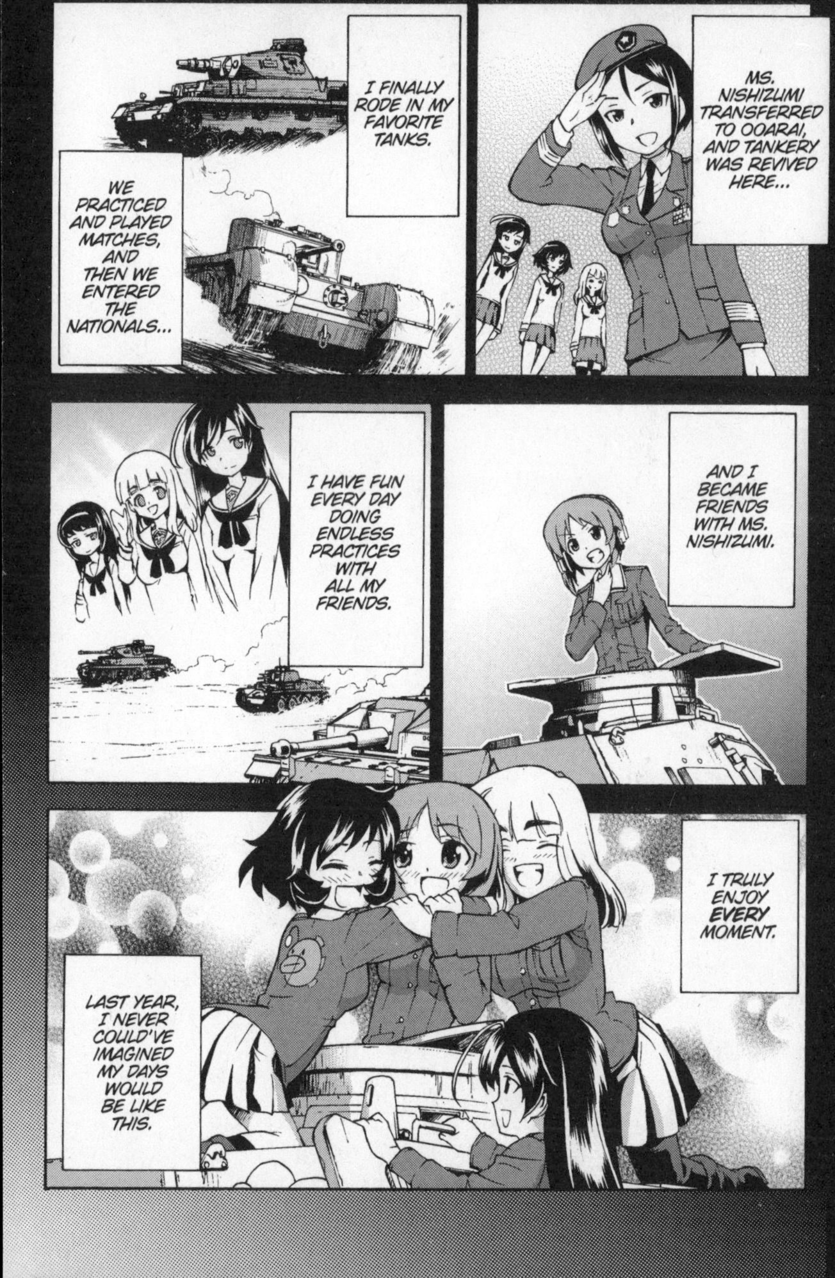
MS. NISHIZUMI TRANSFERRED TO OOARAI, AND TANKERY WAS REVIVED HERE...
I FINALLY RODE IN MY FAVORITE TANKS.
WE PRACTICED AND PLAYED MATCHES, AND THEN WE ENTERED THE NATIONALS...
AND I BECAME FRIENDS WITH MS. NISHIZUMI.
I HAVE FUN EVERY DAY DOING ENDLESS PRACTICES WITH ALL MY FRIENDS.
I TRULY ENJOY EVERY MOMENT.
LAST YEAR, I NEVER COULD'VE IMAGINED MY DAYS WOULD BE LIKE THIS.

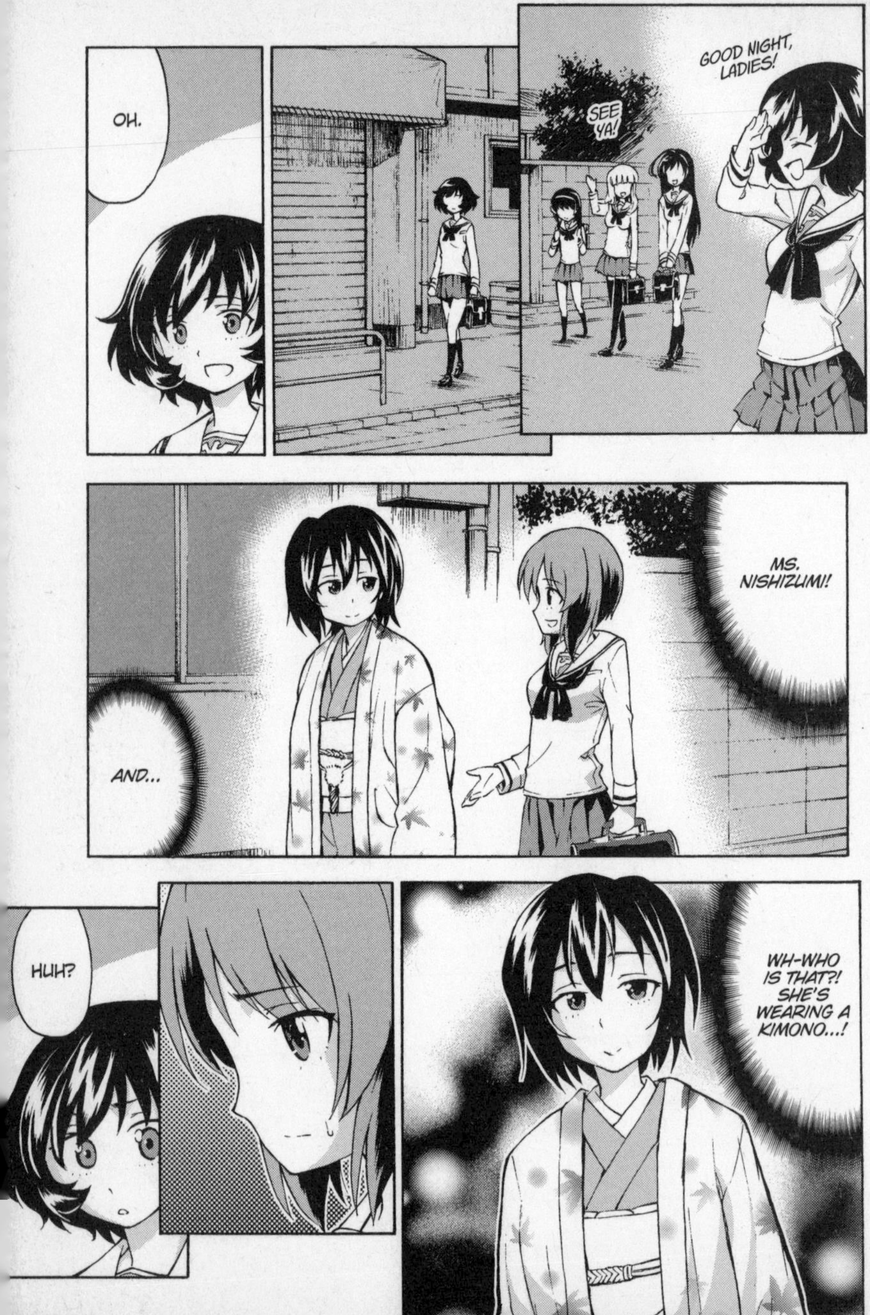
GOOD NIGHT, LADIES!
SEE YA!
OH.
MS. NISHIZUMI!
AND...
WH-WHO IS THAT?! SHE'S WEARING A KIMONO...!
HUH?

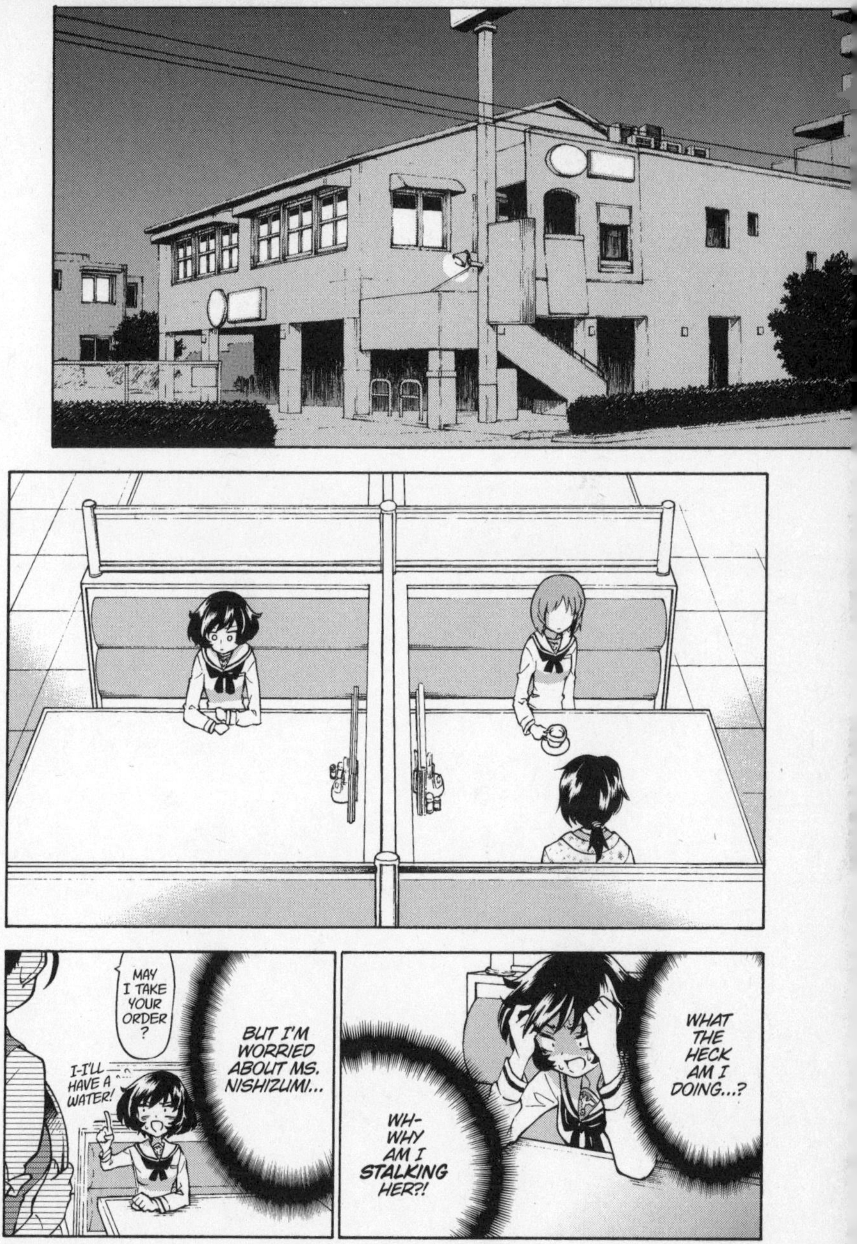
WHAT THE HECK AM I DOING...?
WH- WHY AM I STALKING HER?!
BUT I'M WORRIED ABOUT MS. NISHIZUMI...
MAY I TAKE YOUR ORDER?
I-I'LL HAVE A WATER!

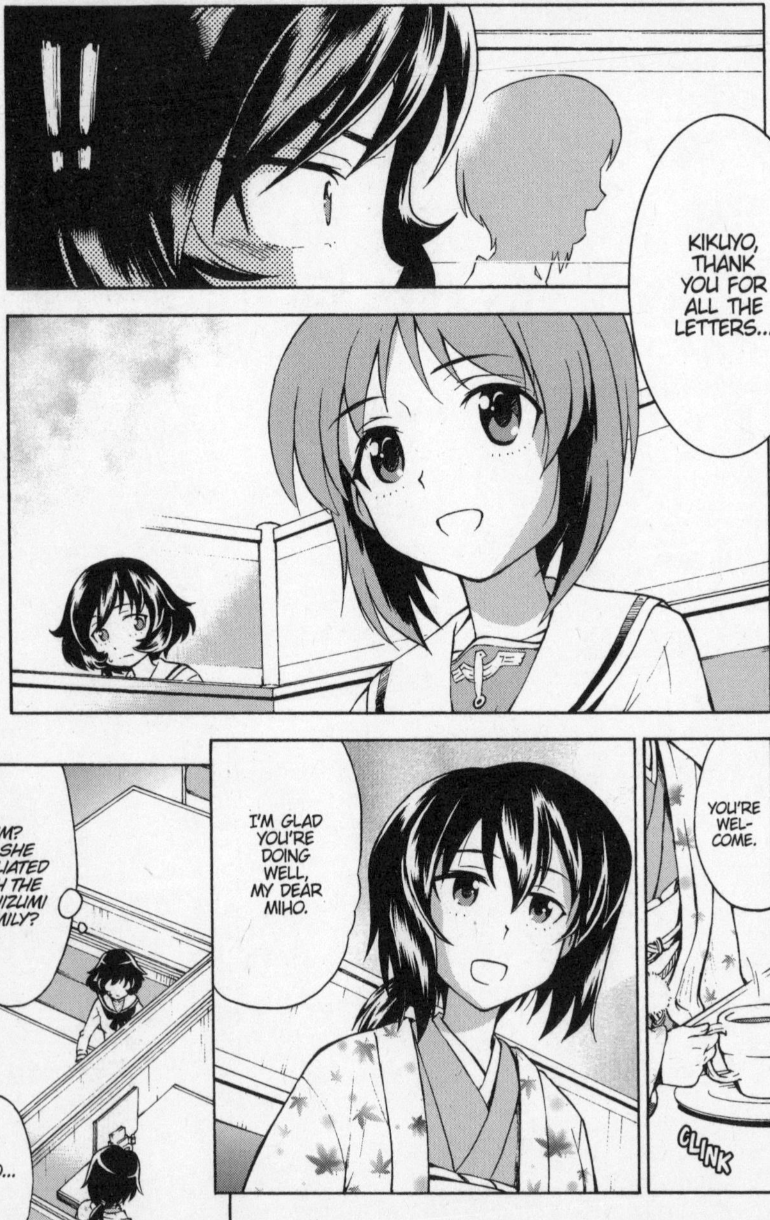
!!
KIKUYO, THANK YOU FOR ALL THE LETTERS...
YOU'RE WEL-COME.
CLINK
I'M GLAD YOU'RE DOING WELL, MY DEAR MIHO.
HM? IS SHE AFFILIATED WITH THE NISHIZUMI FAMILY?
ALSO...

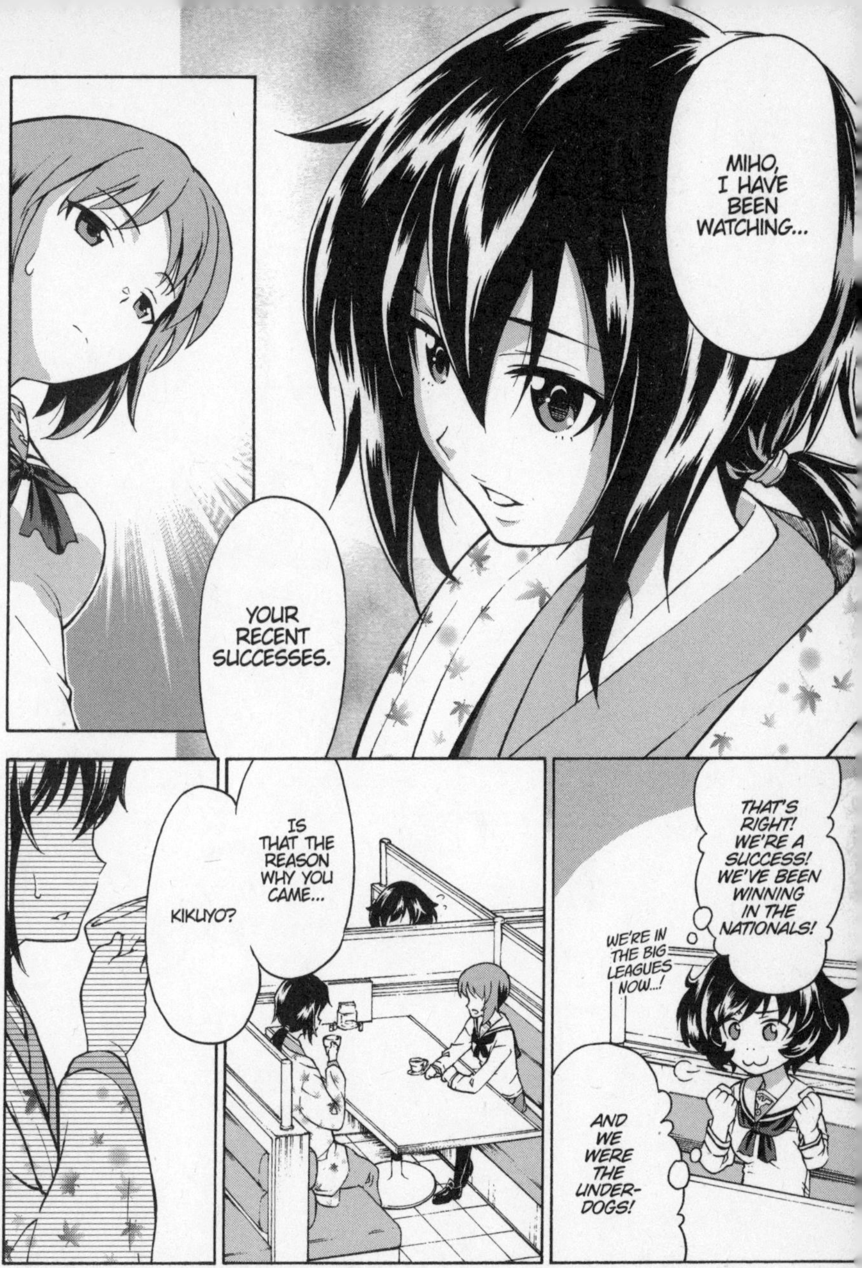
MIHO, I HAVE BEEN WATCHING...
YOUR RECENT SUCCESSES.
THAT'S RIGHT! WE'RE A SUCCESS! WE'VE BEEN WINNING IN THE NATIONALS!
WE'RE IN THE BIG LEAGUES NOW...!
AND WE WERE THE UNDER-DOGS!
IS THAT THE REASON WHY YOU CAME...
KIKUYO?

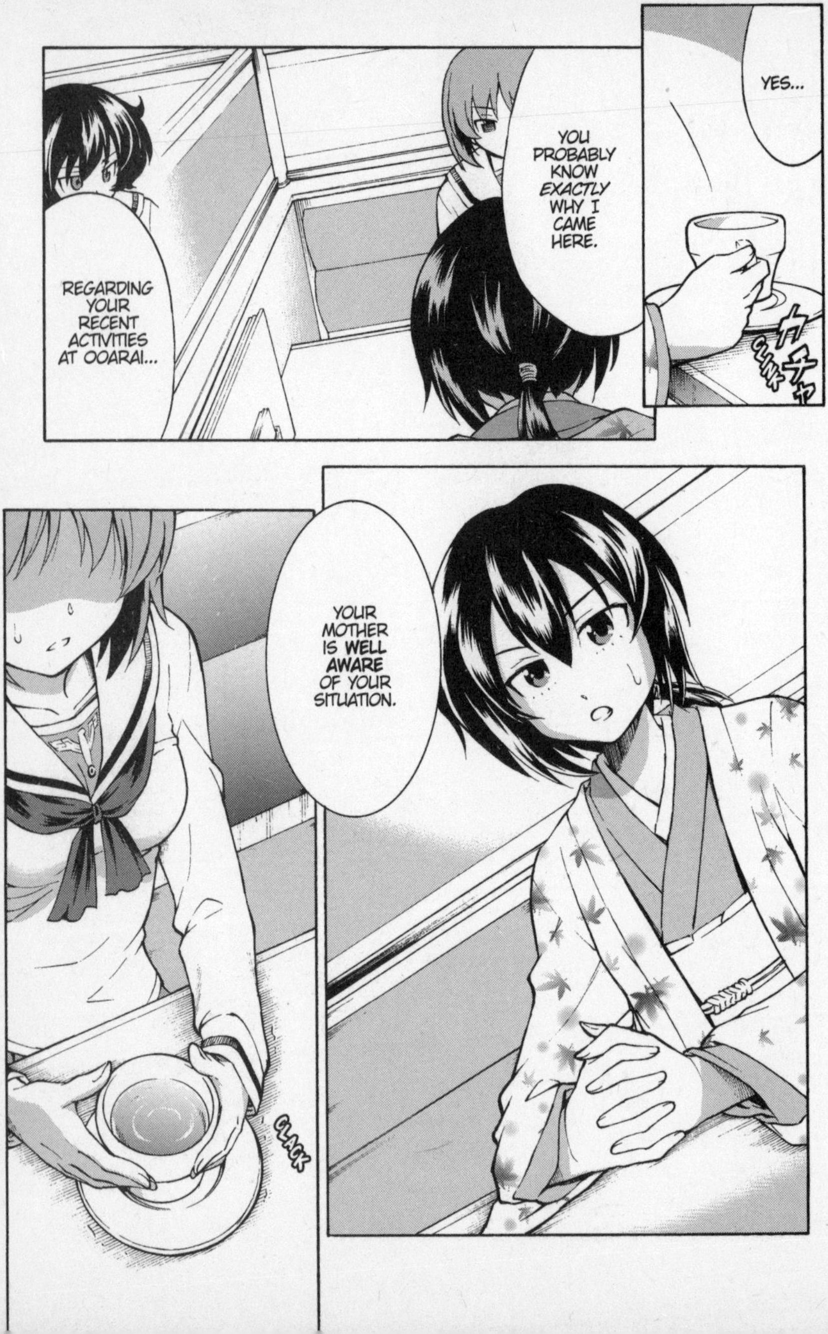

YES...
カチャ
CLINK
YOU PROBABLY KNOW *EXACTLY* WHY I CAME HERE.
REGARDING YOUR RECENT ACTIVITIES AT OOARAI...
YOUR MOTHER IS **WELL AWARE** OF YOUR SITUATION.
CLACK

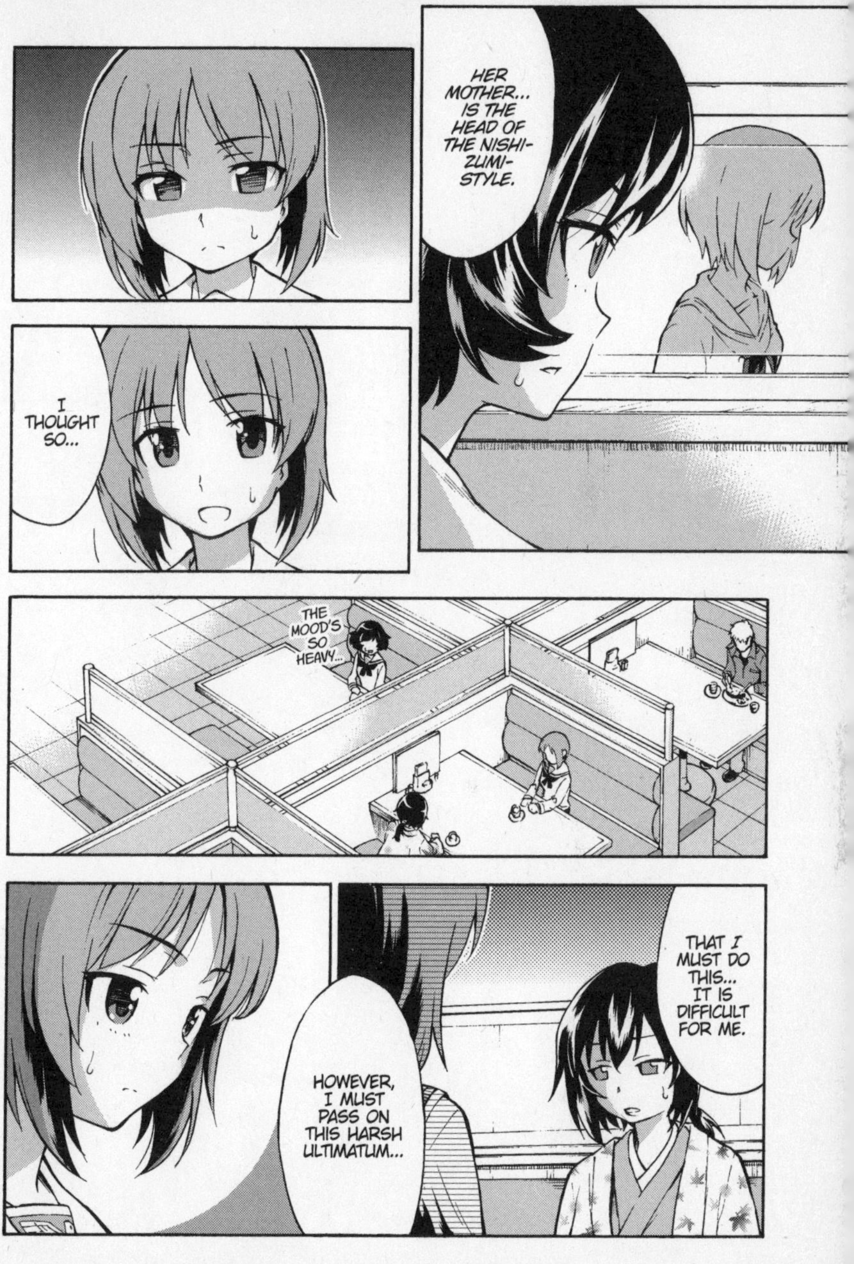
HER MOTHER... IS THE HEAD OF THE NISHI-ZUMI-STYLE.
I THOUGHT SO...
THE MOOD'S SO HEAVY...
THAT I MUST DO THIS... IT IS DIFFICULT FOR ME.
HOWEVER, I MUST PASS ON THIS HARSH ULTIMATUM...

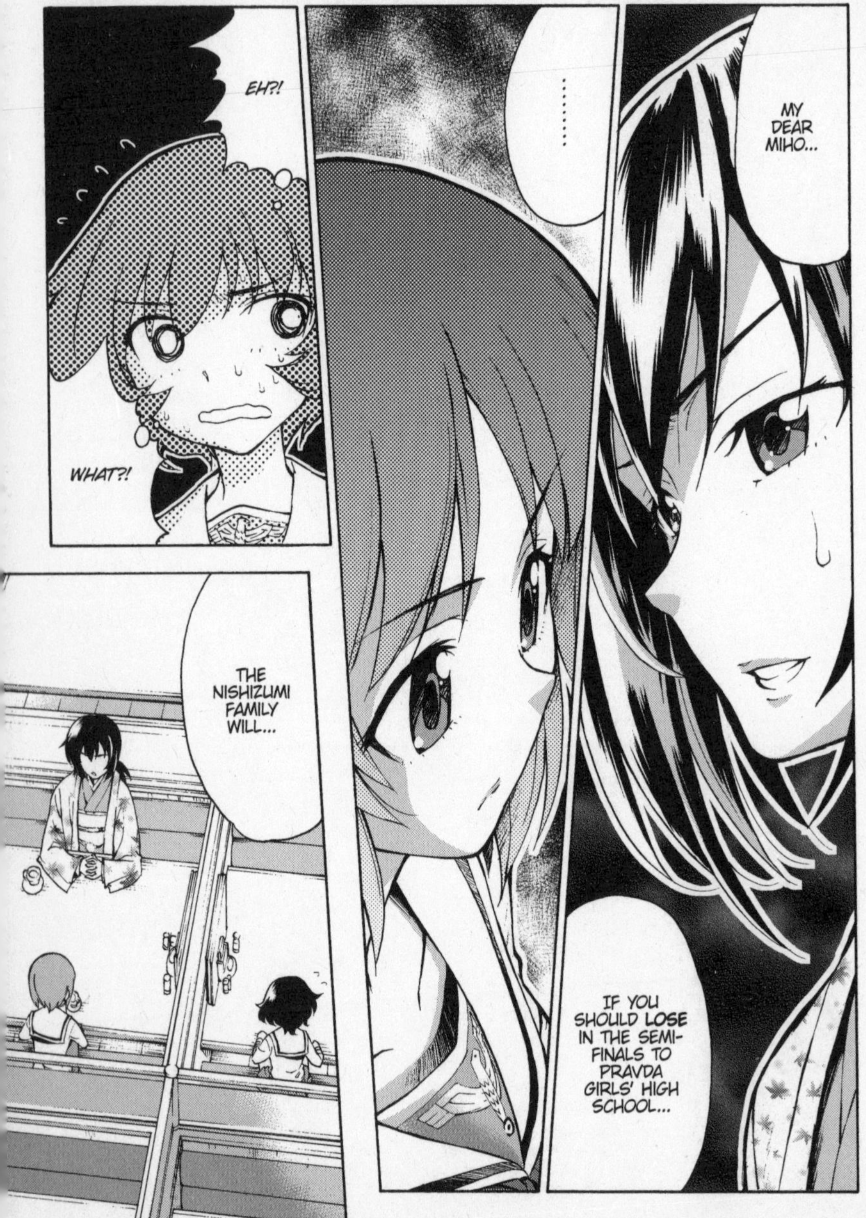

MY DEAR MIHO...
IF YOU SHOULD LOSE IN THE SEMI-FINALS TO PRAVDA GIRLS' HIGH SCHOOL...
......
EH?!
WHAT?!
THE NISHIZUMI FAMILY WILL...

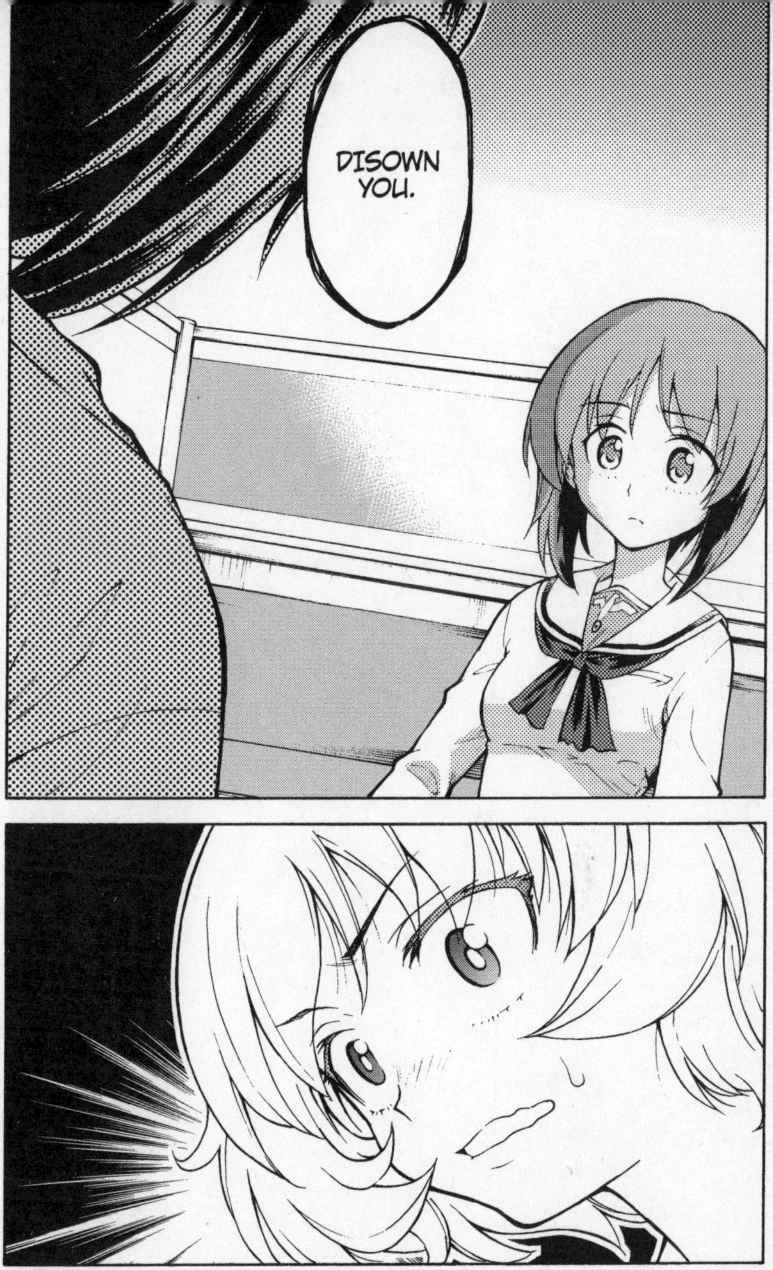
DISOWN YOU.

CHAPTER 11 Semi-Finals Against Pravda Girls' High School! Begins!!

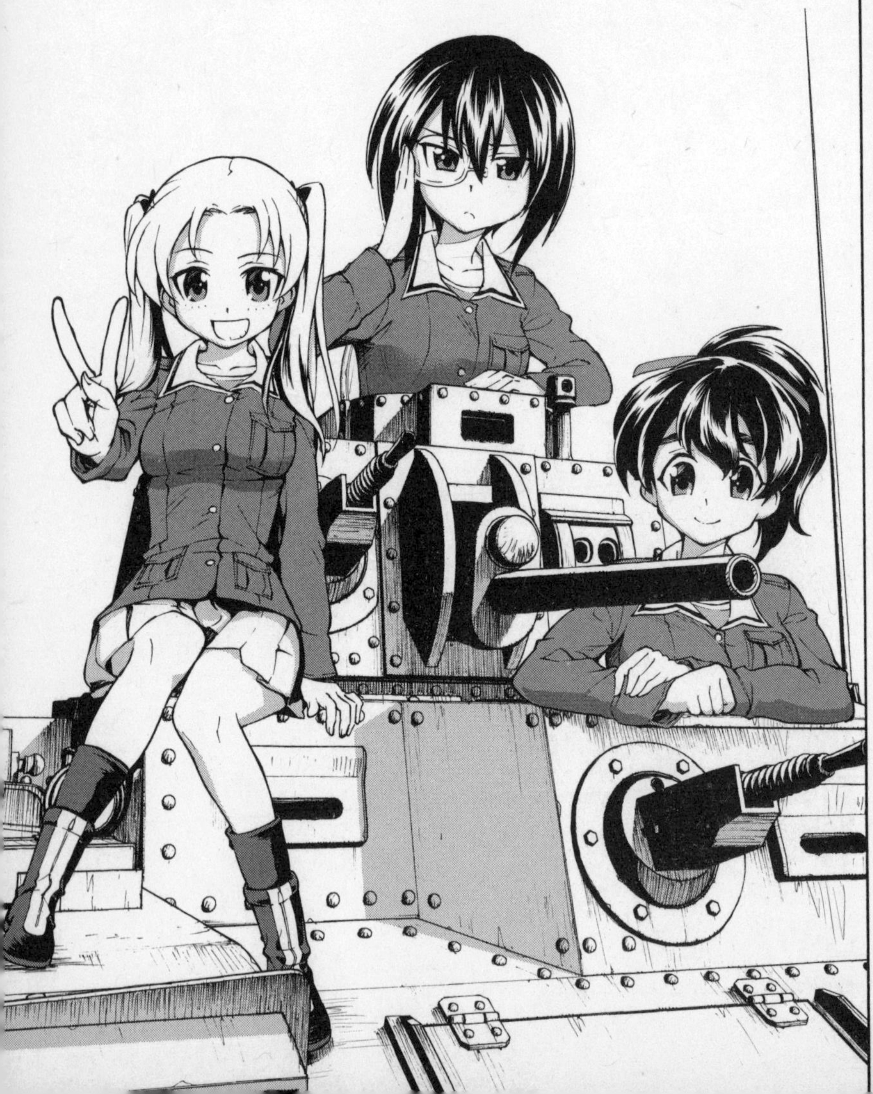

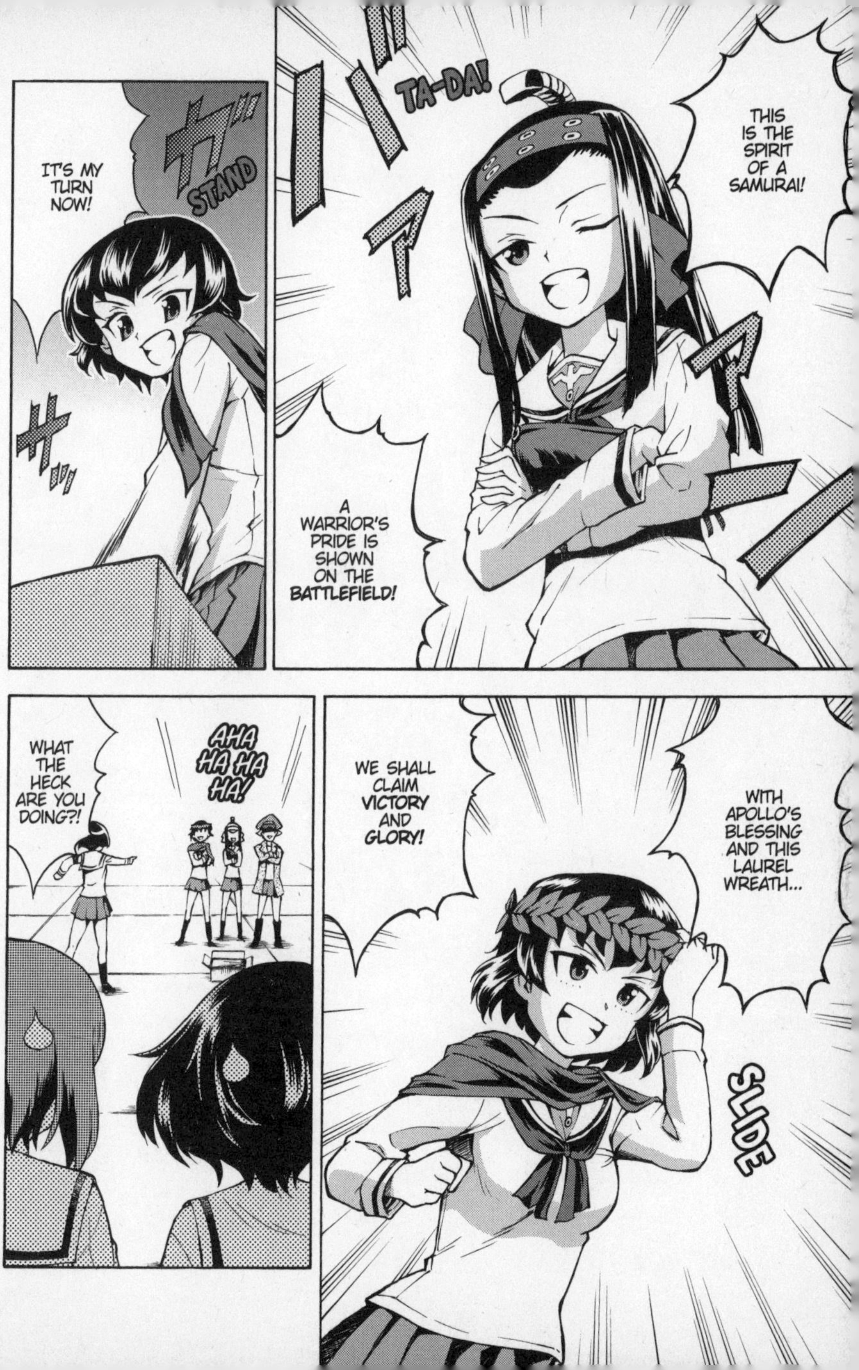

THIS IS THE SPIRIT OF A SAMURAI!
TA-DA!
A WARRIOR'S PRIDE IS SHOWN ON THE BATTLEFIELD!
STAND
IT'S MY TURN NOW!
WITH APOLLO'S BLESSING AND THIS LAUREL WREATH...
WE SHALL CLAIM VICTORY AND GLORY!
SLIDE
AHA HA HA HA HA!
WHAT THE HECK ARE YOU DOING?!

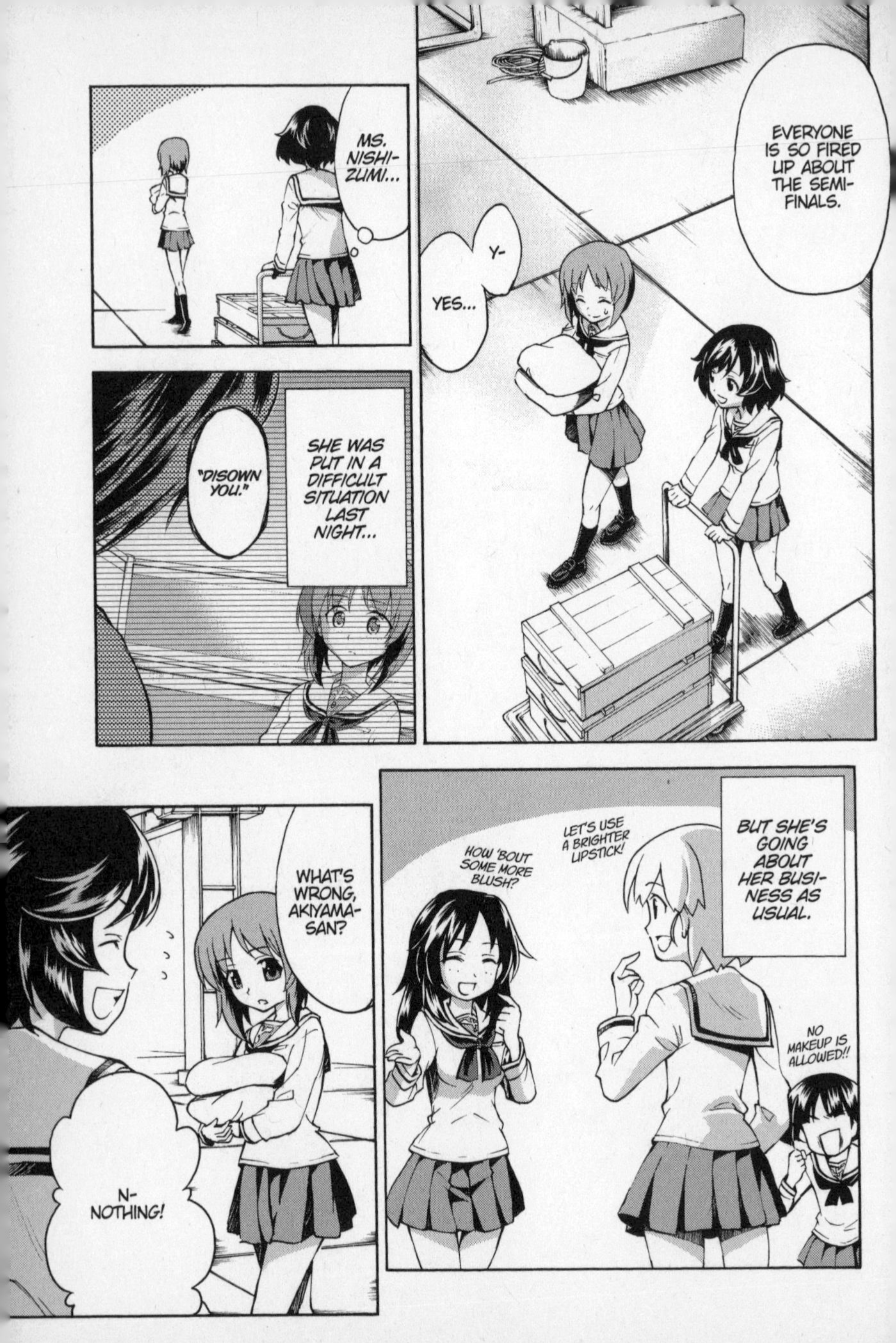
EVERYONE IS SO FIRED UP ABOUT THE SEMI-FINALS.
Y- YES...
MS. NISHI-ZUMI...
SHE WAS PUT IN A DIFFICULT SITUATION LAST NIGHT...
"DISOWN YOU."
BUT SHE'S GOING ABOUT HER BUSI-NESS AS USUAL.
LET'S USE A BRIGHTER LIPSTICK!
HOW 'BOUT SOME MORE BLUSH?
NO MAKEUP IS ALLOWED!!
WHAT'S WRONG, AKIYAMA-SAN?
N-NOTHING!

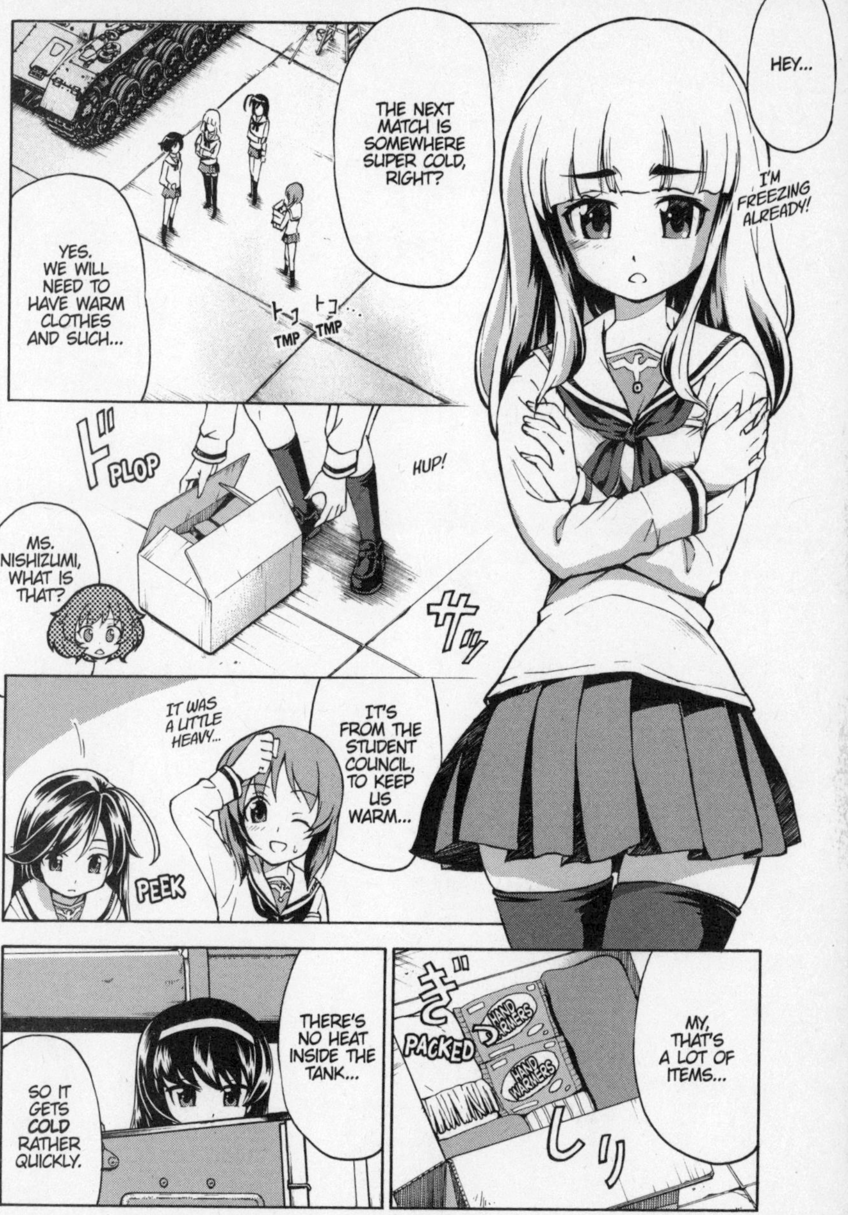

HEY...
I'M FREEZING ALREADY!
THE NEXT MATCH IS SOMEWHERE SUPER COLD, RIGHT?
YES. WE WILL NEED TO HAVE WARM CLOTHES AND SUCH...
TMP TMP
HUP!
PLOP
MS. NISHIZUMI, WHAT IS THAT?
IT'S FROM THE STUDENT COUNCIL, TO KEEP US WARM...
IT WAS A LITTLE HEAVY...
PEEK
MY, THAT'S A LOT OF ITEMS...
PACKED
HAND WARMERS
HAND WARMERS
THERE'S NO HEAT INSIDE THE TANK...
SO IT GETS COLD RATHER QUICKLY.

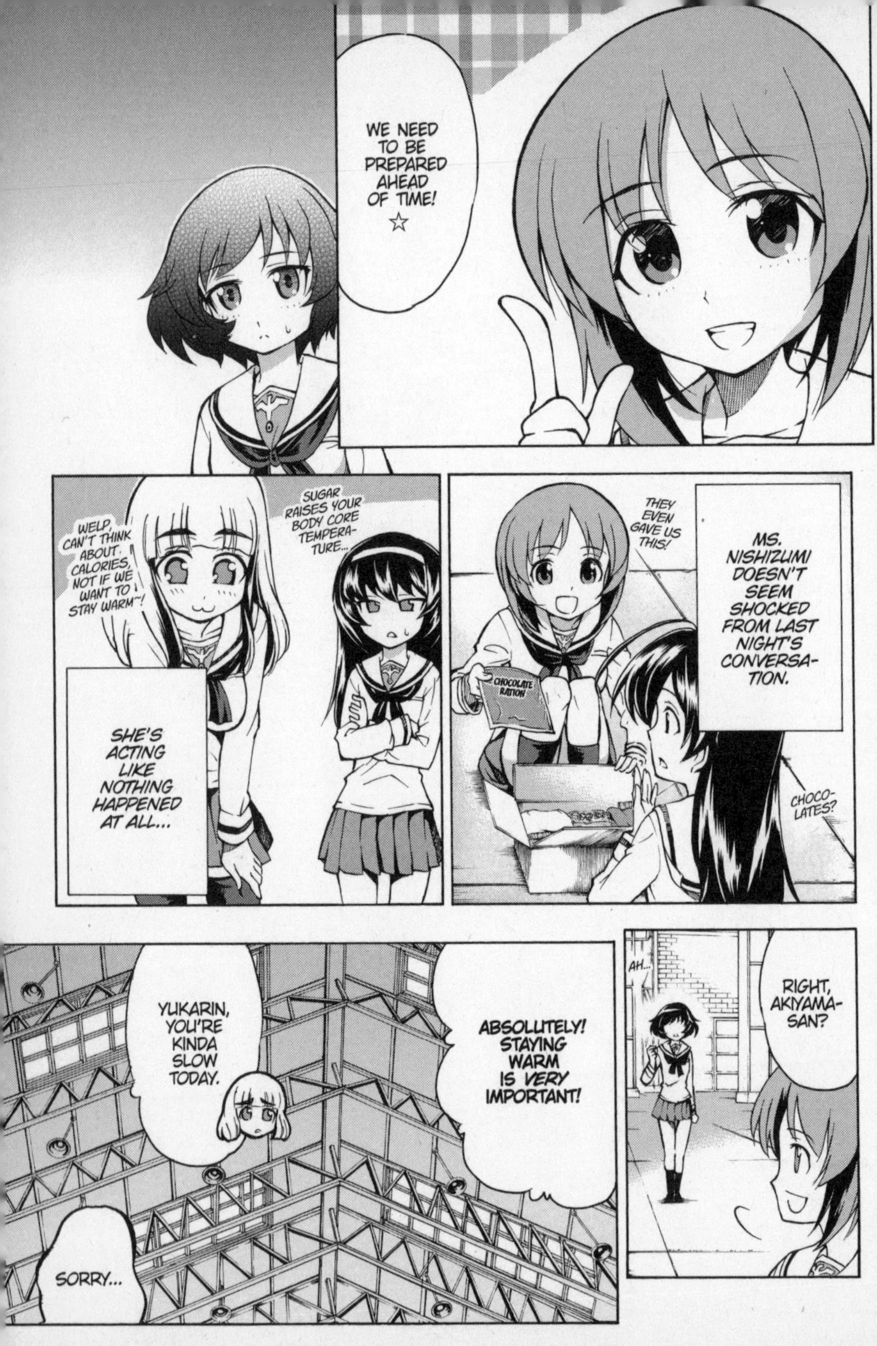
WE NEED TO BE PREPARED AHEAD OF TIME! ☆
MS. NISHIZUMI DOESN'T SEEM SHOCKED FROM LAST NIGHT'S CONVERSA-TION.
THEY EVEN GAVE US THIS!
CHOCOLATE RATION
CHOCO-LATES?
SUGAR RAISES YOUR BODY CORE TEMPERA-TURE...
WELP, CAN'T THINK ABOUT CALORIES, NOT IF WE WANT TO STAY WARM~!
SHE'S ACTING LIKE NOTHING HAPPENED AT ALL...
RIGHT, AKIYAMA-SAN?
AH...
ABSOLUTELY! STAYING WARM IS *VERY* IMPORTANT!
YUKARIN, YOU'RE KINDA SLOW TODAY.
SORRY...

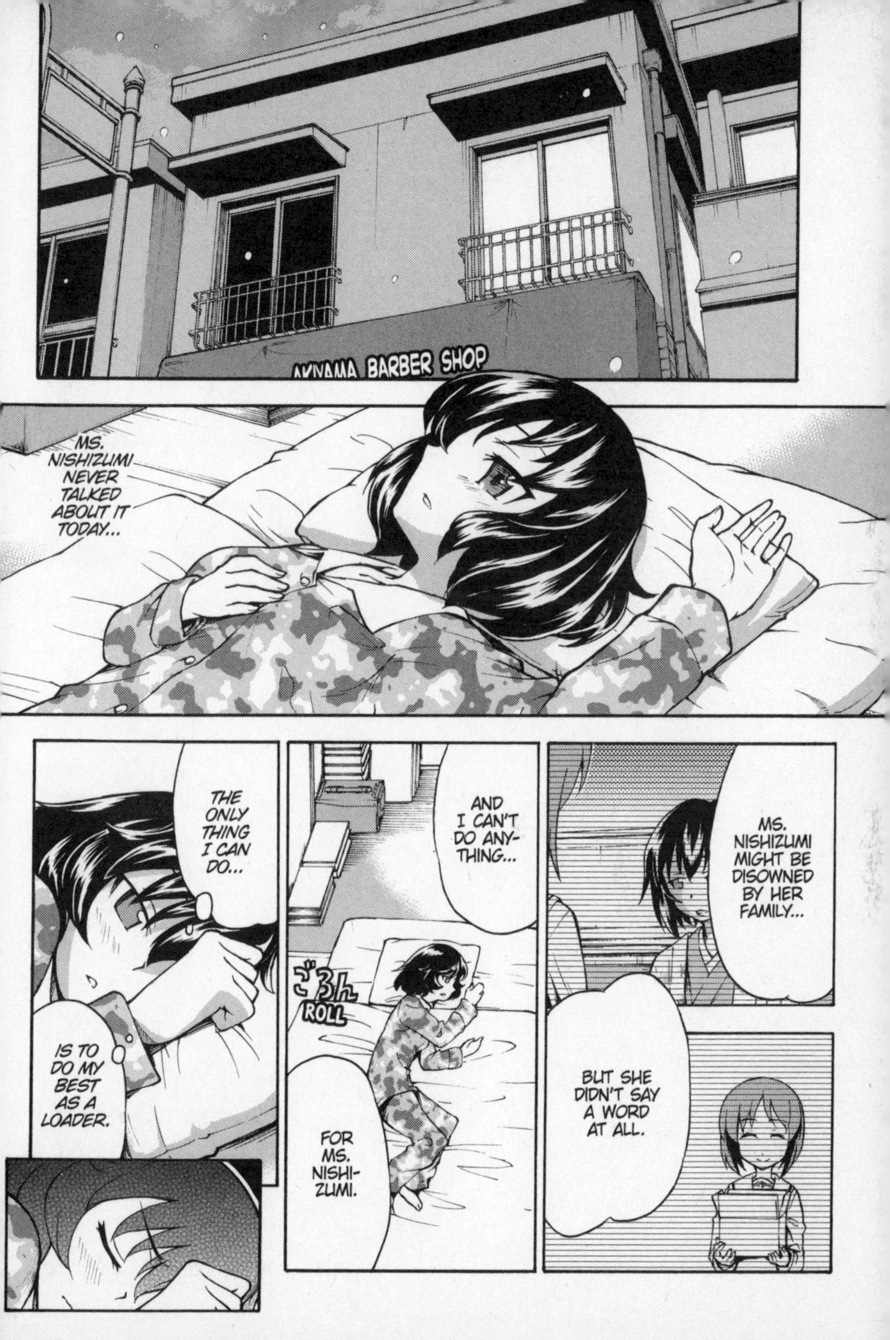
AKIYAMA BARBER SHOP
MS. NISHIZUMI NEVER TALKED ABOUT IT TODAY...
MS. NISHIZUMI MIGHT BE DISOWNED BY HER FAMILY...
BUT SHE DIDN'T SAY A WORD AT ALL.
AND I CAN'T DO ANY-THING...
ごろん
ROLL
FOR MS. NISHI-ZUMI.
THE ONLY THING I CAN DO...
IS TO DO MY BEST AS A LOADER.

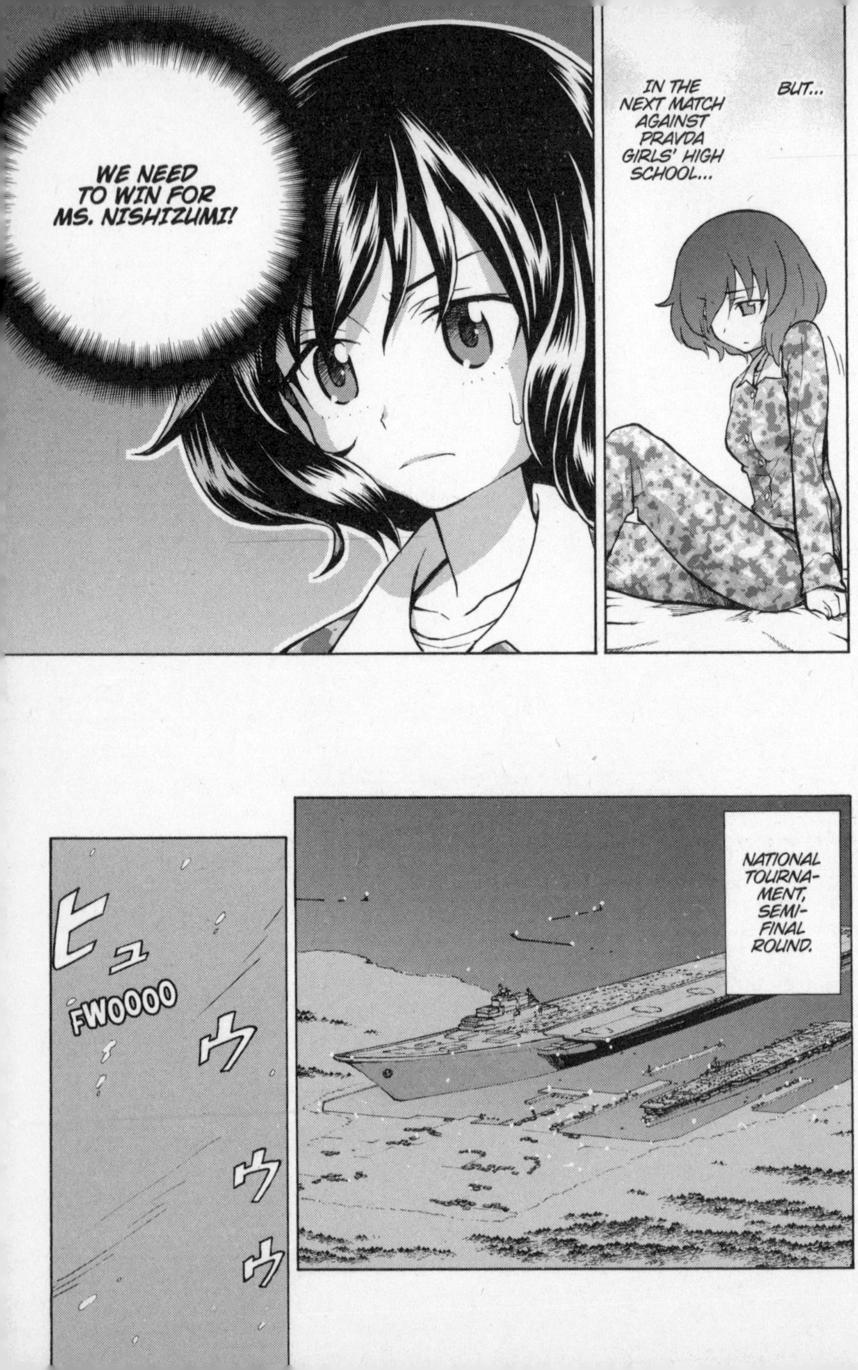
BUT...
IN THE NEXT MATCH AGAINST PRAVDA GIRLS' HIGH SCHOOL...
WE NEED TO WIN FOR MS. NISHIZUMI!
NATIONAL TOURNAMENT, SEMIFINAL ROUND.
ヒュウウウ
FWOOOO

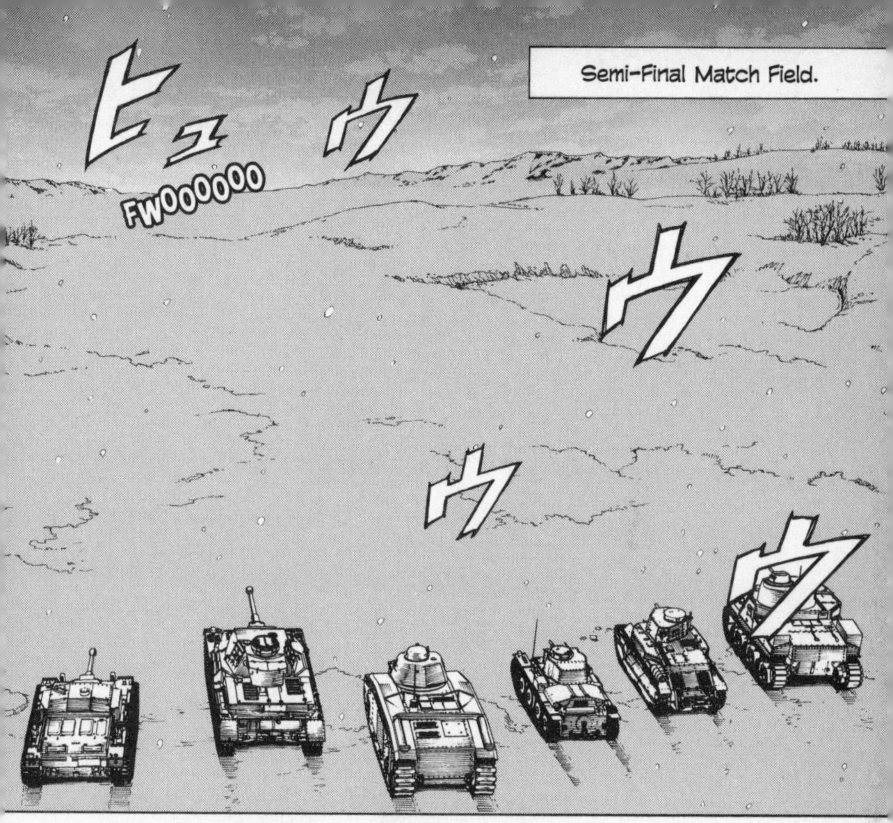
Semi-Final Match Field.
ヒュウウウウ
FWOOOOOO
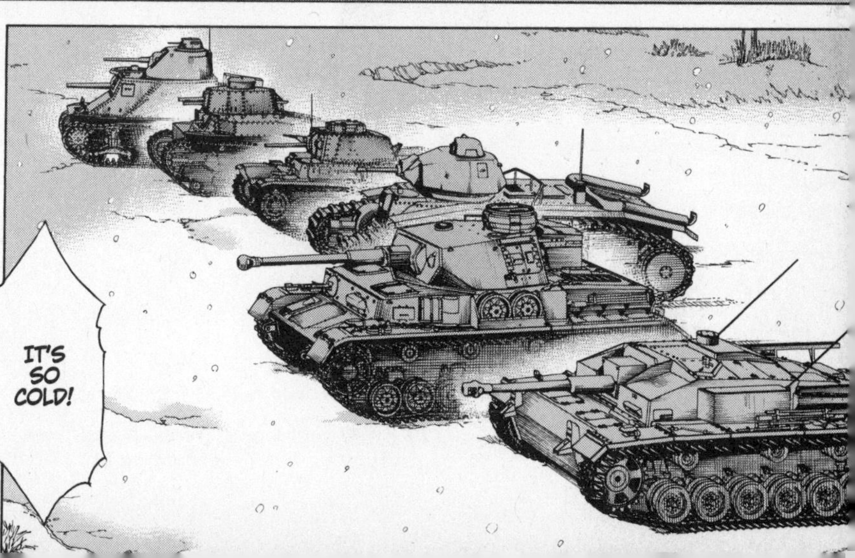
IT'S SO COLD!

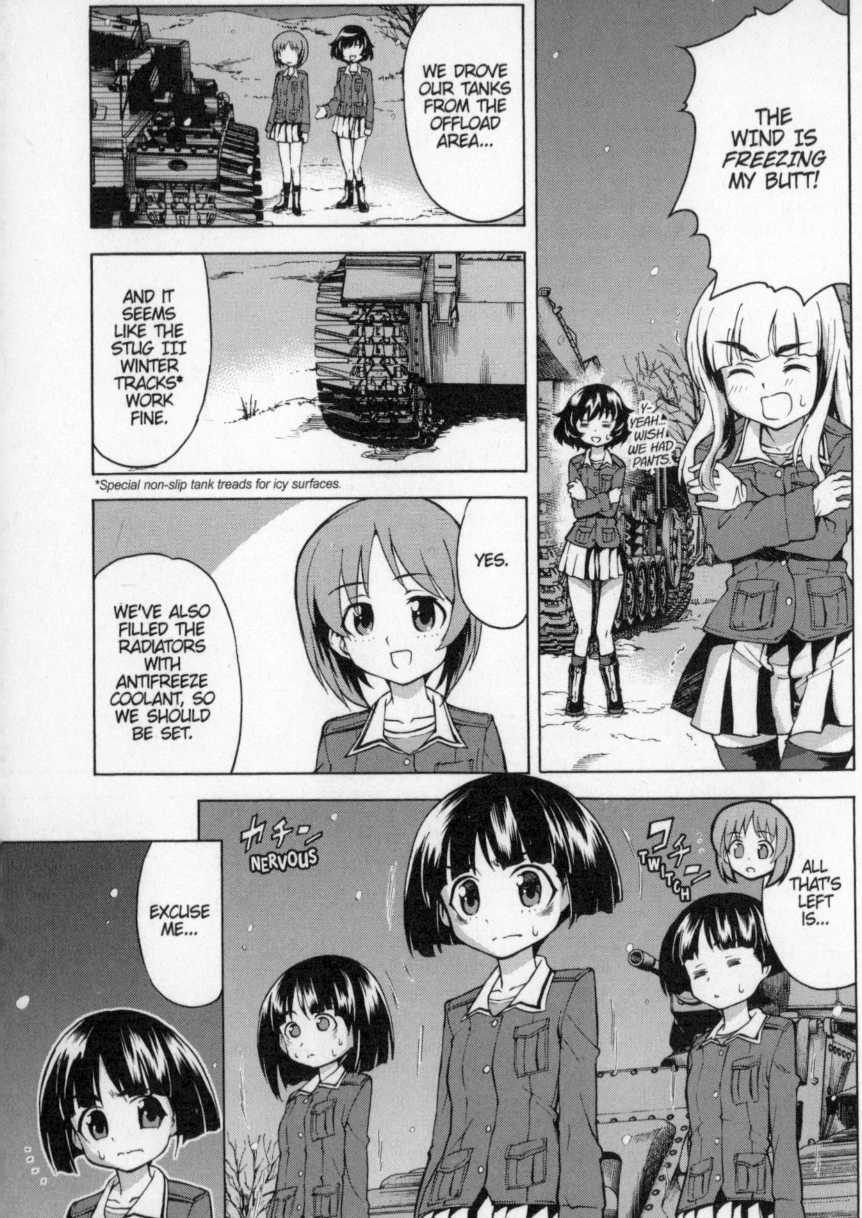
THE WIND IS FREEZING MY BUTT!
Y-YEAH... WISH WE HAD PANTS.
WE DROVE OUR TANKS FROM THE OFFLOAD AREA...
AND IT SEEMS LIKE THE STUG III WINTER TRACKS* WORK FINE.
YES.
WE'VE ALSO FILLED THE RADIATORS WITH ANTIFREEZE COOLANT, SO WE SHOULD BE SET.
ALL THAT'S LEFT IS...
TWITCH
NERVOUS
EXCUSE ME...
*Special non-slip tank treads for icy surfaces.

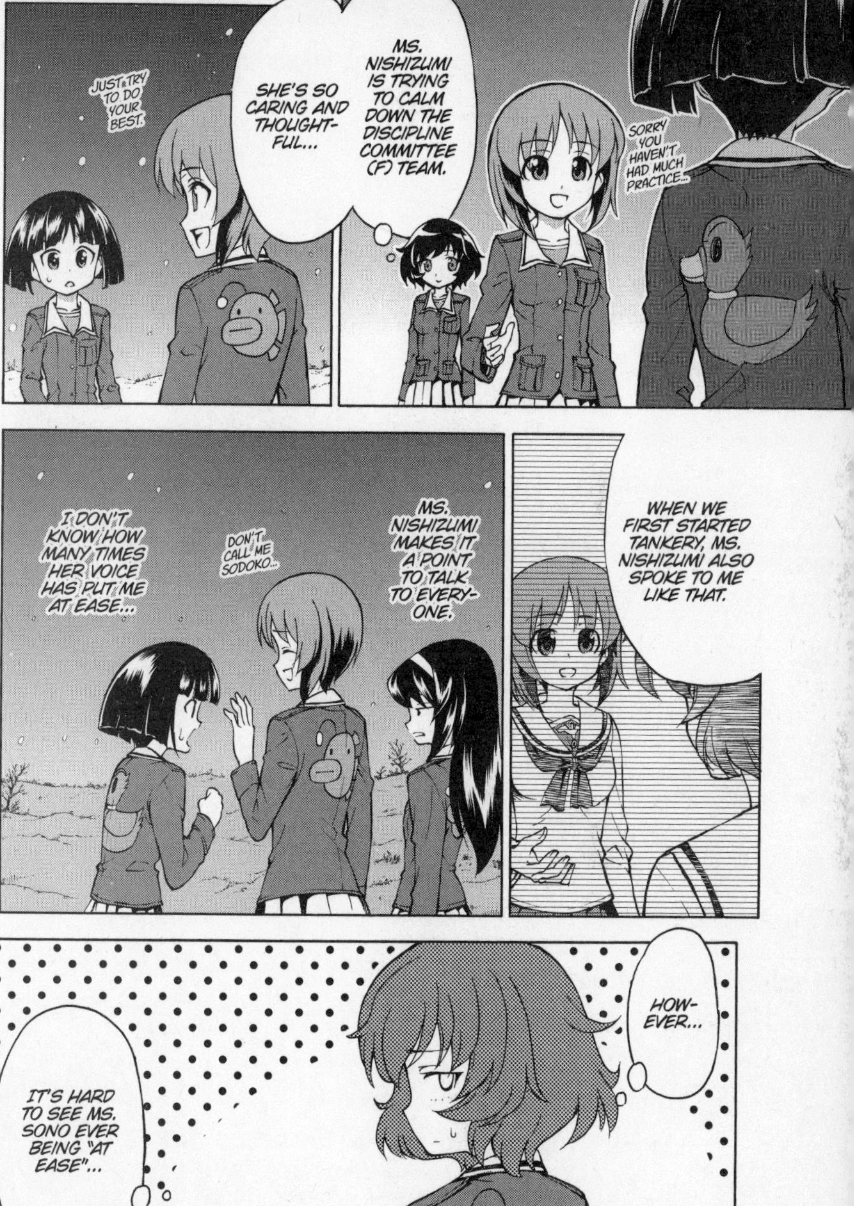
SORRY YOU HAVEN'T HAD MUCH PRACTICE...
MS. NISHIZUMI IS TRYING TO CALM DOWN THE DISCIPLINE COMMITTEE (F) TEAM.
SHE'S SO CARING AND THOUGHT-FUL...
JUST TRY TO DO YOUR BEST.
WHEN WE FIRST STARTED TANKERY, MS. NISHIZUMI ALSO SPOKE TO ME LIKE THAT.
MS. NISHIZUMI MAKES IT A POINT TO TALK TO EVERY-ONE.
DON'T CALL ME SODOKO...
I DON'T KNOW HOW MANY TIMES HER VOICE HAS PUT ME AT EASE...
HOW-EVER...
IT'S HARD TO SEE MS. SONO EVER BEING "AT EASE"...

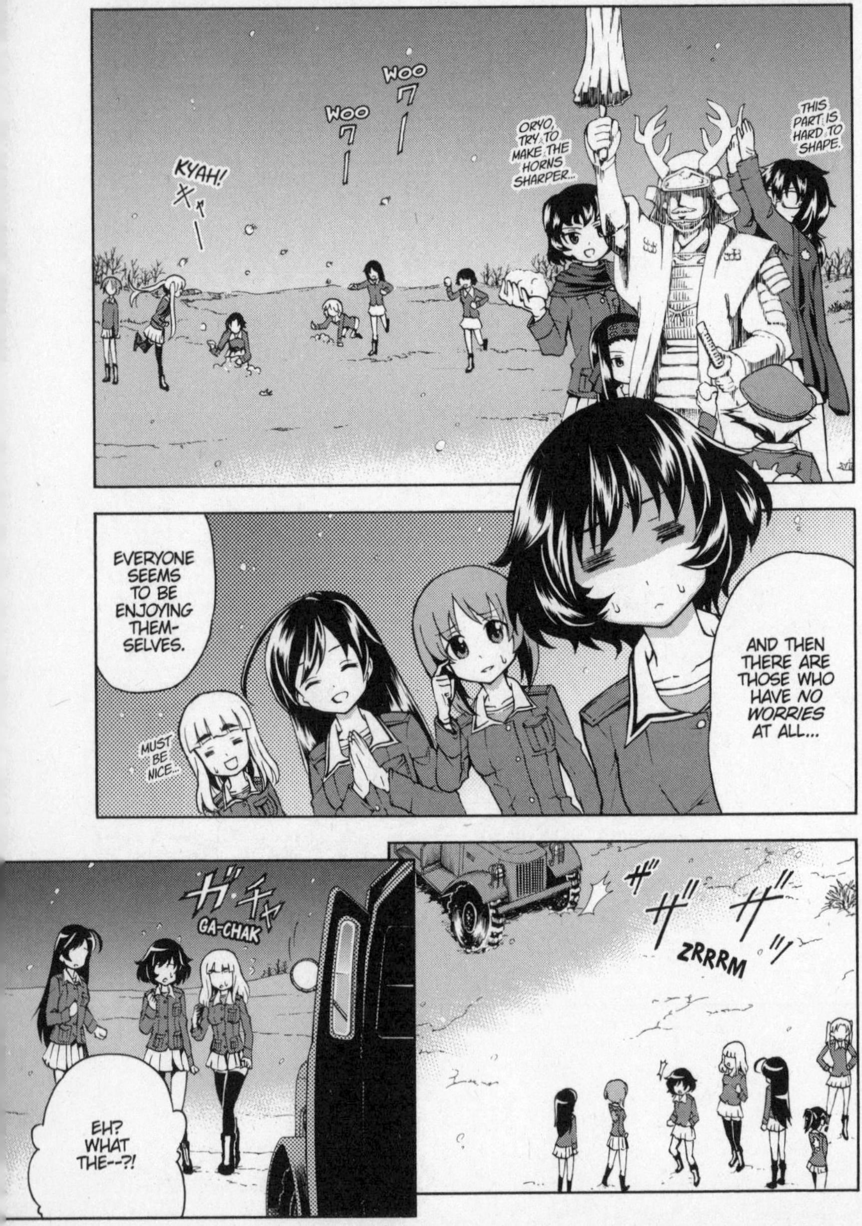
THIS PART IS HARD TO SHAPE.
ORYO, TRY TO MAKE THE HORNS SHARPER...
WOO
ワー
WOO
ワー
KYAH!
キャー
AND THEN THERE ARE THOSE WHO HAVE *NO WORRIES* AT ALL...
EVERYONE SEEMS TO BE ENJOYING THEM-SELVES.
MUST BE NICE...
ザザザッ
ZRRRM
ガチャ
GA-CHAK
EH? WHAT THE--?!

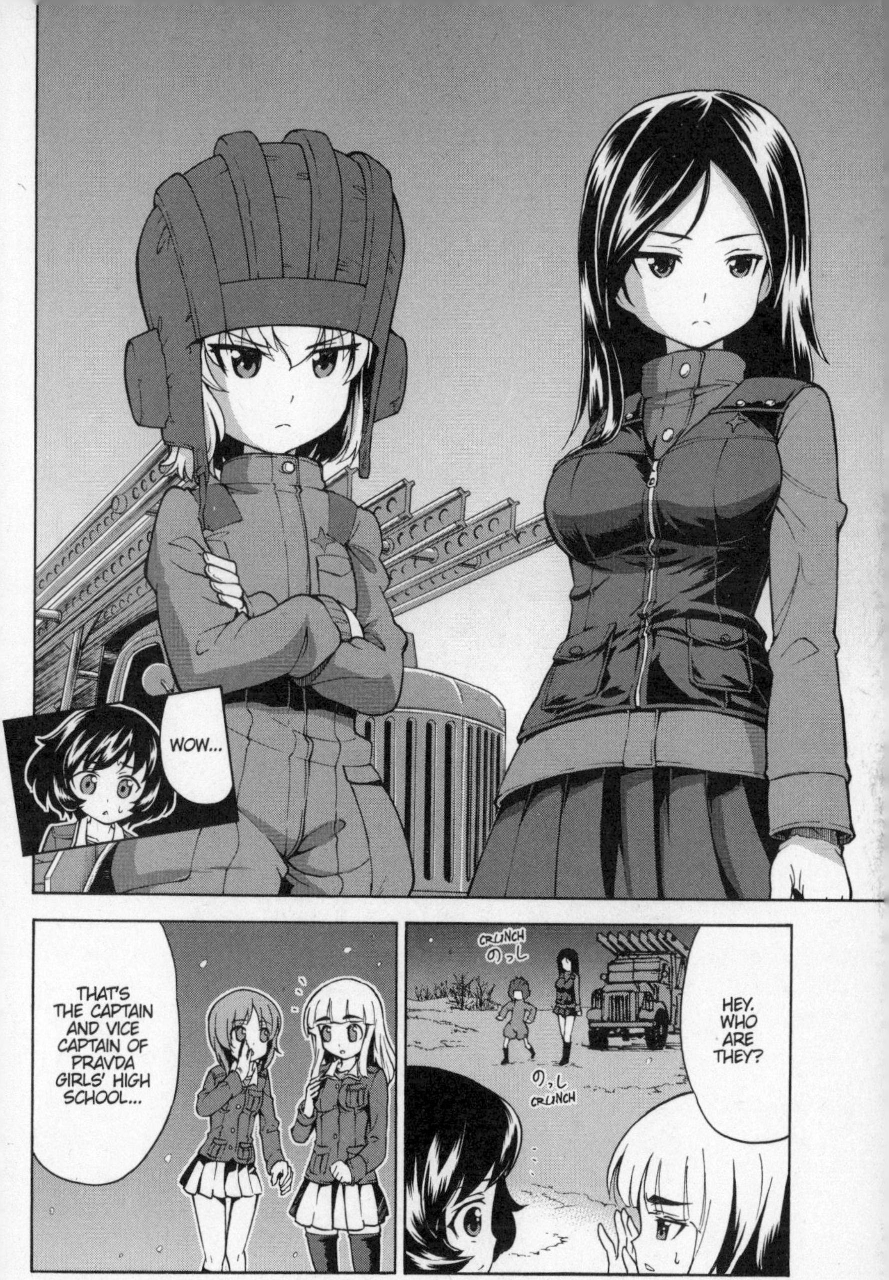
WOW...
HEY. WHO ARE THEY?
CRUNCH のっし
のっし CRUNCH
THAT'S THE CAPTAIN AND VICE CAPTAIN OF PRAVDA GIRLS' HIGH SCHOOL...

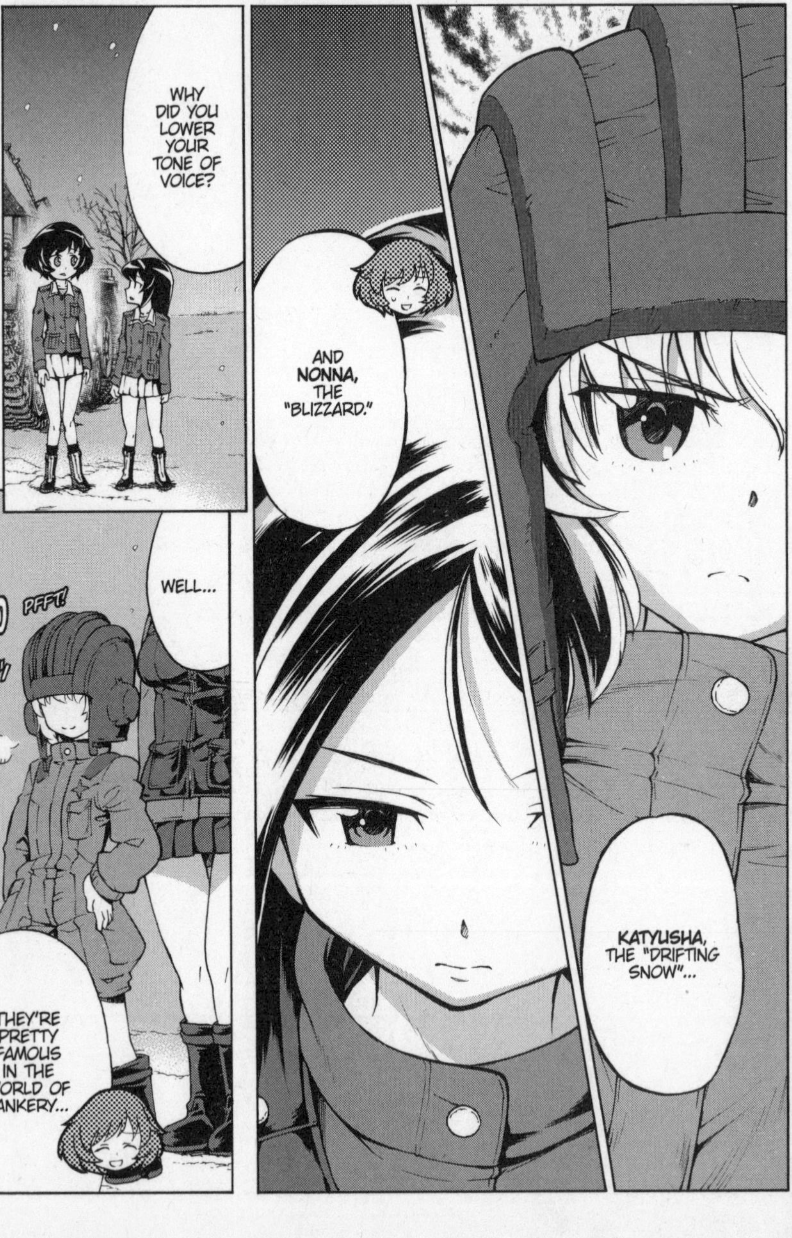
KATYUSHA, THE "DRIFTING SNOW"...
AND NONNA, THE "BLIZZARD."
WHY DID YOU LOWER YOUR TONE OF VOICE?
WELL...
PFFT!
フッ
THEY'RE PRETTY FAMOUS IN THE WORLD OF TANKERY...

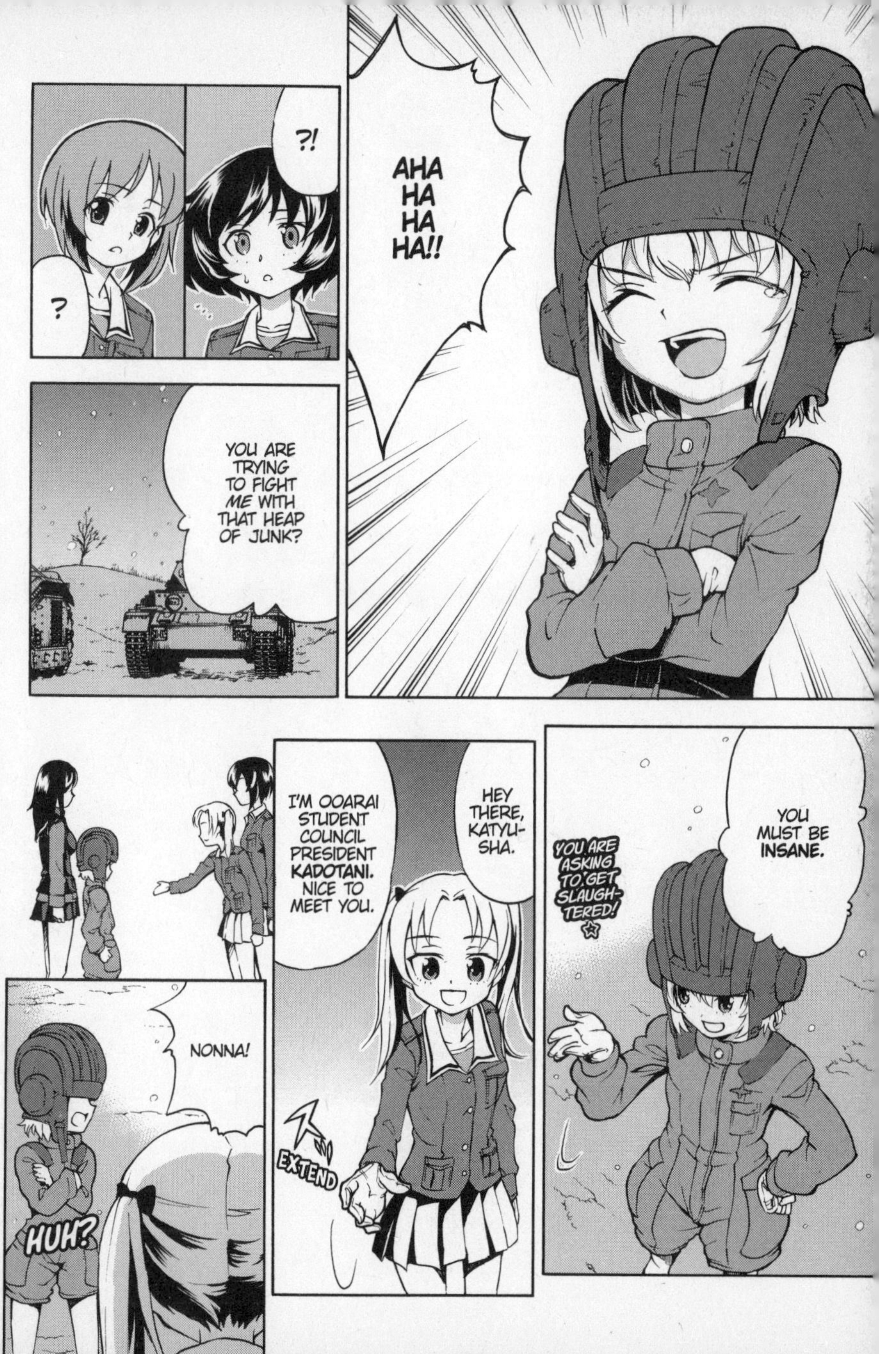

AHA HA HA HA!!
?!
?
YOU ARE TRYING TO FIGHT *ME* WITH THAT HEAP OF JUNK?
YOU MUST BE INSANE.
YOU ARE ASKING TO GET SLAUGHTERED! ☆
HEY THERE, KATYUSHA.
I'M OOARAI STUDENT COUNCIL PRESIDENT KADOTANI. NICE TO MEET YOU.
EXTEND
NONNA!
HUH?

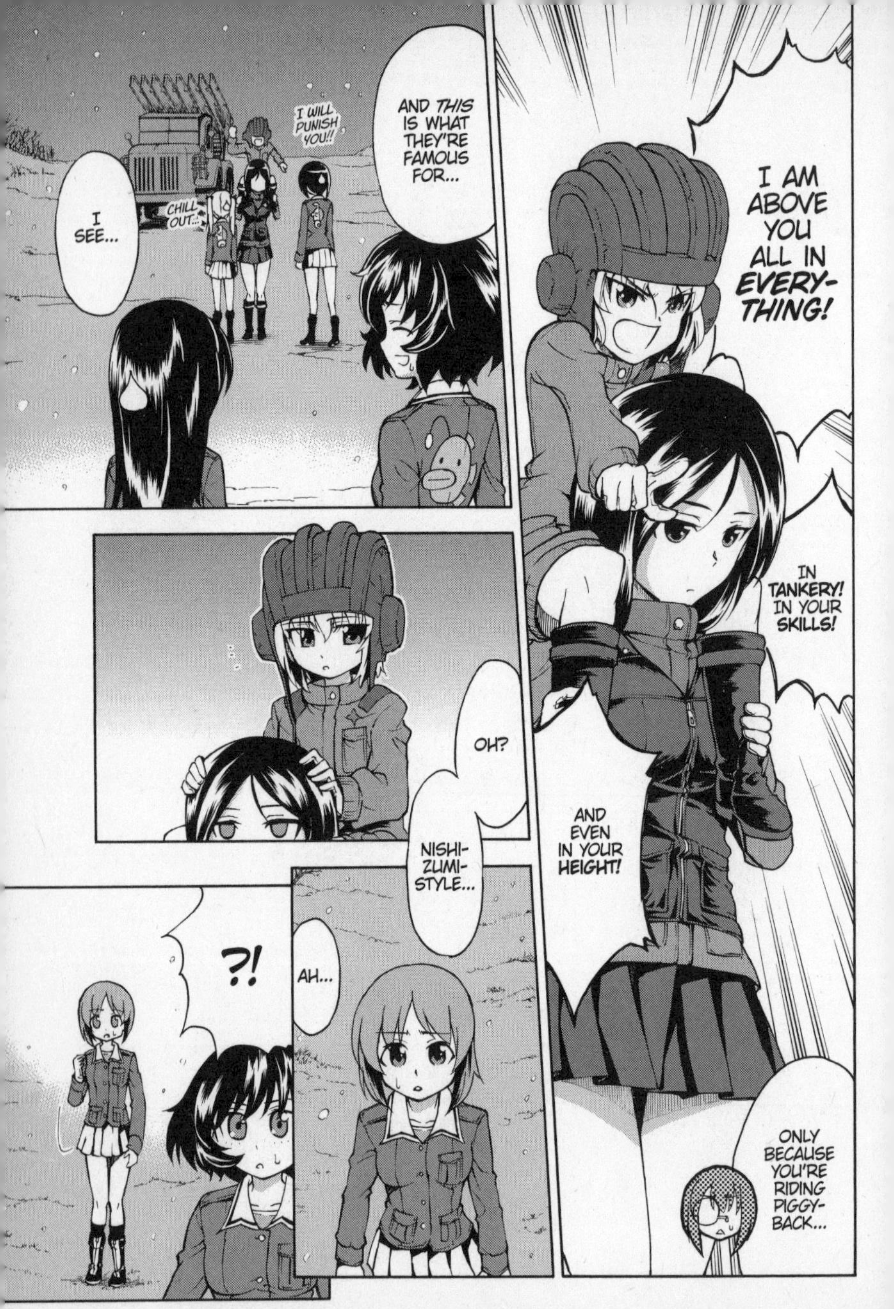
I AM ABOVE YOU ALL IN EVERY-THING!
IN TANKERY! IN YOUR SKILLS!
AND EVEN IN YOUR HEIGHT!
ONLY BECAUSE YOU'RE RIDING PIGGY-BACK...
AND THIS IS WHAT THEY'RE FAMOUS FOR...
I WILL PUNISH YOU!!
CHILL OUT...
I SEE...
OH?
NISHI-ZUMI-STYLE...
AH...
?!

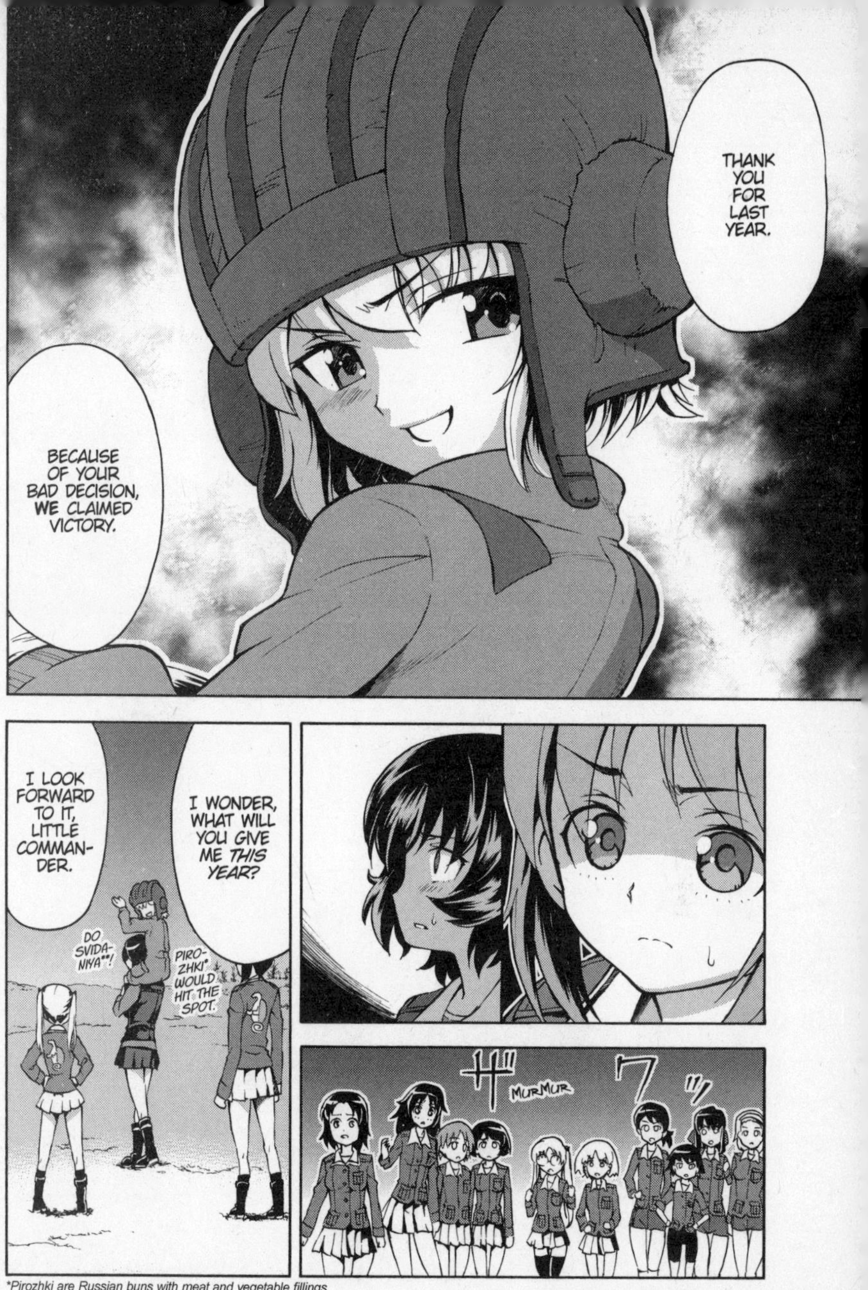
THANK YOU FOR LAST YEAR.
BECAUSE OF YOUR BAD DECISION, WE CLAIMED VICTORY.
ザワッ
MURMUR
I WONDER, WHAT WILL YOU GIVE ME *THIS YEAR?*
I LOOK FORWARD TO IT, LITTLE COMMANDER.
PIROZHKI* WOULD HIT THE SPOT.
DO SVIDANIYA**!

*Pirozhki are Russian buns with meat and vegetable fillings.
**"Do svidaniya" is Russian for "goodbye."

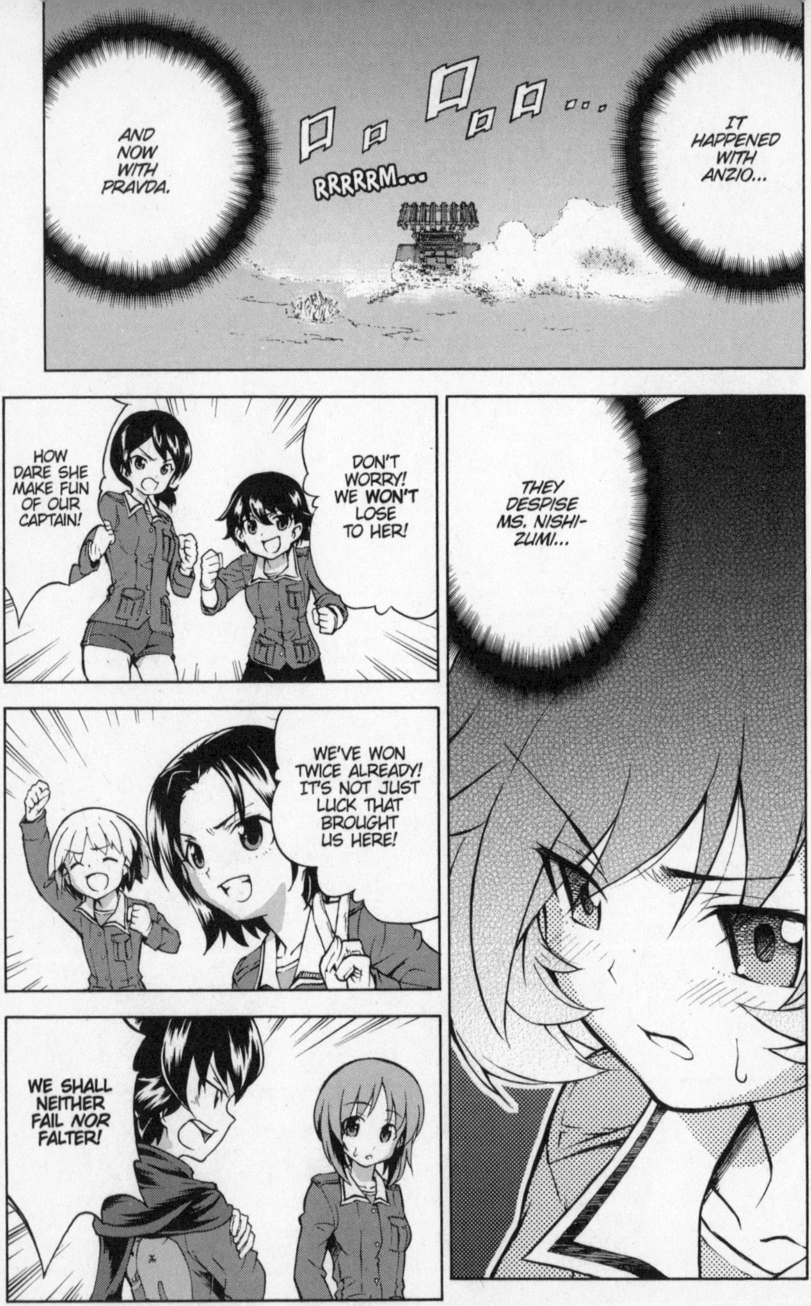
IT HAPPENED WITH ANZIO...
RRRRRM...
AND NOW WITH PRAVDA.
THEY DESPISE MS. NISHIZUMI...
DON'T WORRY! WE WON'T LOSE TO HER!
HOW DARE SHE MAKE FUN OF OUR CAPTAIN!
WE'VE WON TWICE ALREADY! IT'S NOT JUST LUCK THAT BROUGHT US HERE!
WE SHALL NEITHER FAIL NOR FALTER!

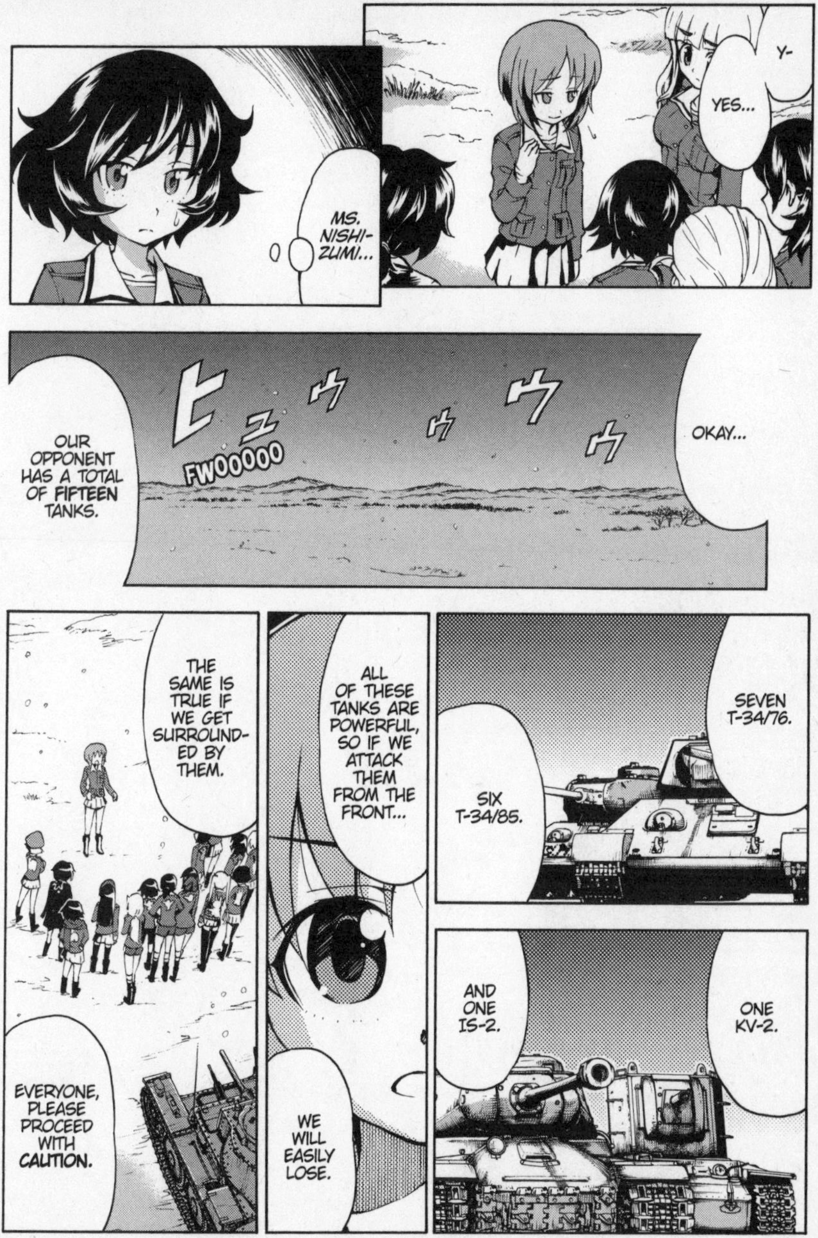
Y-
YES...
MS. NISHIZUMI...
OKAY...
ヒュウゥウゥ
FWOOOOO
OUR OPPONENT HAS A TOTAL OF FIFTEEN TANKS.
SEVEN T-34/76.
SIX T-34/85.
ONE KV-2.
AND ONE IS-2.
ALL OF THESE TANKS ARE POWERFUL, SO IF WE ATTACK THEM FROM THE FRONT...
WE WILL EASILY LOSE.
THE SAME IS TRUE IF WE GET SURROUNDED BY THEM.
EVERYONE, PLEASE PROCEED WITH CAUTION.

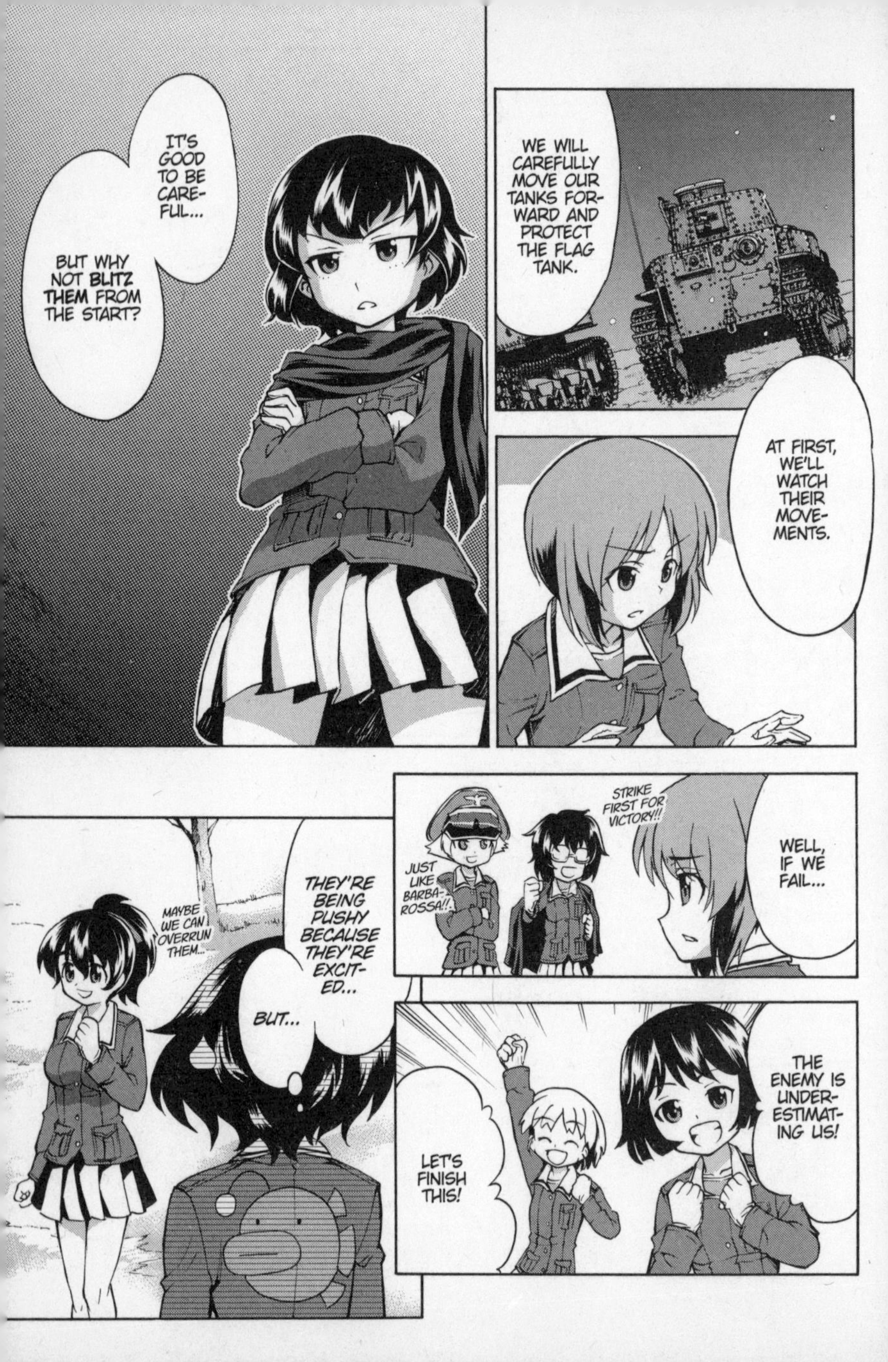
WE WILL CAREFULLY MOVE OUR TANKS FOR-WARD AND PROTECT THE FLAG TANK.
AT FIRST, WE'LL WATCH THEIR MOVE-MENTS.
IT'S GOOD TO BE CARE-FUL...
BUT WHY NOT **BLITZ THEM** FROM THE START?
WELL, IF WE FAIL...
STRIKE FIRST FOR VICTORY!!
JUST LIKE BARBA-ROSSA!!
THE ENEMY IS UNDER-ESTIMAT-ING US!
LET'S FINISH THIS!
THEY'RE BEING PUSHY BECAUSE THEY'RE EXCIT-ED...
BUT...
MAYBE WE CAN OVERRUN THEM...

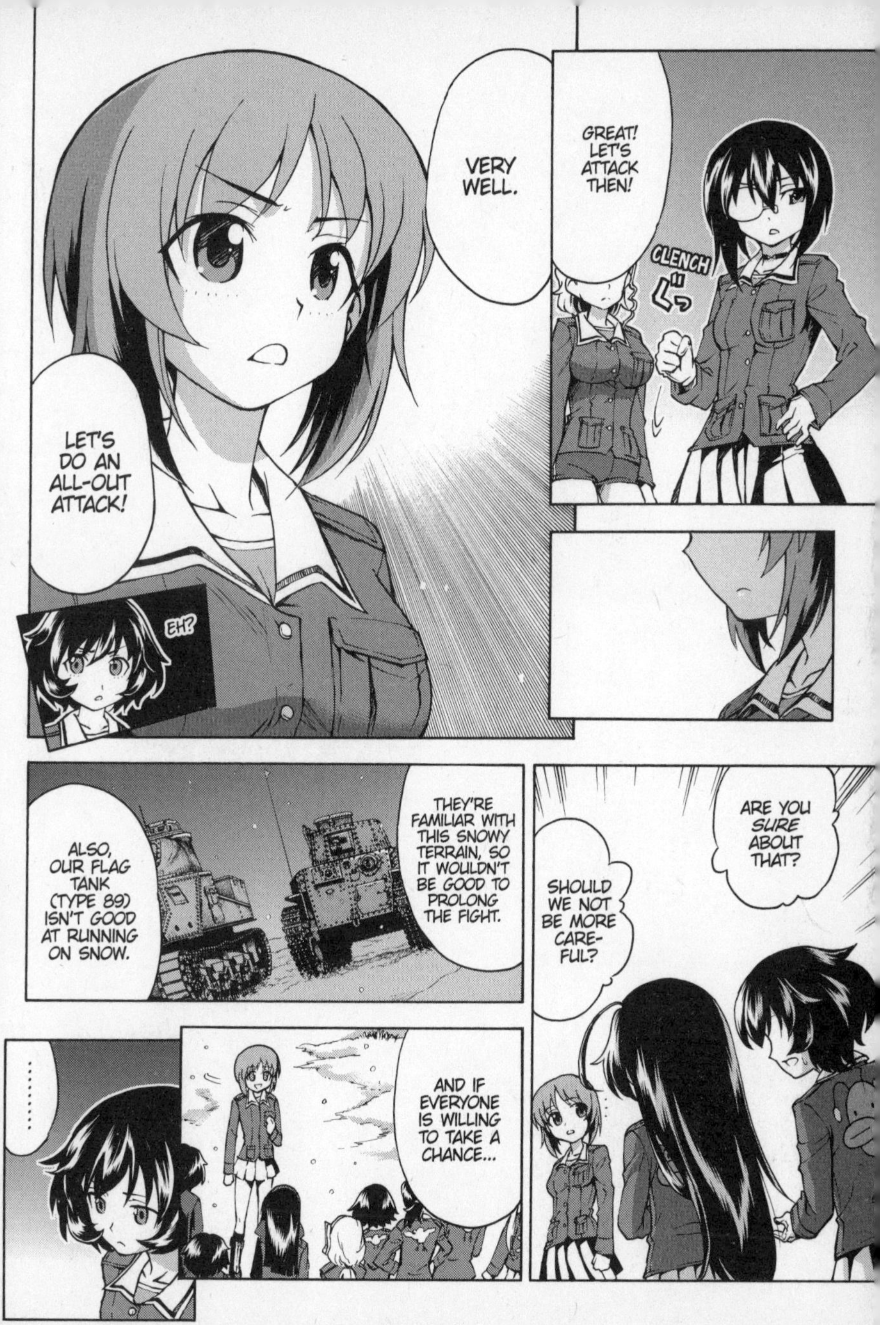

GREAT! LET'S ATTACK THEN!
CLENCH
ぐっ
VERY WELL.
LET'S DO AN ALL-OUT ATTACK!
EH?
ARE YOU SURE ABOUT THAT?
SHOULD WE NOT BE MORE CARE-FUL?
THEY'RE FAMILIAR WITH THIS SNOWY TERRAIN, SO IT WOULDN'T BE GOOD TO PROLONG THE FIGHT.
ALSO, OUR FLAG TANK (TYPE 89) ISN'T GOOD AT RUNNING ON SNOW.
AND IF EVERYONE IS WILLING TO TAKE A CHANCE...
....

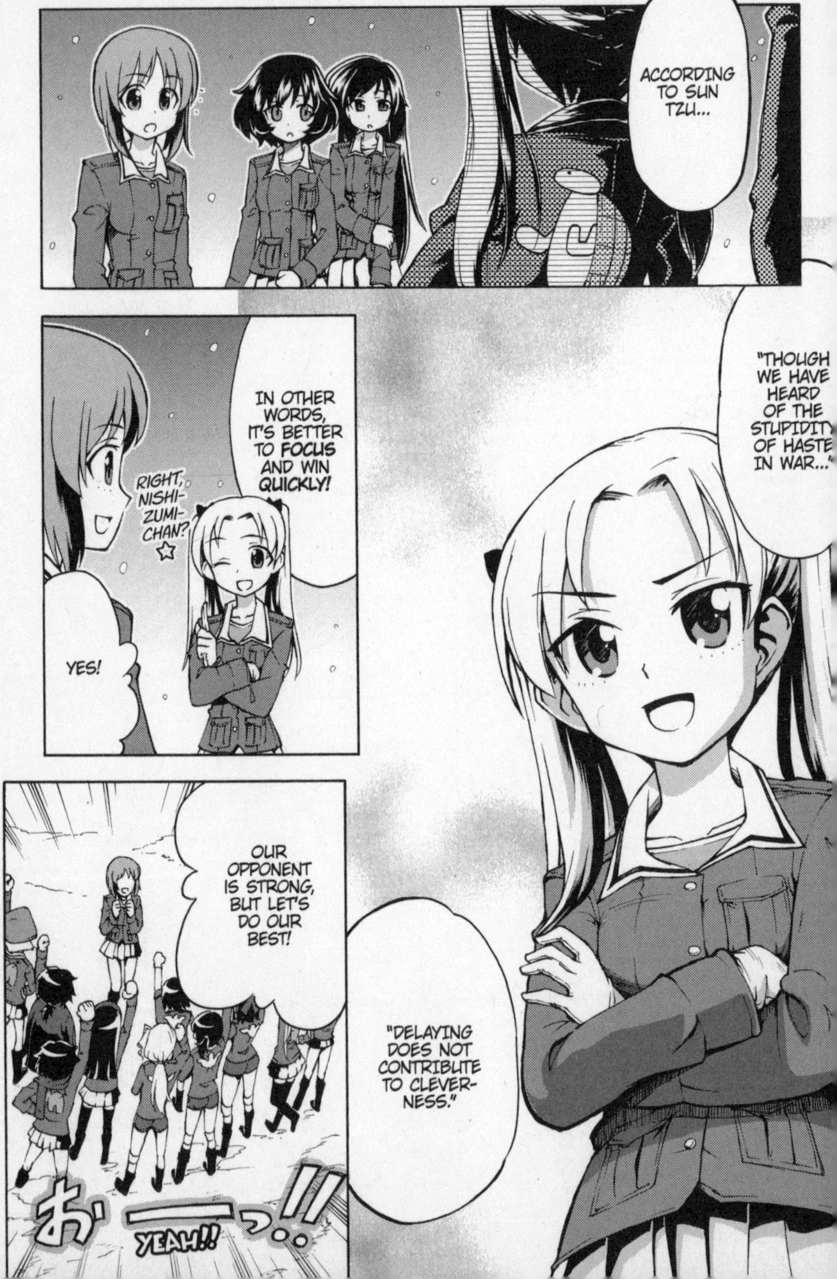
ACCORDING TO SUN TZU...
"THOUGH WE HAVE HEARD OF THE STUPIDITY OF HASTE IN WAR..."
"DELAYING DOES NOT CONTRIBUTE TO CLEVER-NESS."
IN OTHER WORDS, IT'S BETTER TO FOCUS AND WIN QUICKLY!
RIGHT, NISHI-ZUMI-CHAN? ☆
YES!
OUR OPPONENT IS STRONG, BUT LET'S DO OUR BEST!
お――っ!!
YEAH!!

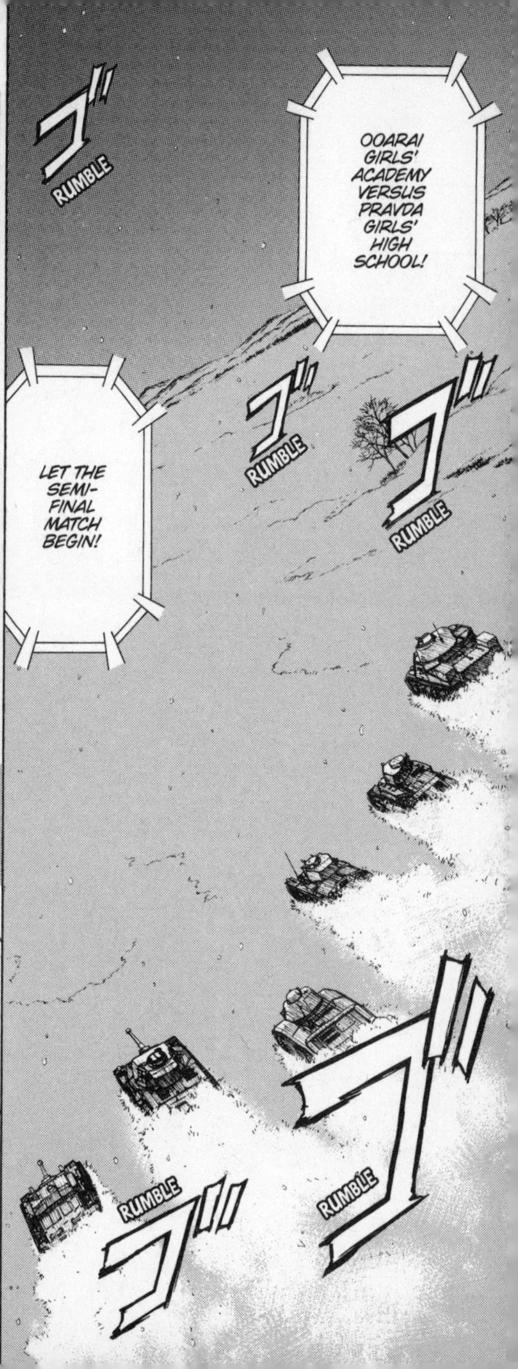
ゴ
RUMBLE
OOARAI GIRLS' ACADEMY VERSUS PRAVDA GIRLS' HIGH SCHOOL!
ゴ
RUMBLE
ゴ
RUMBLE
LET THE SEMI-FINAL MATCH BEGIN!
ゴ
RUMBLE
ゴ
RUMBLE

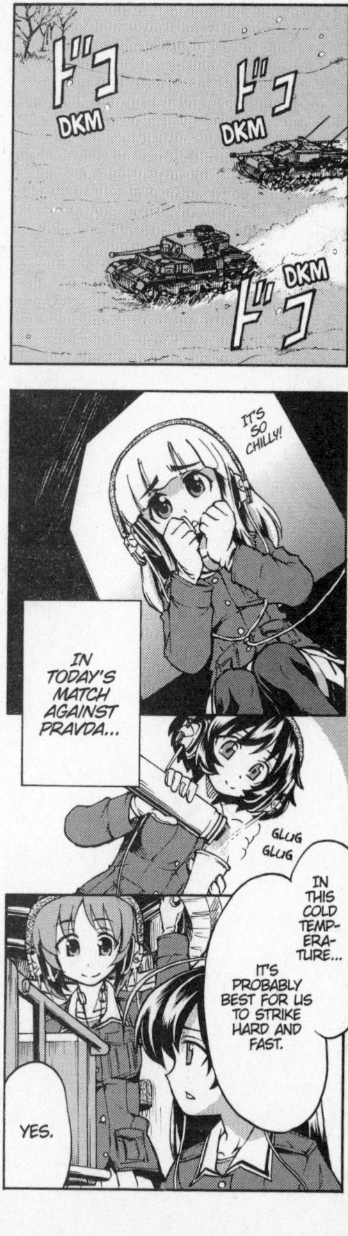
ドコ
DKM
ドコ
DKM
DKM
ドコ
IT'S SO CHILLY!
IN TODAY'S MATCH AGAINST PRAVDA...
GLUG GLUG
IN THIS COLD TEMPERATURE...
IT'S PROBABLY BEST FOR US TO STRIKE HARD AND FAST.
YES.

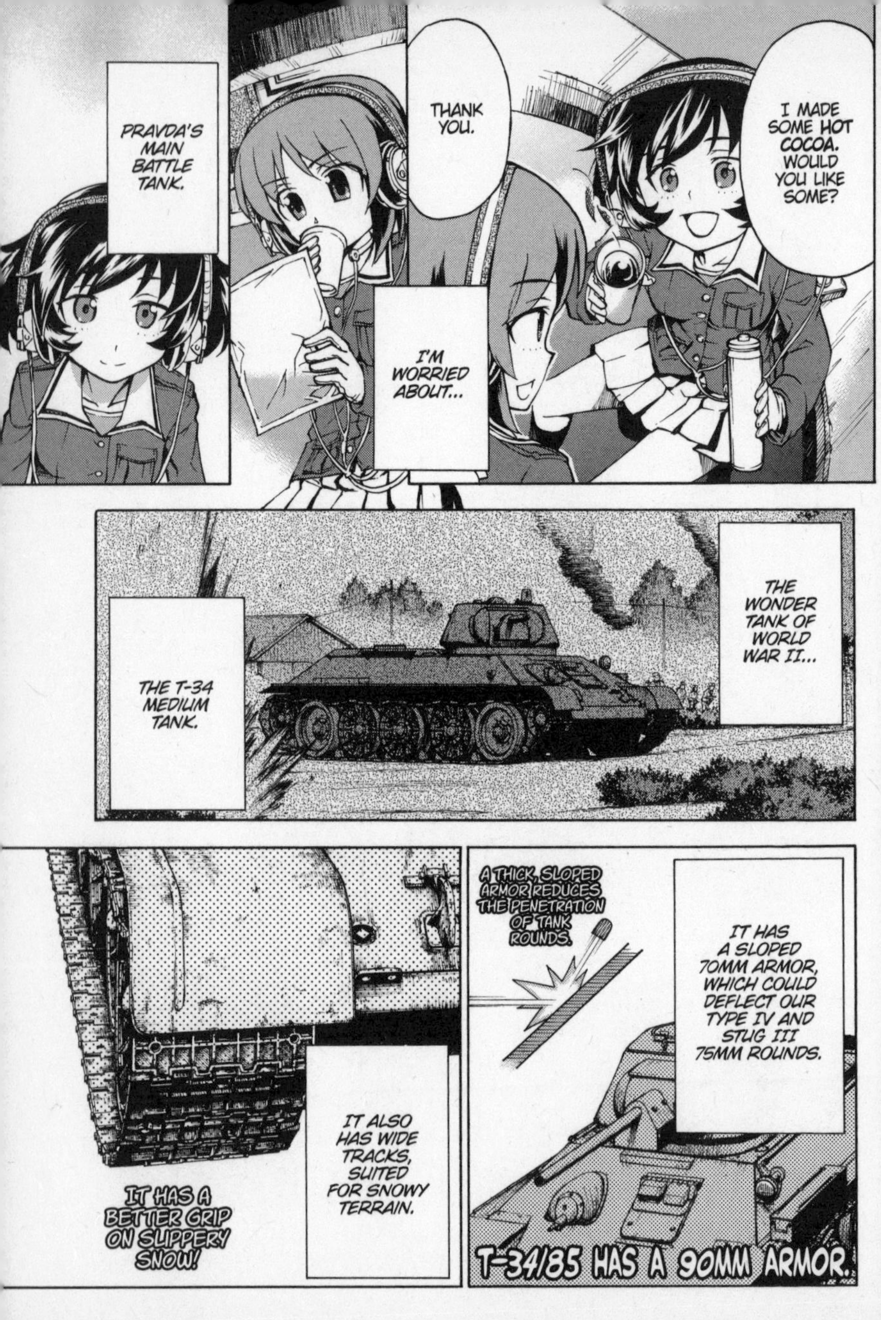
I MADE SOME HOT COCOA. WOULD YOU LIKE SOME?
THANK YOU.
I'M WORRIED ABOUT...
PRAVDA'S MAIN BATTLE TANK.
THE WONDER TANK OF WORLD WAR II...
THE T-34 MEDIUM TANK.
IT HAS A SLOPED 70MM ARMOR, WHICH COULD DEFLECT OUR TYPE IV AND STUG III 75MM ROUNDS.
A THICK, SLOPED ARMOR REDUCES THE PENETRATION OF TANK ROUNDS.
T-34/85 HAS A 90MM ARMOR.
IT ALSO HAS WIDE TRACKS, SUITED FOR SNOWY TERRAIN.
IT HAS A BETTER GRIP ON SLIPPERY SNOW!

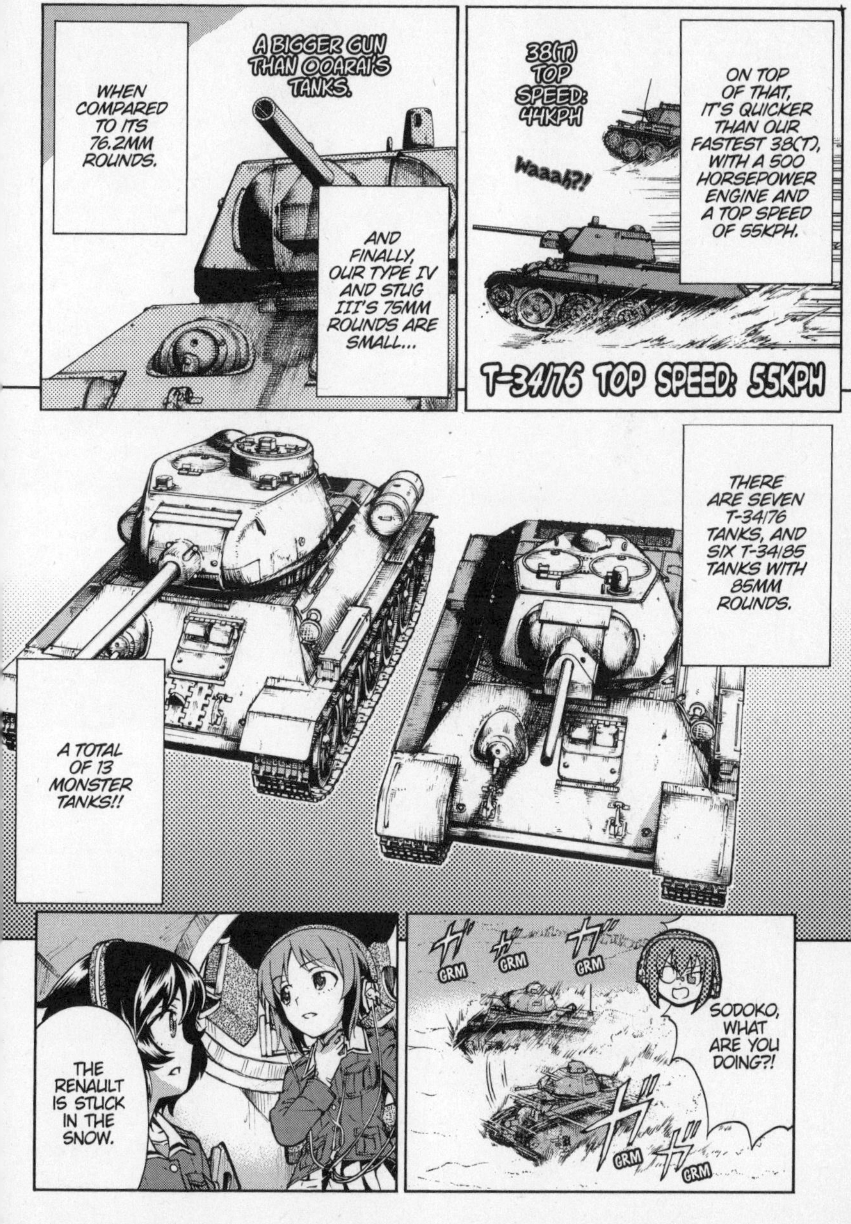
ON TOP OF THAT, IT'S QUICKER THAN OUR FASTEST 38(T), WITH A 500 HORSEPOWER ENGINE AND A TOP SPEED OF 55KPH.
38(T) TOP SPEED: 44KPH
Waaah?!
T-34/76 TOP SPEED: 55KPH
AND FINALLY, OUR TYPE IV AND STUG III'S 75MM ROUNDS ARE SMALL...
WHEN COMPARED TO ITS 76.2MM ROUNDS.
A BIGGER GUN THAN OOARAI'S TANKS.
THERE ARE SEVEN T-34/76 TANKS, AND SIX T-34/85 TANKS WITH 85MM ROUNDS.
A TOTAL OF 13 MONSTER TANKS!!
GRM
GRM
GRM
SODOKO, WHAT ARE YOU DOING?!
GRM
GRM
THE RENAULT IS STUCK IN THE SNOW.

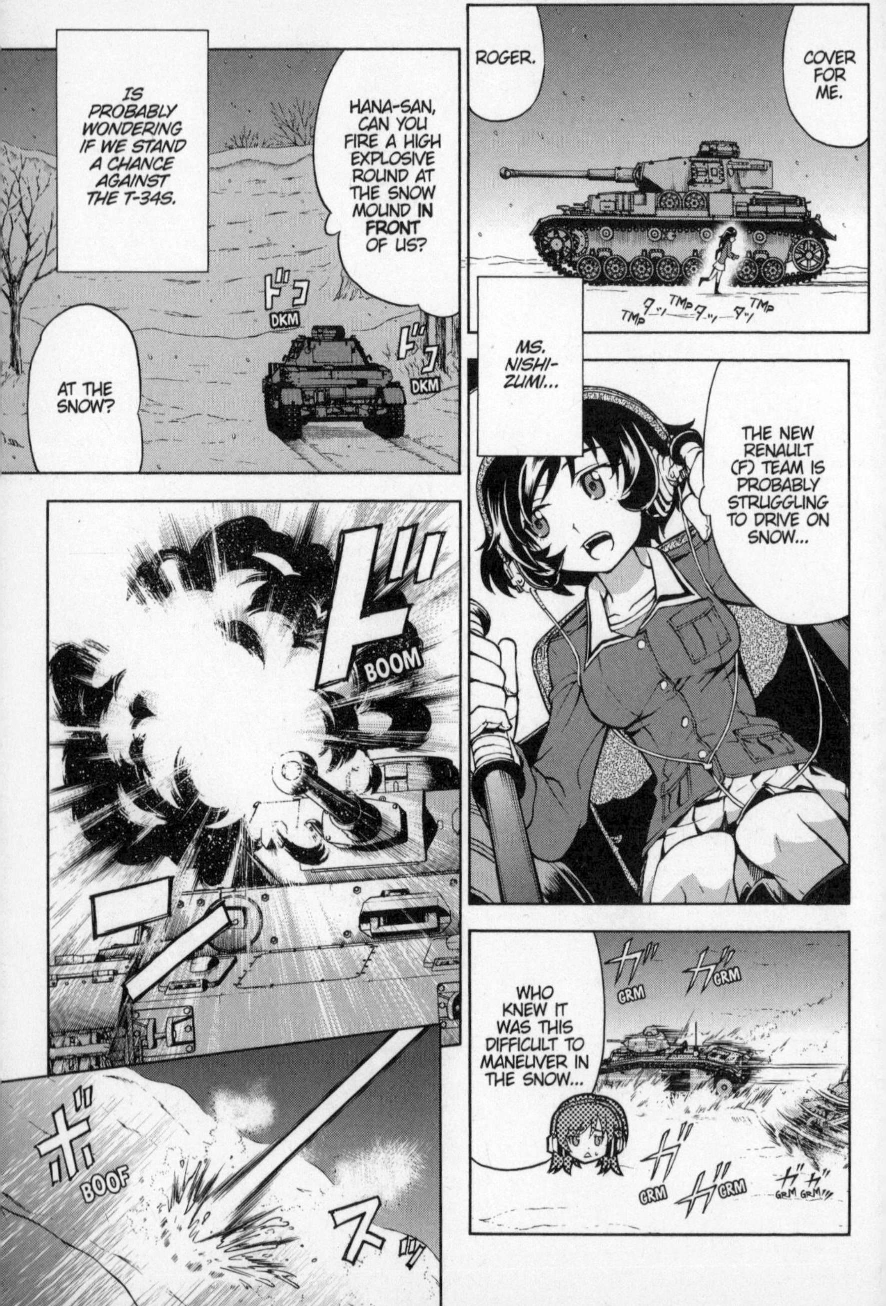
COVER FOR ME.
ROGER.
TMP TMP TMP
HANA-SAN, CAN YOU FIRE A HIGH EXPLOSIVE ROUND AT THE SNOW MOUND IN FRONT OF US?
IS PROBABLY WONDERING IF WE STAND A CHANCE AGAINST THE T-34S.
DKM
DKM
AT THE SNOW?
MS. NISHIZUMI...
THE NEW RENAULT (F) TEAM IS PROBABLY STRUGGLING TO DRIVE ON SNOW...
BOOM
BOOF
GRM
GRM
WHO KNEW IT WAS THIS DIFFICULT TO MANEUVER IN THE SNOW...
GRM
GRM
GRM GRM

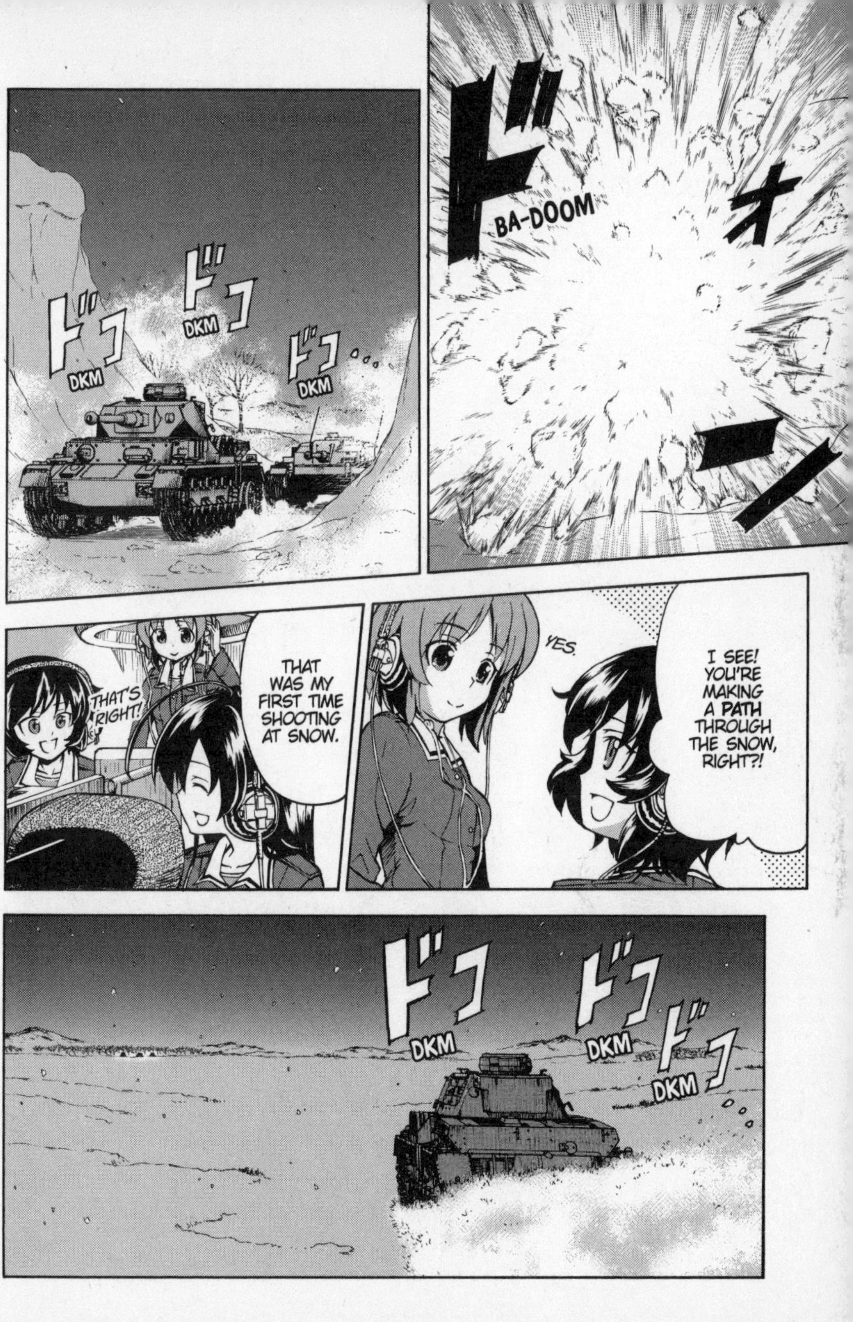
BA-DOOM
DKM
DKM
DKM
I SEE! YOU'RE MAKING A PATH THROUGH THE SNOW, RIGHT?!
YES.
THAT WAS MY FIRST TIME SHOOTING AT SNOW.
THAT'S RIGHT!
DKM
DKM
DKM

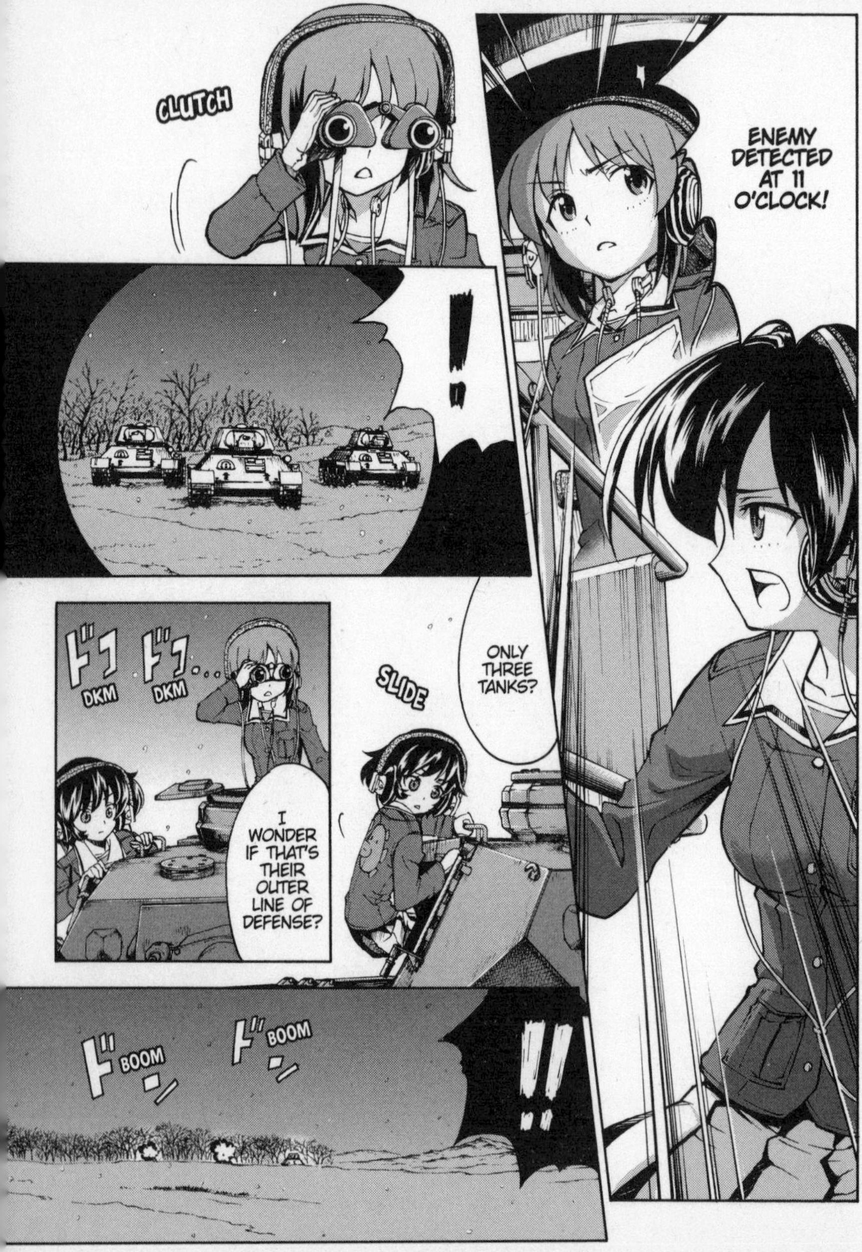
ENEMY DETECTED AT 11 O'CLOCK!
ONLY THREE TANKS?
CLUTCH
!!
ドッ DKM
ドッ DKM
SLIDE
I WONDER IF THAT'S THEIR OUTER LINE OF DEFENSE?
ド BOOM
ド BOOM
!!

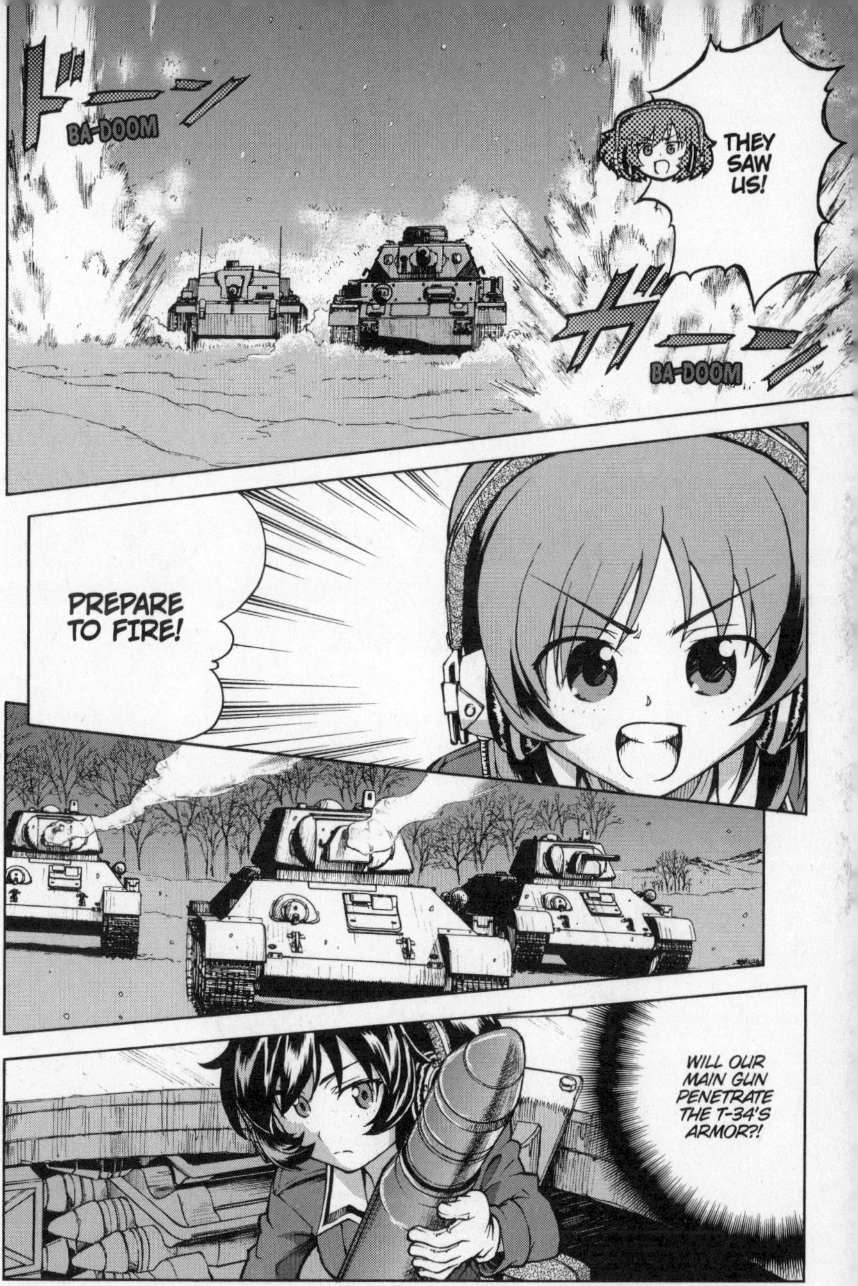
THEY SAW US!
BA-DOOM
BA-DOOM
PREPARE TO FIRE!
WILL OUR MAIN GUN PENETRATE THE T-34'S ARMOR?!

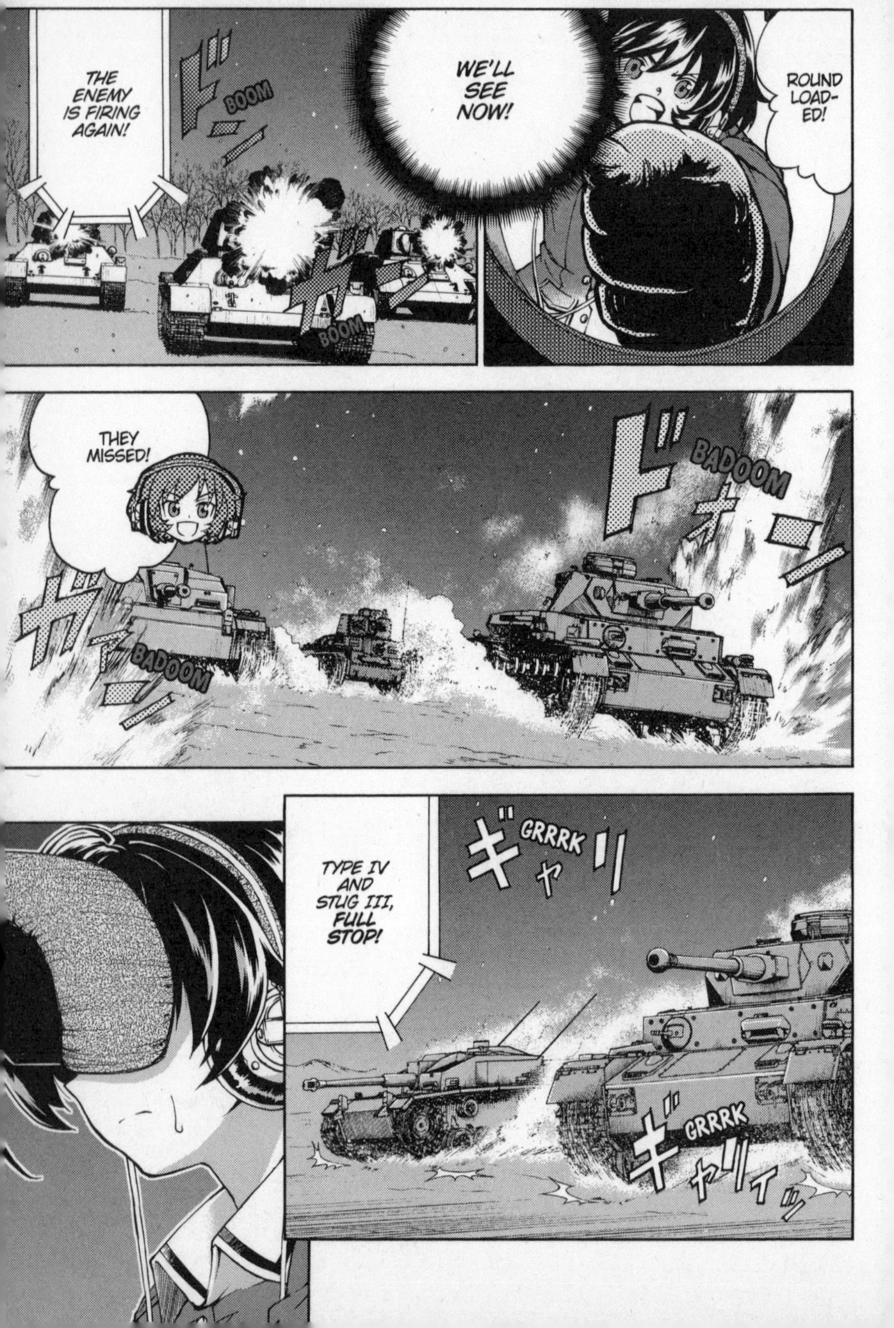
ROUND LOAD-ED!
WE'LL SEE NOW!
THE ENEMY IS FIRING AGAIN!
BOOM
BOOM
BADOOM
THEY MISSED!
BADOOM
GRRRK
TYPE IV AND STUG III, FULL STOP!
GRRRK

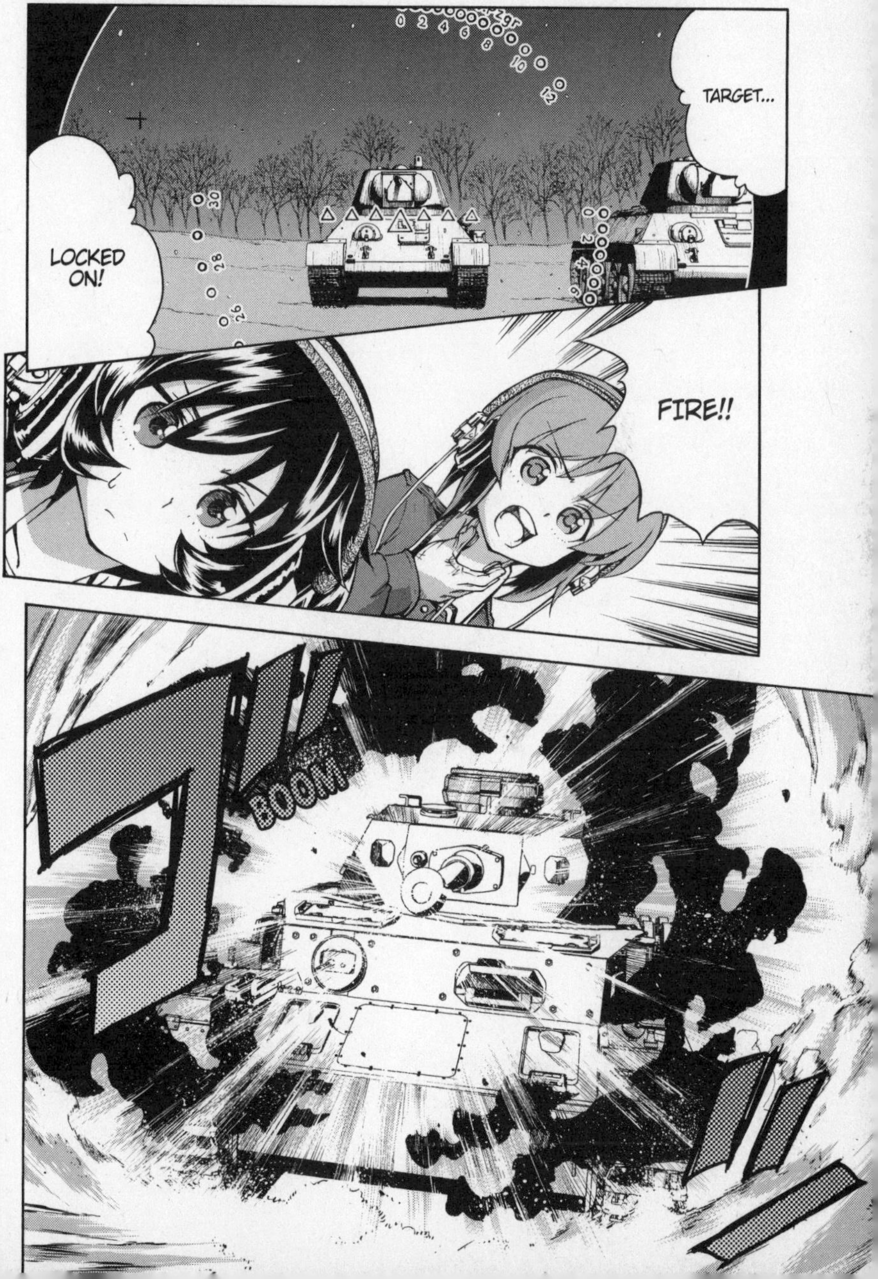
TARGET...
LOCKED ON!
FIRE!!
BOOM!

CHAPTER 12 Do Or Die! In a Big Pinch!!

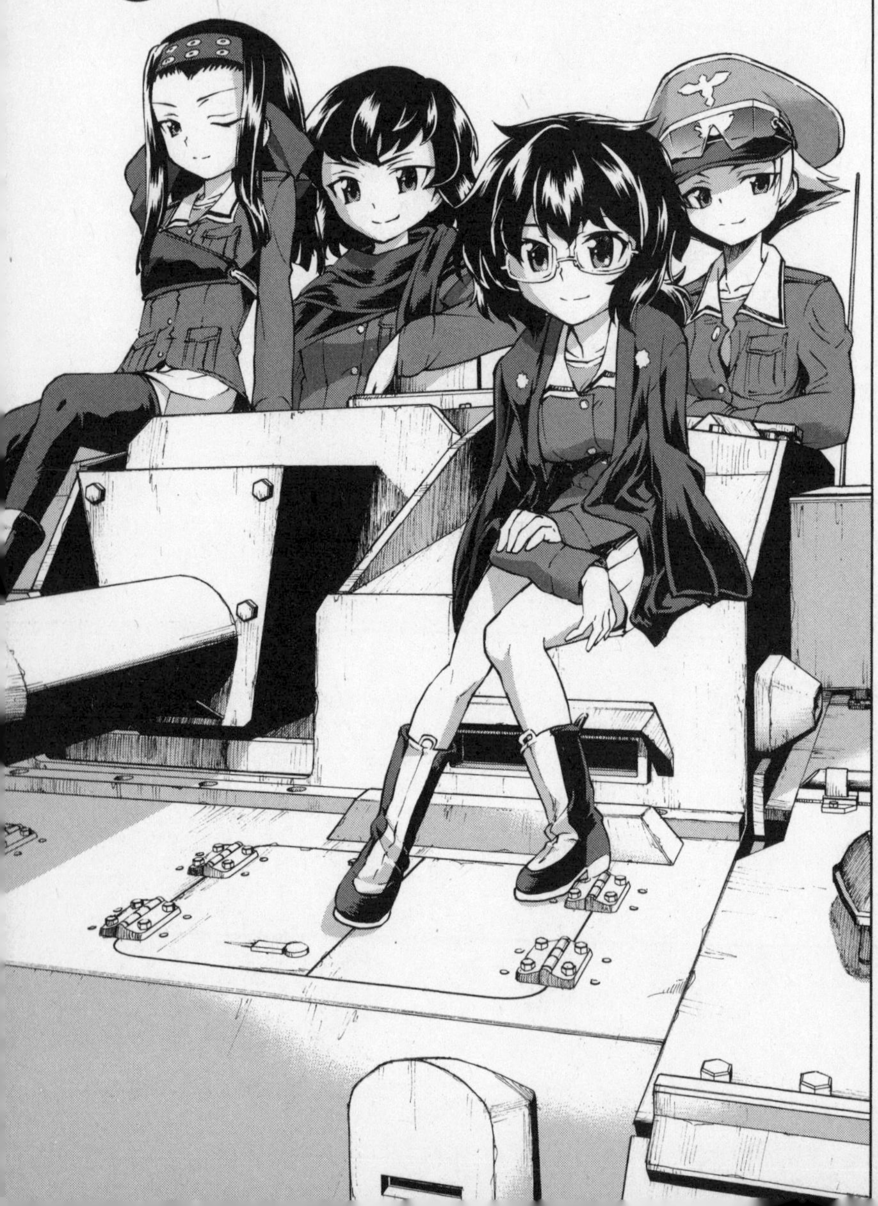

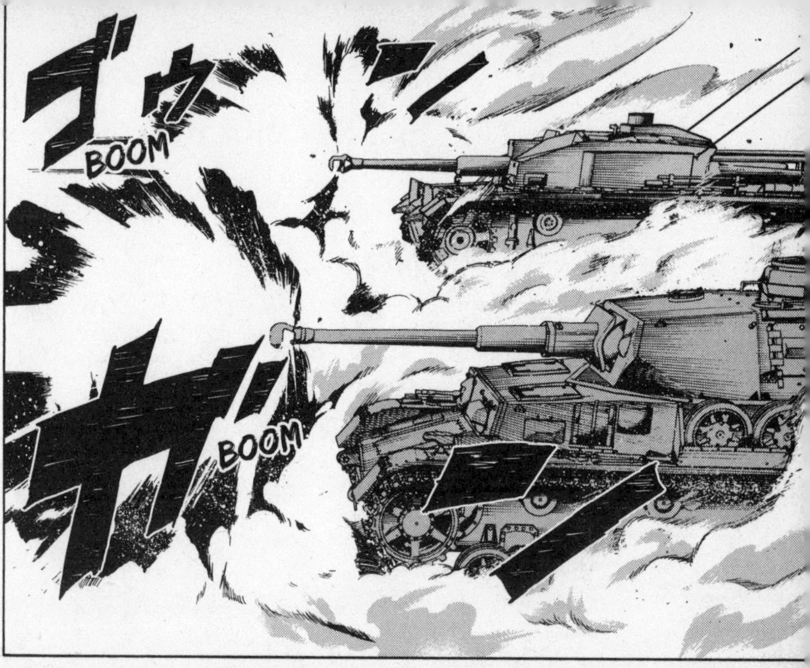
BOOM
BOOM
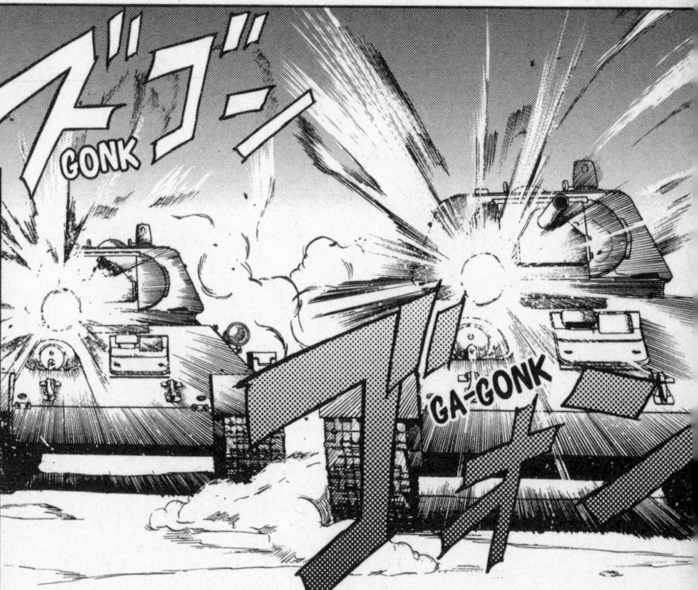
GONK
GA-GONK
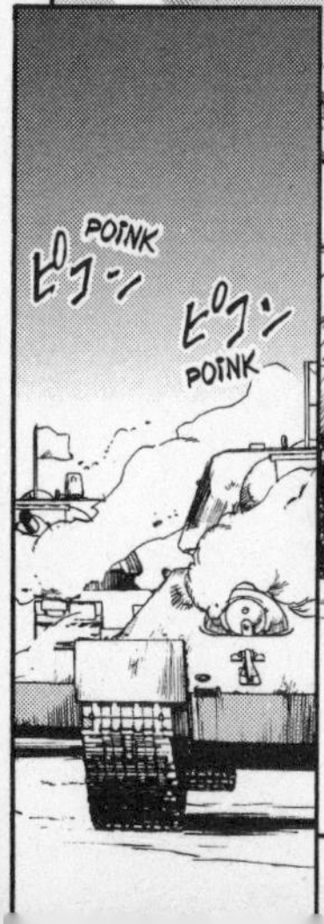
POINK
POINK

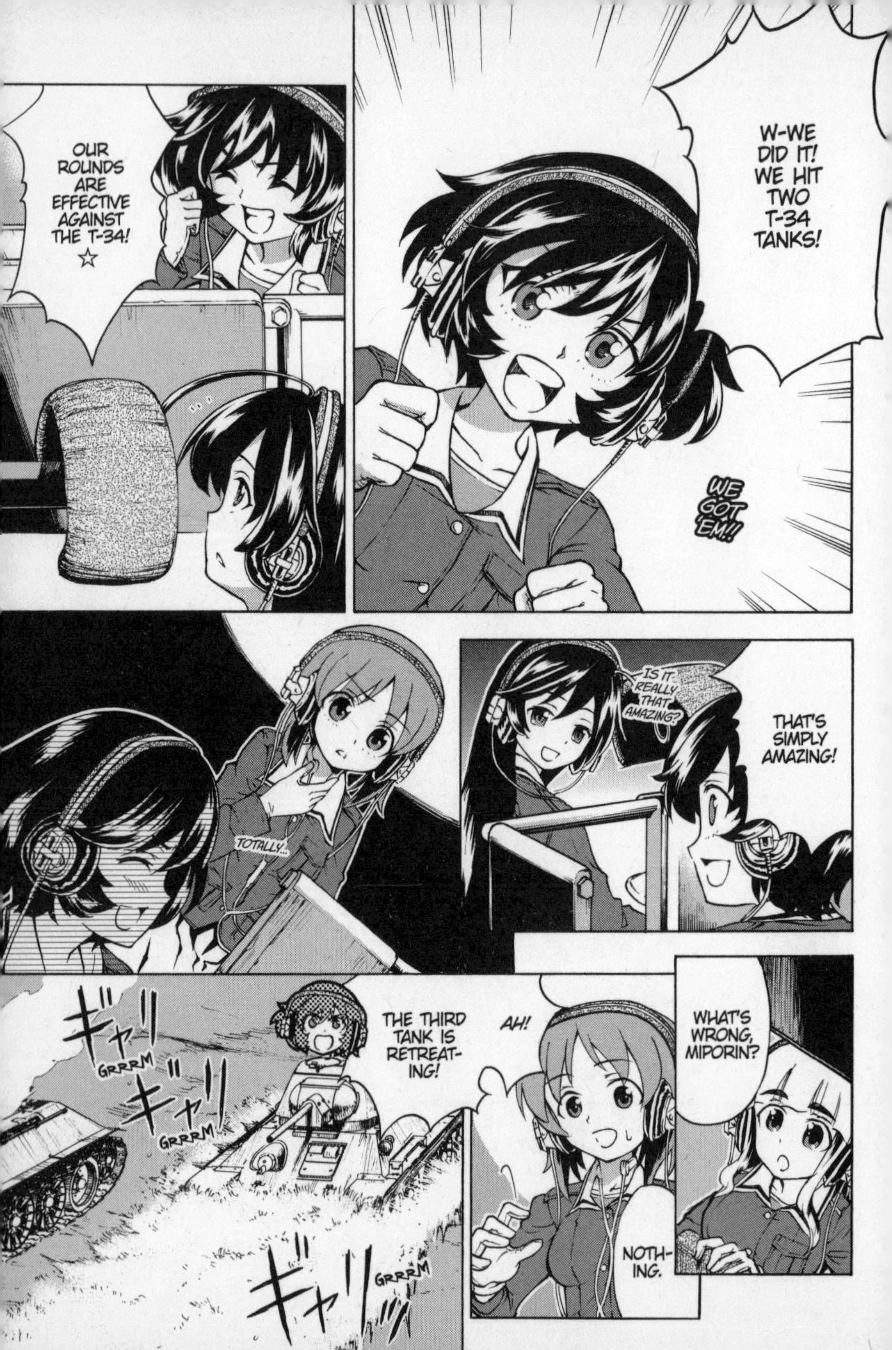
W-WE DID IT! WE HIT TWO T-34 TANKS!
WE GOT 'EM!!
OUR ROUNDS ARE EFFECTIVE AGAINST THE T-34! ☆
THAT'S SIMPLY AMAZING!
IS IT REALLY THAT AMAZING?
TOTALLY...
WHAT'S WRONG, MIPORIN?
AH!
NOTH-ING.
THE THIRD TANK IS RETREAT-ING!
ギャリ
GRRRM
ギャリ
GRRRM
ギャリ
GRRRM

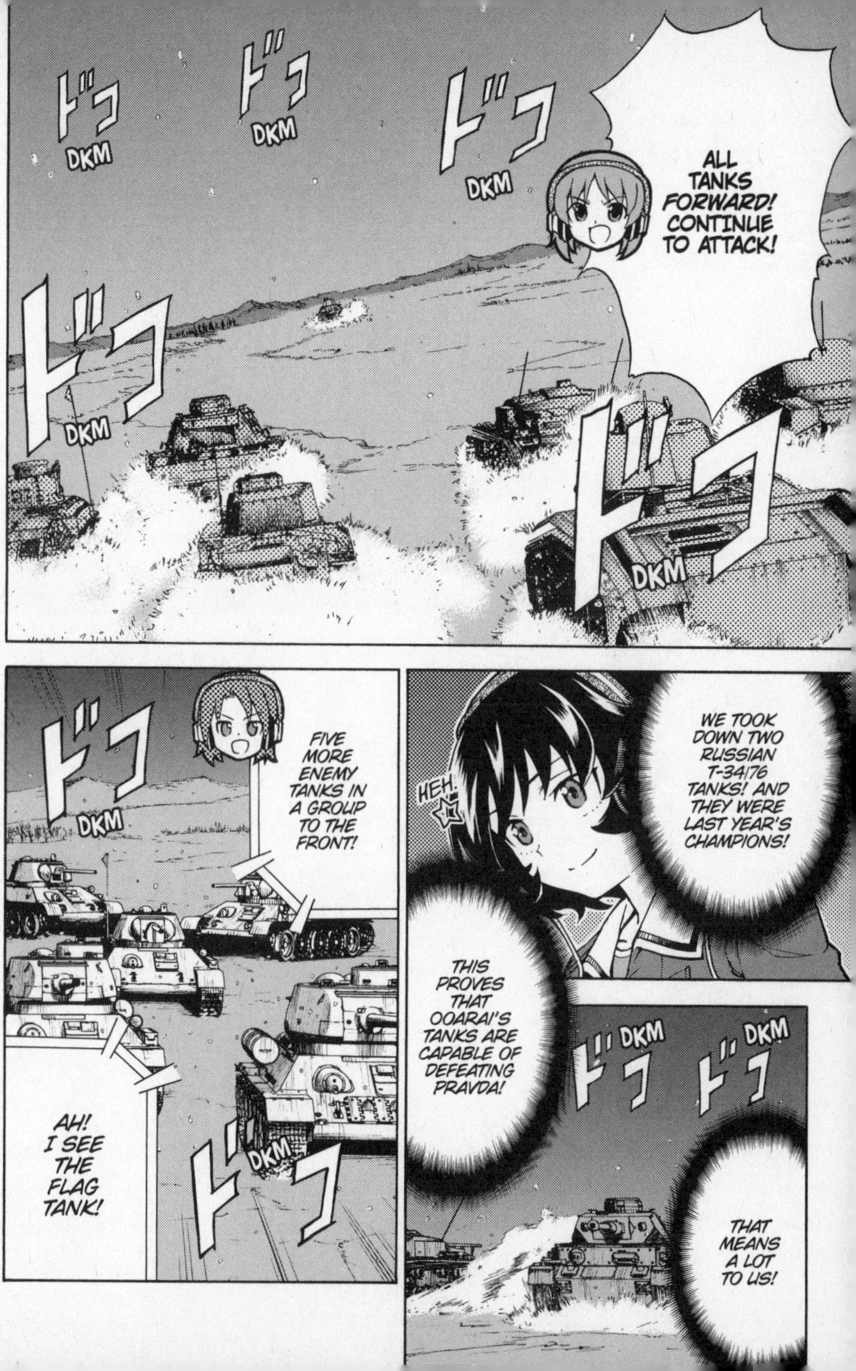
ALL TANKS FORWARD! CONTINUE TO ATTACK!
ドッ
DKM
ドッ
DKM
ドッ
DKM
ドッ
DKM
ドッ
DKM
HEH.
WE TOOK DOWN TWO RUSSIAN T-34/76 TANKS! AND THEY WERE LAST YEAR'S CHAMPIONS!
THIS PROVES THAT OOARAI'S TANKS ARE CAPABLE OF DEFEATING PRAVDA!
ドッ
DKM
ドッ
DKM
THAT MEANS A LOT TO US!
FIVE MORE ENEMY TANKS IN A GROUP TO THE FRONT!
ドッ
DKM
ドッ
DKM
AH! I SEE THE FLAG TANK!

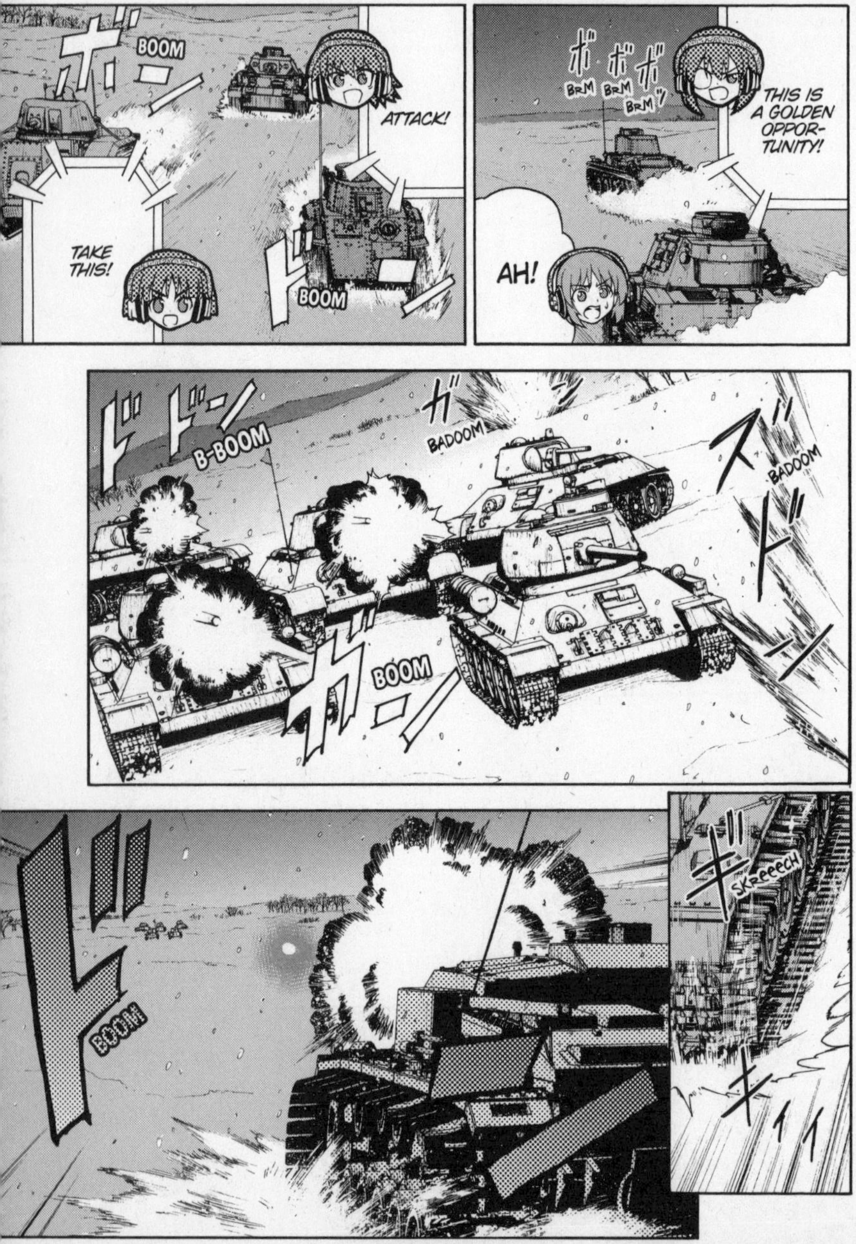
THIS IS A GOLDEN OPPORTUNITY!
BRM BRM BRM
AH!
ATTACK!
BOOM
BOOM
TAKE THIS!
BADOOM
BADOOM
B-BOOM
BOOM
SKREEECH
BOOM

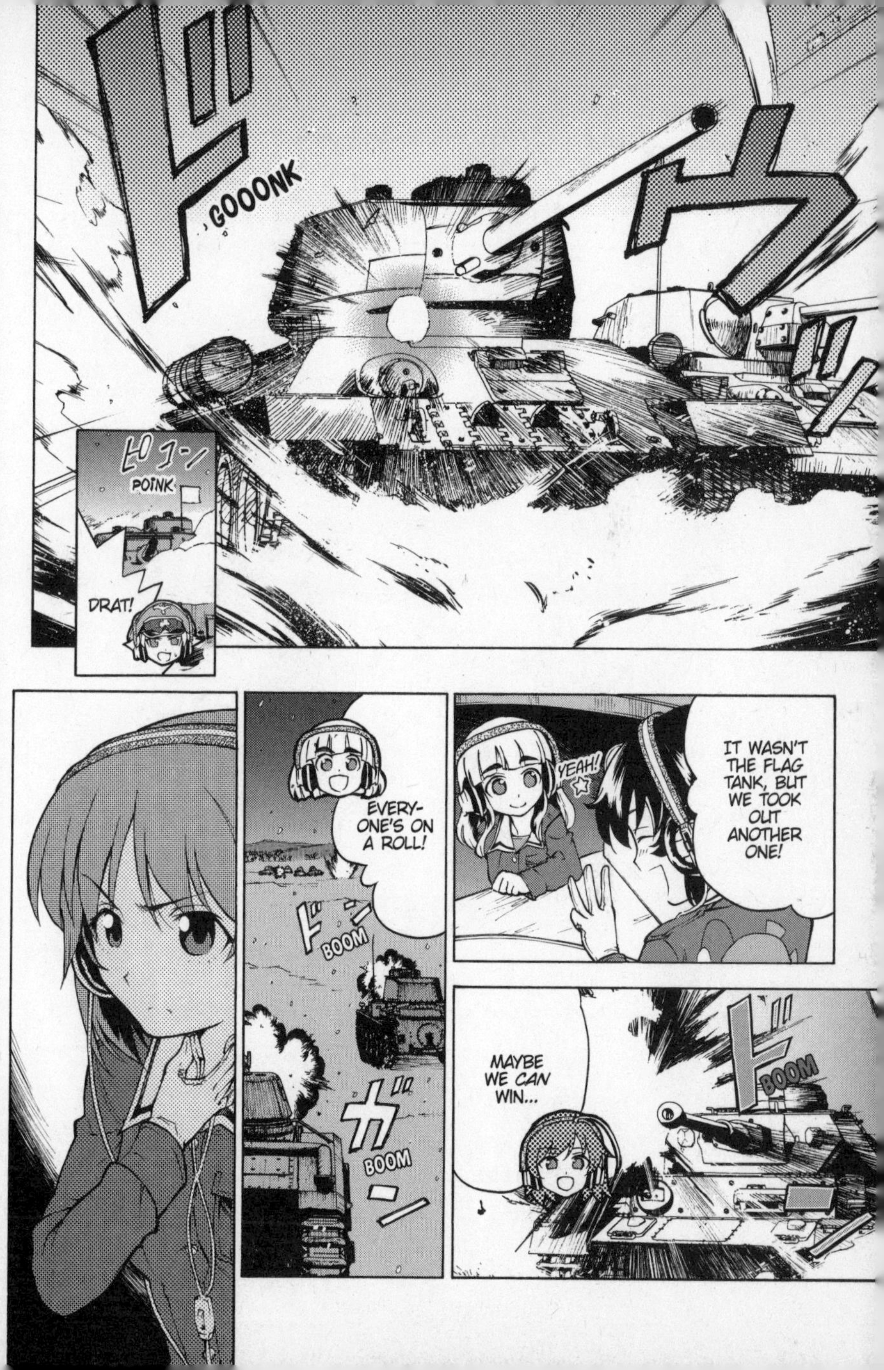

GOOONK
POINK
DRAT!
YEAH!
IT WASN'T THE FLAG TANK, BUT WE TOOK OUT ANOTHER ONE!
MAYBE WE CAN WIN...
BOOM
EVERY-ONE'S ON A ROLL!
BOOM
BOOM

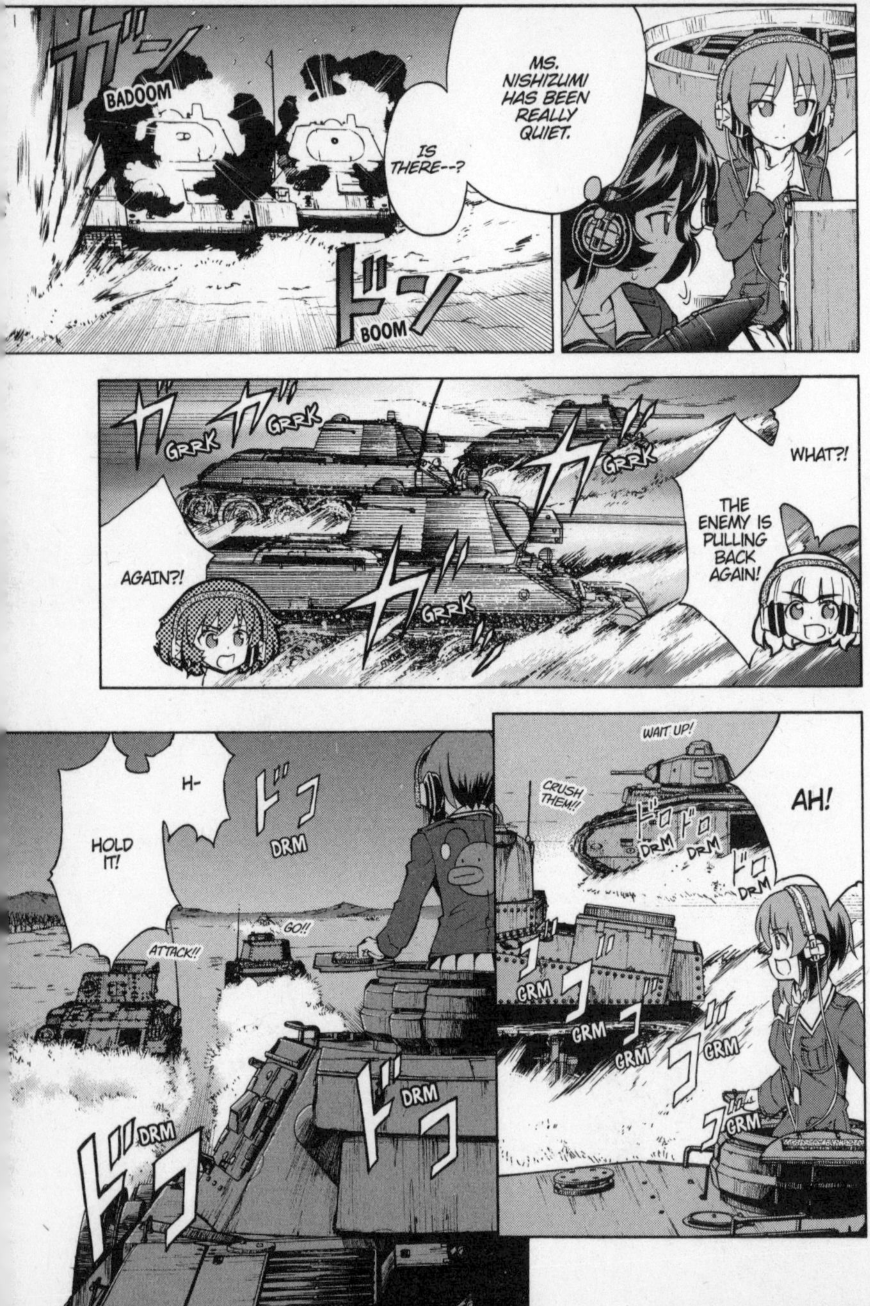
MS. NISHIZUMI HAS BEEN REALLY QUIET.
IS THERE--?
BADOOM
BOOM
WHAT?!
THE ENEMY IS PULLING BACK AGAIN!
GRRK
GRRK
GRRK
GRRK
AGAIN?!
WAIT UP!
AH!
CRUSH THEM!!
DRM
DRM
DRM
GRM
GRM
GRM
GRM
GRM
H-
DRM
HOLD IT!
GO!!
ATTACK!!
DRM
DRM

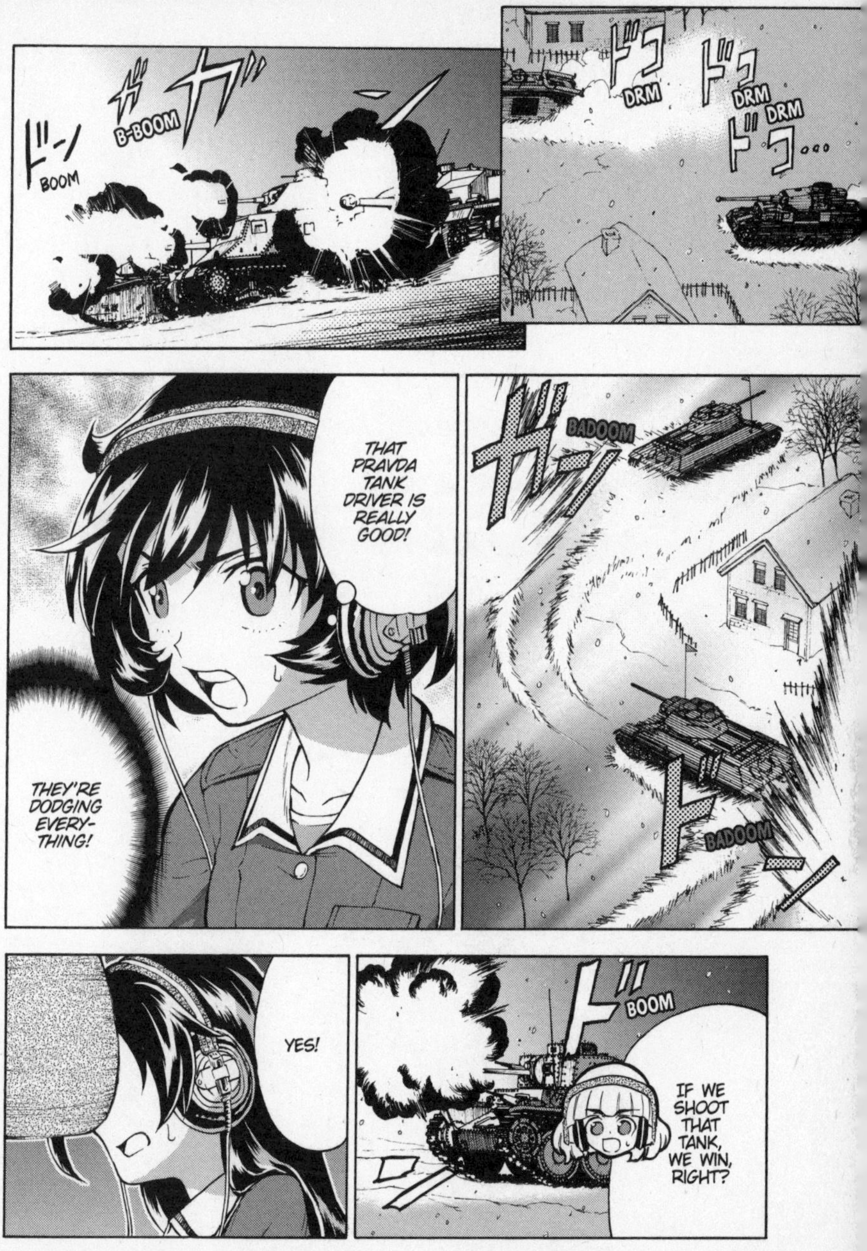
DRM
DRM
DRM
B-BOOM
BOOM
BADOOM
BADOOM
THAT PRAVDA TANK DRIVER IS REALLY GOOD!
THEY'RE DODGING EVERYTHING!
BOOM
IF WE SHOOT THAT TANK, WE WIN, RIGHT?
YES!

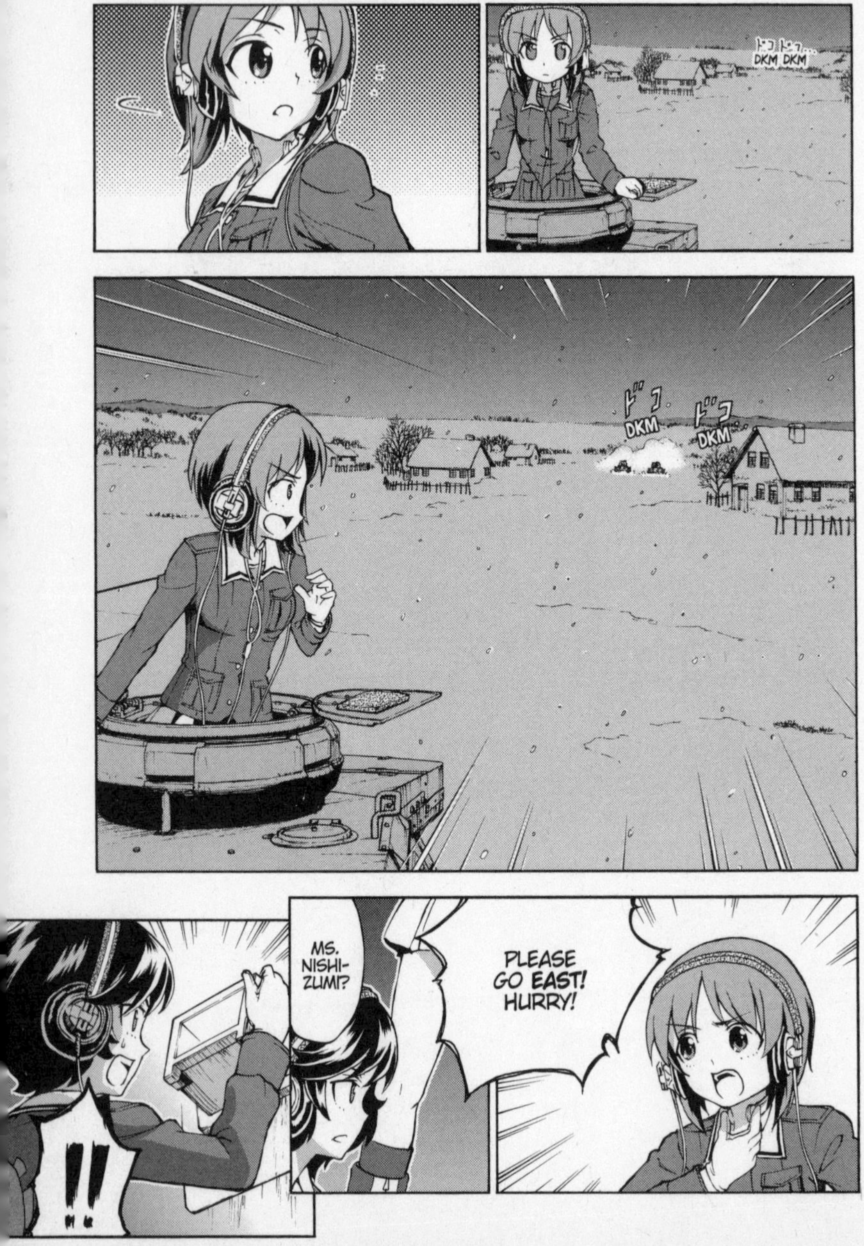
ドコドコ…
DKM DKM
ドコ
DKM
ドコ
DKM
PLEASE GO EAST! HURRY!
MS. NISHI-ZUMI?
!!

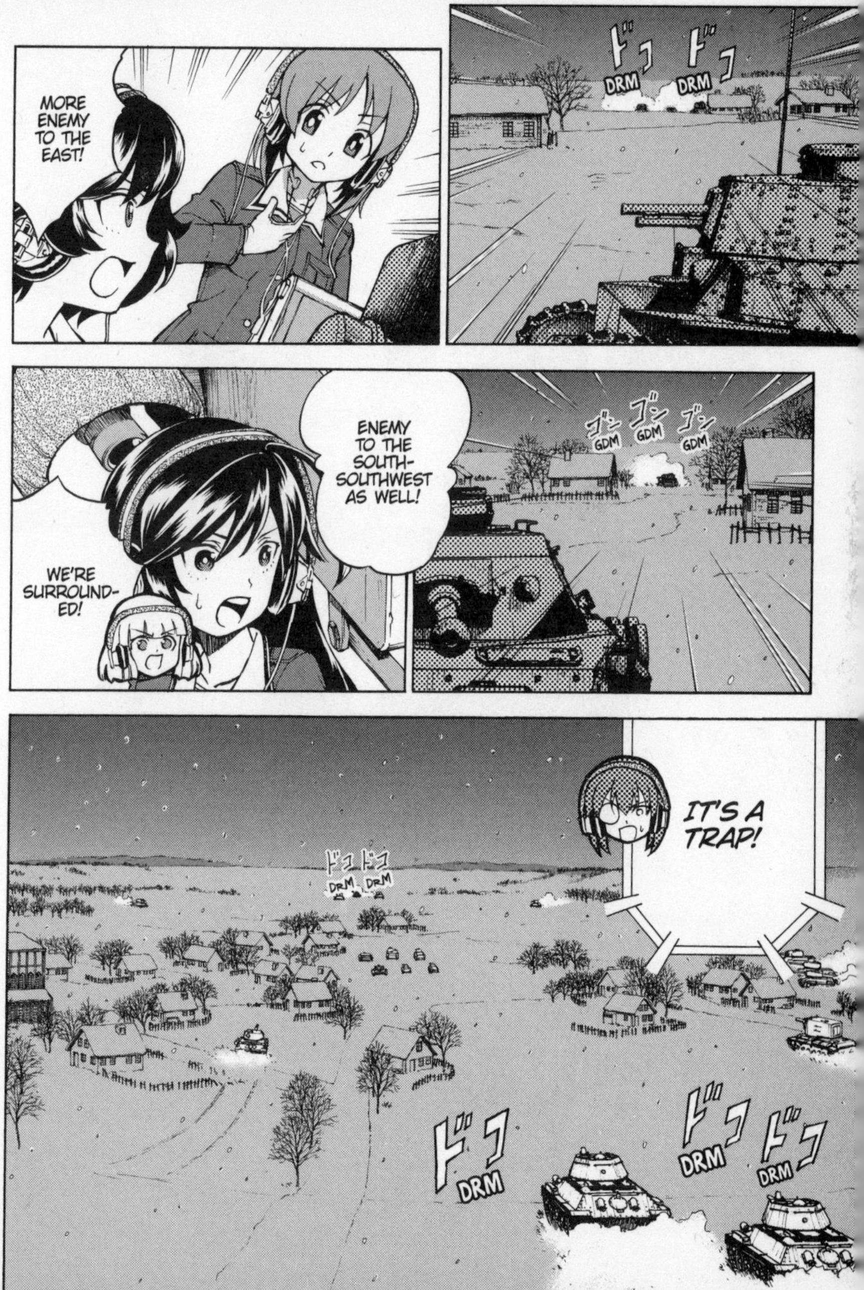

ドコ ドコ
DRM DRM
MORE ENEMY TO THE EAST!
ゴン ゴン ゴン
GDM GDM GDM
ENEMY TO THE SOUTH-SOUTHWEST AS WELL!
WE'RE SURROUND-ED!
IT'S A TRAP!
ドコ ドコ
DRM DRM
ドコ
DRM
ドコ
DRM
ドコ
DRM

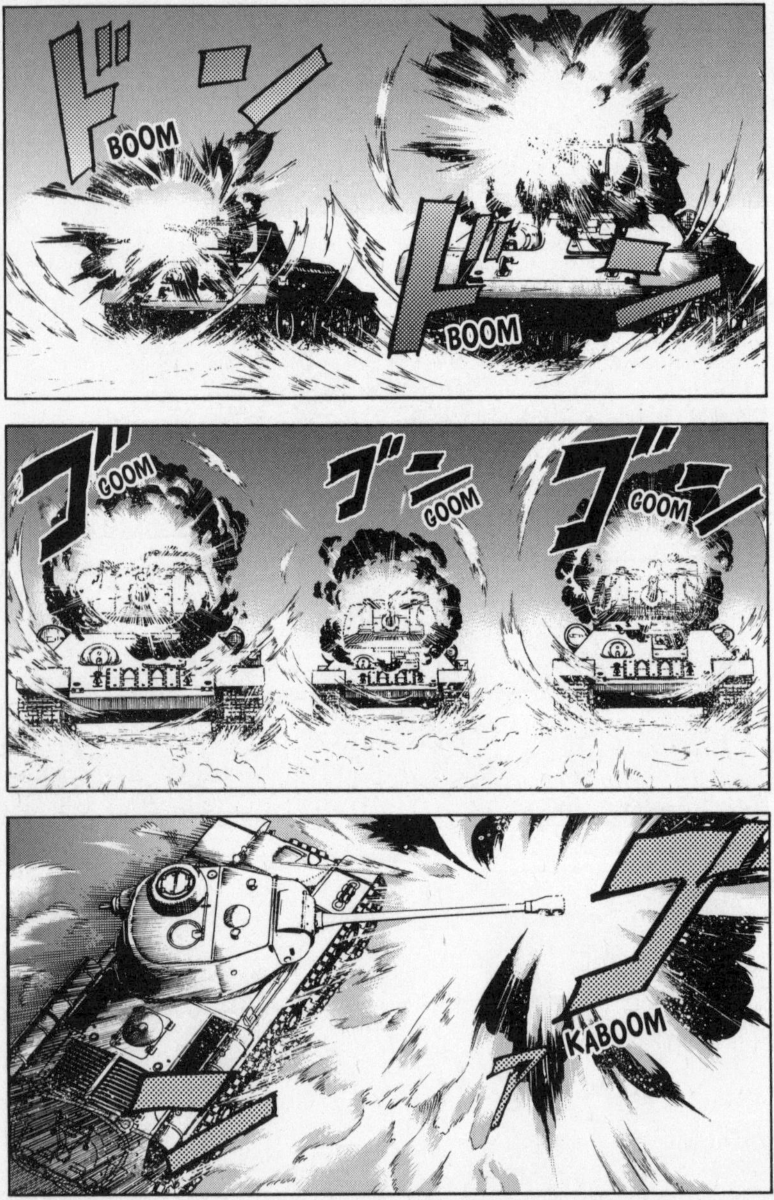
BOOM
ドーン
BOOM
GOOM
GOOM
GOOM
KABOOM

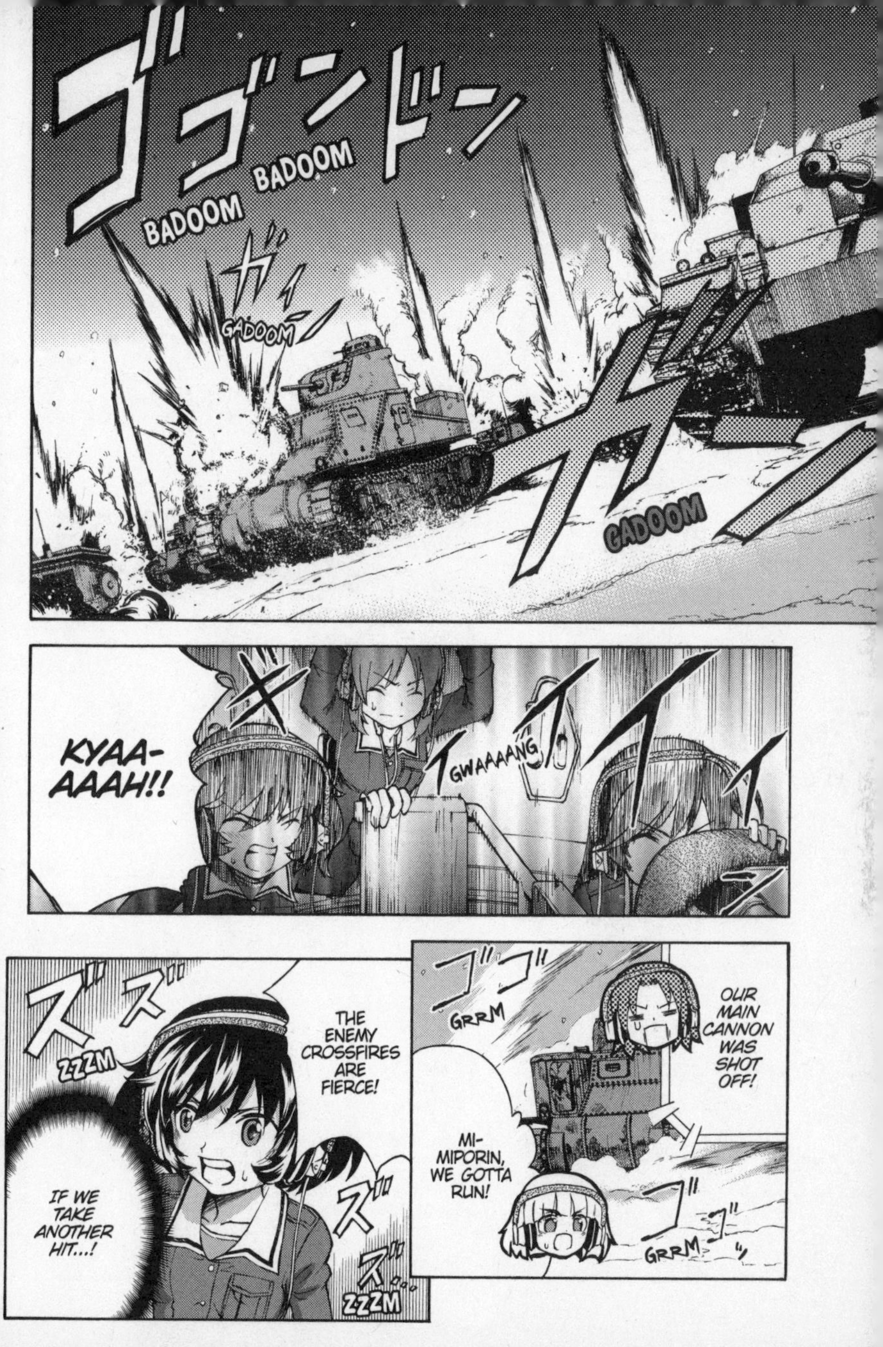
BADOOM
BADOOM
GADOOM
GADOOM
KYAA-AAAH!!
GWAAAANG
GRRM
OUR MAIN CANNON WAS SHOT OFF!
MI-MIPORIN, WE GOTTA RUN!
GRRM
ZZZM
THE ENEMY CROSSFIRES ARE FIERCE!
IF WE TAKE ANOTHER HIT...!
ZZZM

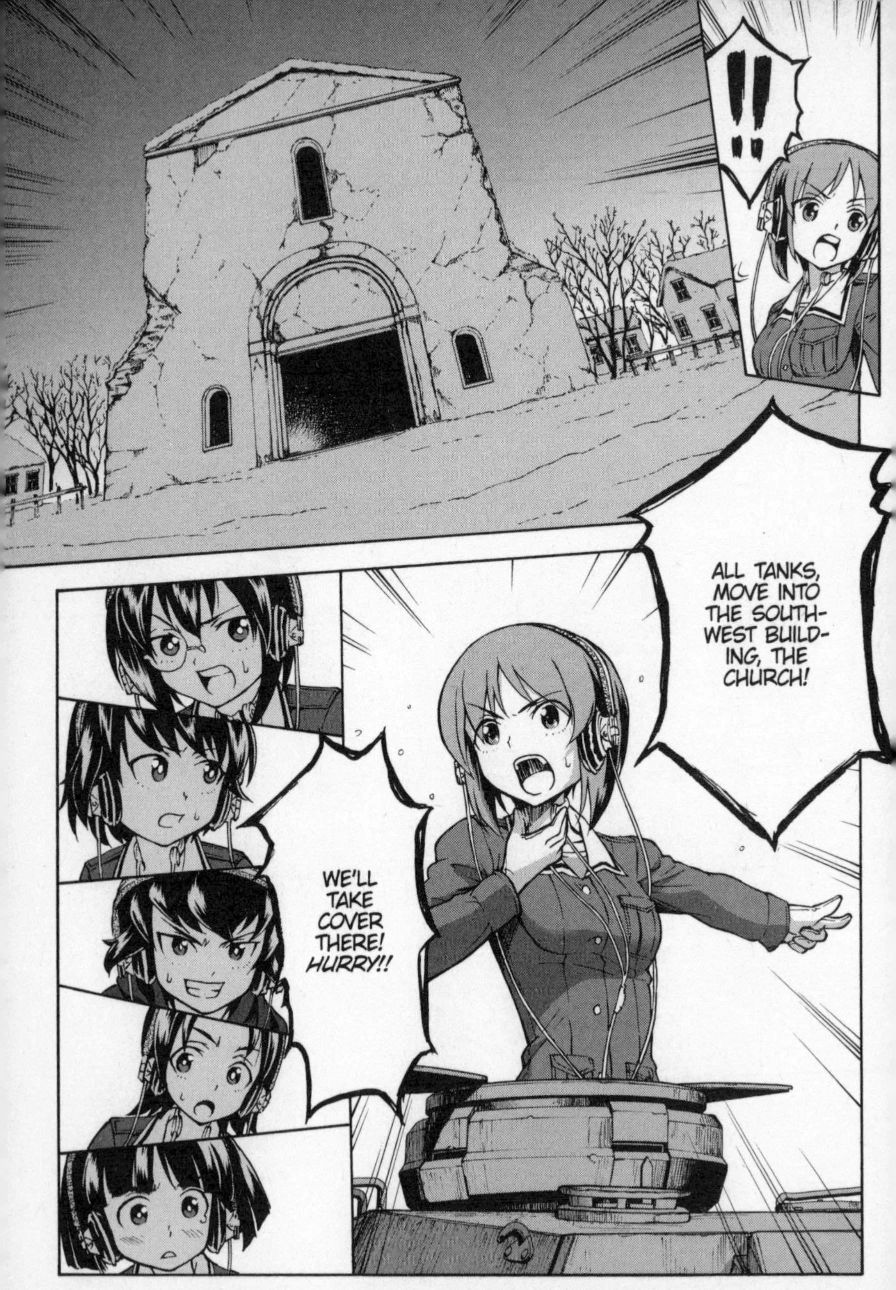
!!
ALL TANKS, MOVE INTO THE SOUTH-WEST BUILD-ING, THE CHURCH!
WE'LL TAKE COVER THERE! HURRY!!

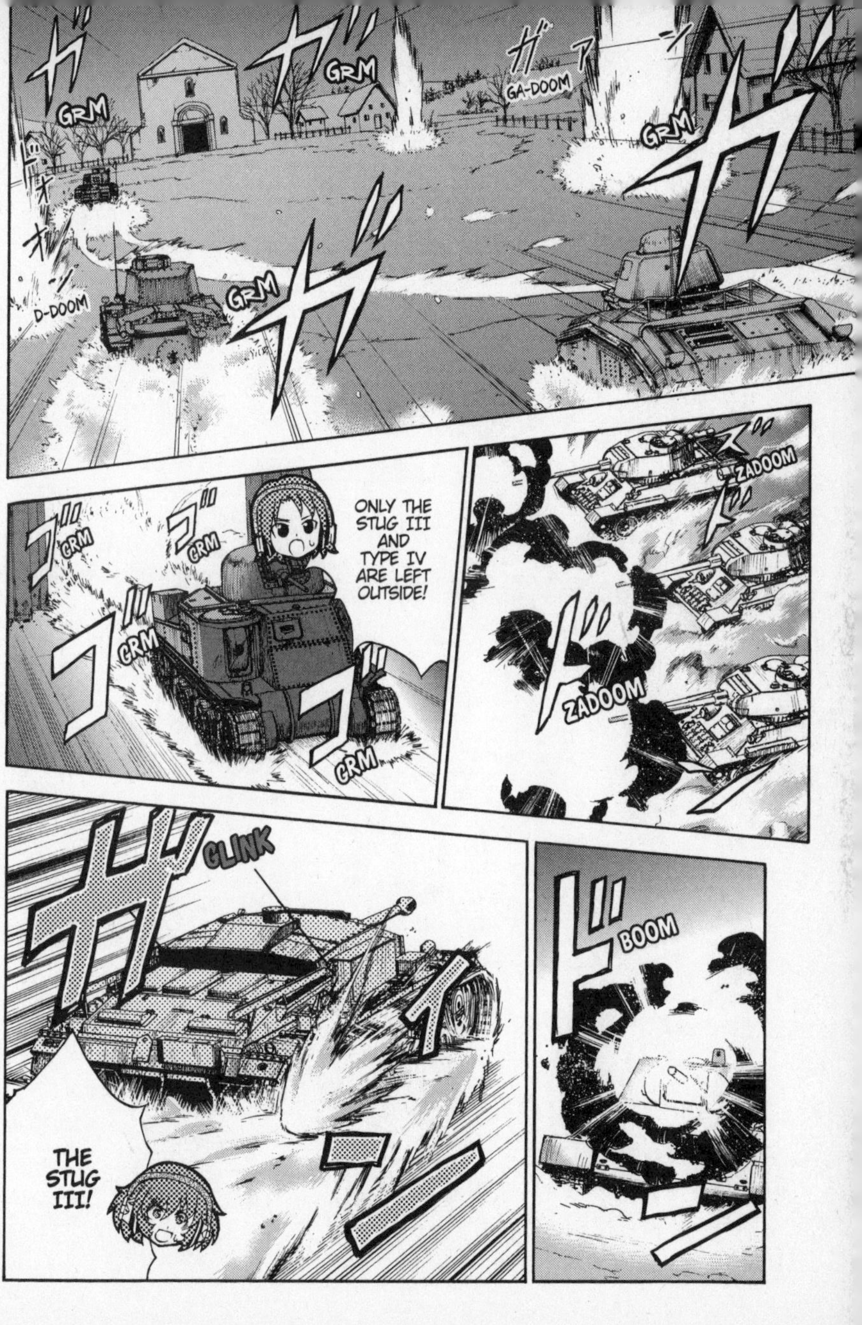

GA-DOOM
GRM
GRM
GRM
GRM
D-DOOM
ZADOOM
ZADOOM
ONLY THE STUG III AND TYPE IV ARE LEFT OUTSIDE!
GRM
GRM
GRM
GRM
BOOM
GLINK
THE STUG III!

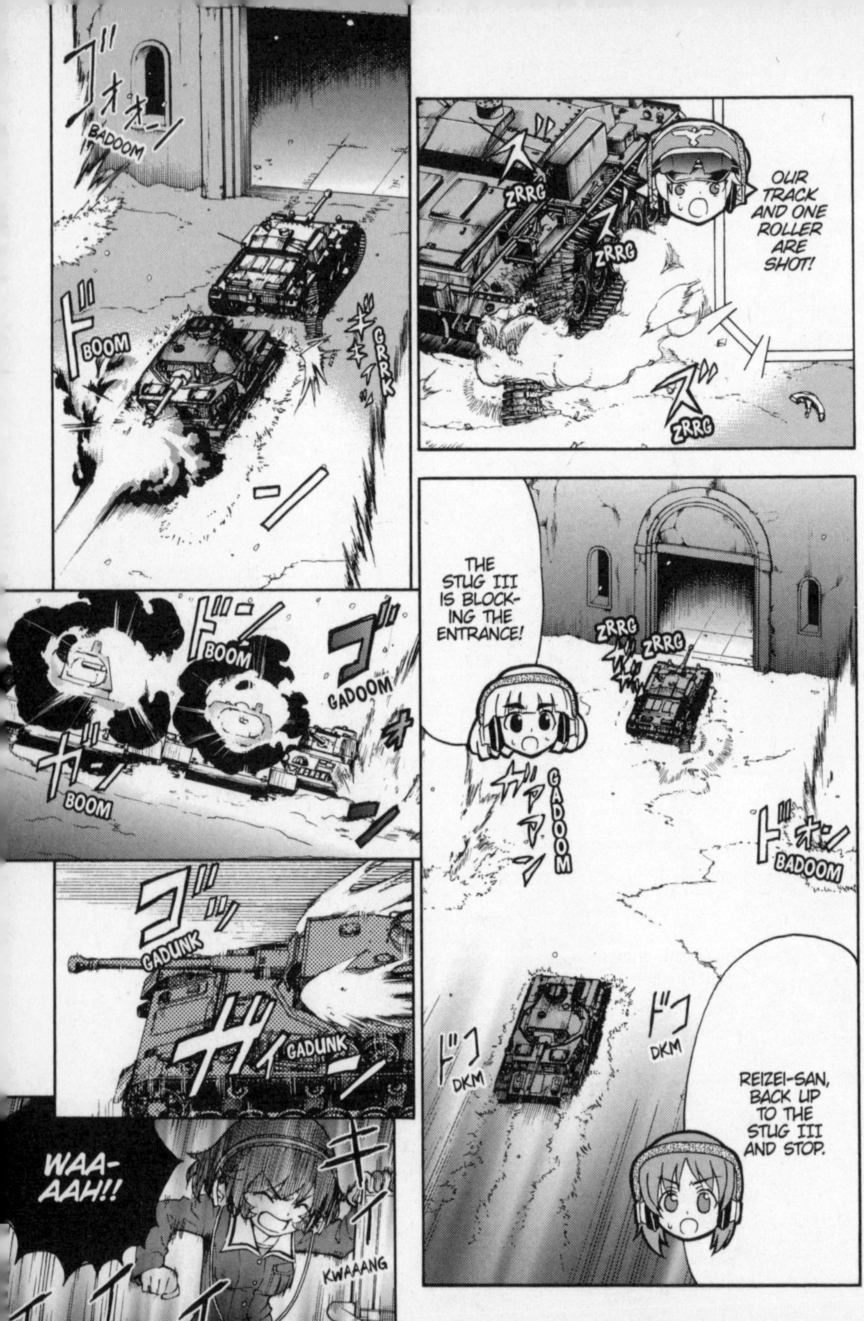
ZRRG
OUR TRACK AND ONE ROLLER ARE SHOT!
ZRRG
ZRRG
BADOOM
BOOM
GRRK
THE STUG III IS BLOCKING THE ENTRANCE!
ZRRG
ZRRG
GADOOOM
BADOOM
DKM
DKM
REIZEI-SAN, BACK UP TO THE STUG III AND STOP.
BOOM
GADOOM
BOOM
GADUNK
GADUNK
KWAAANG
WAA-AAH!!

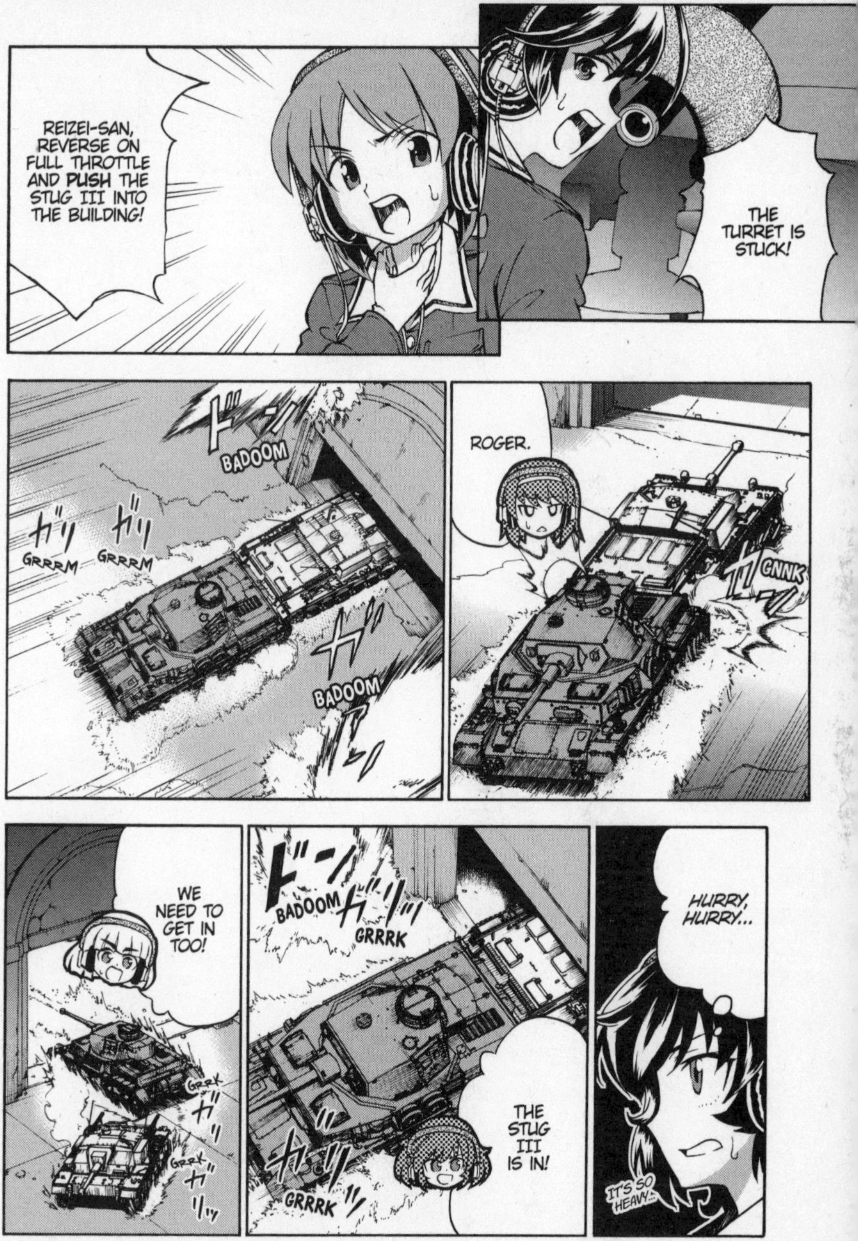
THE TURRET IS STUCK!
REIZEI-SAN, REVERSE ON FULL THROTTLE AND PUSH THE STUG III INTO THE BUILDING!
ROGER.
GNNK
BADOOM
GRRRM
GRRRM
BADOOM
HURRY, HURRY...
IT'S SO HEAVY...
BADOOM
GRRRK
THE STUG III IS IN!
GRRRK
WE NEED TO GET IN TOO!
GRRK
GRRK

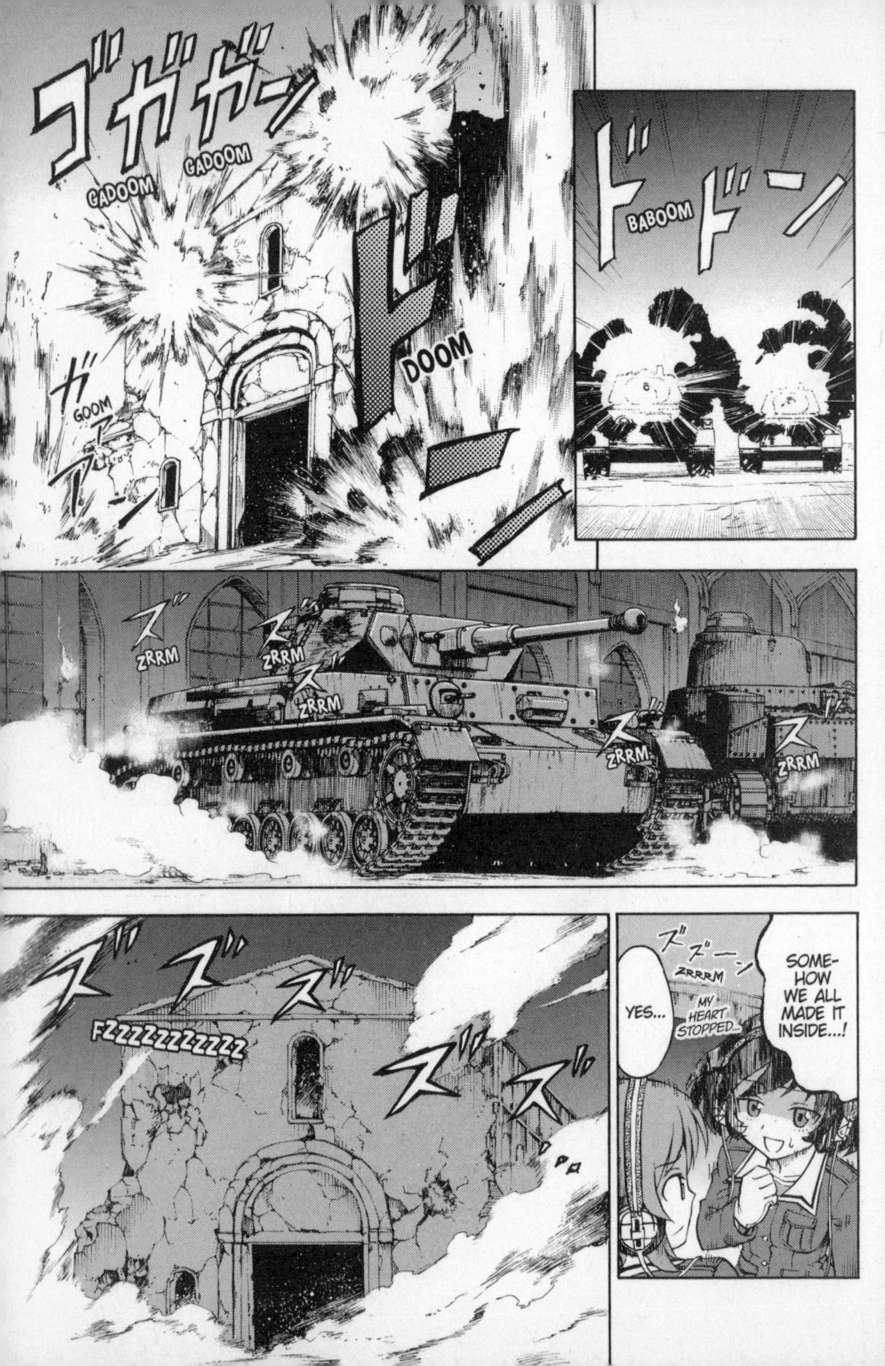
ドドーン
BABOOM
ゴガガーン
GADOOM
GADOOM
ドン
DOOM
ガアア
GOOM
ズ
ZRRM
ズ
ZRRM
ズ
ZRRM
ズ
ZRRM
ズ
ZRRM
ズズーン
ZRRRM
SOME-HOW WE ALL MADE IT INSIDE...!
MY HEART STOPPED...
YES...
ズズズ
FZZZZZZZZZZ
ズズ

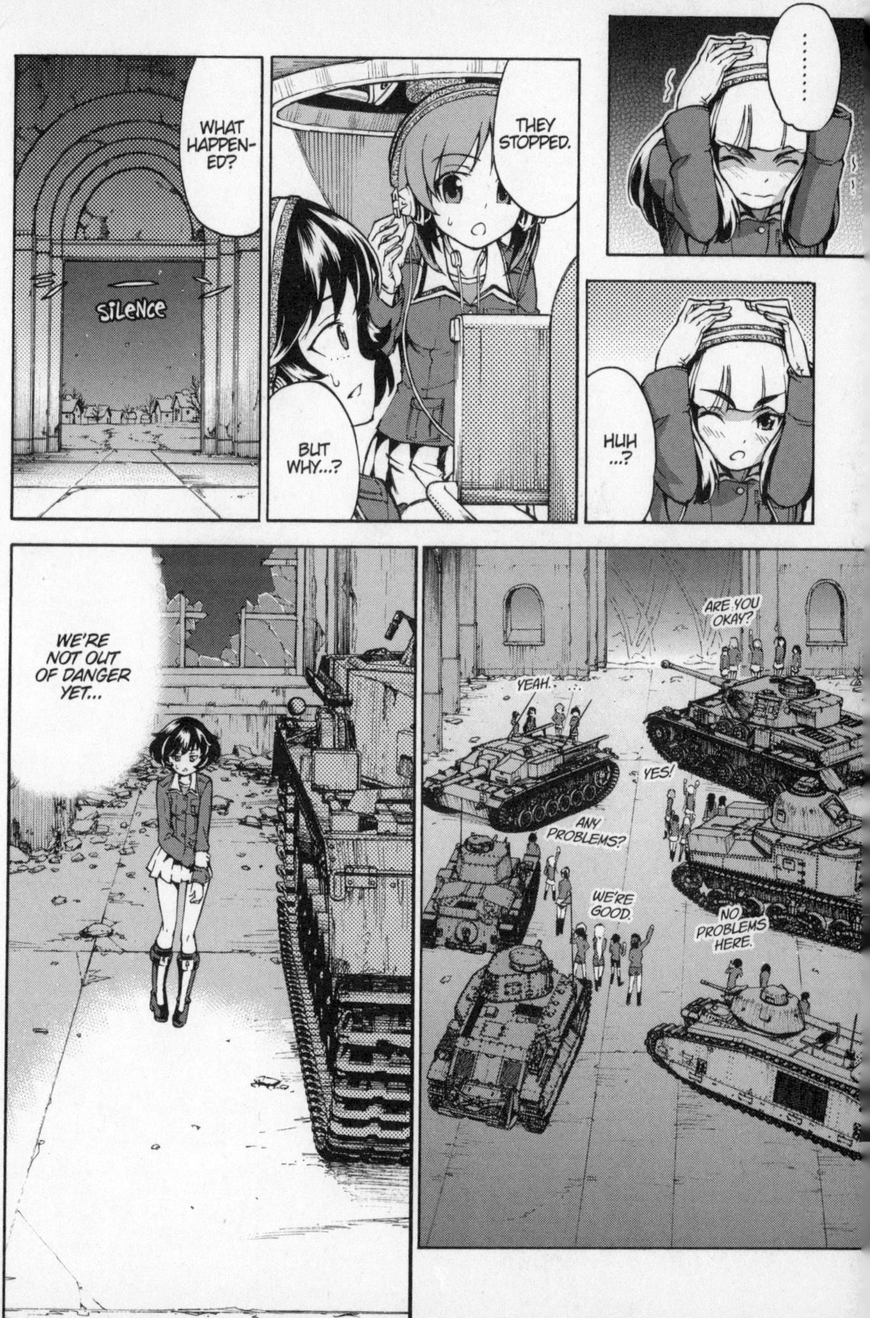
......
HUH ...?
THEY STOPPED.
BUT WHY...?
WHAT HAPPEN-ED?
SILENCE
ARE YOU OKAY?
YEAH.
...
YES!
ANY PROBLEMS?
WE'RE GOOD.
NO PROBLEMS HERE.
WE'RE NOT OUT OF DANGER YET...

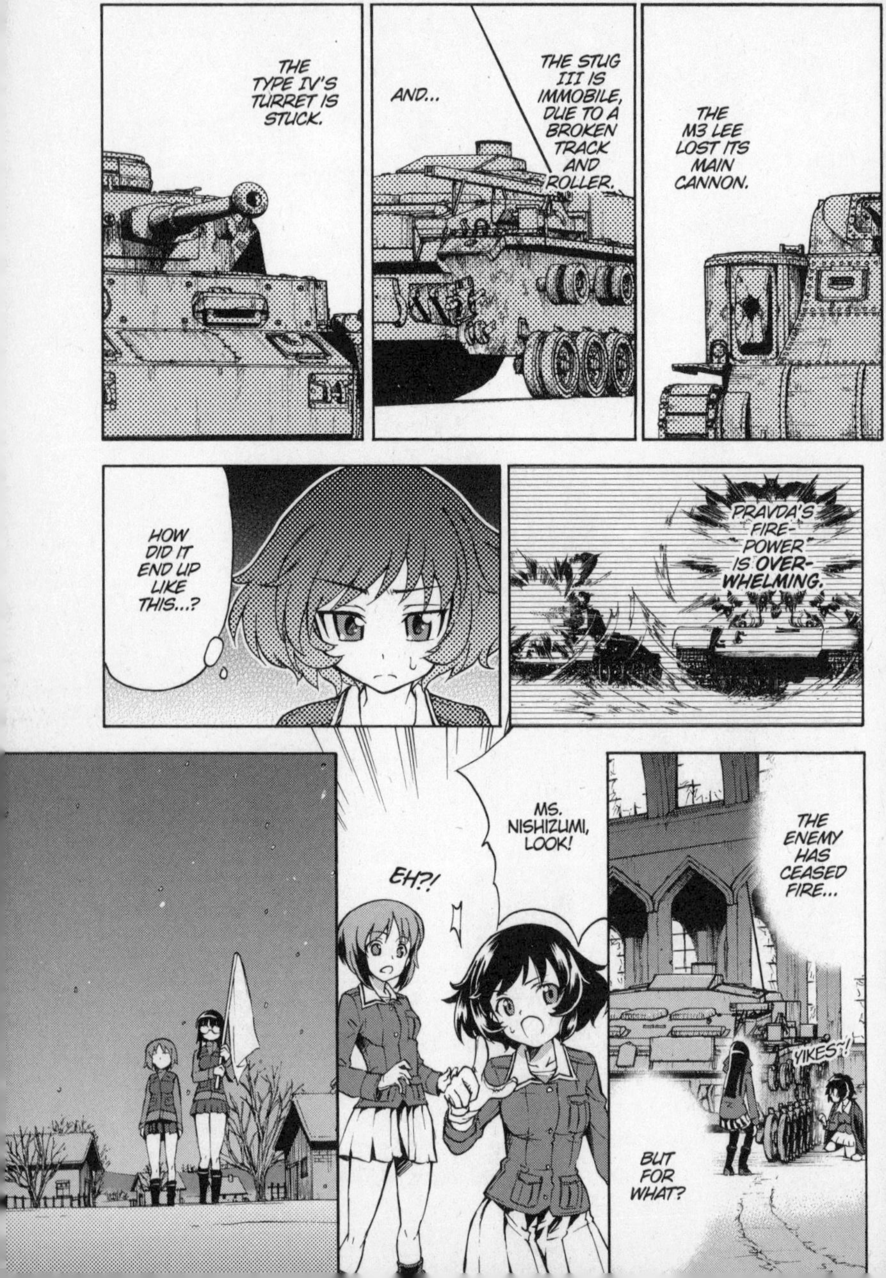

THE M3 LEE LOST ITS MAIN CANNON.
THE STUG III IS IMMOBILE, DUE TO A BROKEN TRACK AND ROLLER.
AND...
THE TYPE IV'S TURRET IS STUCK.
PRAVDA'S FIRE-POWER IS OVER-WHELMING.
HOW DID IT END UP LIKE THIS...?
THE ENEMY HAS CEASED FIRE...
YIKES~!
BUT FOR WHAT?
MS. NISHIZUMI, LOOK!
EH?!

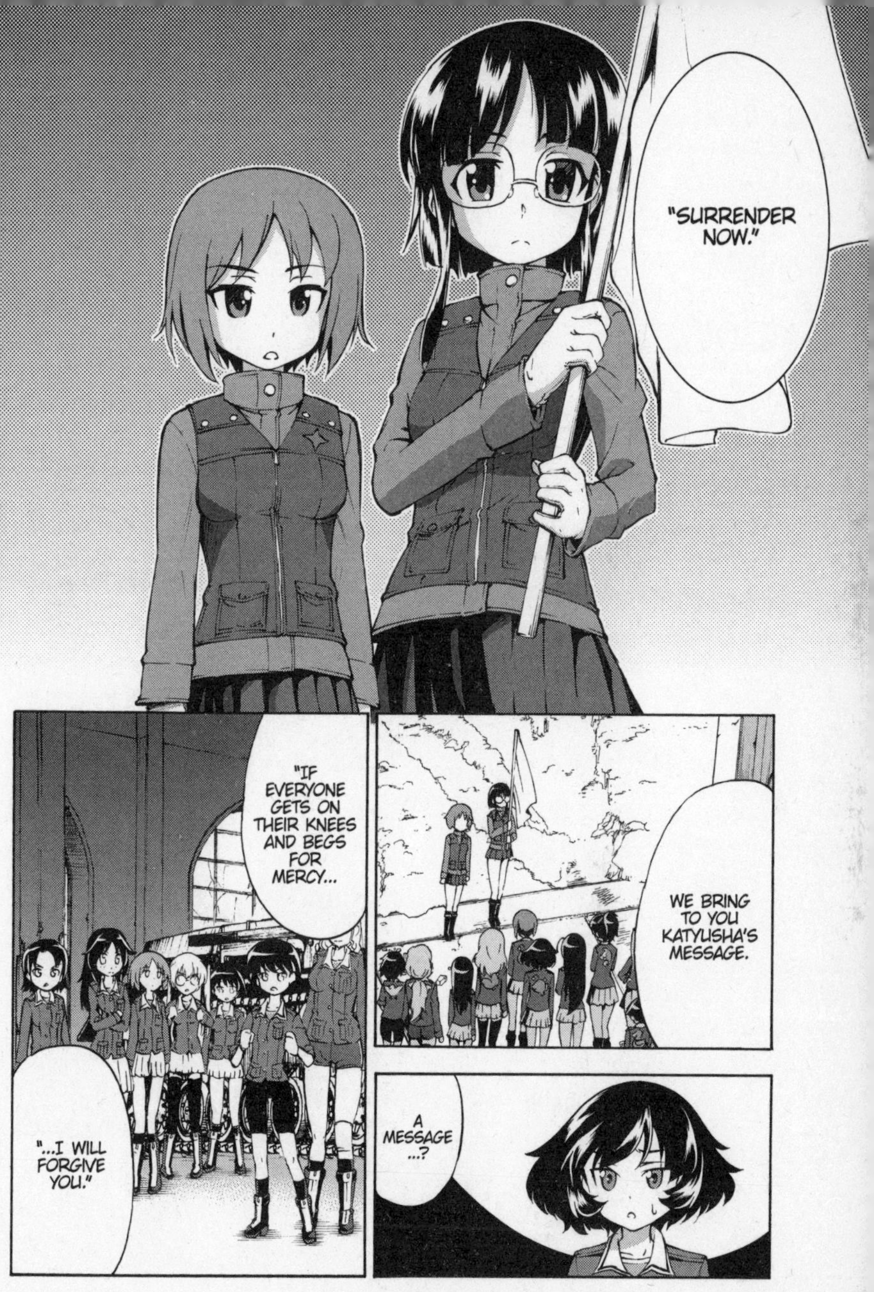
"SURRENDER NOW."
WE BRING TO YOU KATYUSHA'S MESSAGE.
A MESSAGE ...?
"IF EVERYONE GETS ON THEIR KNEES AND BEGS FOR MERCY...
"...I WILL FORGIVE YOU."

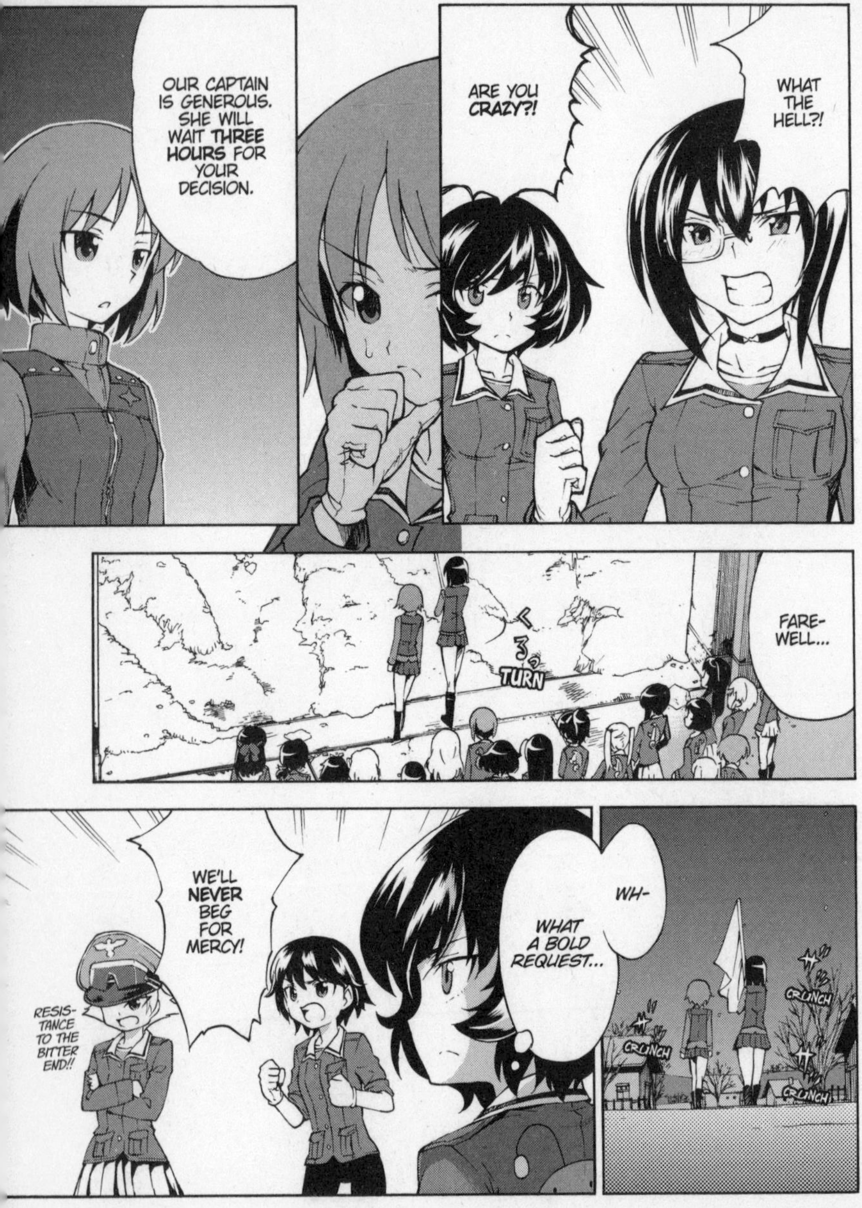

WHAT THE HELL?!
ARE YOU CRAZY?!
OUR CAPTAIN IS GENEROUS. SHE WILL WAIT THREE HOURS FOR YOUR DECISION.
FARE-WELL...
くる TURN
CRUNCH
CRUNCH
CRUNCH
WH-
WHAT A BOLD REQUEST...
WE'LL NEVER BEG FOR MERCY!
RESIS-TANCE TO THE BITTER END!!

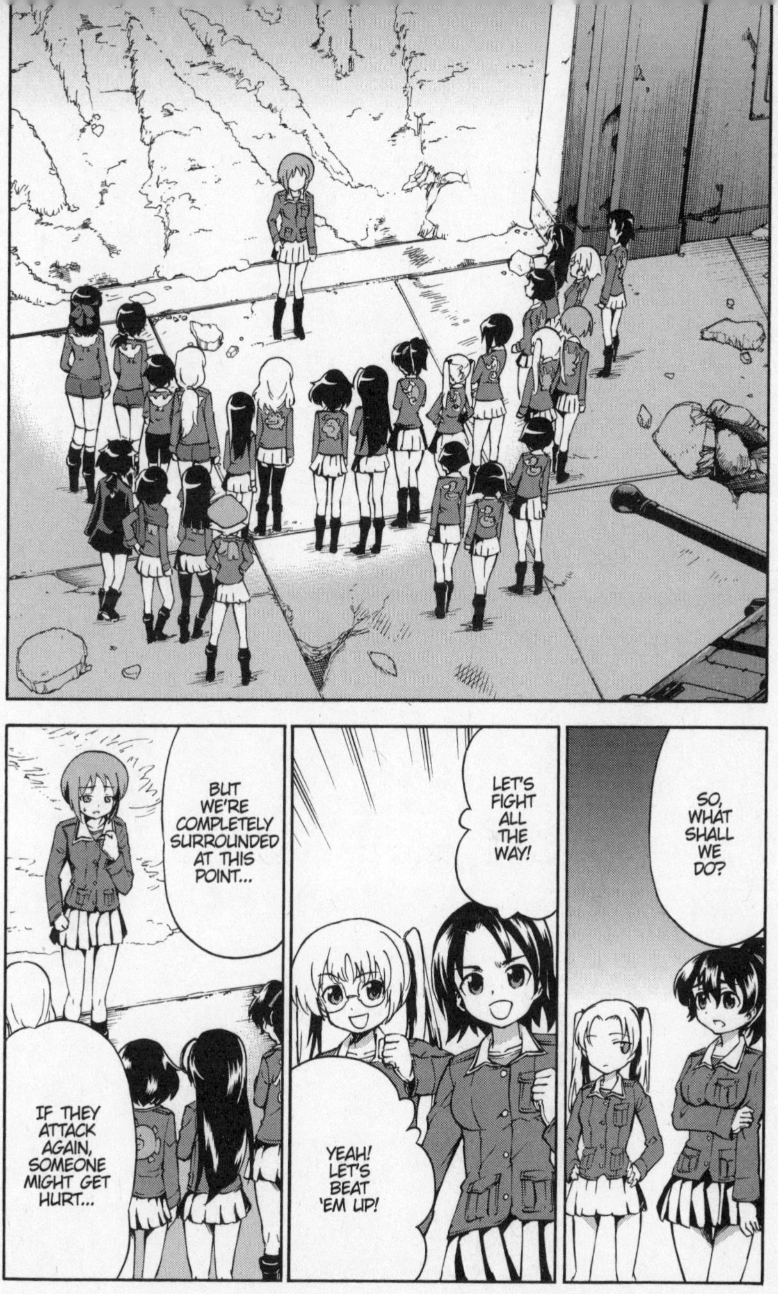
SO, WHAT SHALL WE DO?
LET'S FIGHT ALL THE WAY!
YEAH! LET'S BEAT 'EM UP!
BUT WE'RE COMPLETELY SURROUNDED AT THIS POINT...
IF THEY ATTACK AGAIN, SOMEONE MIGHT GET HURT...

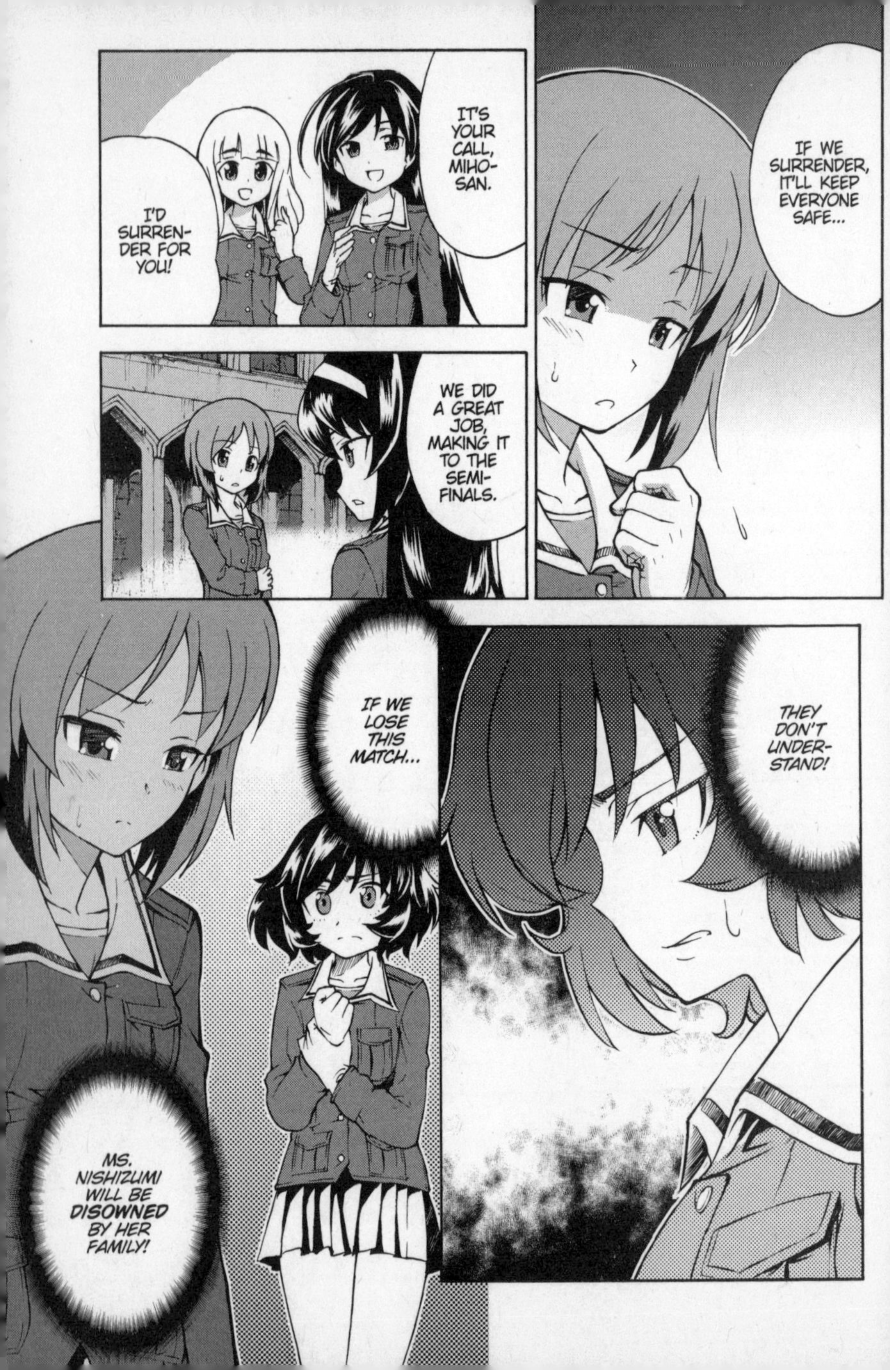
IF WE SURRENDER, IT'LL KEEP EVERYONE SAFE...
IT'S YOUR CALL, MIHO-SAN.
I'D SURRENDER FOR YOU!
WE DID A GREAT JOB, MAKING IT TO THE SEMI-FINALS.
THEY DON'T UNDERSTAND!
IF WE LOSE THIS MATCH...
MS. NISHIZUMI WILL BE **DISOWNED** BY HER FAMILY!

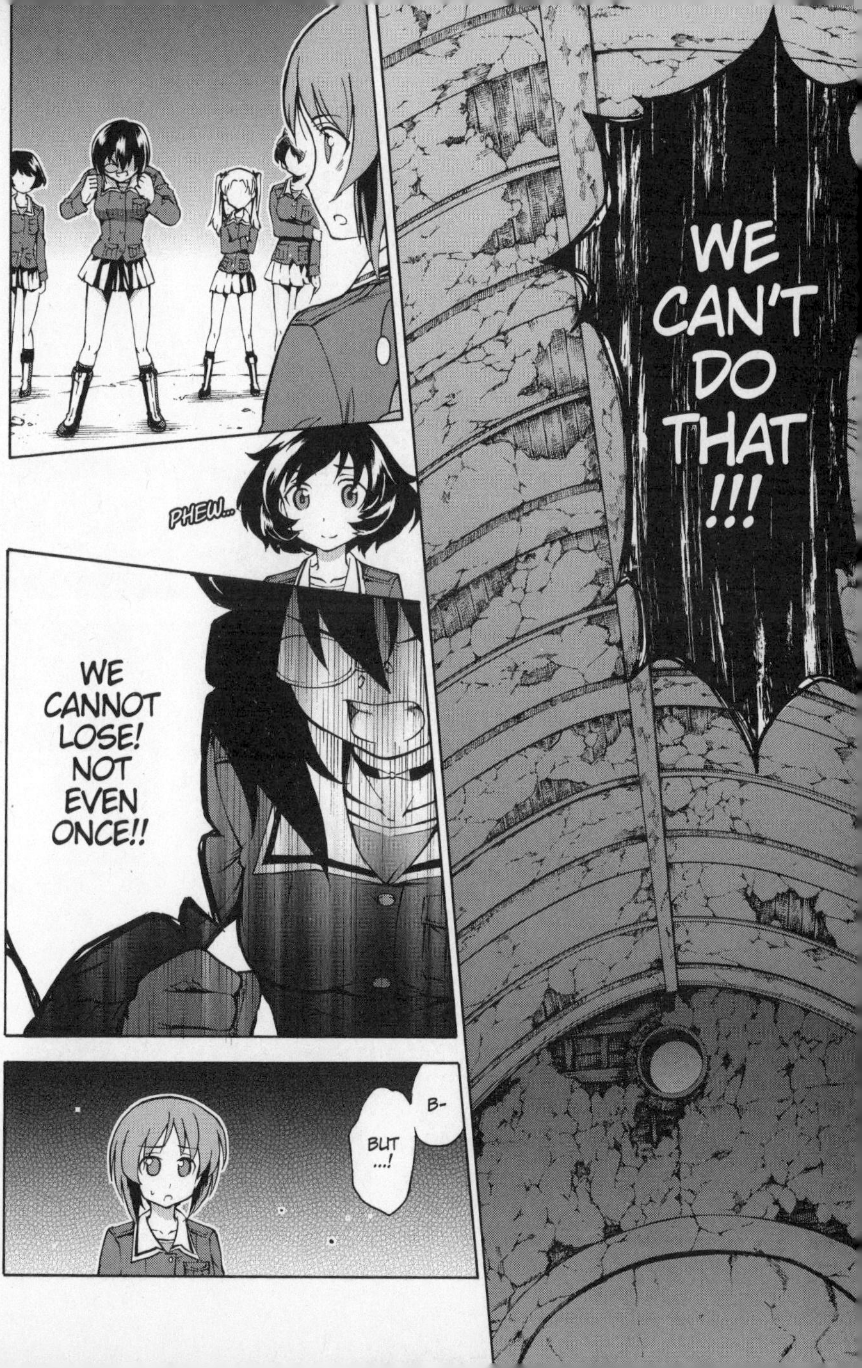

WE CAN'T DO THAT!!!
PHEW...
WE CANNOT LOSE! NOT EVEN ONCE!!
B-
BUT ...!

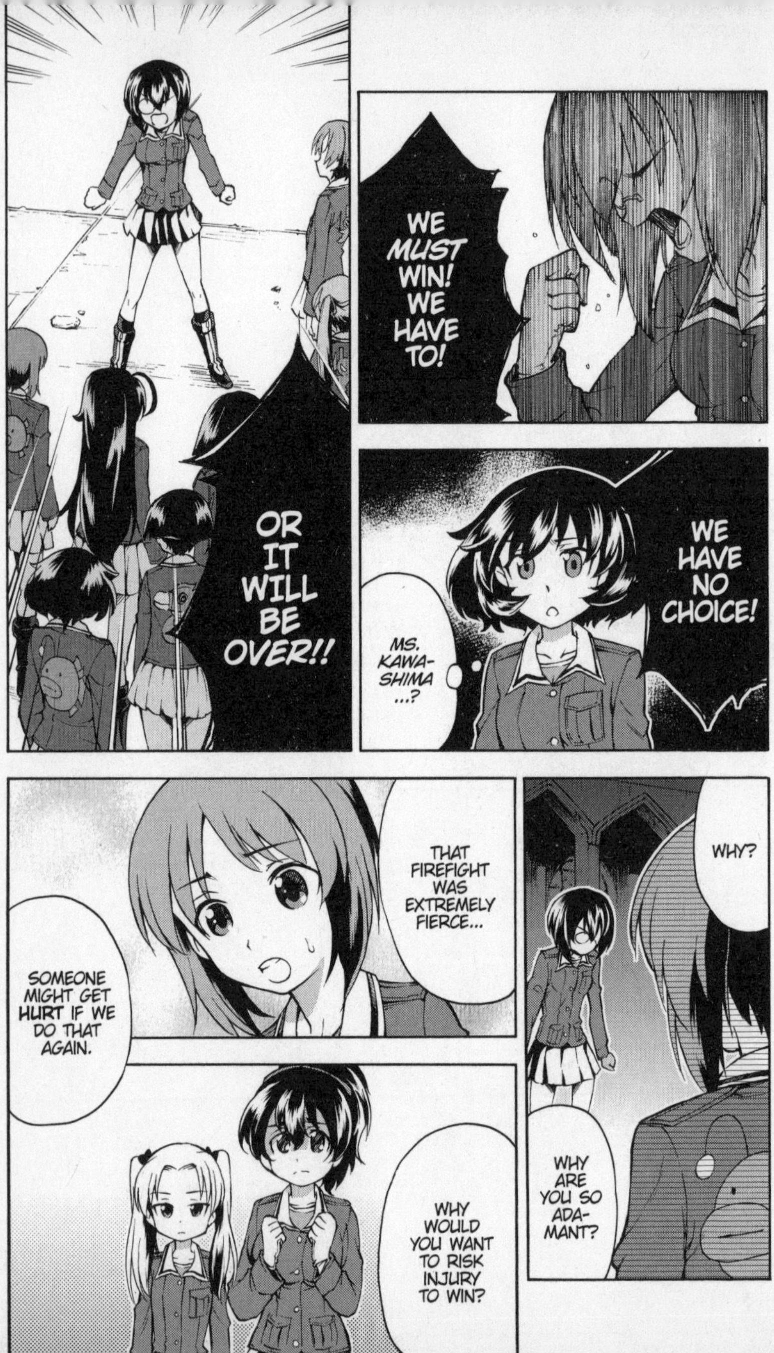
WE MUST WIN! WE HAVE TO!
WE HAVE NO CHOICE!
MS. KAWASHIMA ...?
OR IT WILL BE OVER!!
WHY?
WHY ARE YOU SO ADAMANT?
THAT FIREFIGHT WAS EXTREMELY FIERCE...
SOMEONE MIGHT GET HURT IF WE DO THAT AGAIN.
WHY WOULD YOU WANT TO RISK INJURY TO WIN?

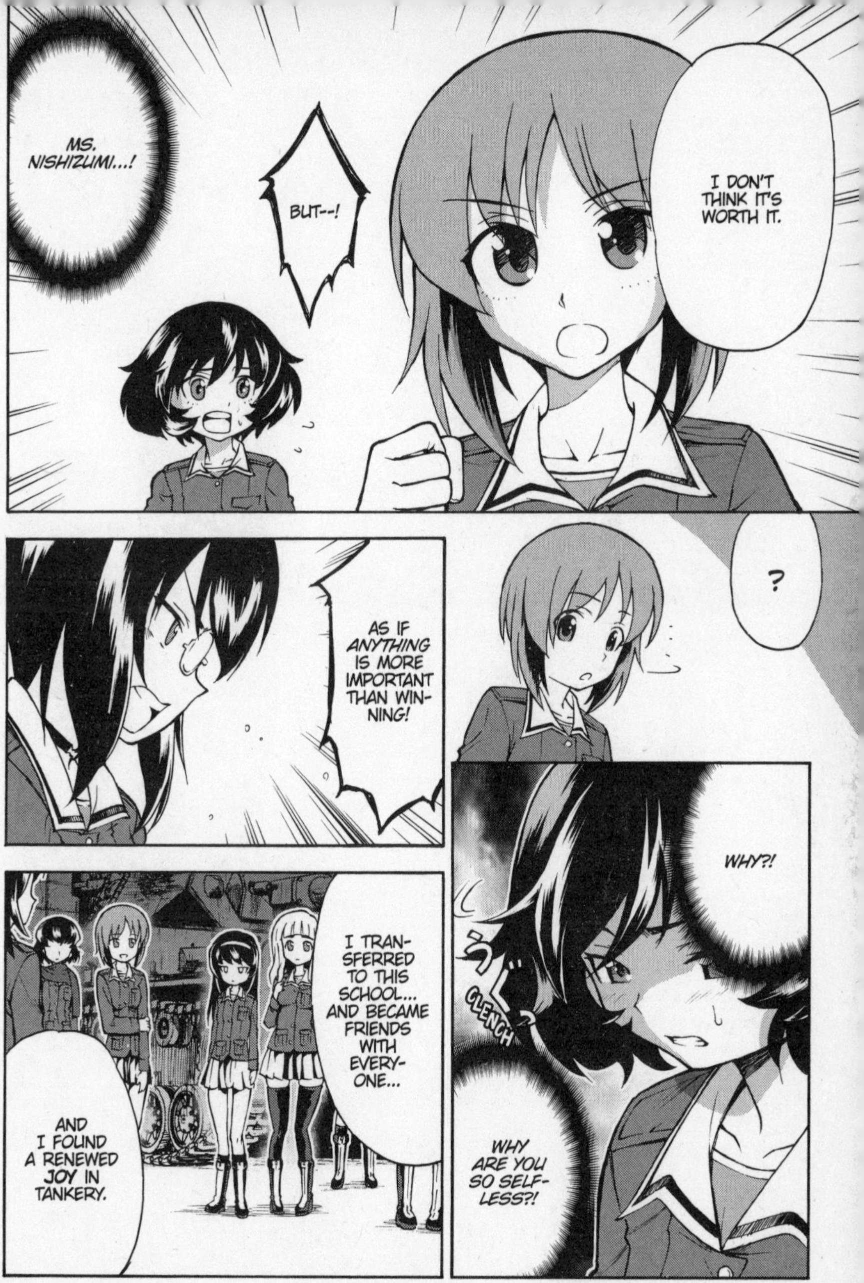

I DON'T THINK IT'S WORTH IT.
BUT--!
MS. NISHIZUMI...!
?
AS IF *ANYTHING* IS MORE IMPORTANT THAN WIN-NING!
WHY?!
CLENCH
WHY ARE YOU SO SELF-LESS?!
I TRAN-SFERRED TO THIS SCHOOL... AND BECAME FRIENDS WITH EVERY-ONE...
AND I FOUND A RENEWED *JOY* IN TANKERY.

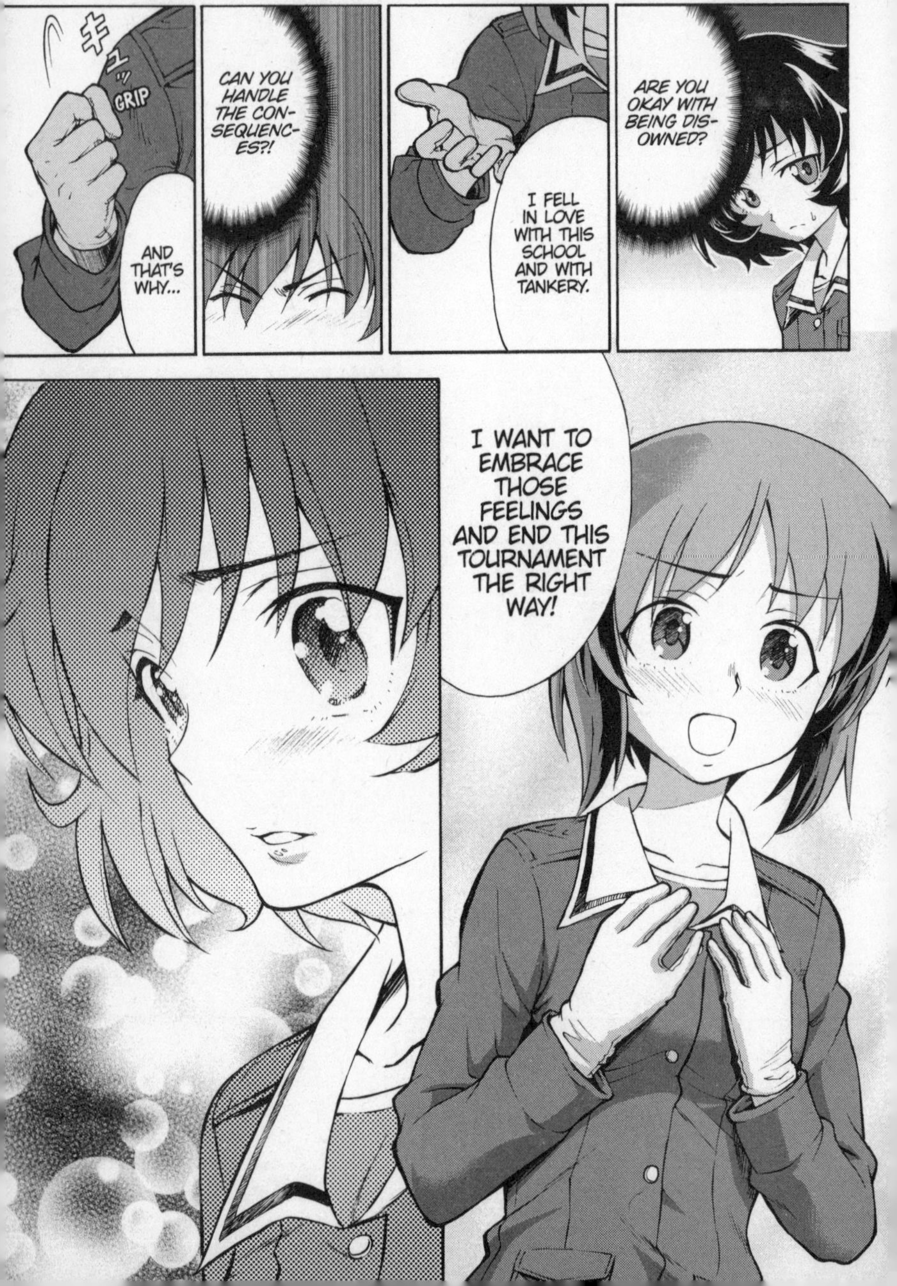
ARE YOU OKAY WITH BEING DIS-OWNED?
I FELL IN LOVE WITH THIS SCHOOL AND WITH TANKERY.
CAN YOU HANDLE THE CON-SEQUENC-ES?!
キュッ
GRIP
AND THAT'S WHY...
I WANT TO EMBRACE THOSE FEELINGS AND END THIS TOURNAMENT THE RIGHT WAY!

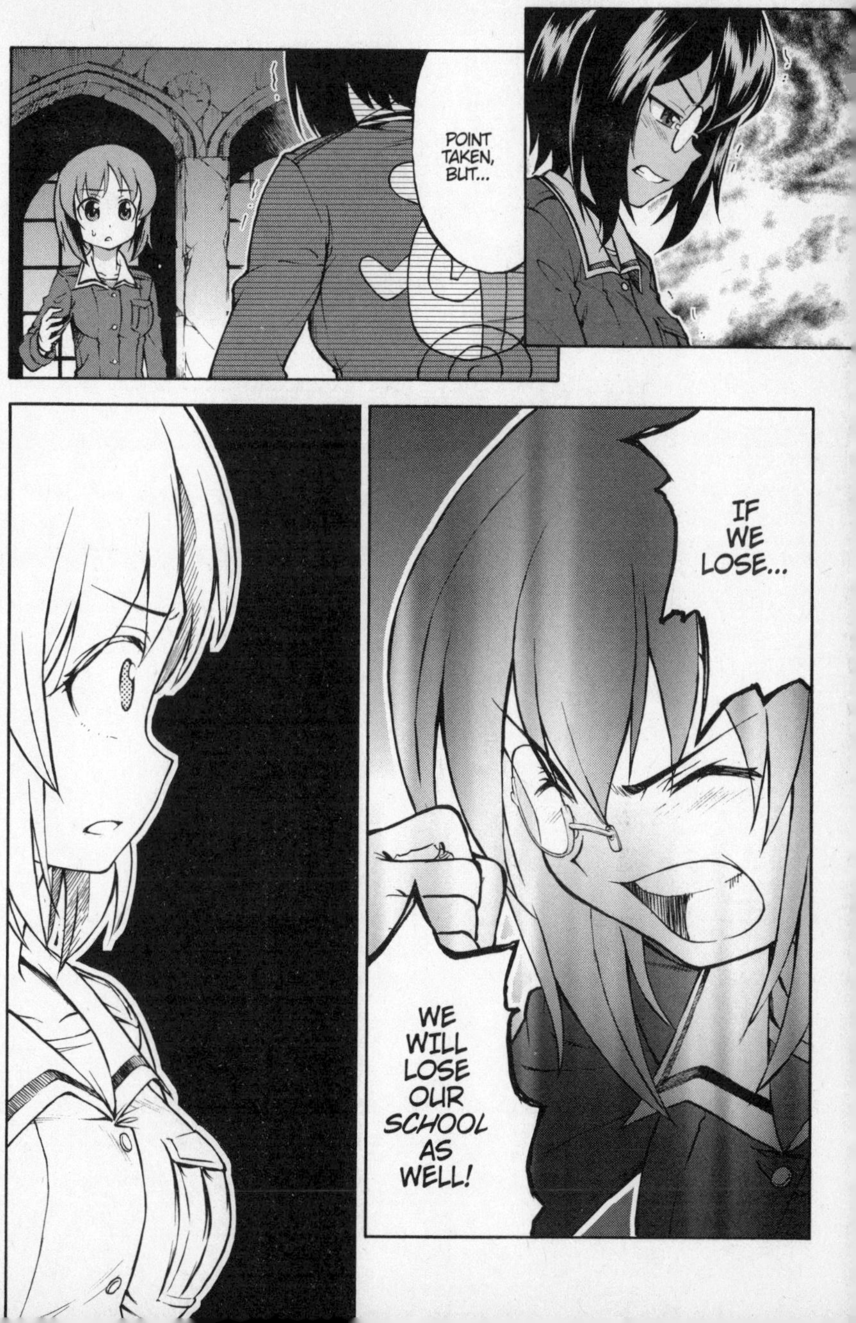
POINT TAKEN, BUT...
IF WE LOSE...
WE WILL LOSE OUR SCHOOL AS WELL!

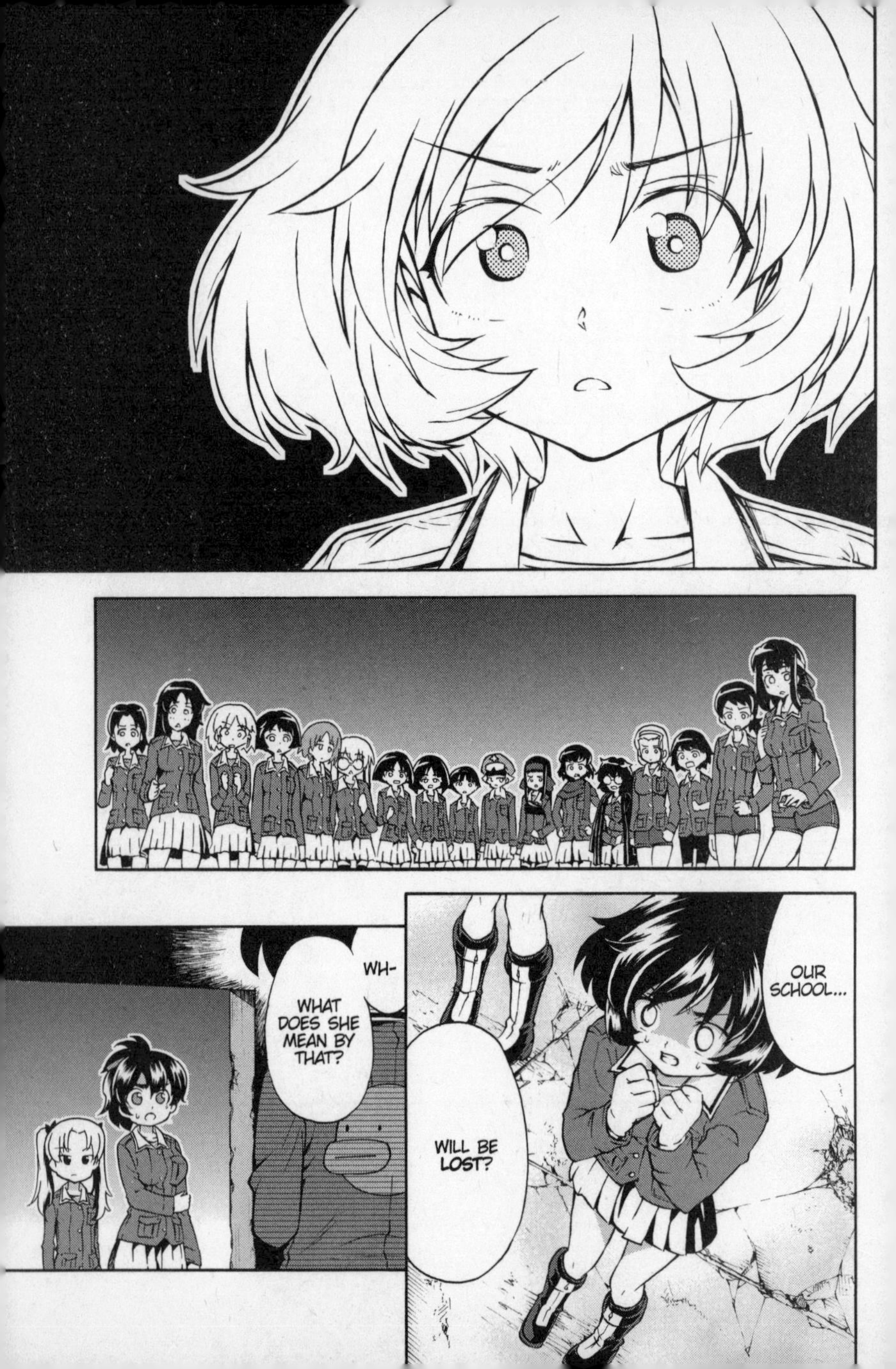
OUR SCHOOL...
WILL BE LOST?
WH-
WHAT DOES SHE MEAN BY THAT?

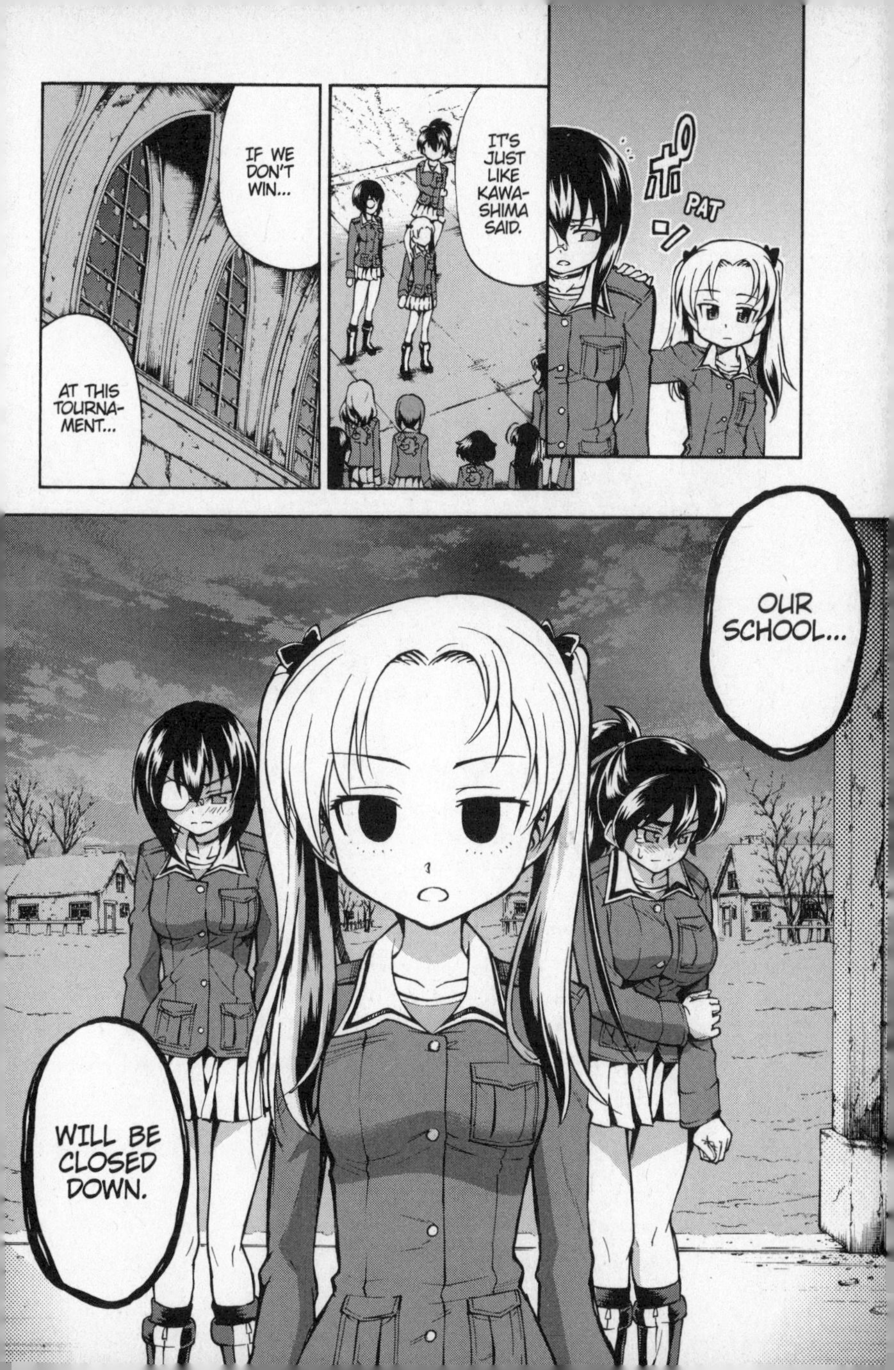
ポ
PAT
IT'S JUST LIKE KAWA-SHIMA SAID.
IF WE DON'T WIN...
AT THIS TOURNA-MENT...
OUR SCHOOL...
WILL BE CLOSED DOWN.

ガールズ&パンツァー
GIRLS und PANZER

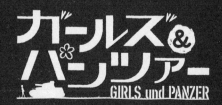

CHAPTER 13 Captain! We'll Dance!!

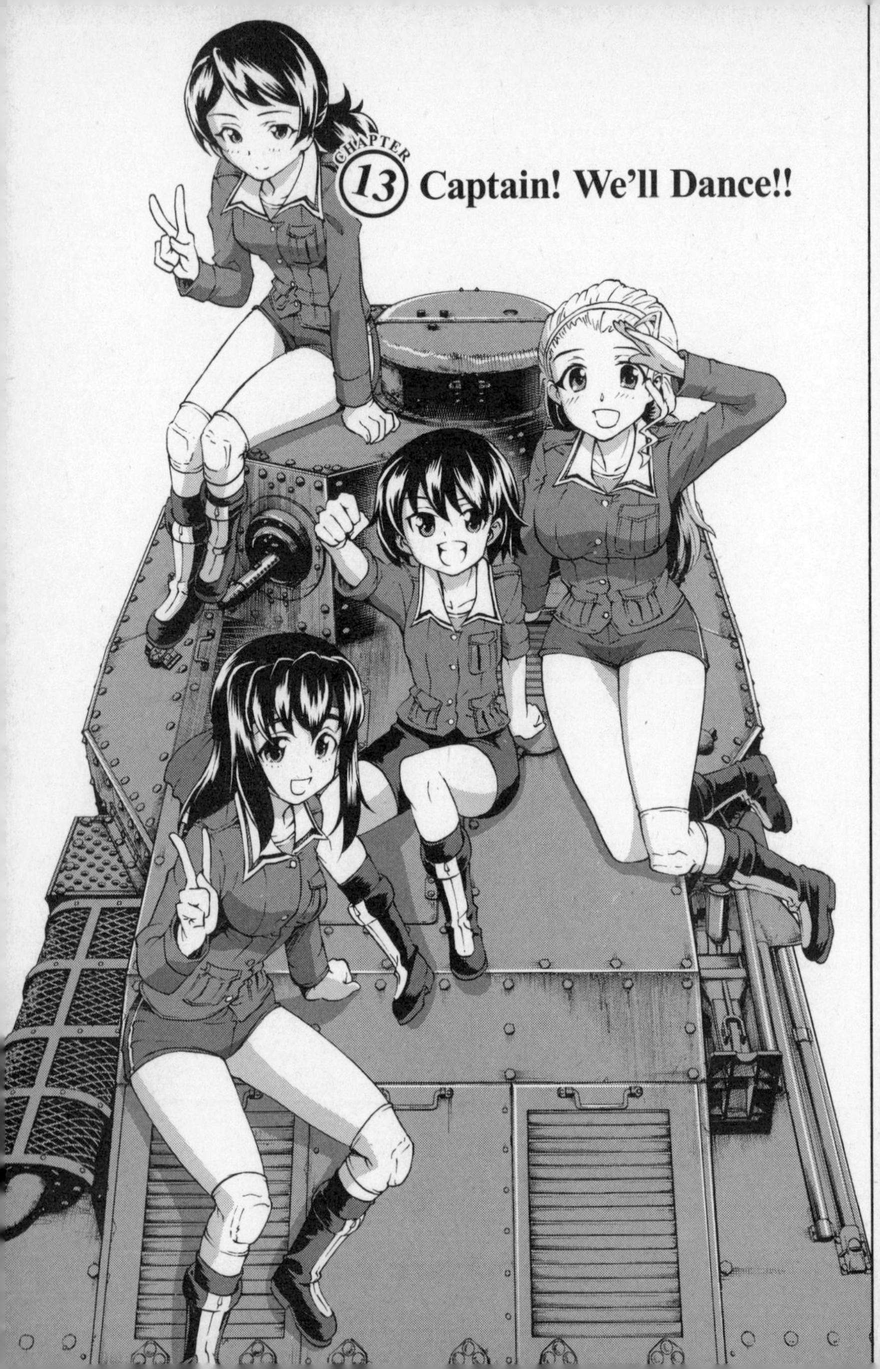

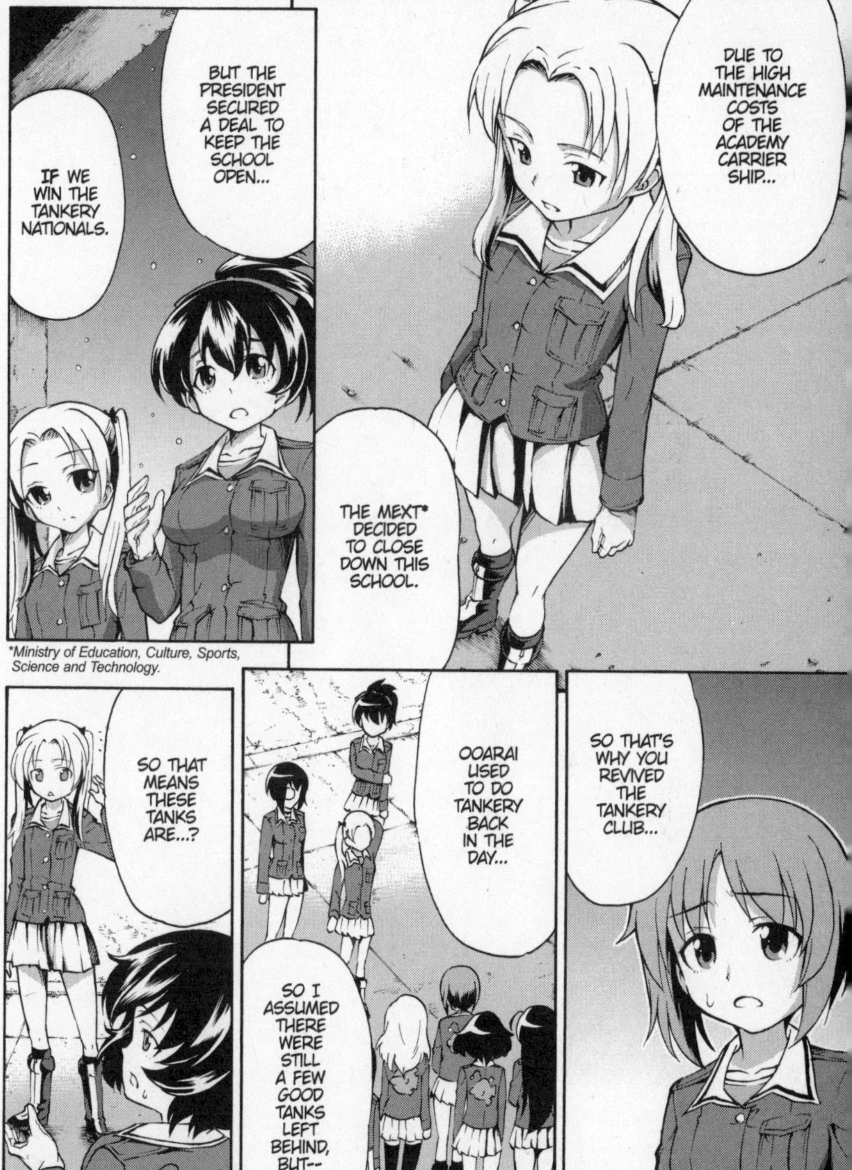
DUE TO THE HIGH MAINTENANCE COSTS OF THE ACADEMY CARRIER SHIP...
THE MEXT* DECIDED TO CLOSE DOWN THIS SCHOOL.
BUT THE PRESIDENT SECURED A DEAL TO KEEP THE SCHOOL OPEN...
IF WE WIN THE TANKERY NATIONALS.
SO THAT'S WHY YOU REVIVED THE TANKERY CLUB...
OOARAI USED TO DO TANKERY BACK IN THE DAY...
SO I ASSUMED THERE WERE STILL A FEW GOOD TANKS LEFT BEHIND, BUT--
SO THAT MEANS THESE TANKS ARE...?

*Ministry of Education, Culture, Sports, Science and Technology.

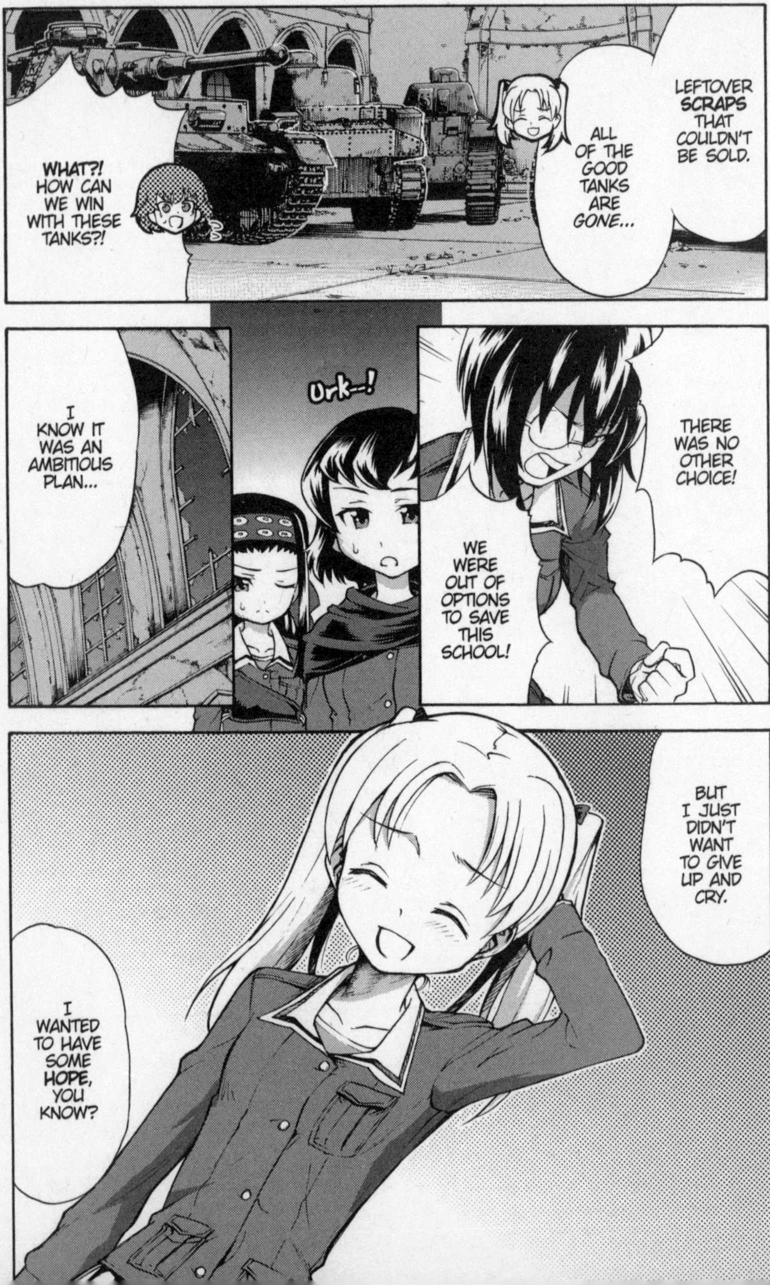
LEFTOVER SCRAPS THAT COULDN'T BE SOLD.
ALL OF THE GOOD TANKS ARE GONE...
WHAT?! HOW CAN WE WIN WITH THESE TANKS?!
THERE WAS NO OTHER CHOICE!
WE WERE OUT OF OPTIONS TO SAVE THIS SCHOOL!
Urk--!
I KNOW IT WAS AN AMBITIOUS PLAN...
BUT I JUST DIDN'T WANT TO GIVE UP AND CRY.
I WANTED TO HAVE SOME HOPE, YOU KNOW?

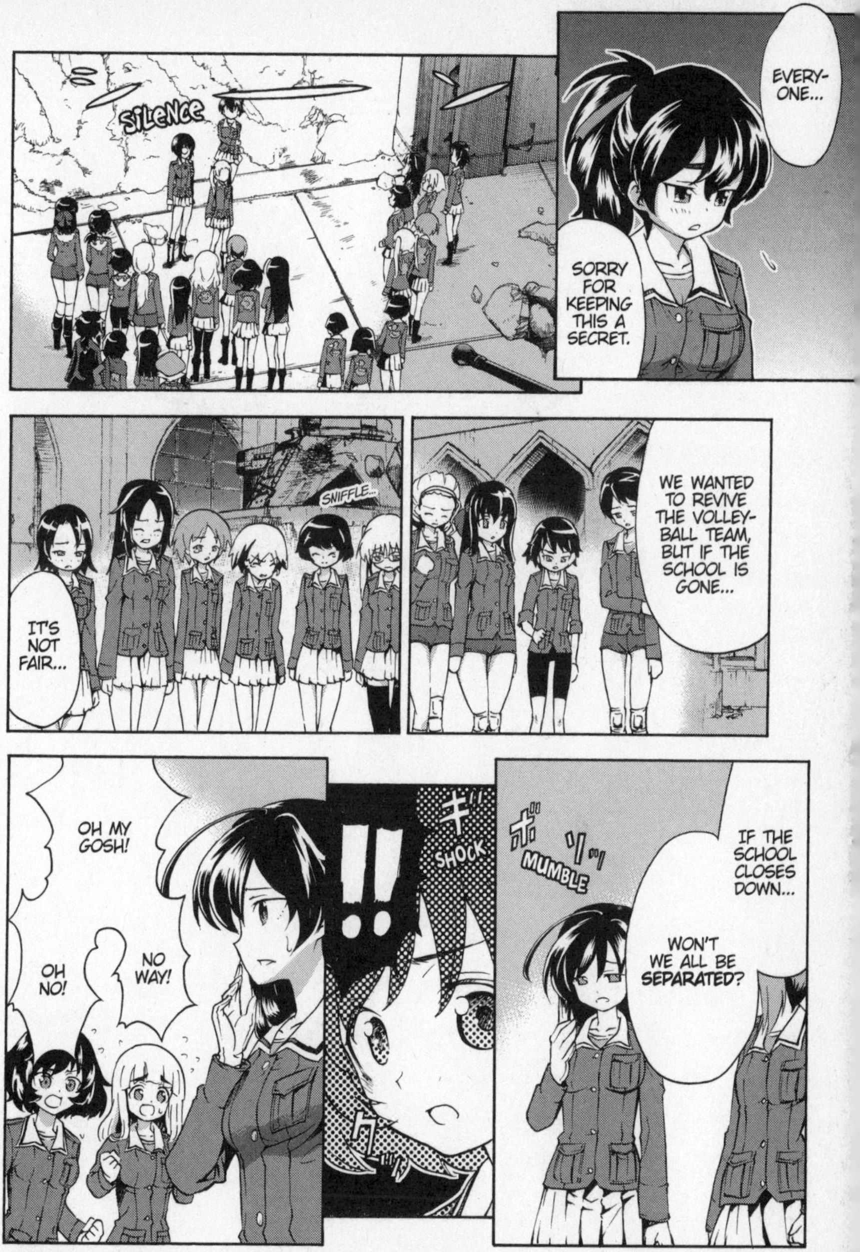
EVERY-ONE...
SORRY FOR KEEPING THIS A SECRET.
SILENCE
WE WANTED TO REVIVE THE VOLLEY-BALL TEAM, BUT IF THE SCHOOL IS GONE...
SNIFFLE...
IT'S NOT FAIR...
MUMBLE
IF THE SCHOOL CLOSES DOWN...
WON'T WE ALL BE SEPARATED?
SHOCK
!!
OH MY GOSH!
NO WAY!
OH NO!

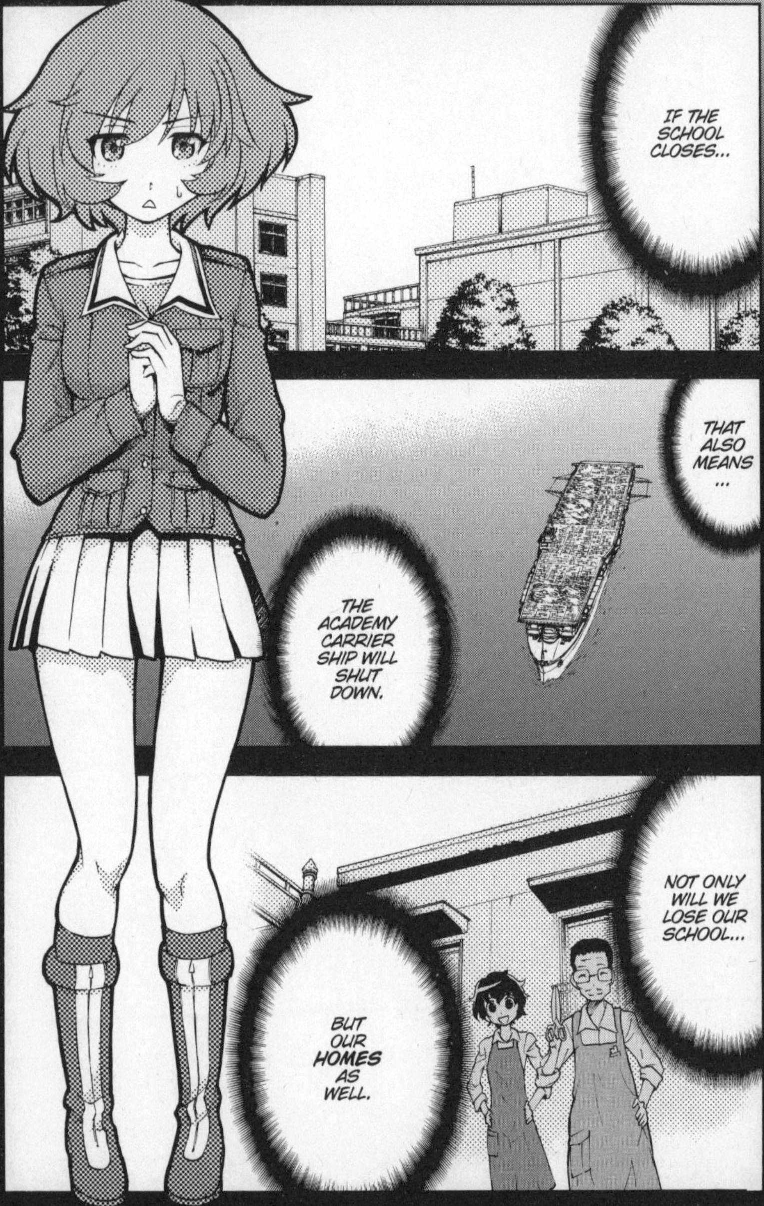
IF THE SCHOOL CLOSES...
THAT ALSO MEANS ...
THE ACADEMY CARRIER SHIP WILL SHUT DOWN.
NOT ONLY WILL WE LOSE OUR SCHOOL...
BUT OUR HOMES AS WELL.

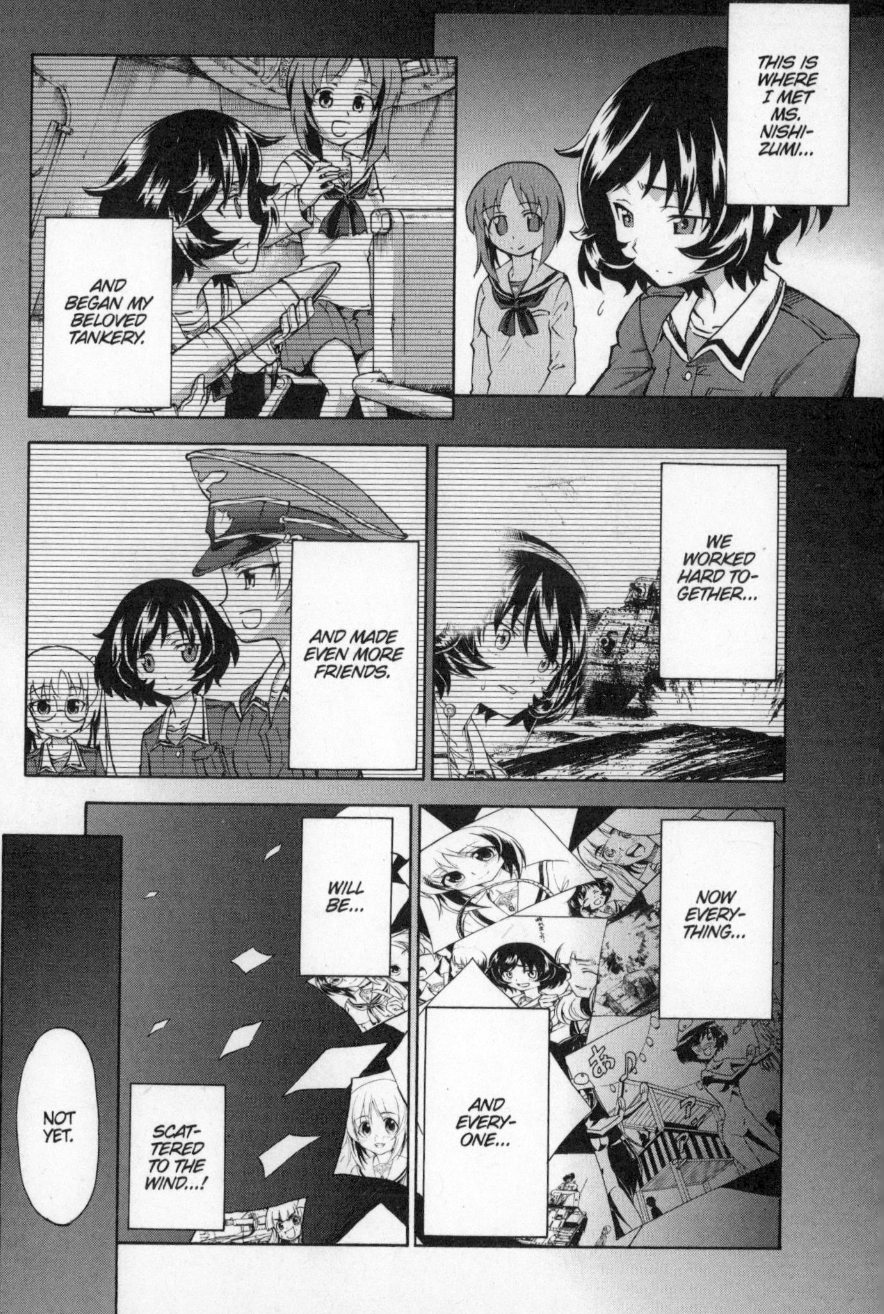
THIS IS WHERE I MET MS. NISHIZUMI...
AND BEGAN MY BELOVED TANKERY.
WE WORKED HARD TOGETHER...
AND MADE EVEN MORE FRIENDS.
NOW EVERYTHING...
AND EVERYONE...
WILL BE...
SCATTERED TO THE WIND...!
NOT YET.

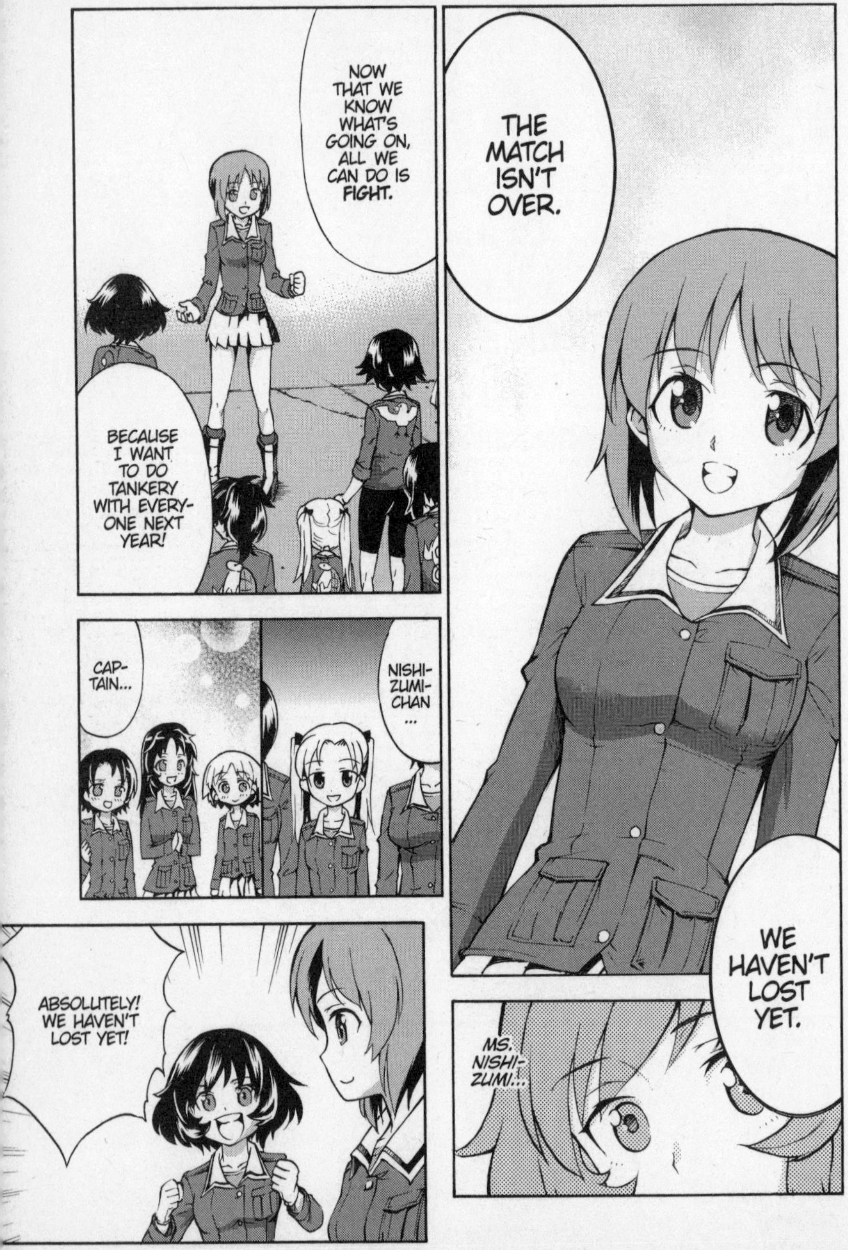
THE MATCH ISN'T OVER.
WE HAVEN'T LOST YET.
NOW THAT WE KNOW WHAT'S GOING ON, ALL WE CAN DO IS FIGHT.
BECAUSE I WANT TO DO TANKERY WITH EVERY-ONE NEXT YEAR!
NISHI-ZUMI-CHAN...
CAP-TAIN...
MS. NISHI-ZUMI...
ABSOLUTELY! WE HAVEN'T LOST YET!

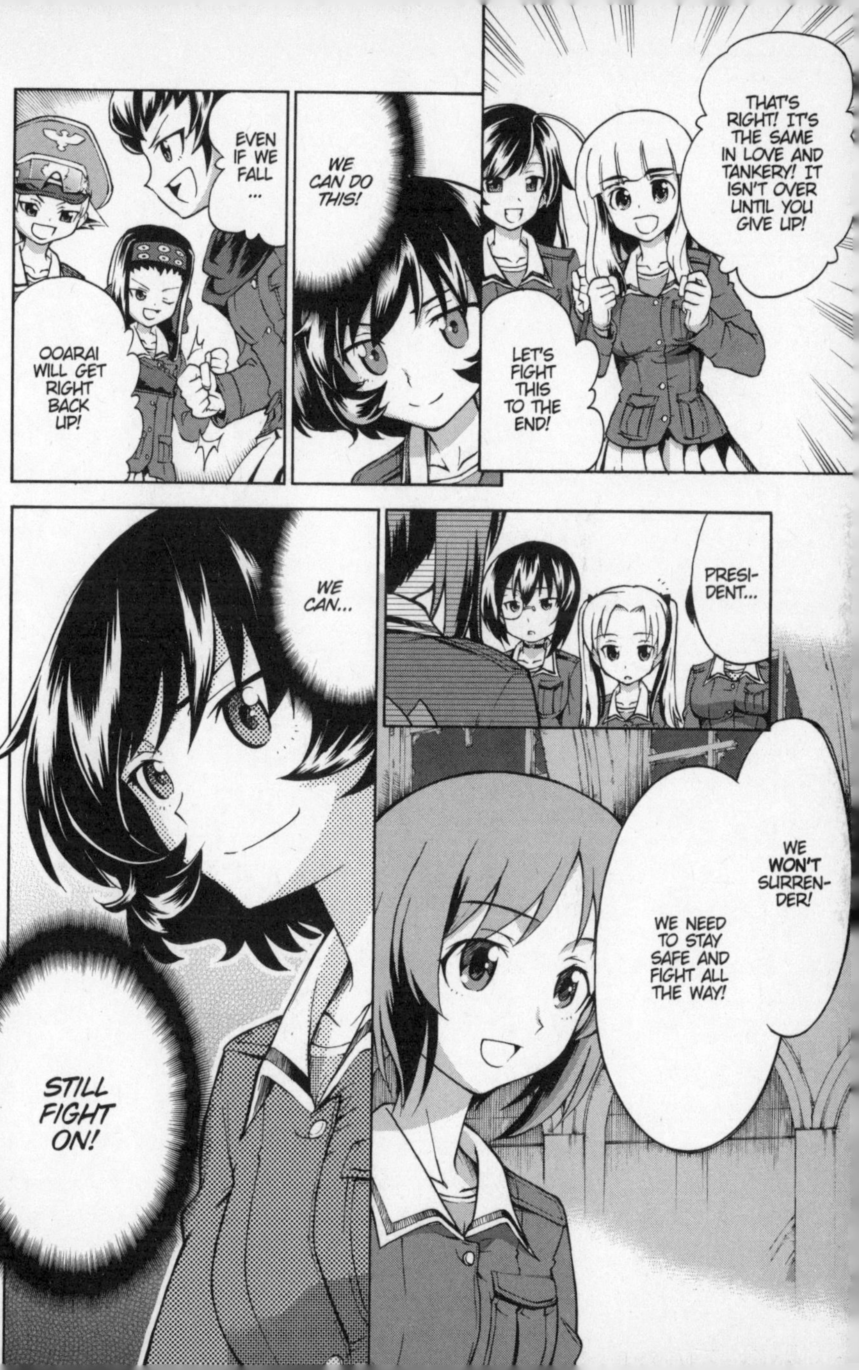
THAT'S RIGHT! IT'S THE SAME IN LOVE AND TANKERY! IT ISN'T OVER UNTIL YOU GIVE UP!
LET'S FIGHT THIS TO THE END!
WE CAN DO THIS!
EVEN IF WE FALL ...
OOARAI WILL GET RIGHT BACK UP!
PRESI-DENT...
WE WON'T SURREN-DER!
WE NEED TO STAY SAFE AND FIGHT ALL THE WAY!
WE CAN...
STILL FIGHT ON!

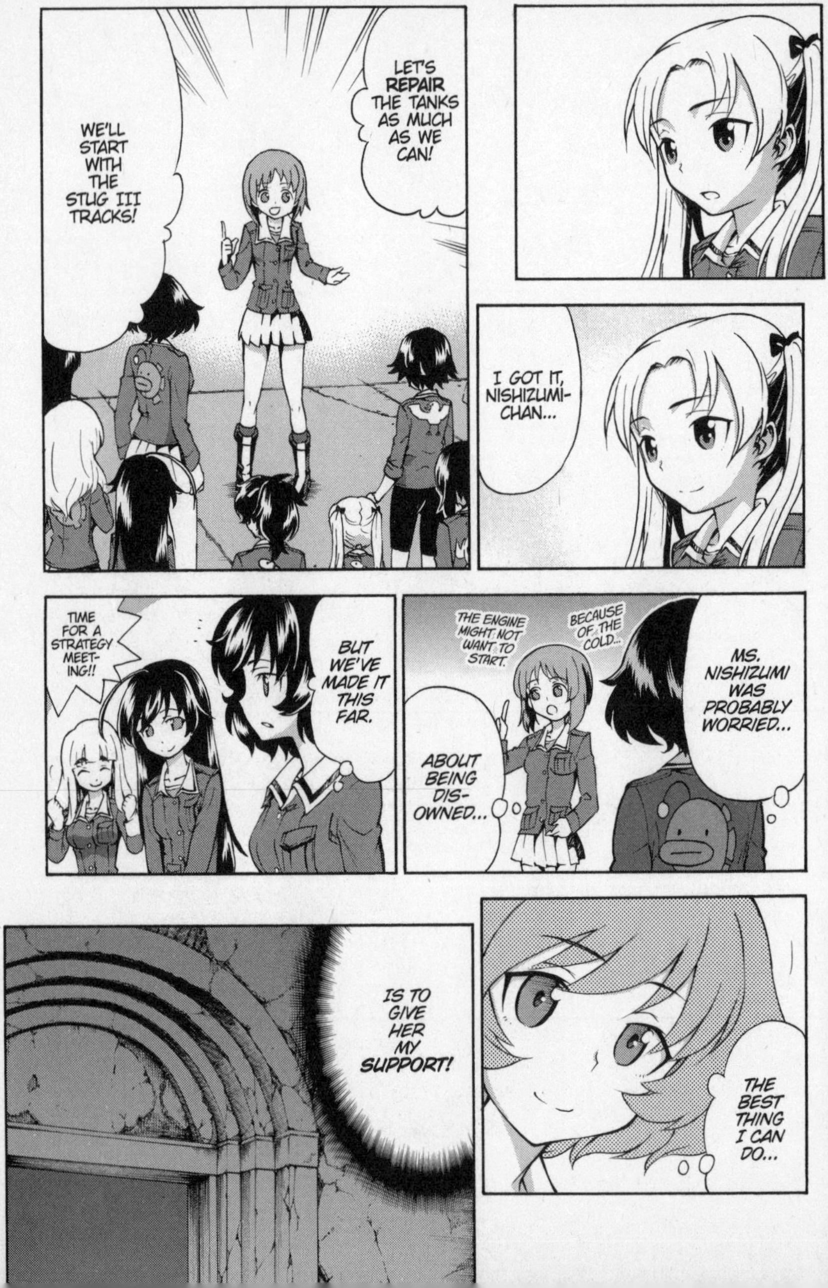
I GOT IT, NISHIZUMI-CHAN...
LET'S REPAIR THE TANKS AS MUCH AS WE CAN!
WE'LL START WITH THE STUG III TRACKS!
MS. NISHIZUMI WAS PROBABLY WORRIED...
BECAUSE OF THE COLD...
THE ENGINE MIGHT NOT WANT TO START.
ABOUT BEING DIS-OWNED...
BUT WE'VE MADE IT THIS FAR.
TIME FOR A STRATEGY MEET-ING!!
THE BEST THING I CAN DO...
IS TO GIVE HER MY SUPPORT!

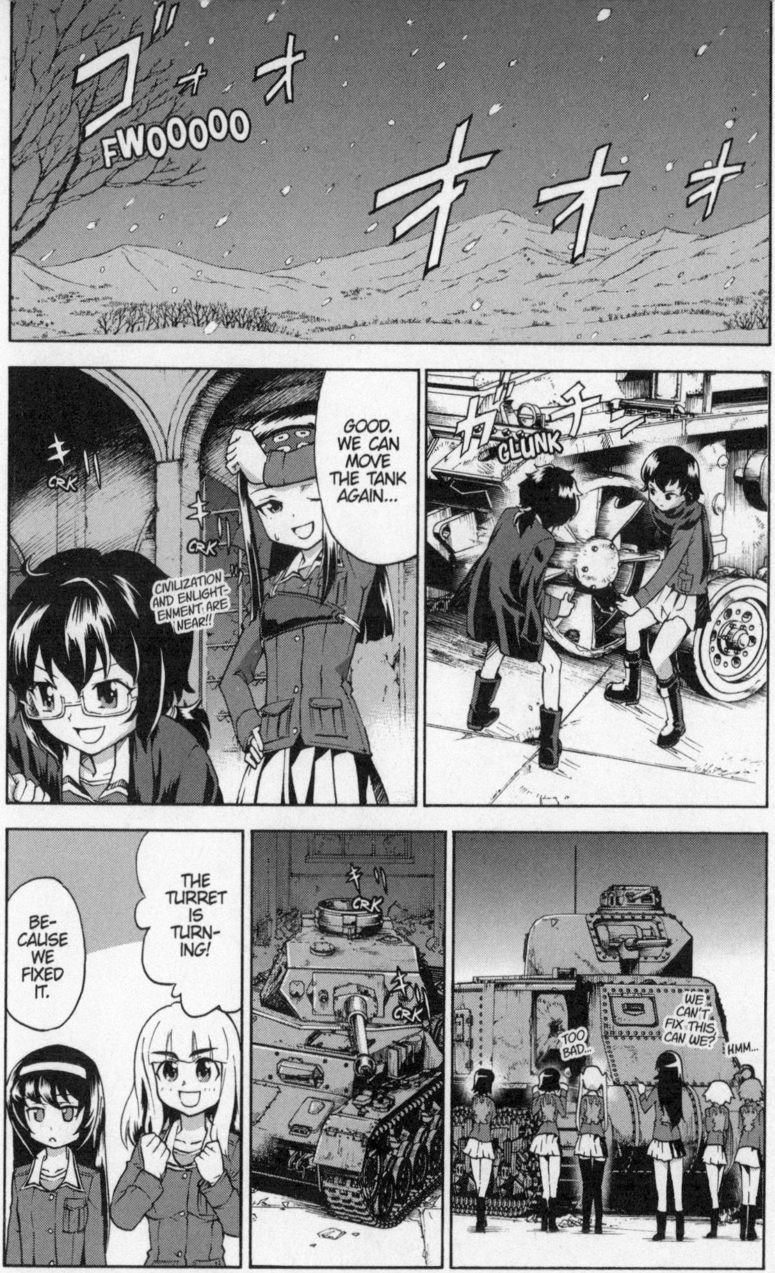
ゴォオ
FWOOOOO
オオォ
ガチン
GLUNK
GOOD. WE CAN MOVE THE TANK AGAIN...
キリ
CRK
キリ
CRK
CIVILIZATION AND ENLIGHTENMENT ARE NEAR!!
HMM...
WE CAN'T FIX THIS, CAN WE?
TOO BAD...
キリ
CRK
キリ
CRK
THE TURRET IS TURNING!
BECAUSE WE FIXED IT.

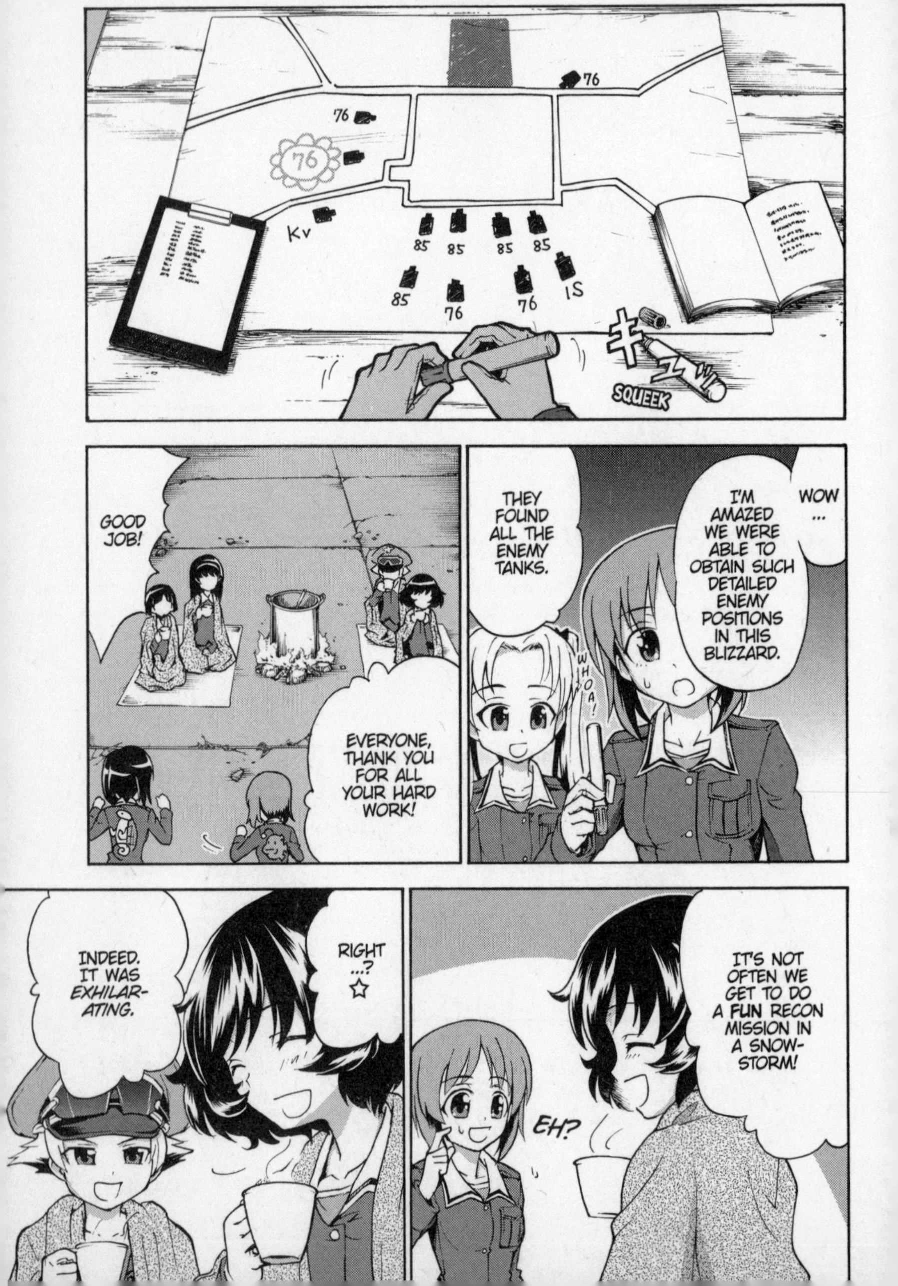
76
76
76
Kv
85
85
85
85
85
76
76
IS
SQUEEK
WOW ...
I'M AMAZED WE WERE ABLE TO OBTAIN SUCH DETAILED ENEMY POSITIONS IN THIS BLIZZARD.
THEY FOUND ALL THE ENEMY TANKS.
WHOA!
GOOD JOB!
EVERYONE, THANK YOU FOR ALL YOUR HARD WORK!
IT'S NOT OFTEN WE GET TO DO A FUN RECON MISSION IN A SNOW-STORM!
EH?
RIGHT ...? ☆
INDEED. IT WAS EXHILAR-ATING.

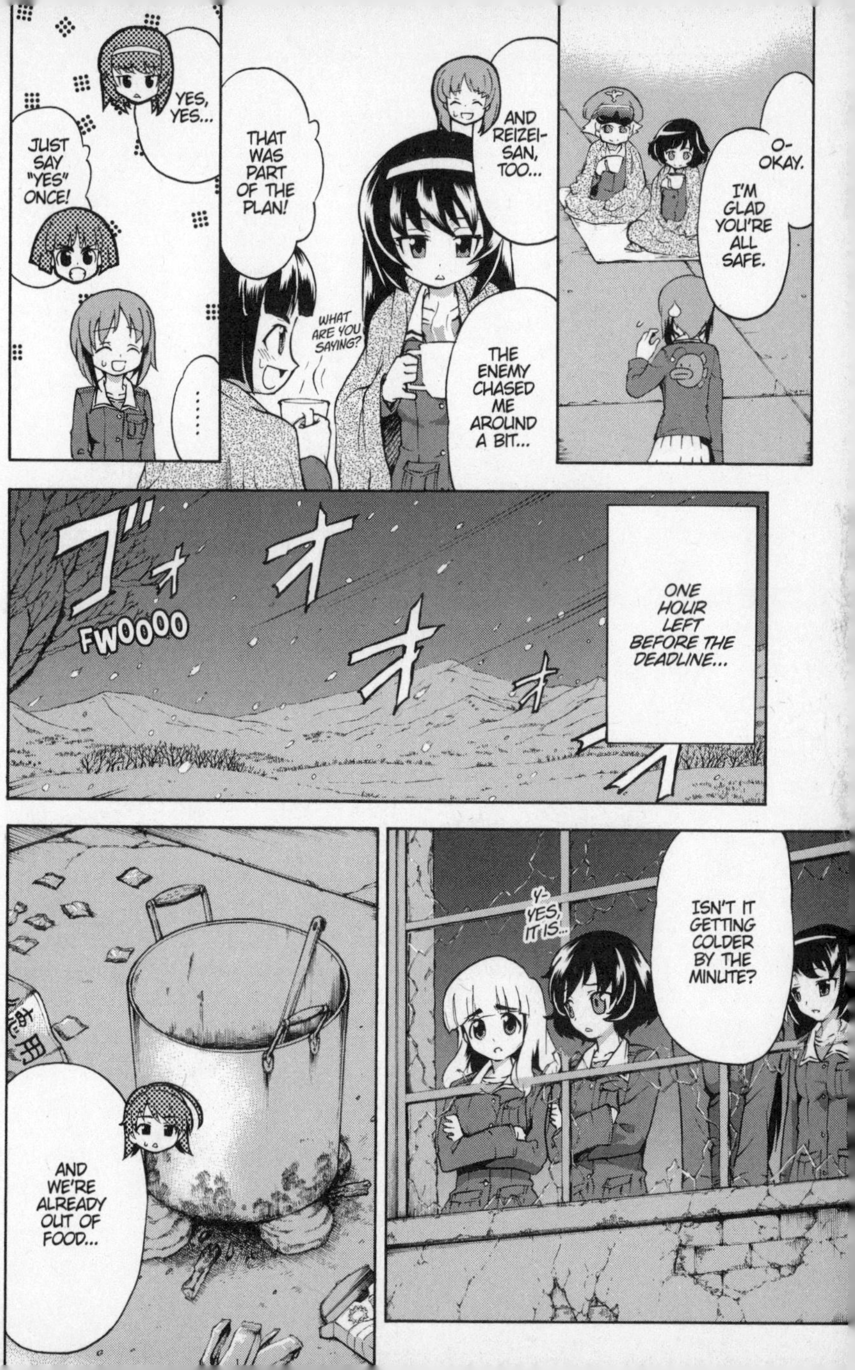
O-OKAY.
I'M GLAD YOU'RE ALL SAFE.
AND REIZEI-SAN, TOO...
THE ENEMY CHASED ME AROUND A BIT...
THAT WAS PART OF THE PLAN!
WHAT ARE YOU SAYING?
YES, YES...
JUST SAY "YES" ONCE!
......
ゴォオオオ
FWOOOO
ONE HOUR LEFT BEFORE THE DEADLINE...
ISN'T IT GETTING COLDER BY THE MINUTE?
Y-YES, IT IS...
AND WE'RE ALREADY OUT OF FOOD...

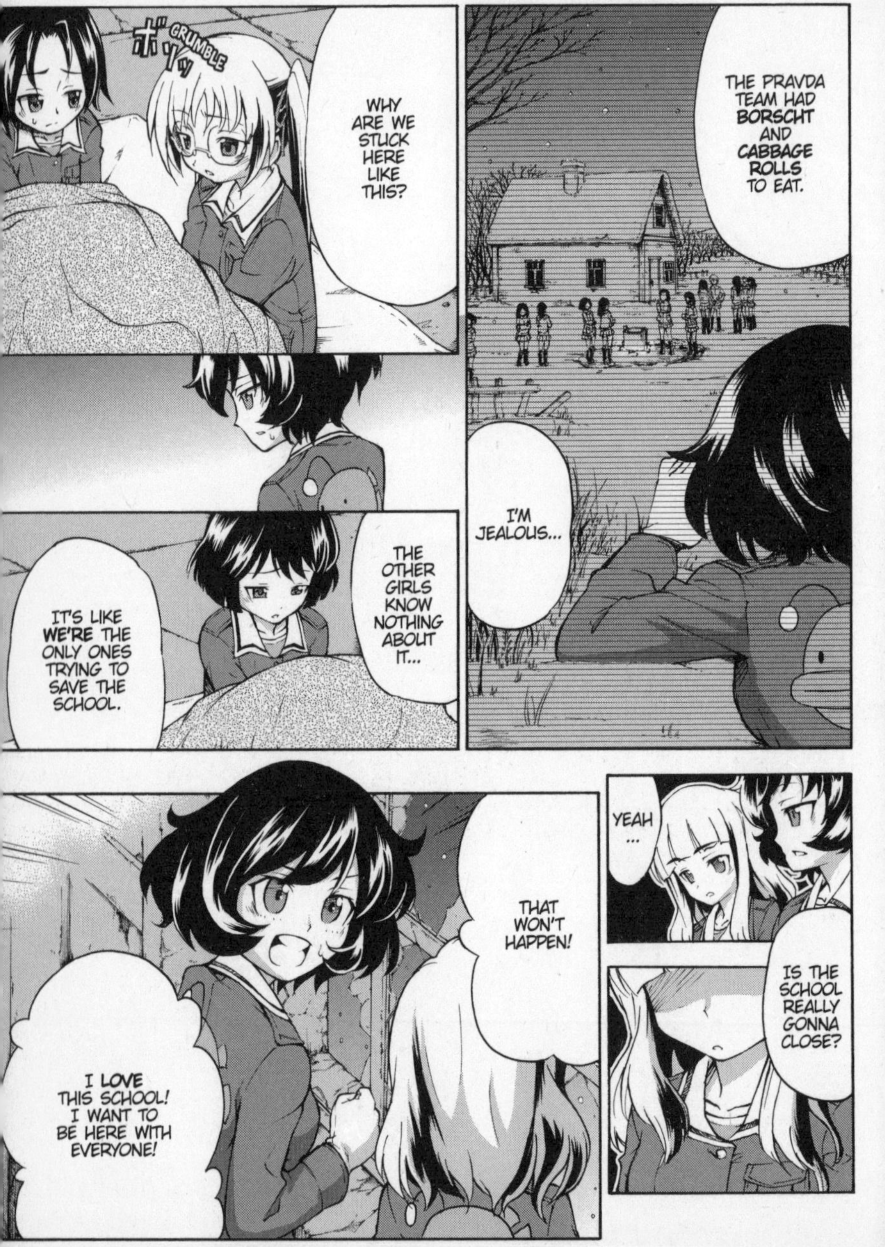
THE PRAVDA TEAM HAD BORSCHT AND CABBAGE ROLLS TO EAT.
I'M JEALOUS...
ボソッ
CRUMBLE
WHY ARE WE STUCK HERE LIKE THIS?
THE OTHER GIRLS KNOW NOTHING ABOUT IT...
IT'S LIKE WE'RE THE ONLY ONES TRYING TO SAVE THE SCHOOL.
YEAH ...
IS THE SCHOOL REALLY GONNA CLOSE?
THAT WON'T HAPPEN!
I LOVE THIS SCHOOL! I WANT TO BE HERE WITH EVERYONE!

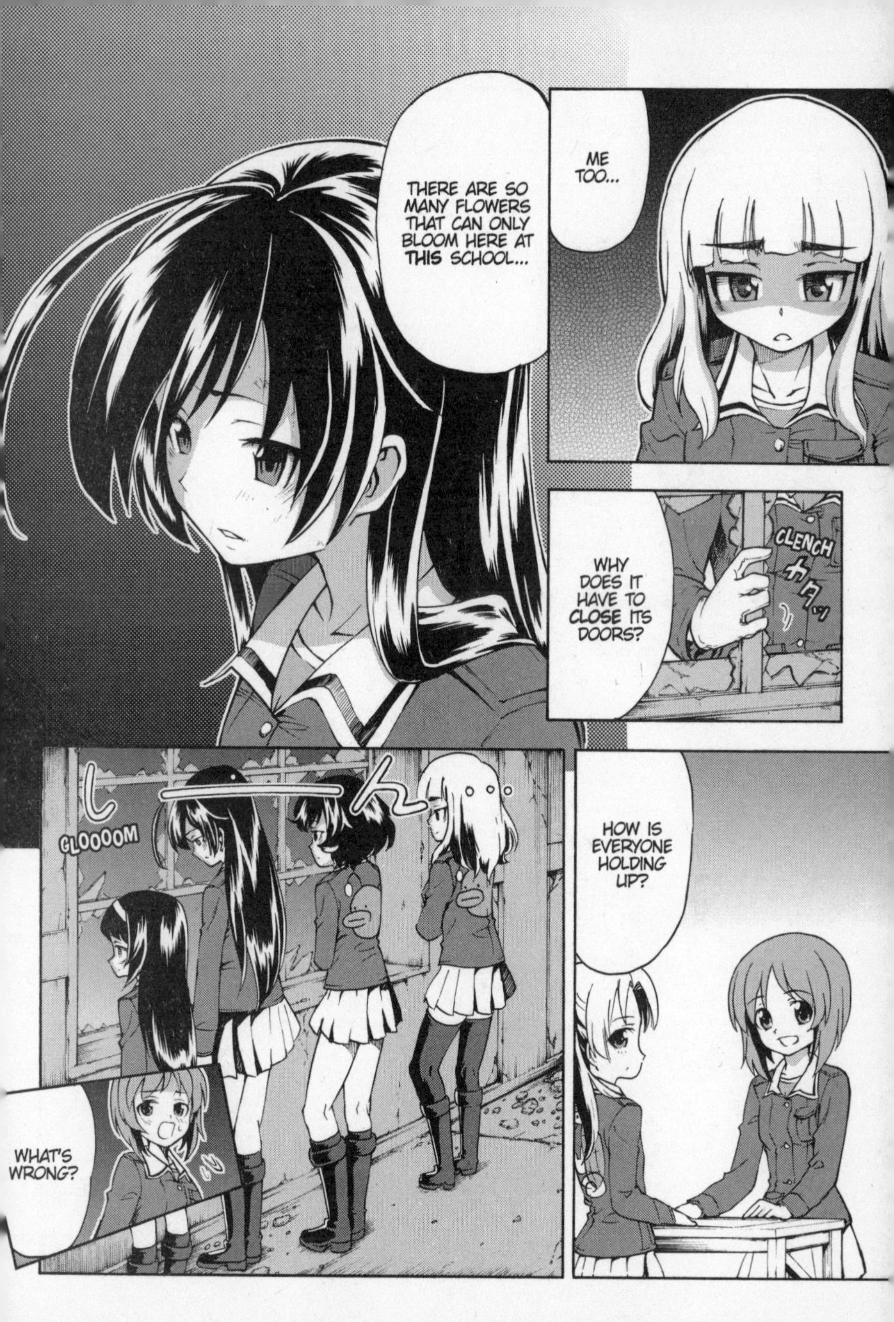
ME TOO...
WHY DOES IT HAVE TO CLOSE ITS DOORS?
CLENCH
カタッ
THERE ARE SO MANY FLOWERS THAT CAN ONLY BLOOM HERE AT **THIS** SCHOOL...
HOW IS EVERYONE HOLDING UP?
しーーん
GLOOOOM
WHAT'S WRONG?

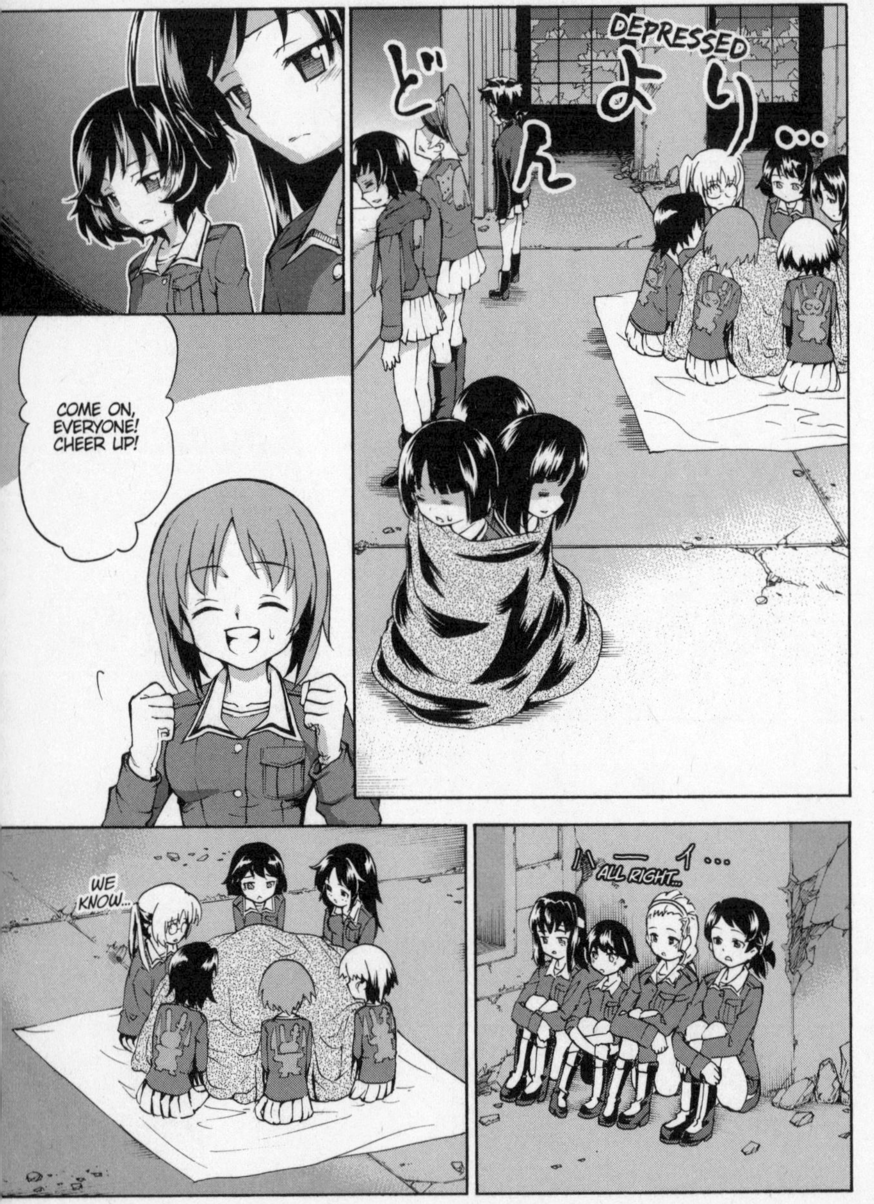
どよ〜ん
DEPRESSED
COME ON, EVERYONE! CHEER UP!
ハーイ...
ALL RIGHT...
WE KNOW...

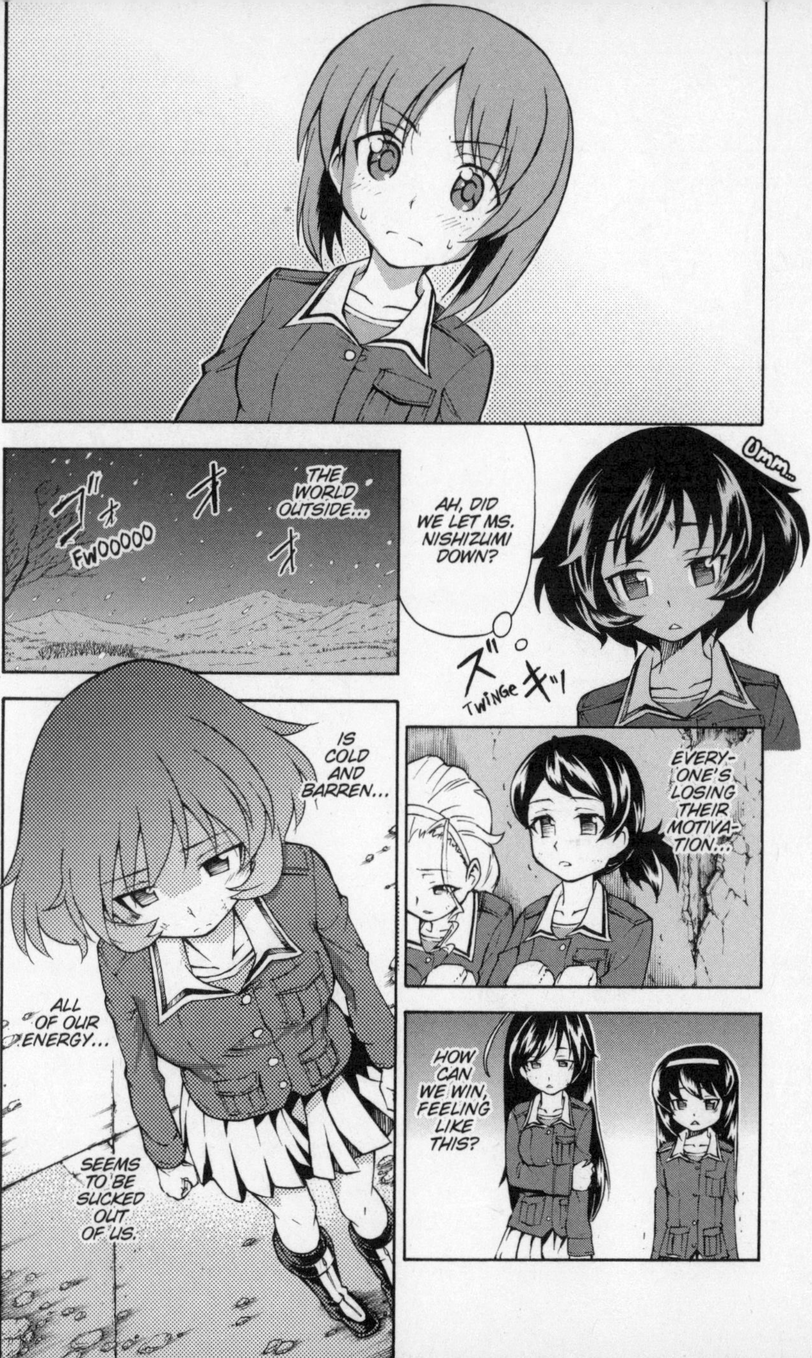
Umm...
AH, DID WE LET MS. NISHIZUMI DOWN?
ズキッ
TWINGE
THE WORLD OUTSIDE...
ゴォォォ
FWOOOOO
EVERY-ONE'S LOSING THEIR MOTIVA-TION...
HOW CAN WE WIN, FEELING LIKE THIS?
IS COLD AND BARREN...
ALL OF OUR ENERGY...
SEEMS TO BE SUCKED OUT OF US.

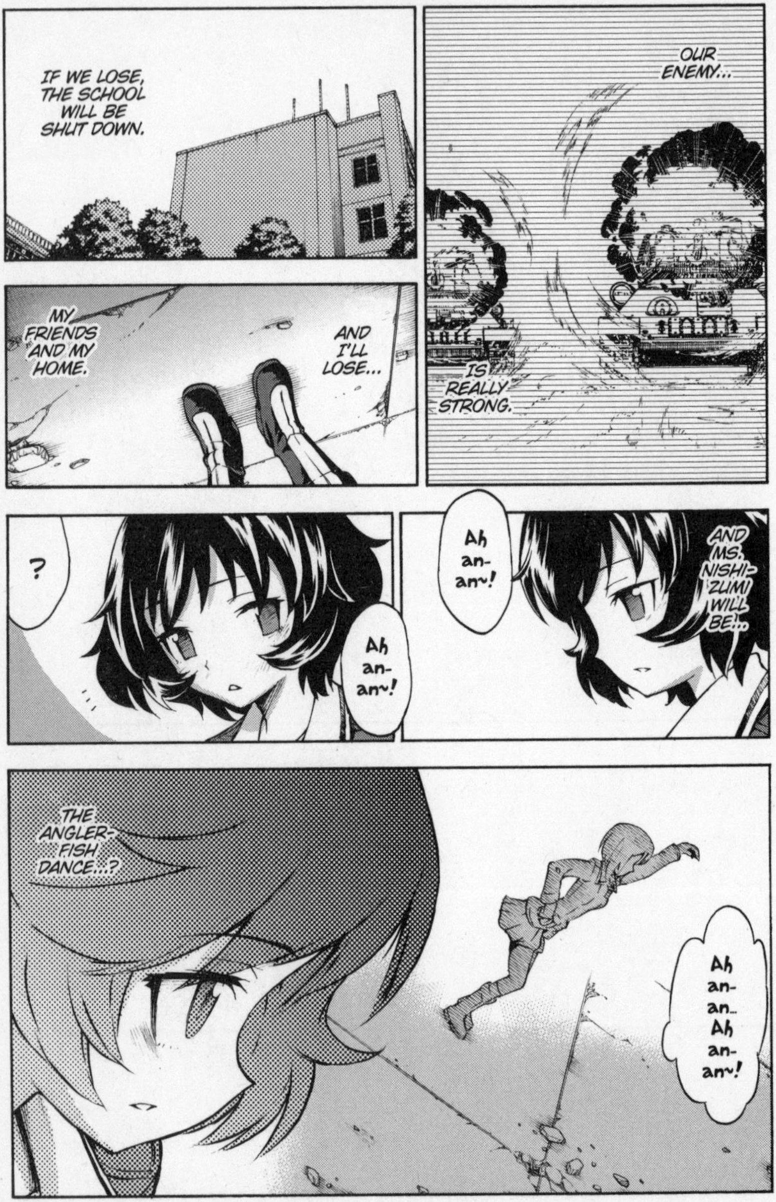
OUR ENEMY...
IS REALLY STRONG.
IF WE LOSE, THE SCHOOL WILL BE SHUT DOWN.
AND I'LL LOSE...
MY FRIENDS AND MY HOME.
AND MS. NISHIZUMI WILL BE...
Ah an-an~!
Ah an-an~!
?
...
Ah an-an.. Ah an-an~!
THE ANGLER-FISH DANCE...?

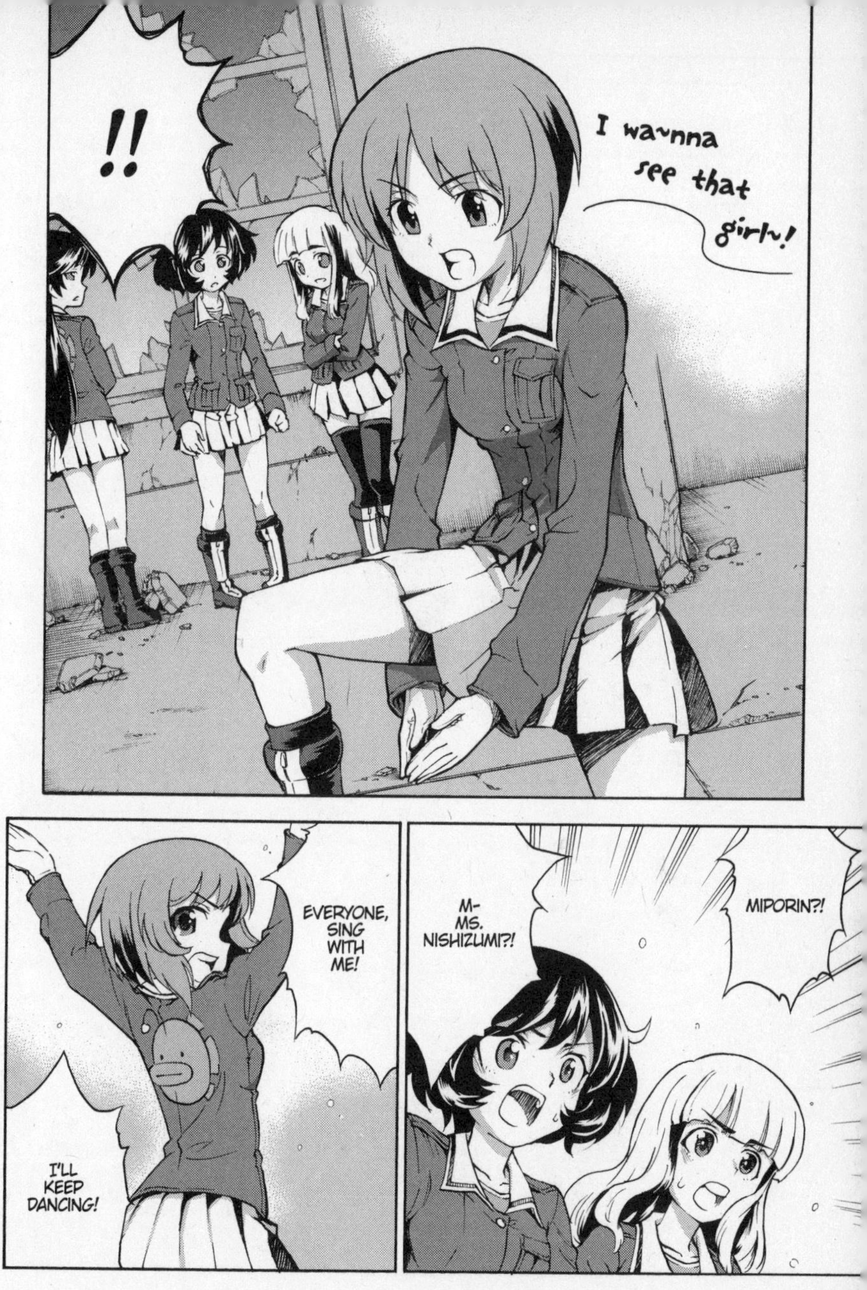
I wa~nna see that girl~!
!!
MIPORIN?!
M-MS. NISHIZUMI?!
EVERYONE, SING WITH ME!
I'LL KEEP DANCING!

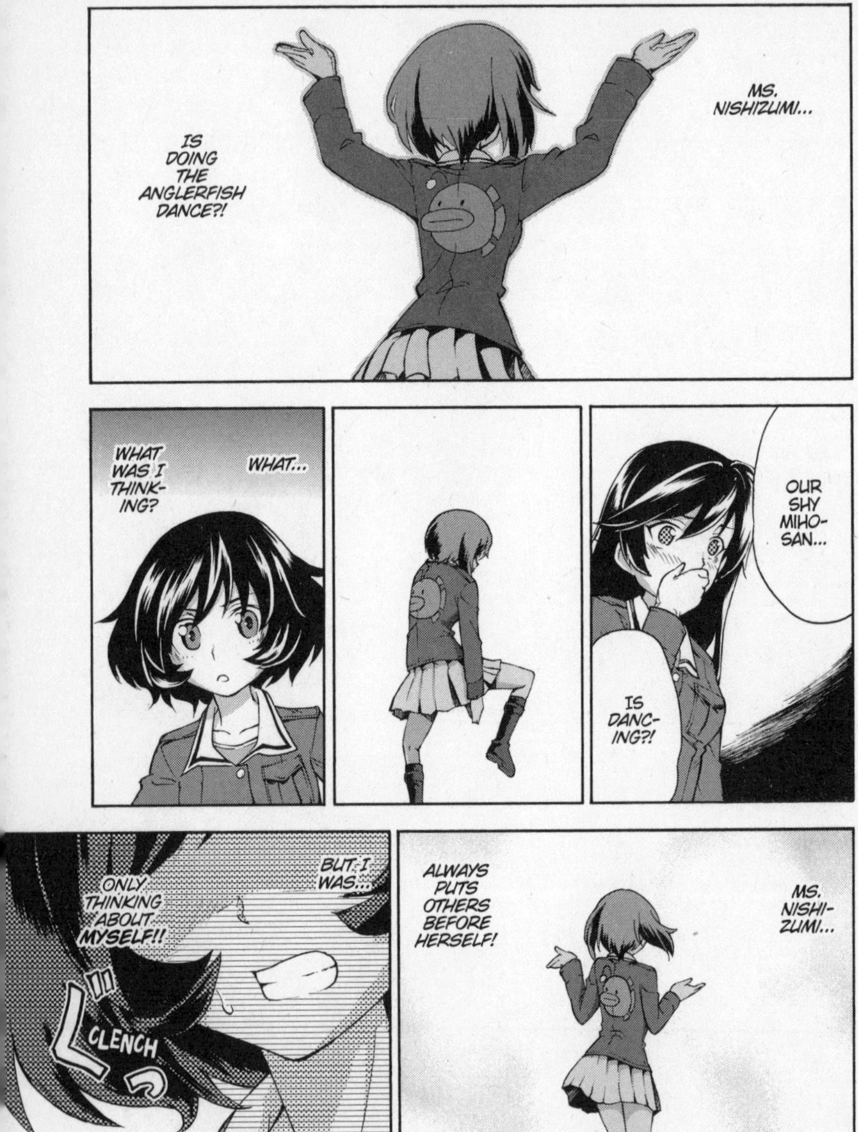
MS. NISHIZUMI...
IS DOING THE ANGLERFISH DANCE?!
OUR SHY MIHO-SAN...
IS DANCING?!
WHAT...
WHAT WAS I THINKING?
MS. NISHIZUMI...
ALWAYS PUTS OTHERS BEFORE HERSELF!
BUT I WAS...
ONLY THINKING ABOUT MYSELF!!
CLENCH

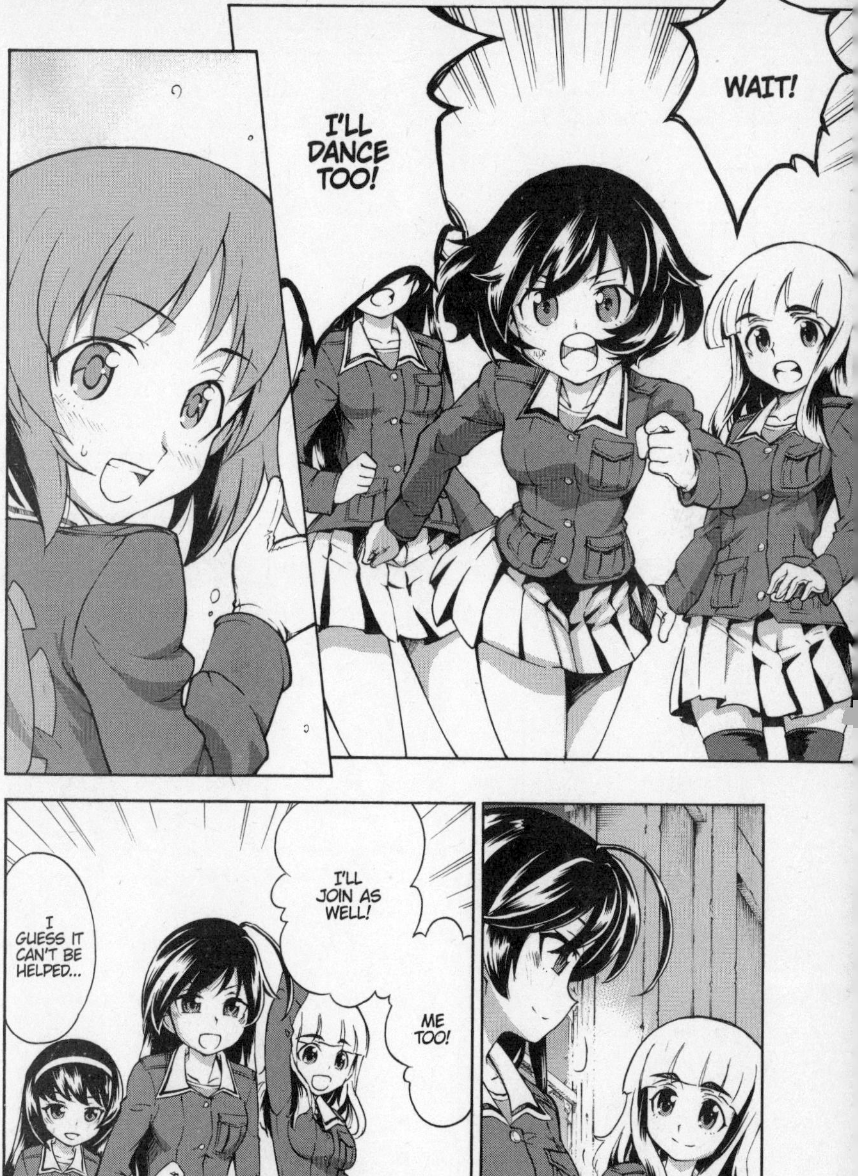
WAIT!
I'LL DANCE TOO!
I'LL JOIN AS WELL!
ME TOO!
I GUESS IT CAN'T BE HELPED...

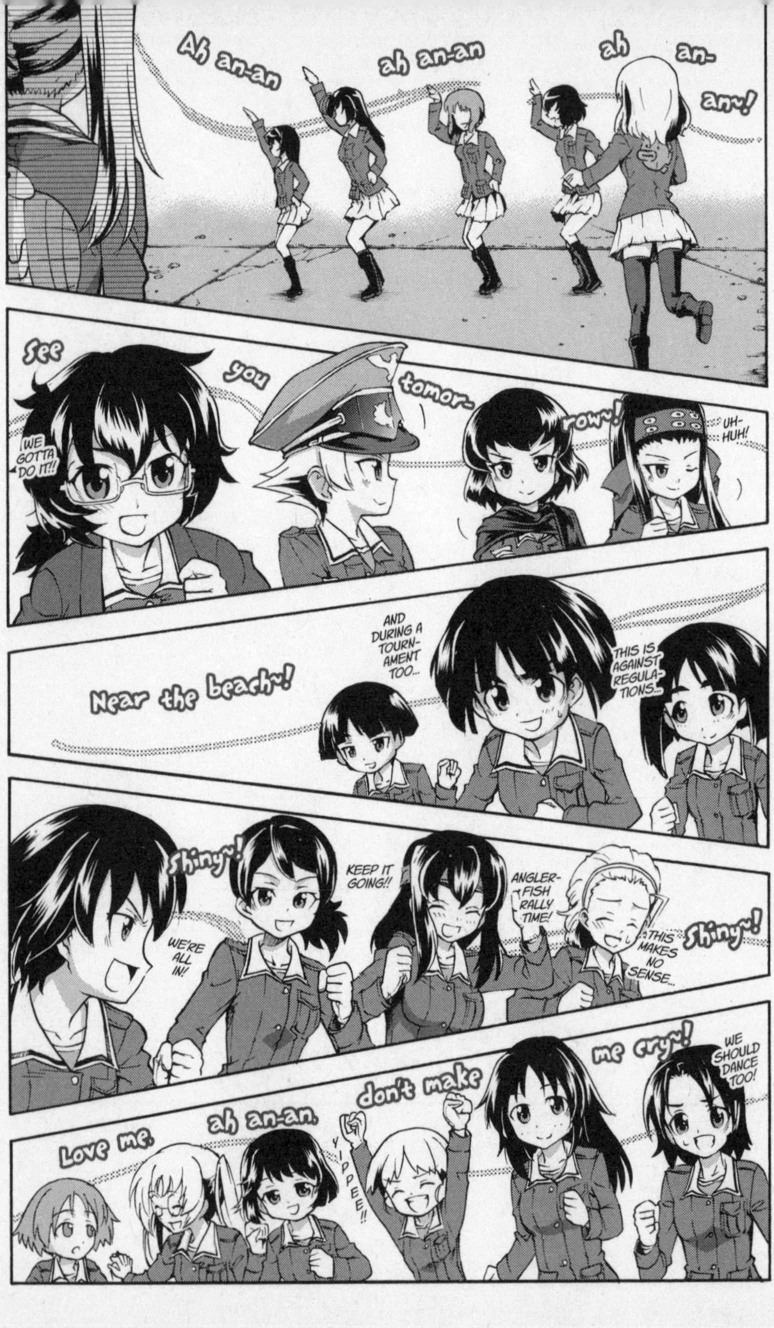
Ah an-an
ah an-an
ah an-
an~!
See you tomor- row~!
UH-HUH!
WE GOTTA DO IT!!
THIS IS AGAINST REGULATIONS...
AND DURING A TOURNAMENT TOO...
Near the beach~!
Shiny~!
THIS MAKES NO SENSE...
ANGLER-FISH RALLY TIME!
KEEP IT GOING!!
Shiny~!
WE'RE ALL IN!
WE SHOULD DANCE TOO!
Love me, ah an-an, don't make me cry~!
YIPPEE!!

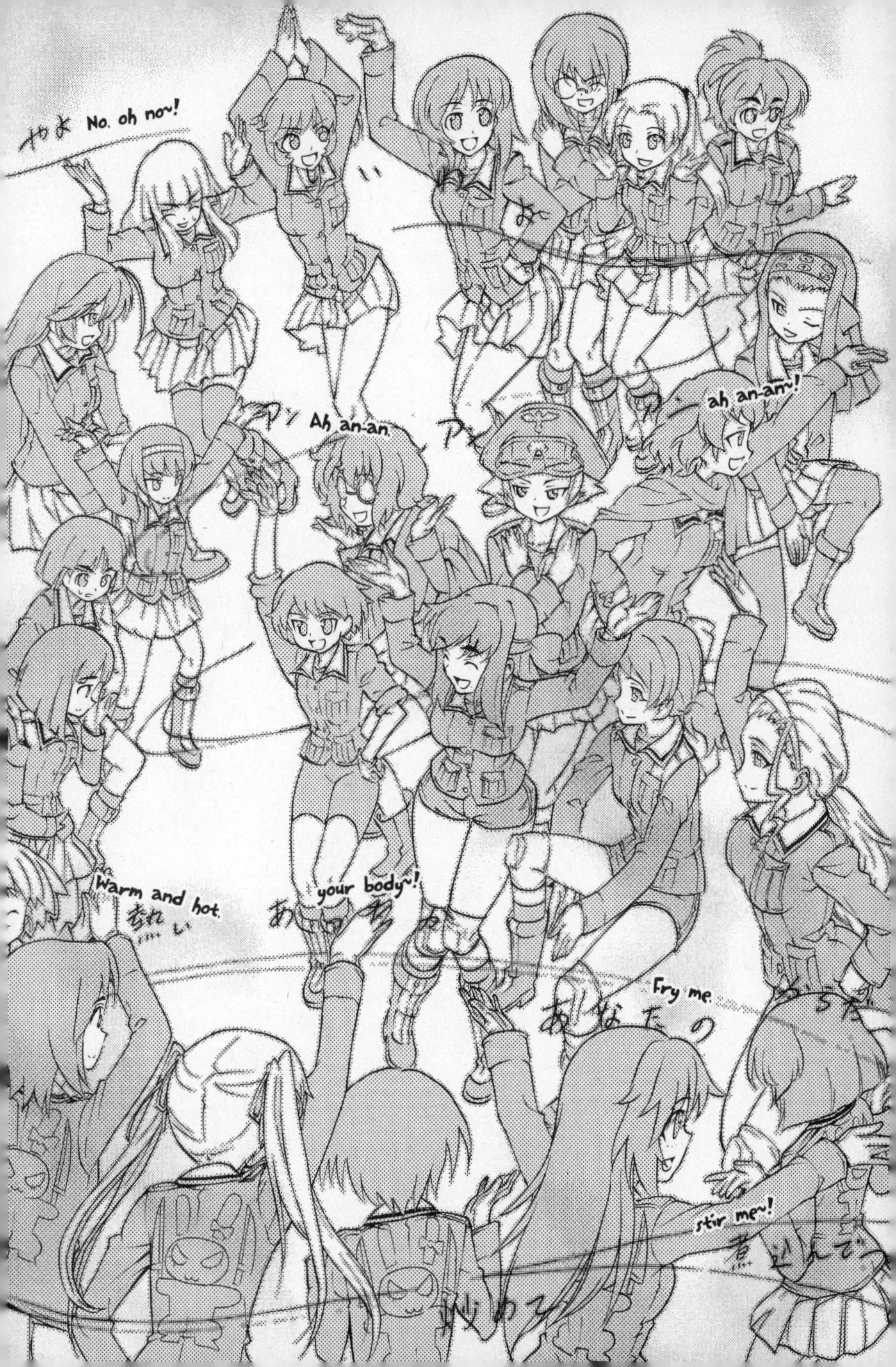

No, oh no~!
ah an-an~!
Ah an-an.
Warm and hot,
your body~!
Fry me,
stir me~!

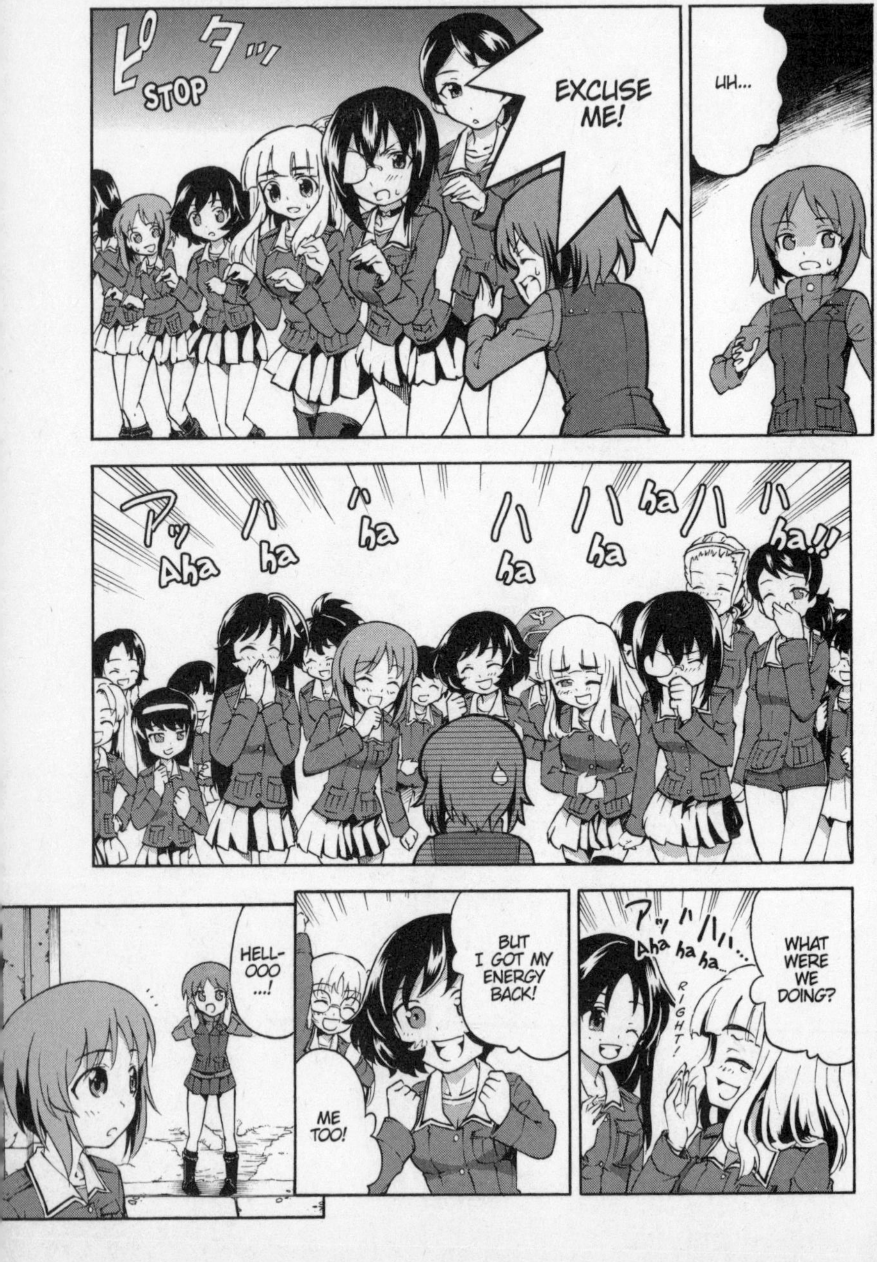
UH...
EXCUSE ME!
ピタッ
STOP
アッハハハハハハ
Aha ha ha ha ha ha ha!!
WHAT WERE WE DOING?
アッハハハ…
Aha ha ha...
RIGHT!
BUT I GOT MY ENERGY BACK!
ME TOO!
HELL-OOO ...!

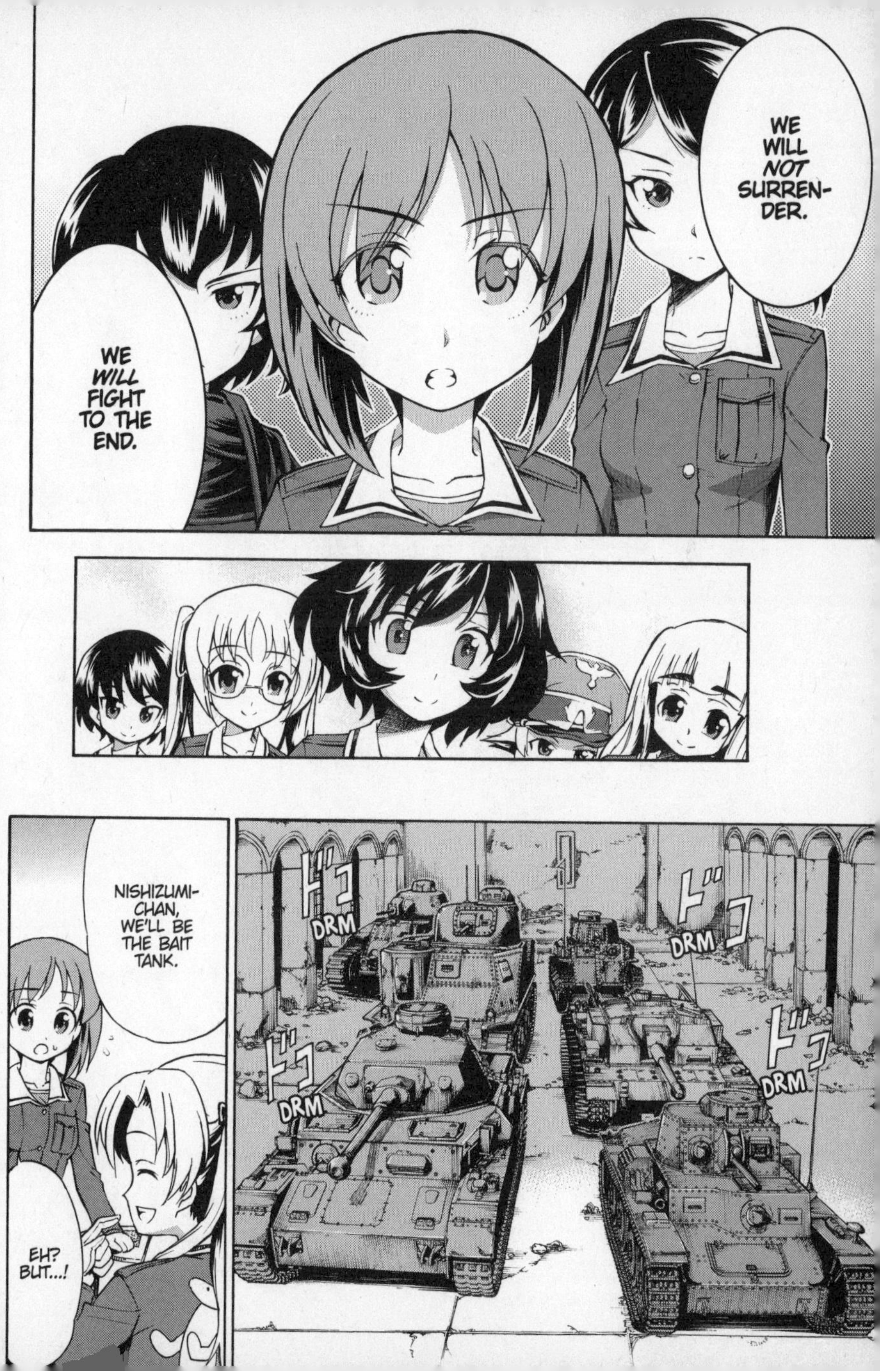
WE WILL NOT SURREN-DER.
WE WILL FIGHT TO THE END.
DRM
DRM
DRM
DRM
NISHIZUMI-CHAN, WE'LL BE THE BAIT TANK.
EH? BUT...!

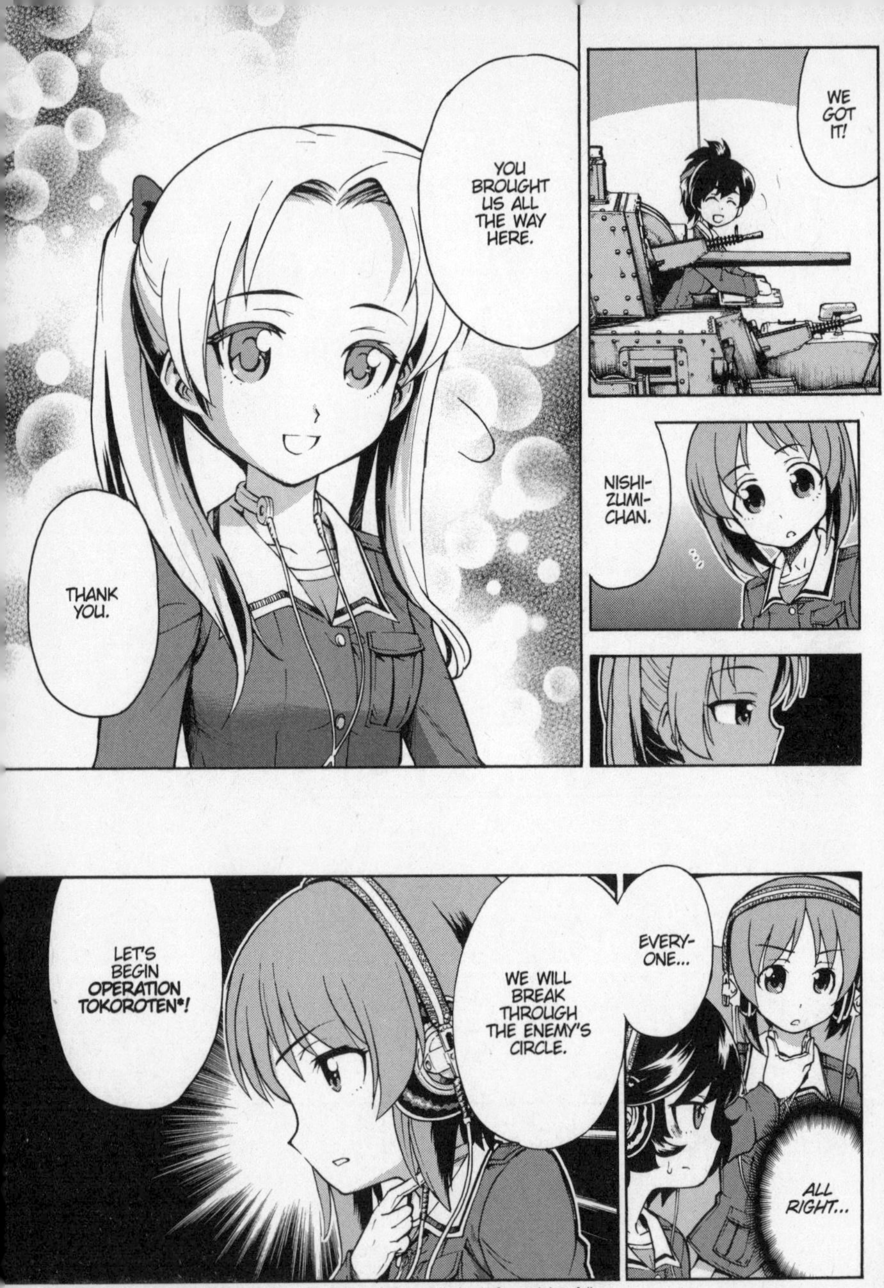
WE GOT IT!
NISHI-ZUMI-CHAN.
YOU BROUGHT US ALL THE WAY HERE.
THANK YOU.
EVERY-ONE...
WE WILL BREAK THROUGH THE ENEMY'S CIRCLE.
LET'S BEGIN OPERATION TOKOROTEN*!
ALL RIGHT...

*Tokoroten is agar jelly, often served in string form by being pushed out of a container full of holes. The tanks here will be exiting the building one at a time, like a long, slippery string of jelly.

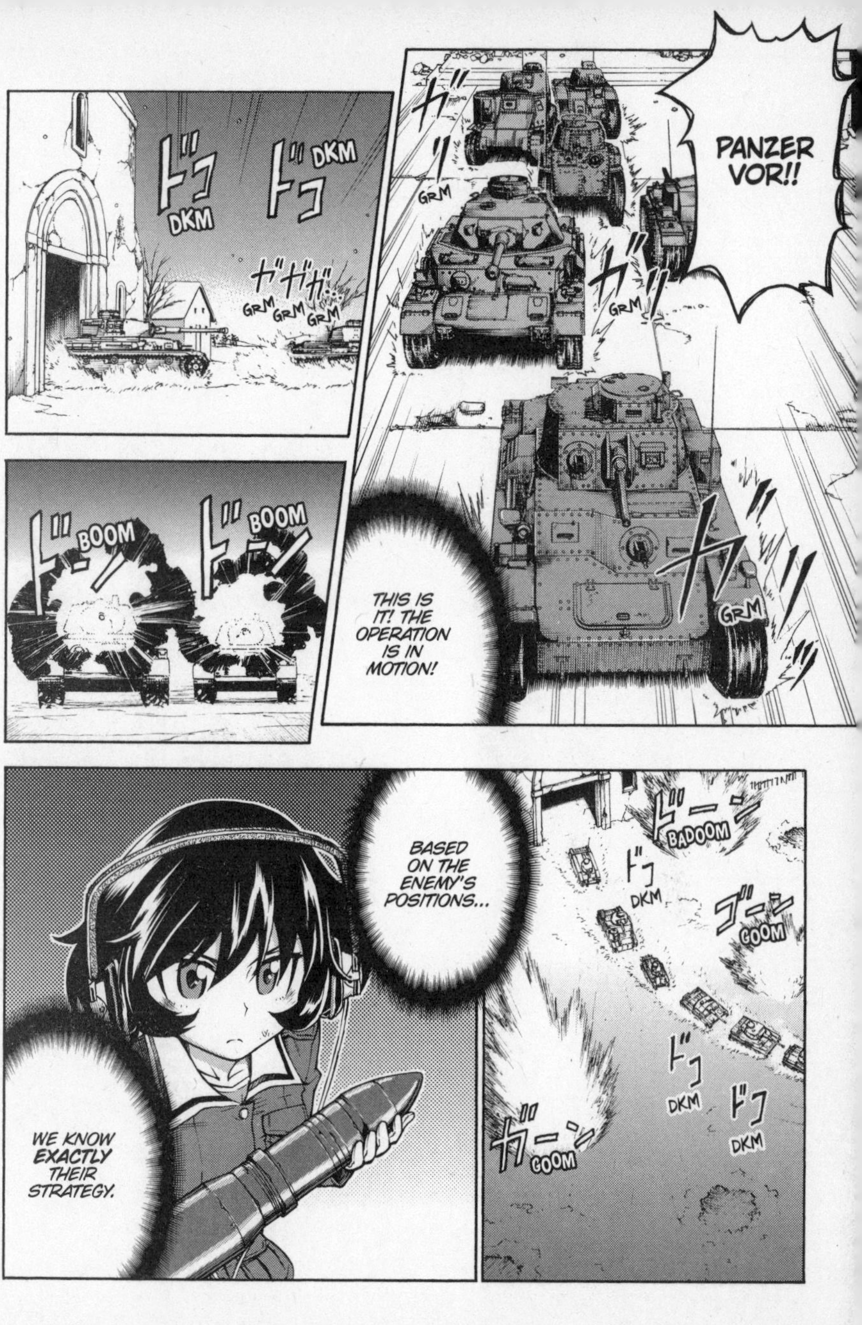
PANZER VOR!!
GRM
GRM
GRM
THIS IS IT! THE OPERATION IS IN MOTION!
DKM
DKM
GRM GRM GRM
BOOM
BOOM
BADOOM
DKM
GOOM
DKM
DKM
GOOM
BASED ON THE ENEMY'S POSITIONS...
WE KNOW EXACTLY THEIR STRATEGY.

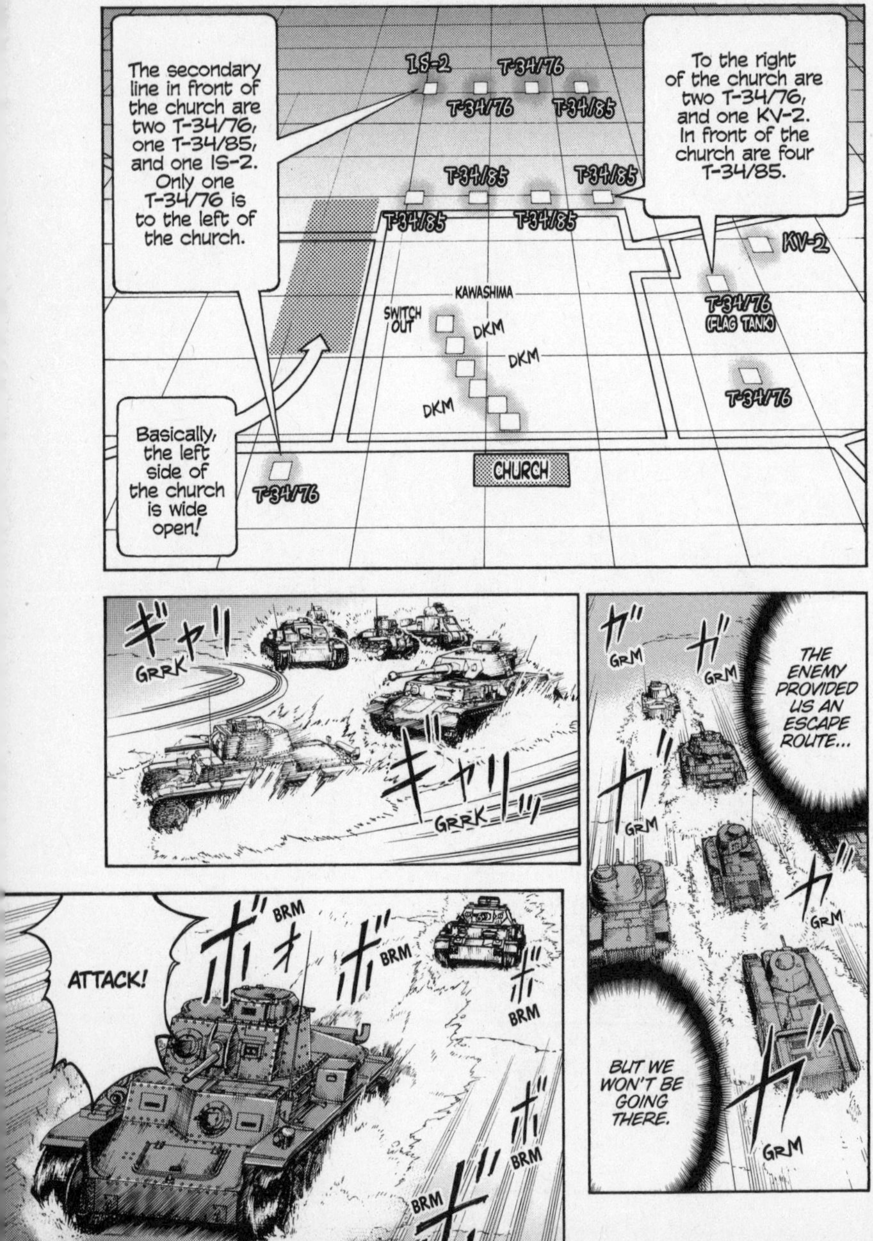

To the right of the church are two T-34/76, and one KV-2. In front of the church are four T-34/85.
IS-2
T-34/76
T-34/76
T-34/85
T-34/85
T-34/85
T-34/85
T-34/85
KV-2
T-34/76 (FLAG TANK)
T-34/76
KAWASHIMA
SWITCH OUT
DKM
DKM
DKM
CHURCH
T-34/76
The secondary line in front of the church are two T-34/76, one T-34/85, and one IS-2. Only one T-34/76 is to the left of the church.
Basically, the left side of the church is wide open!
ガ GRM
ガ GRM
THE ENEMY PROVIDED US AN ESCAPE ROUTE...
ガ GRM
ガ GRM
BUT WE WON'T BE GOING THERE.
ガ GRM
ギャリ GRRK
ギャリッ GRRK
ボオ BRM
ボ BRM
ATTACK!
ボ BRM
ボ BRM
ボ BRM

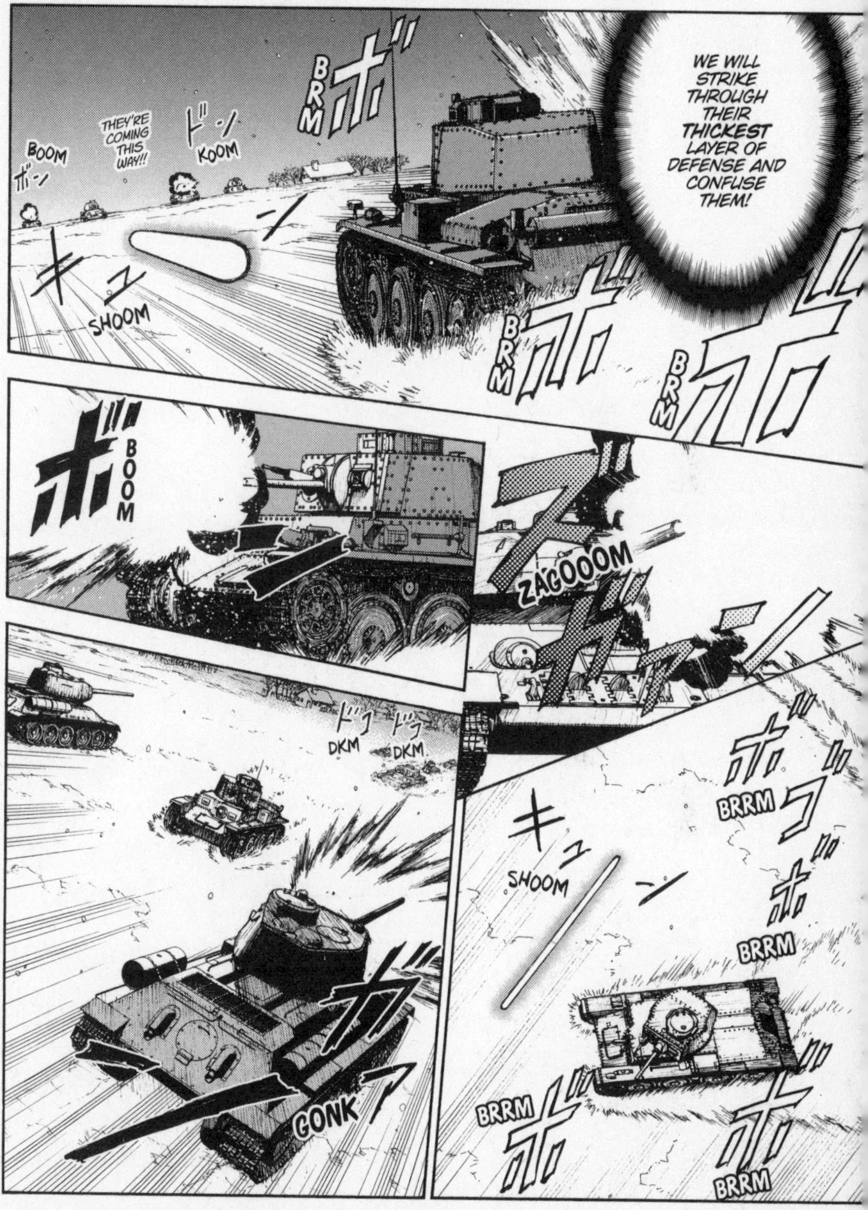
WE WILL STRIKE THROUGH THEIR THICKEST LAYER OF DEFENSE AND CONFUSE THEM!
BRM
BRM
BRM
KOOM
THEY'RE COMING THIS WAY!!
BOOM
SHOOM
ZAGOOOM
BOOM
BRRM
BRRM
SHOOM
BRRM
BRRM
DKM
DKM
GONK

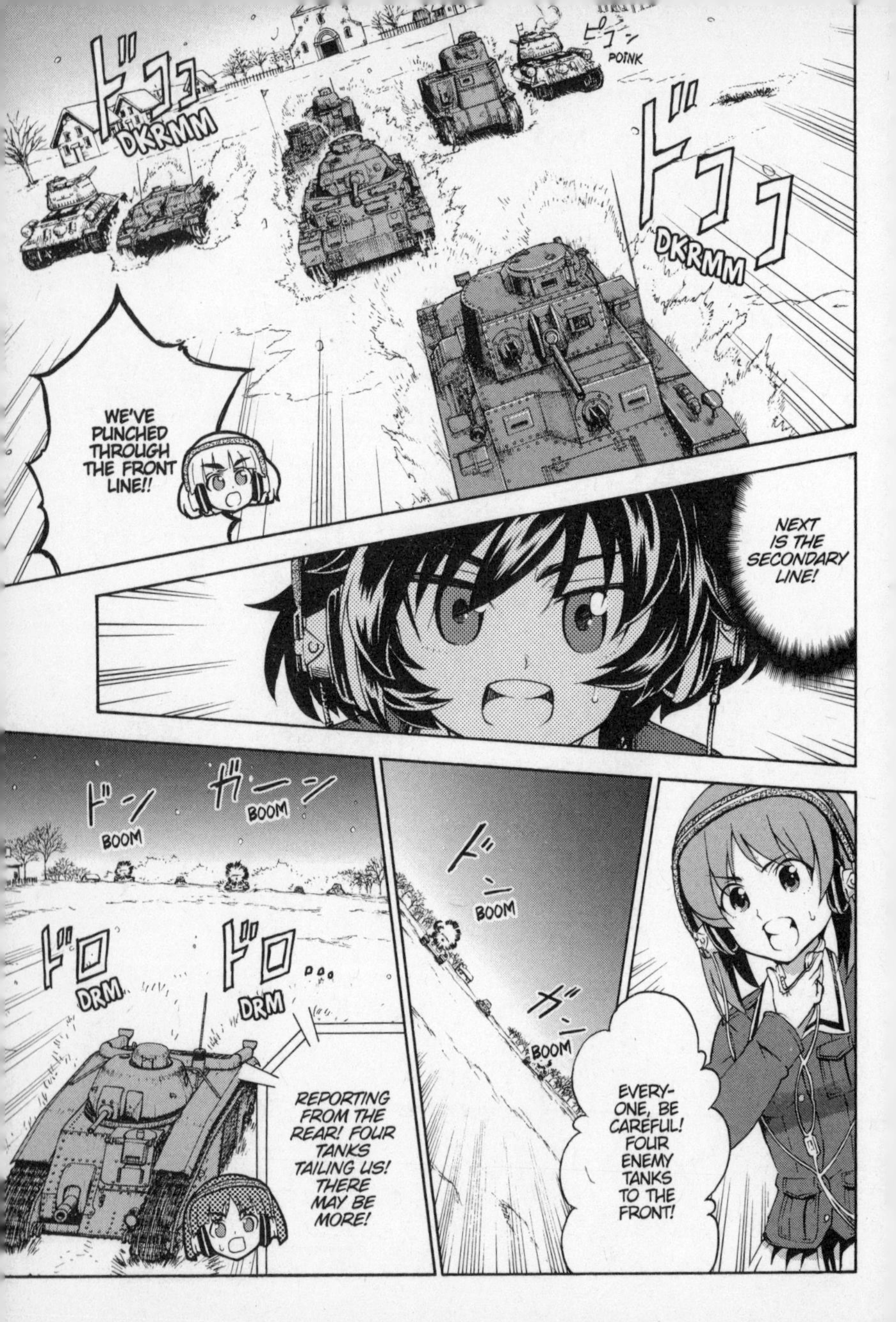
ピコン
POINK
ドゴゴ
DKRMM
ドゴゴ
DKRMM
WE'VE PUNCHED THROUGH THE FRONT LINE!!
NEXT IS THE SECONDARY LINE!
EVERY-ONE, BE CAREFUL! FOUR ENEMY TANKS TO THE FRONT!
ド
BOOM
ガ
BOOM
ガーン
BOOM
ドン
BOOM
ドロ
DRM
ドロ
DRM
REPORTING FROM THE REAR! FOUR TANKS TAILING US! THERE MAY BE MORE!

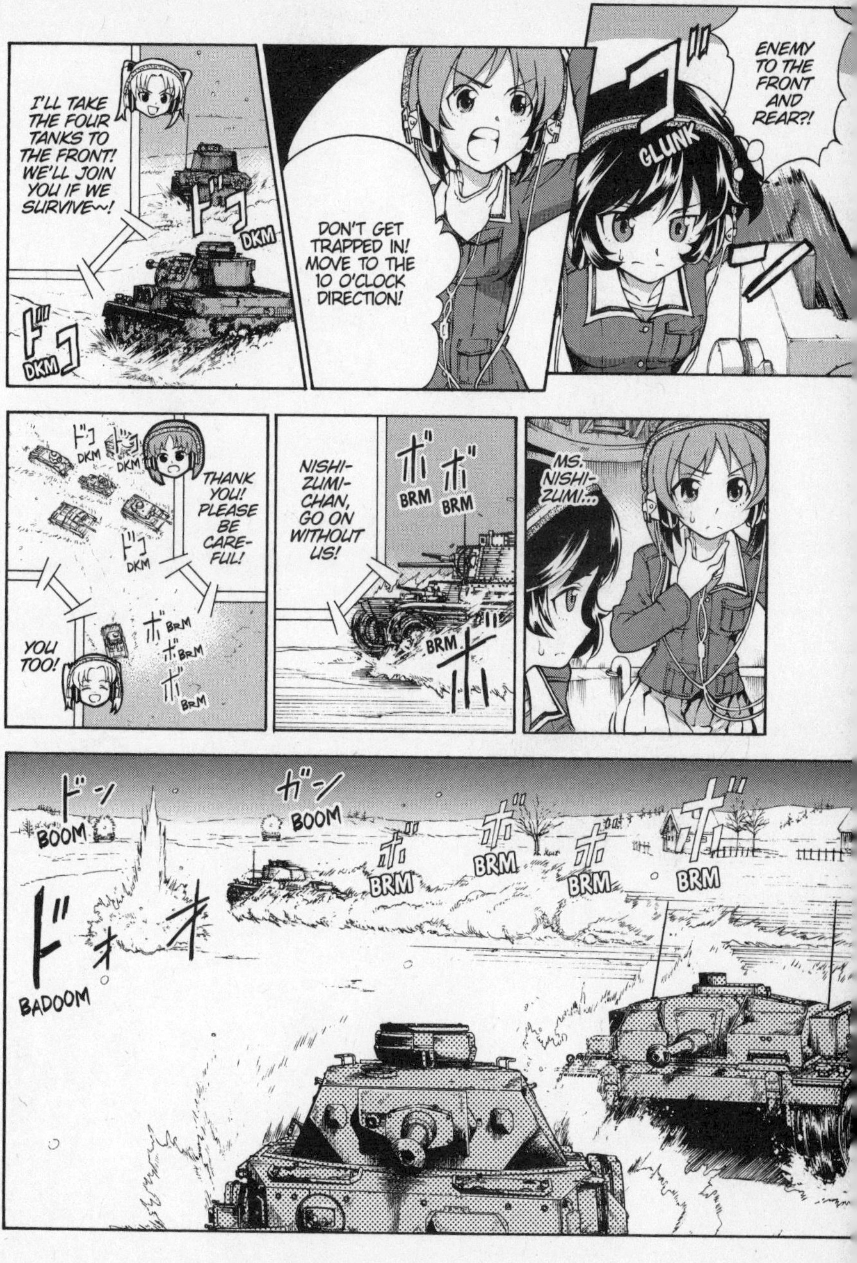

ENEMY TO THE FRONT AND REAR?!
GLUNK
DON'T GET TRAPPED IN! MOVE TO THE 10 O'CLOCK DIRECTION!
I'LL TAKE THE FOUR TANKS TO THE FRONT! WE'LL JOIN YOU IF WE SURVIVE~!
DKM
DKM
MS. NISHIZUMI...
NISHIZUMI-CHAN, GO ON WITHOUT US!
BRM
BRM
BRM
DKM
DKM
THANK YOU! PLEASE BE CAREFUL!
DKM
YOU TOO!
BRM
BRM
BRM
BOOM
BOOM
BRM
BRM
BRM
BRM
BADOOM

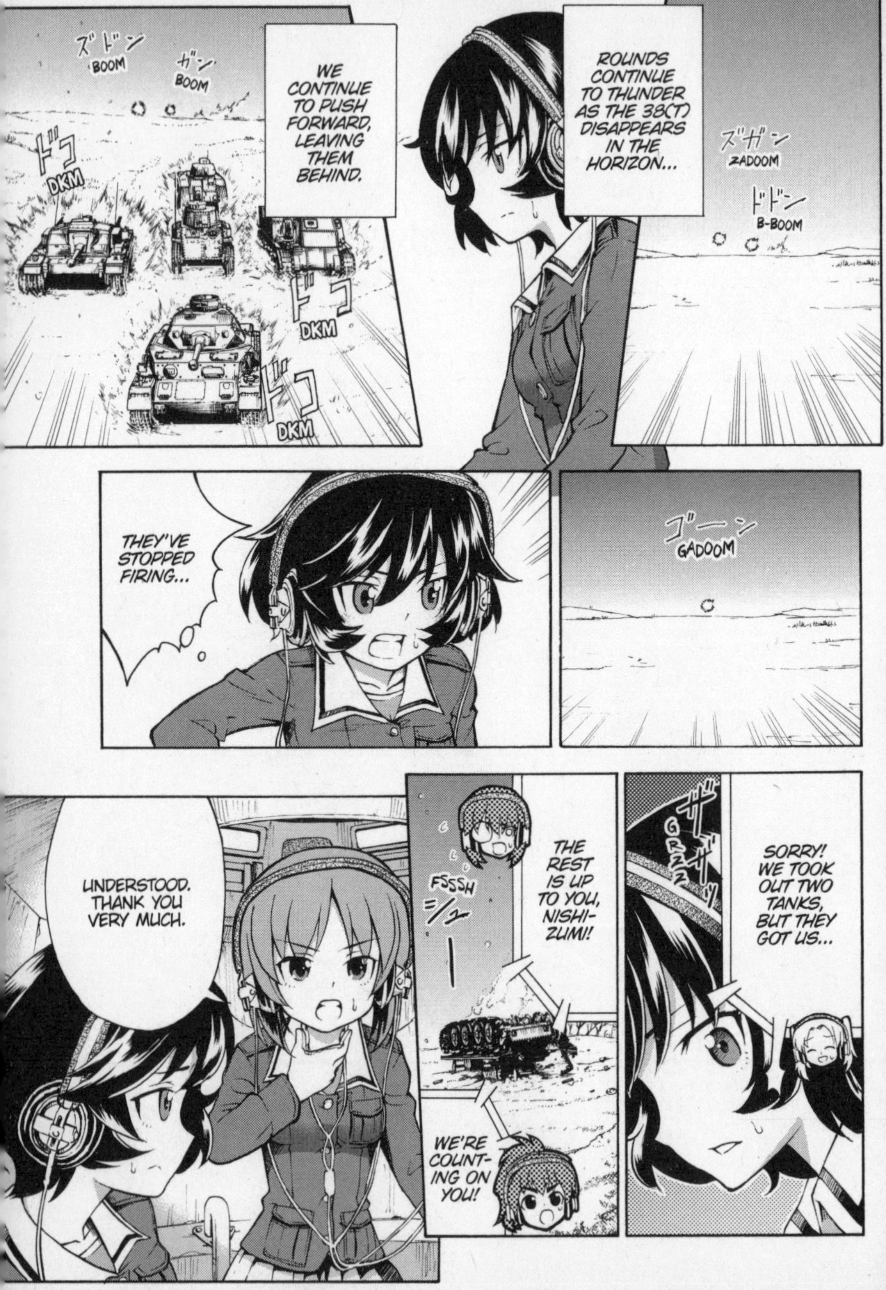
ROUNDS CONTINUE TO THUNDER AS THE 38(T) DISAPPEARS IN THE HORIZON...
ズガン
ZADOOM
ドドン
B-BOOM
WE CONTINUE TO PUSH FORWARD, LEAVING THEM BEHIND.
ガン
BOOM
ズドン
BOOM
ドコ
DKM
ドコ
DKM
ドコ
DKM
ゴーン
GADOOM
THEY'VE STOPPED FIRING...
SORRY! WE TOOK OUT TWO TANKS, BUT THEY GOT US...
ザザッ
GRZZ
THE REST IS UP TO YOU, NISHI-ZUMI!
シュー
FSSSH
WE'RE COUNTING ON YOU!
UNDERSTOOD. THANK YOU VERY MUCH.

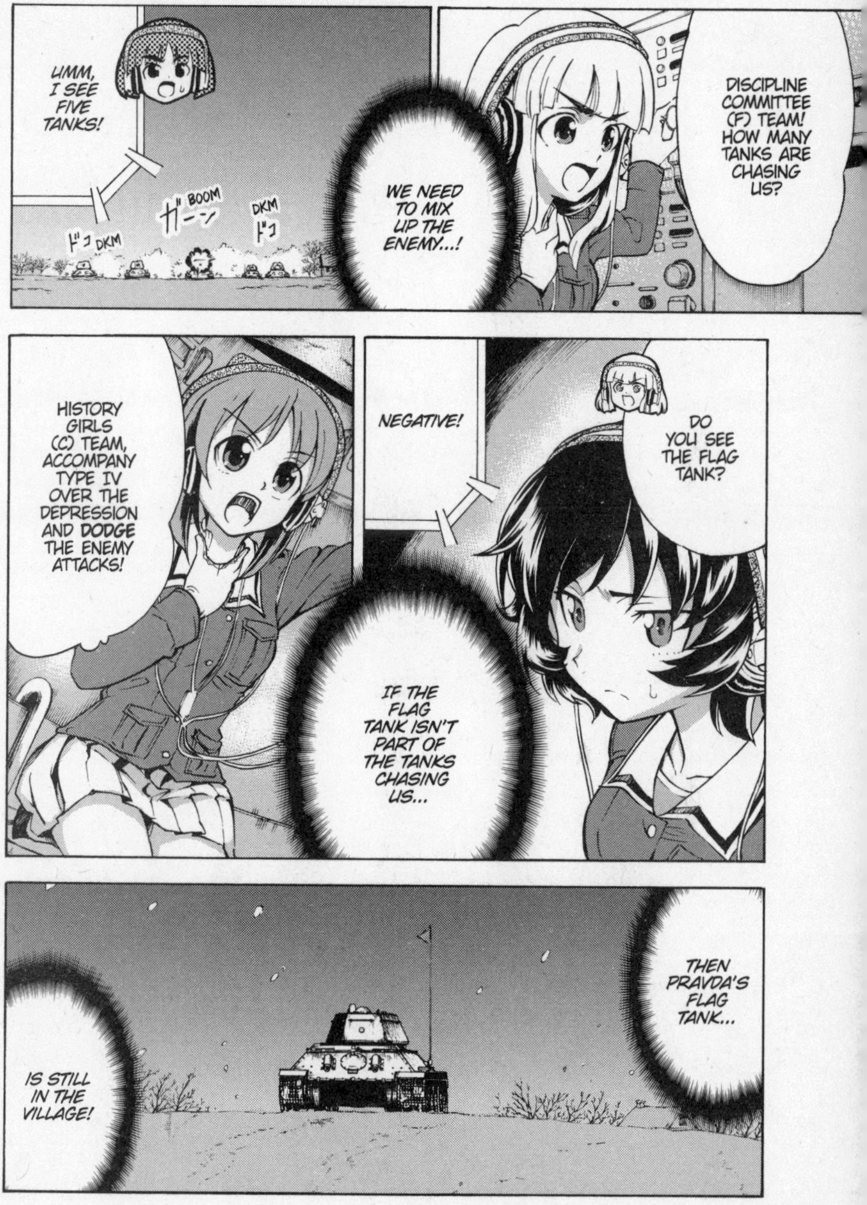
DISCIPLINE COMMITTEE (F) TEAM! HOW MANY TANKS ARE CHASING US?
UMM, I SEE FIVE TANKS!
ガーン BOOM
ドコ DKM
ドコ DKM
WE NEED TO MIX UP THE ENEMY...!
DO YOU SEE THE FLAG TANK?
NEGATIVE!
IF THE FLAG TANK ISN'T PART OF THE TANKS CHASING US...
HISTORY GIRLS (C) TEAM, ACCOMPANY TYPE IV OVER THE DEPRESSION AND DODGE THE ENEMY ATTACKS!
THEN PRAVDA'S FLAG TANK...
IS STILL IN THE VILLAGE!

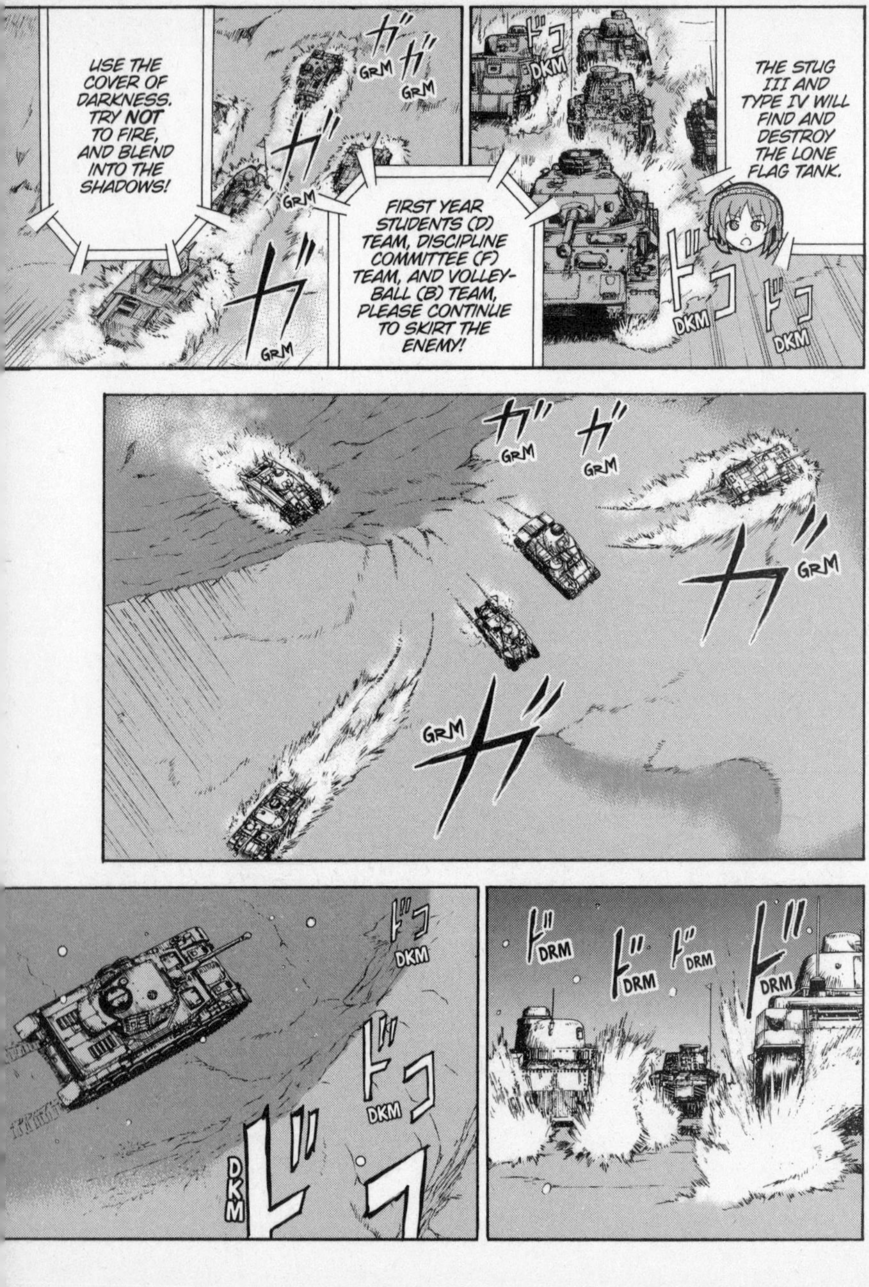
THE STUG III AND TYPE IV WILL FIND AND DESTROY THE LONE FLAG TANK.
DKM
DKM
DKM
DKM
FIRST YEAR STUDENTS (D) TEAM, DISCIPLINE COMMITTEE (F) TEAM, AND VOLLEY-BALL (B) TEAM, PLEASE CONTINUE TO SKIRT THE ENEMY!
GRM
GRM
USE THE COVER OF DARKNESS. TRY NOT TO FIRE, AND BLEND INTO THE SHADOWS!
GRM
GRM
GRM
GRM
GRM
GRM
DRM
DRM
DRM
DRM
DKM
DKM
DKM

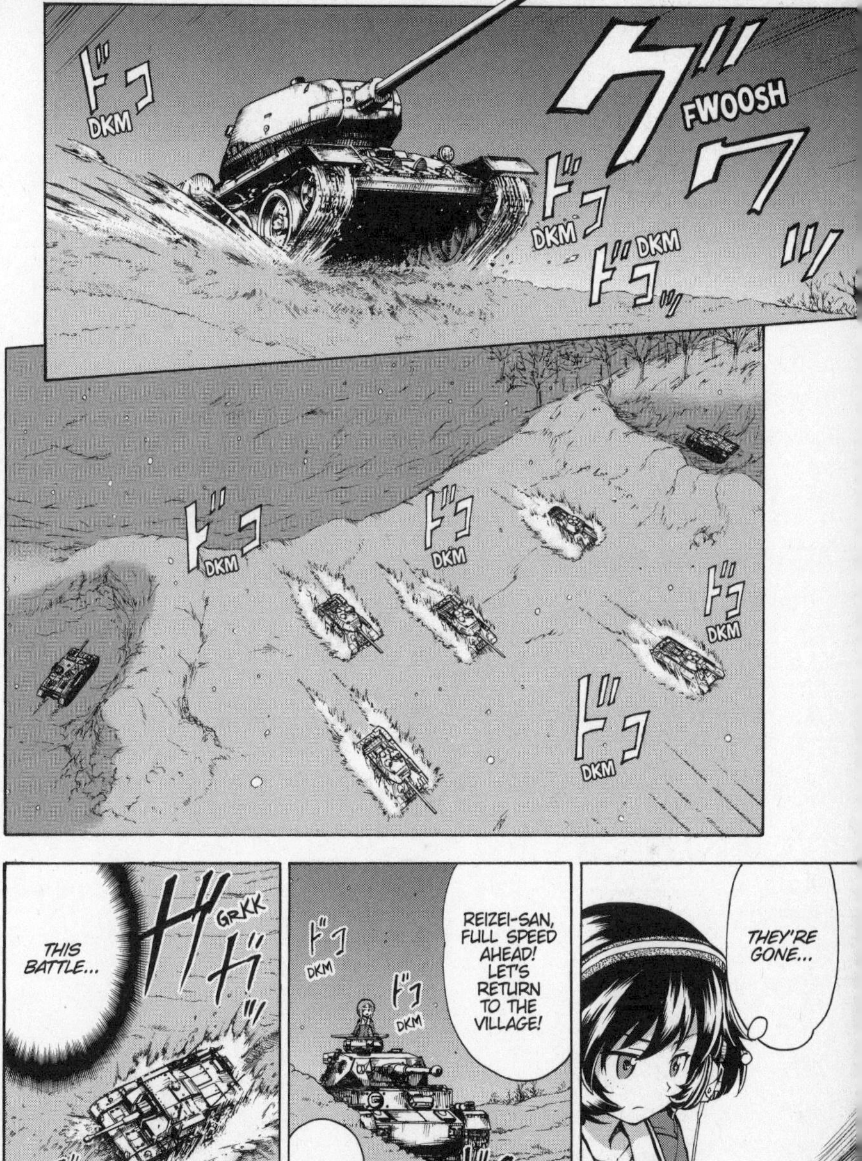
DKM
FWOOSH
DKM
DKM
DKM
DKM
DKM
DKM
THEY'RE GONE...
REIZEI-SAN, FULL SPEED AHEAD! LET'S RETURN TO THE VILLAGE!
DKM
DKM
ROGER.
DKM
THIS BATTLE...
GRKK
ZRRRMMM

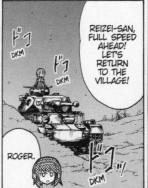

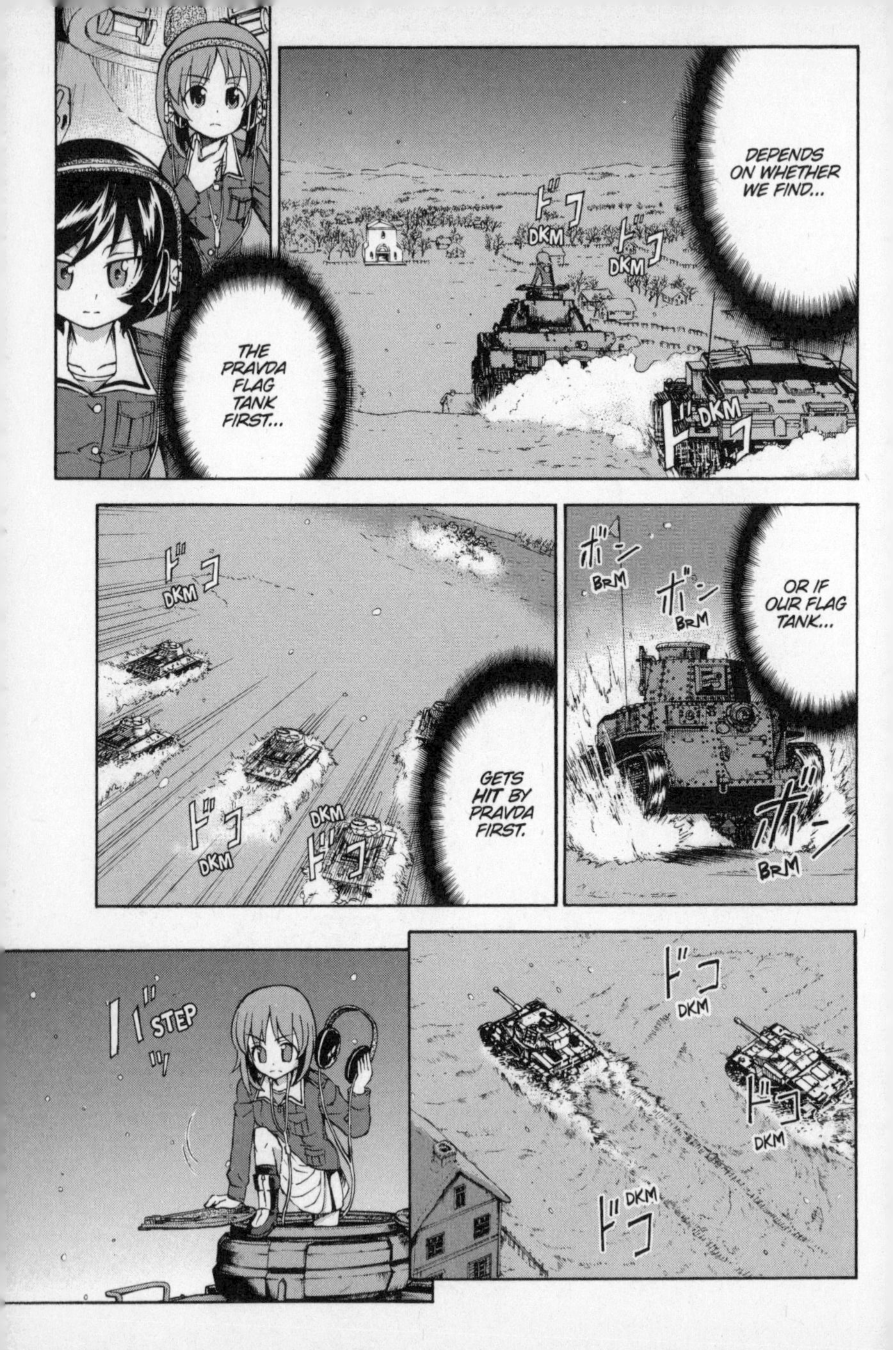
DEPENDS ON WHETHER WE FIND...
ドコ DKM
ドコ DKM
ドコ DKM
THE PRAVDA FLAG TANK FIRST...
OR IF OUR FLAG TANK...
ボン BRM
ボン BRM
ボー BRM
ドコ DKM
GETS HIT BY PRAVDA FIRST.
ドコ DKM
ドコ DKM
ドコ DKM
ドコ DKM
ドコ DKM
STEP

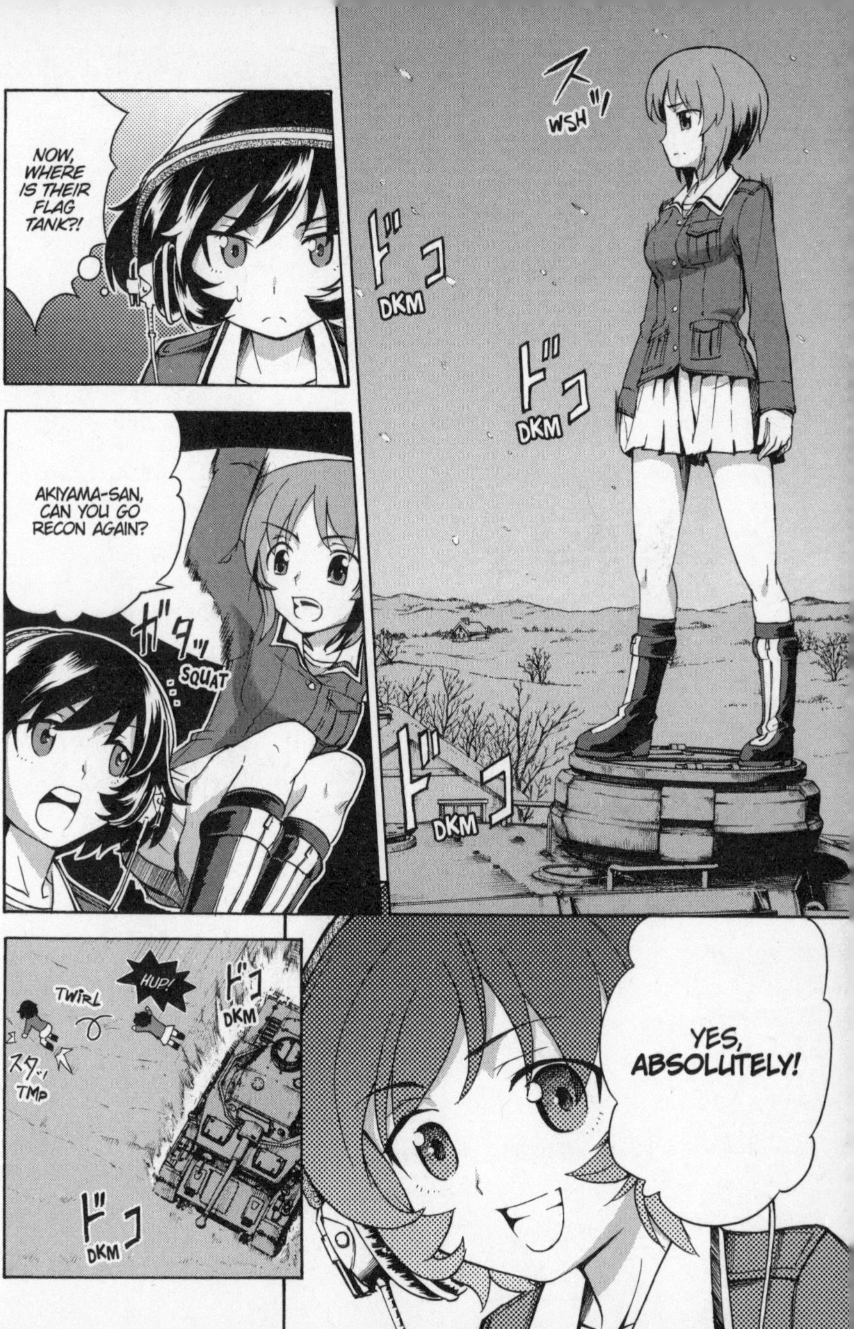

スッ
WSH
ドコ
DKM
ドコ
DKM
ドコ
DKM
NOW, WHERE IS THEIR FLAG TANK?!
AKIYAMA-SAN, CAN YOU GO RECON AGAIN?
ガタッ
SQUAT
YES, ABSOLUTELY!
HUP!
ドコ
DKM
TWIRL
スタッ
TMP
ドコ
DKM

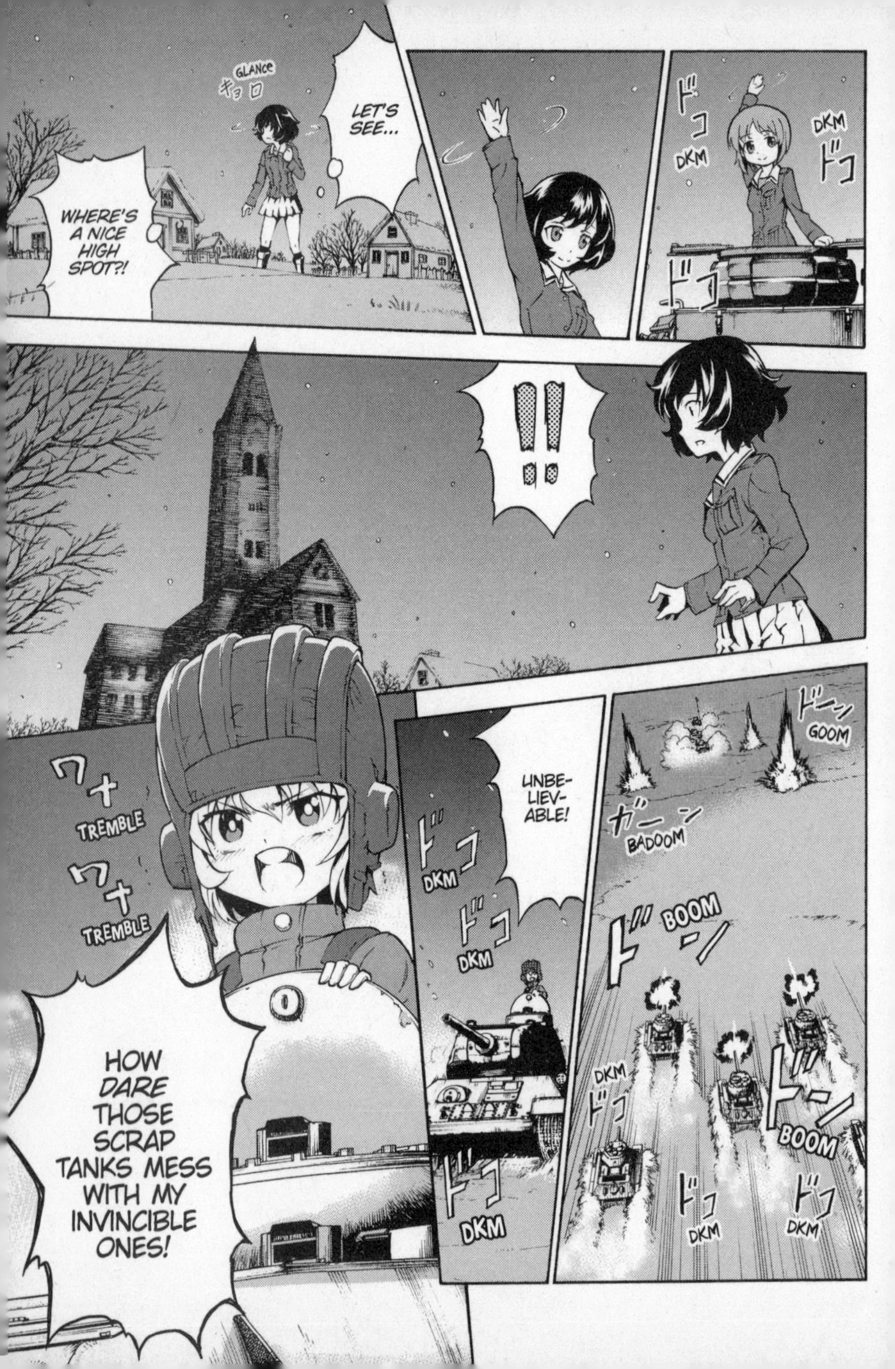
ドコ
DKM
ドコ
DKM
ドコ
GLANCE
キョロ
LET'S SEE...
WHERE'S A NICE HIGH SPOT?!
!!
ドーン
GOOM
ガーン
BADOOM
ドーン
BOOM
ドーン
BOOM
DKM
ドコ
ドコ
DKM
ドコ
DKM
UNBE-LIEV-ABLE!
ドコ
DKM
ドコ
DKM
ドコ
DKM
ワナ
TREMBLE
ワナ
TREMBLE
HOW DARE THOSE SCRAP TANKS MESS WITH MY INVINCIBLE ONES!

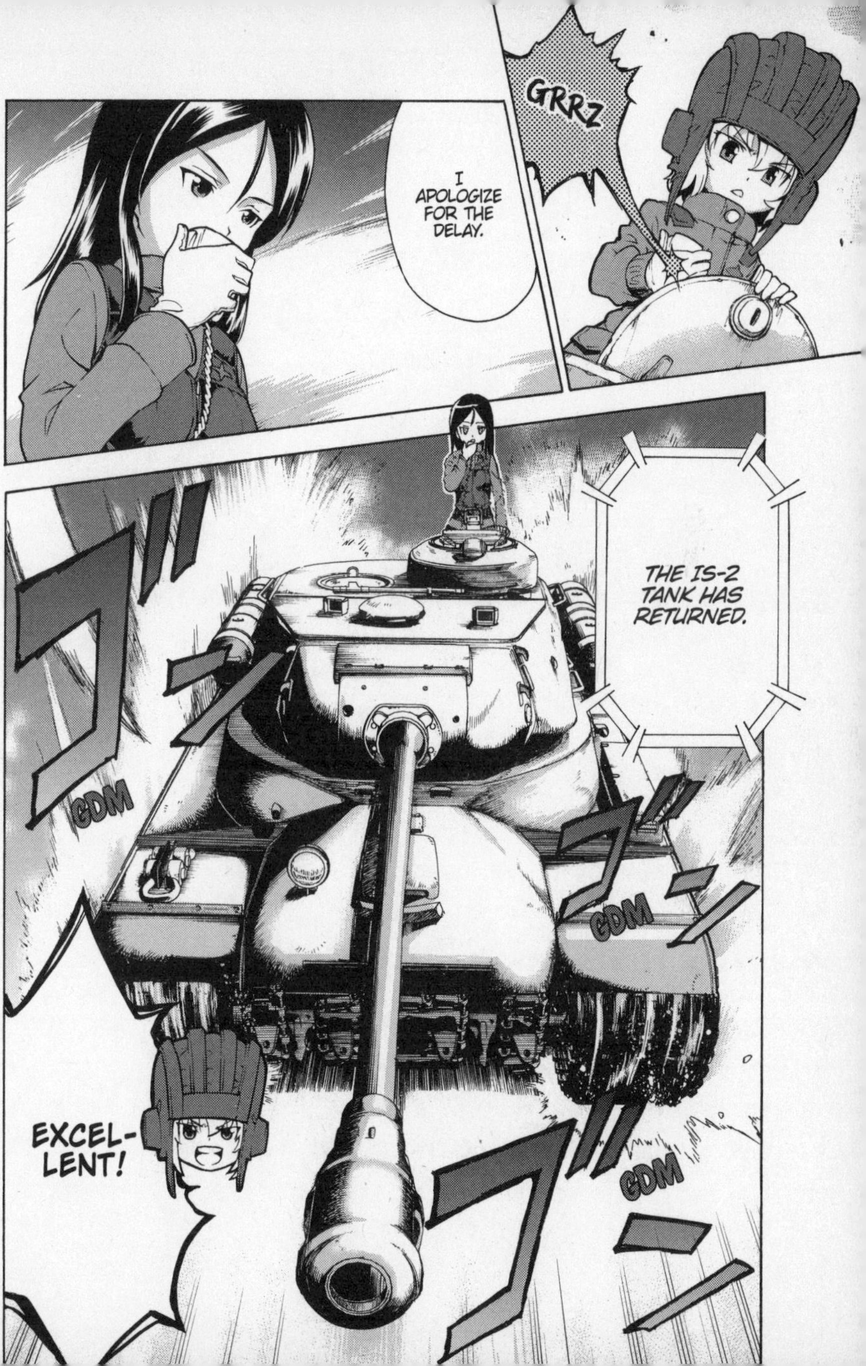
GRRZ
I APOLOGIZE FOR THE DELAY.
THE IS-2 TANK HAS RETURNED.
GDM
GDM
GDM
EXCEL-LENT!

CHAPTER 14 Pravda Match! Showdown!!

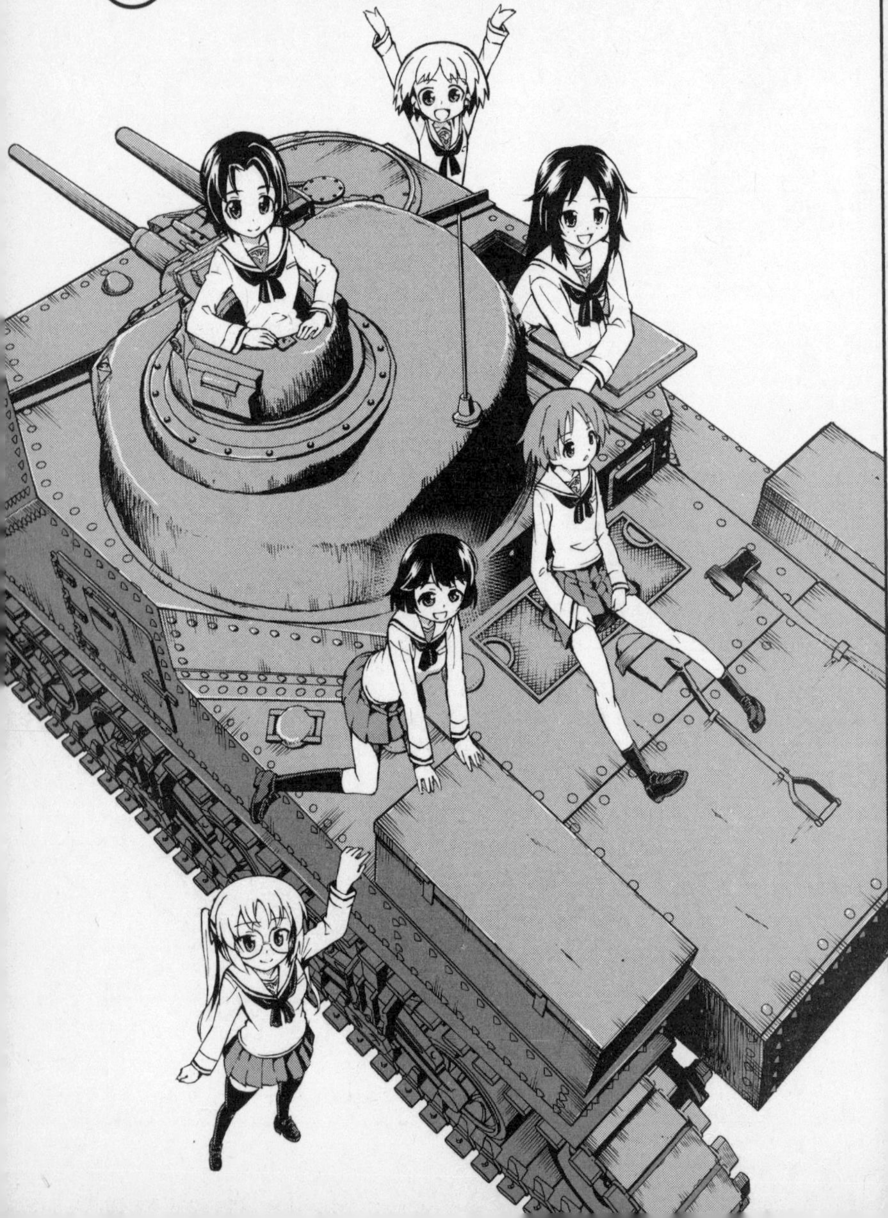

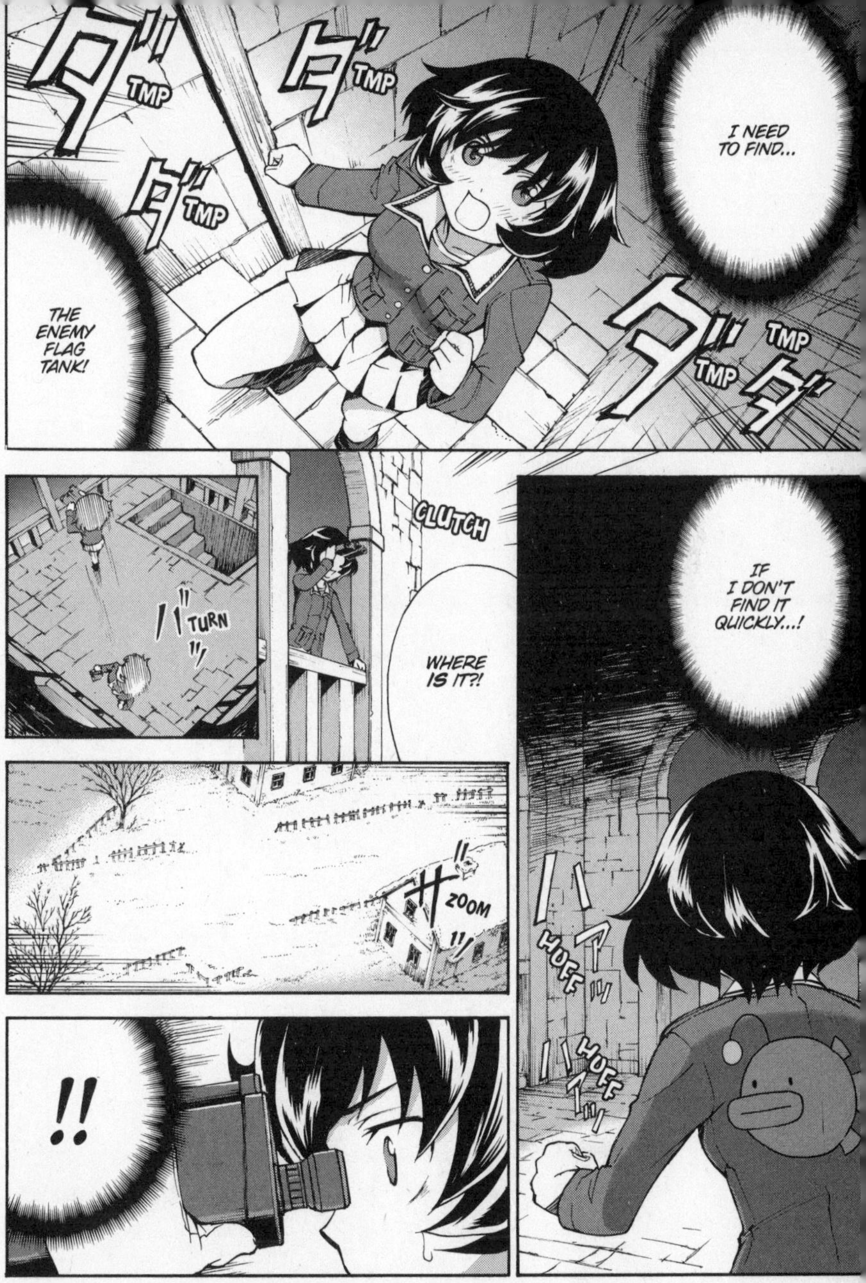
TMP
TMP
TMP
I NEED TO FIND...
TMP
TMP
THE ENEMY FLAG TANK!
IF I DON'T FIND IT QUICKLY...!
HUFF
HUFF
CLUTCH
WHERE IS IT?!
TURN
ZOOM
!!

FOUND IT!

THANK YOU, AKIYAMA-SAN!

!!

ドコ DKM

ドコ DKM

ド コ DKM

ド コ DKM

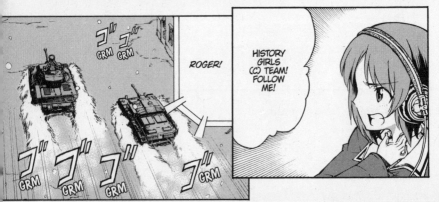

ゴ ゴ CRM CRM

ゴ ゴ ゴ ゴ CRM CRM CRM CRM

ROGER!

HISTORY GIRLS (C) TEAM! FOLLOW ME!

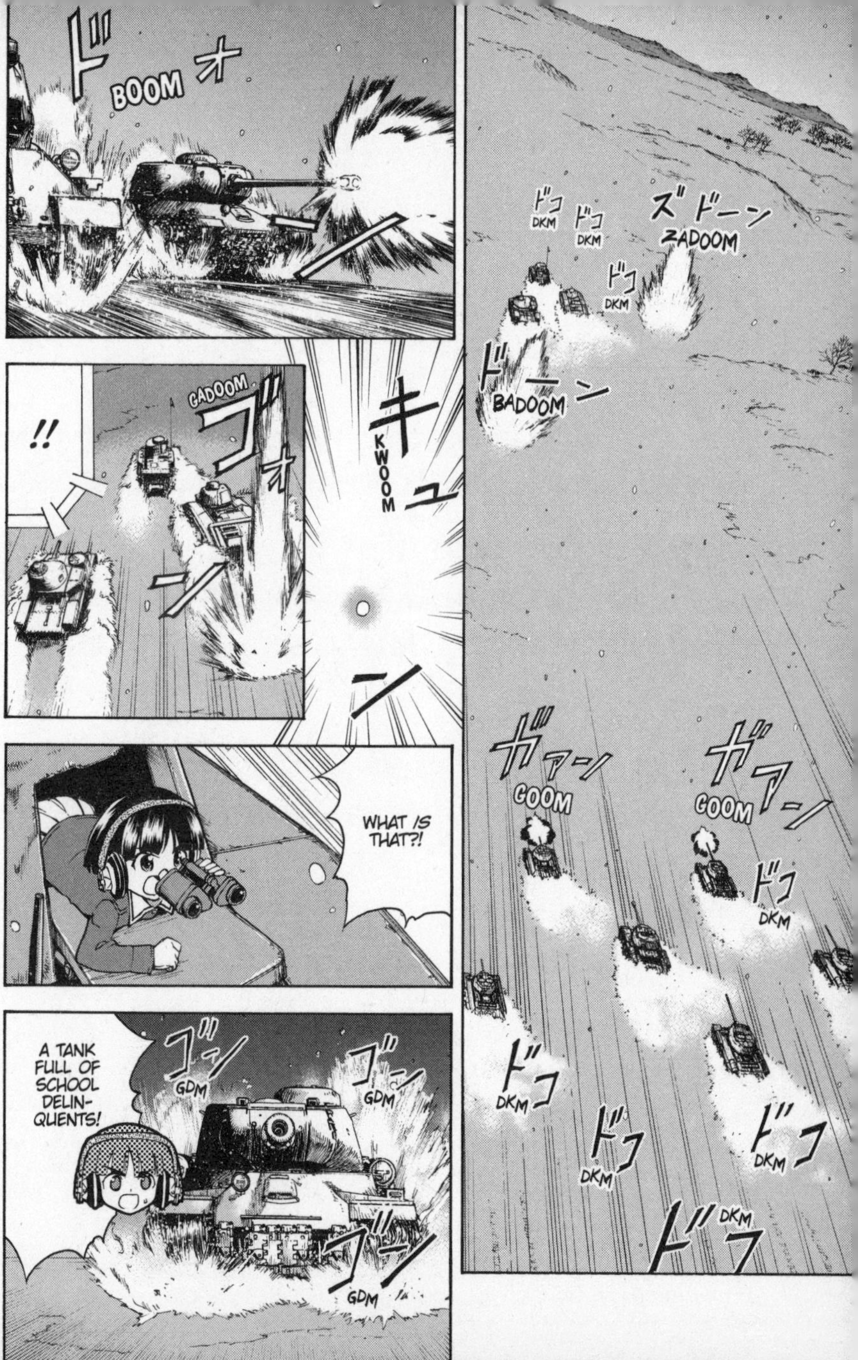
ズドーン
ZADOOM
ドコ
DKM
ドコ
DKM
ドコ
DKM
ドーン
BADOOM
ガァーン
GOOM
ガァーン
GOOM
ドコ
DKM
ドコ
DKM
ドコ
DKM
ドコ
DKM
ドコ
DKM
ドオ
BOOM
キュン
KWOOM
ゴォ
GADOOM
!!
WHAT IS THAT?!
ゴン
GDM
ゴン
GDM
A TANK FULL OF SCHOOL DELIN-QUENTS!
ゴン
GDM

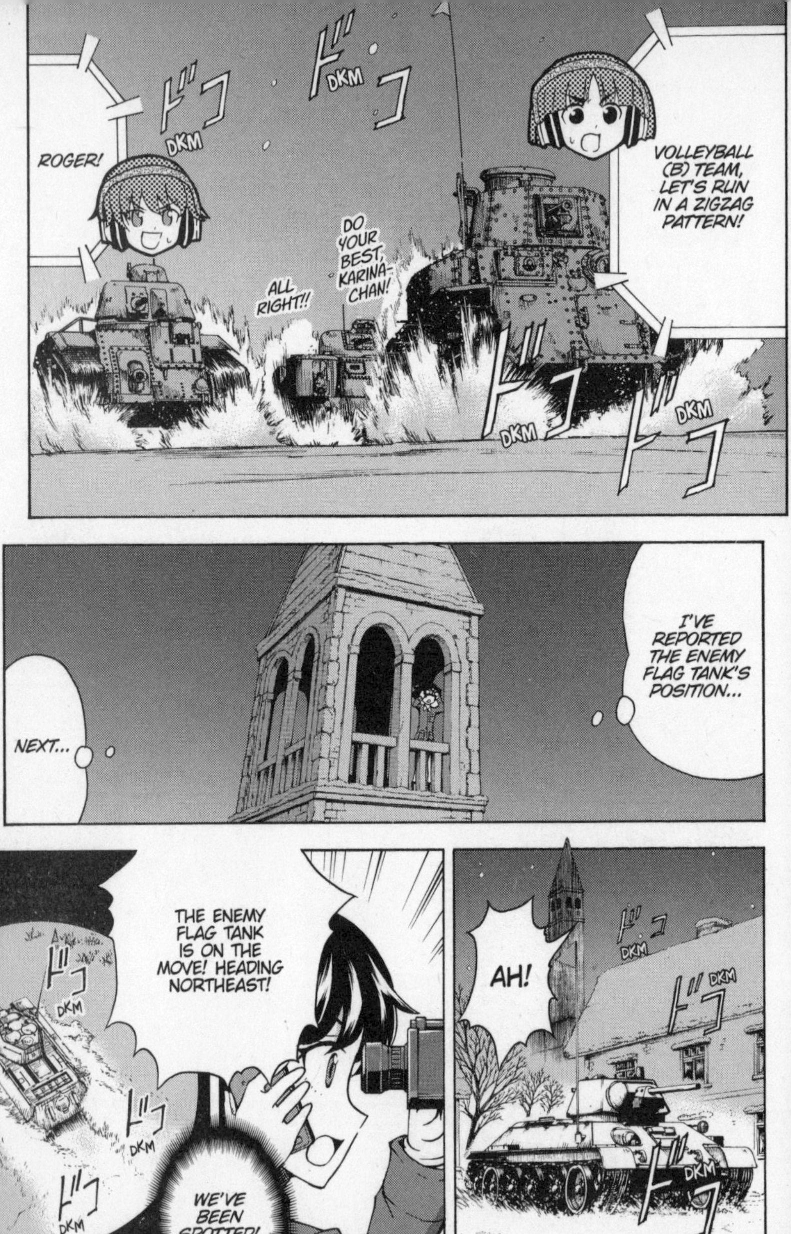
VOLLEYBALL (B) TEAM, LET'S RUN IN A ZIGZAG PATTERN!
DKM
DKM
DO YOUR BEST, KARINA-CHAN!
ALL RIGHT!!
ROGER!
DKM
DKM
I'VE REPORTED THE ENEMY FLAG TANK'S POSITION...
NEXT...
AH!
DKM
DKM
DKM
THE ENEMY FLAG TANK IS ON THE MOVE! HEADING NORTHEAST!
DKM
DKM
DKM
WE'VE BEEN SPOTTED!

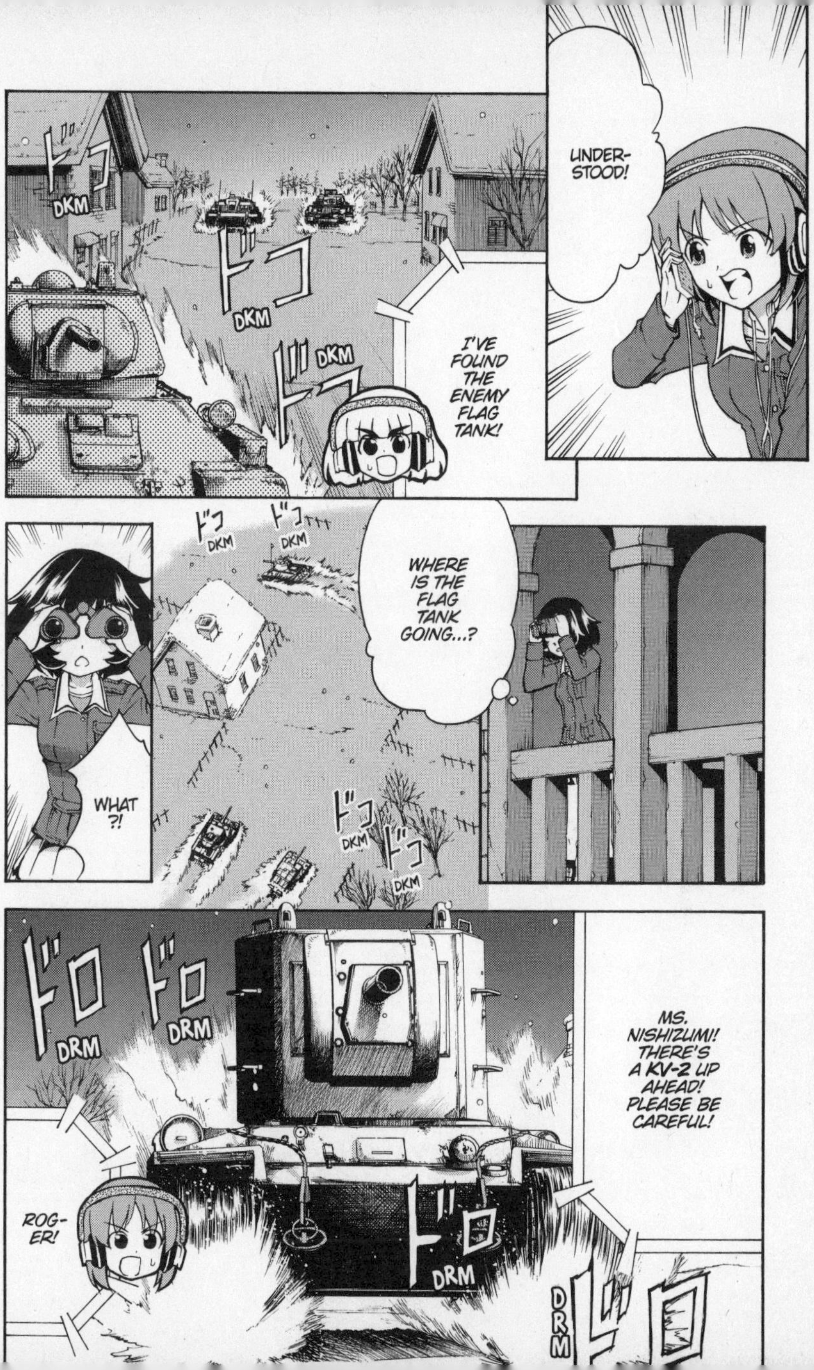
UNDER-
STOOD!
DKM
ドコ
DKM
I'VE FOUND THE ENEMY FLAG TANK!
ドコ
DKM
ドコ
DKM
WHERE IS THE FLAG TANK GOING...?
ドコ
DKM
ドコ
DKM
ドコ
DKM
ドコ
DKM
WHAT ?!
ドロ
DRM
MS. NISHIZUMI! THERE'S A KV-2 UP AHEAD! PLEASE BE CAREFUL!
ドロ
DRM
ドロ
DRM
ドロ
DRM
ROG-
ER!

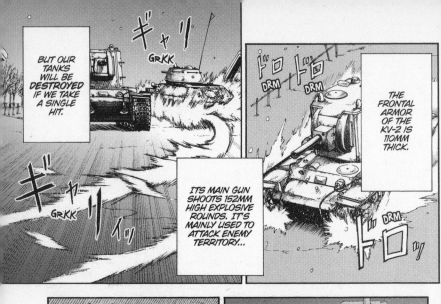

THE FRONTAL ARMOR OF THE KV-2 IS 110MM THICK.
DRM
DRM
ITS MAIN GUN SHOOTS 152MM HIGH EXPLOSIVE ROUNDS. IT'S MAINLY USED TO ATTACK ENEMY TERRITORY...
DRM
GRKK
BUT OUR TANKS WILL BE DESTROYED IF WE TAKE A SINGLE HIT.
GRKK
THERE IT IS!!
GIGAN-TIC!!
DKM
DKM
WE'LL BE OKAY!!
DKM
HOW-EVER!
GET 'EM!!
BOOM
BADOOM
MISS
ALL RIGHT!

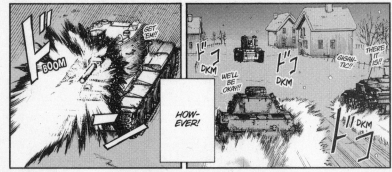

IT TAKES A LONG TIME FOR THE KV-2...

TO RELOAD ITS LARGE ROUNDS.

GRRXXXKKK

OH GOSH!!!

HURRY!!!

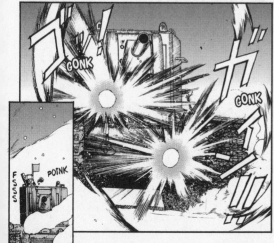

CONK

CONK

POINK

FIRE!

BOOM

BOOM

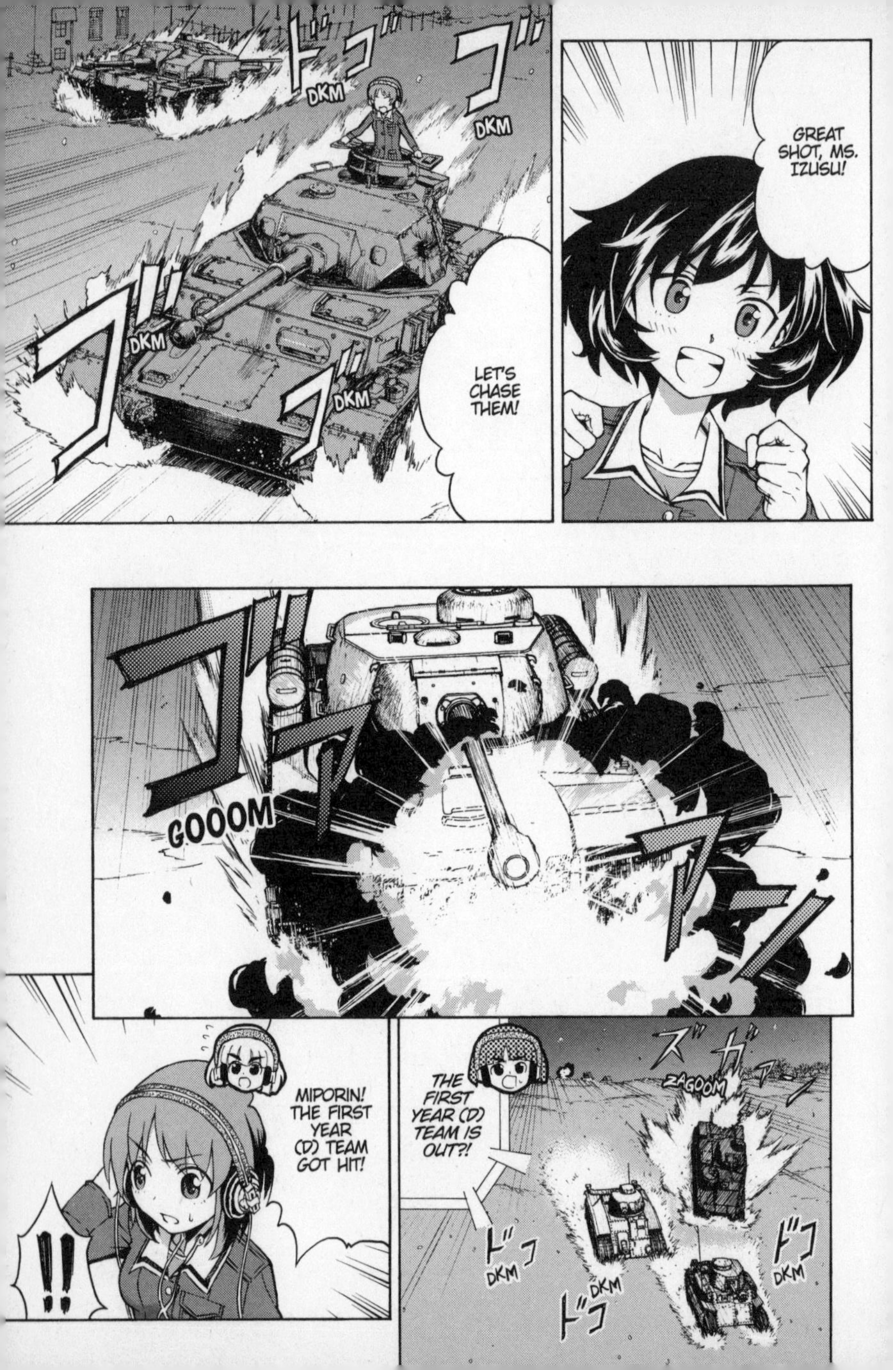
GREAT SHOT, MS. IZUSU!
DKM
DKM
LET'S CHASE THEM!
DKM
DKM
GOOOM
THE FIRST YEAR (D) TEAM IS OUT?!
ZAGOOM
DKM
DKM
DKM
MIPORIN! THE FIRST YEAR (D) TEAM GOT HIT!
!!

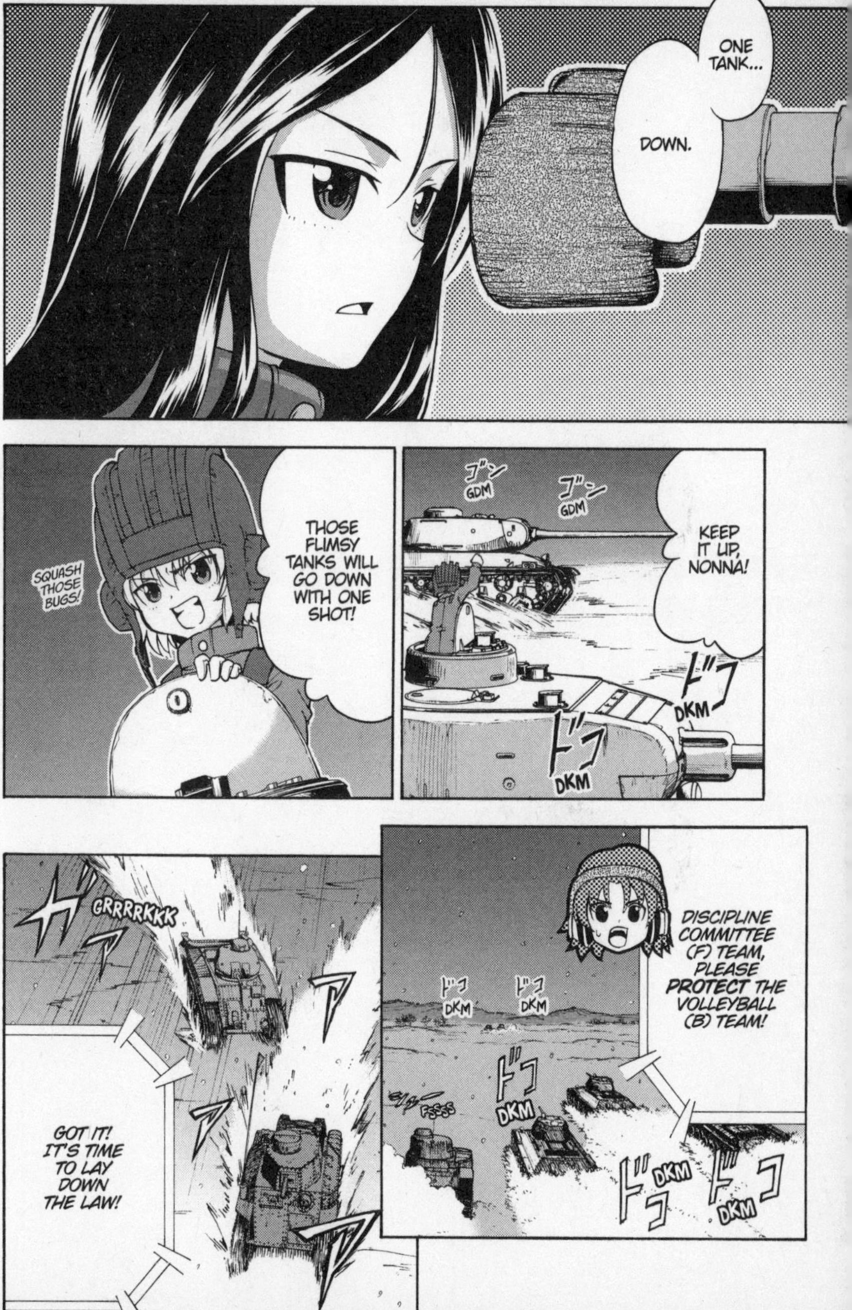
ONE TANK...
DOWN.
ゴン GDM
ゴン GDM
KEEP IT UP, NONNA!
ドコ DKM
ドコ DKM
THOSE FLIMSY TANKS WILL GO DOWN WITH ONE SHOT!
SQUASH THOSE BUGS!
DISCIPLINE COMMITTEE (F) TEAM, PLEASE PROTECT THE VOLLEYBALL (B) TEAM!
ドコ DKM
ドコ DKM
ドコ DKM
FSSS
ドコ DKM
ドコ DKM
ガァ GRRRRKKK
GOT IT! IT'S TIME TO LAY DOWN THE LAW!

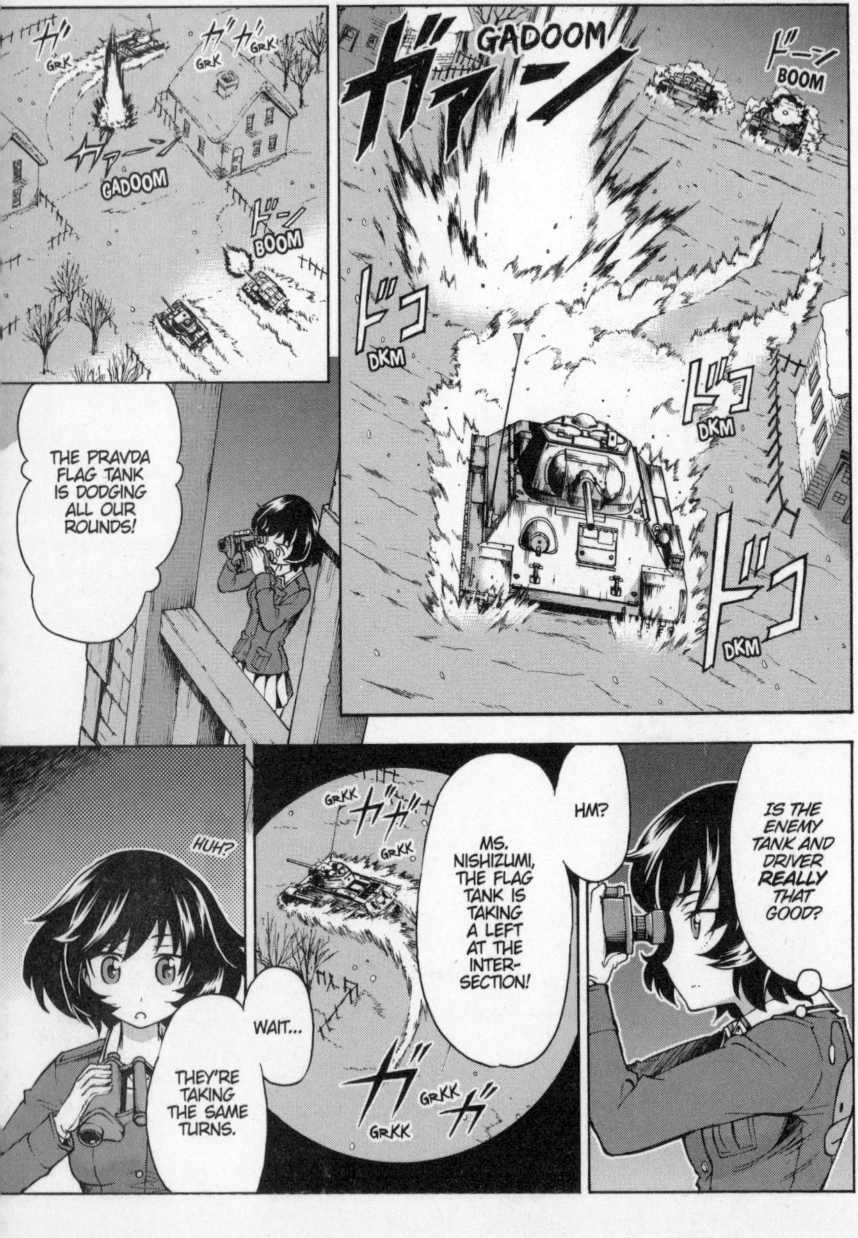
GADOOM
BOOM
DKM
DKM
DKM
GRK
GRK
GRK
GADOOM
BOOM
THE PRAVDA FLAG TANK IS DODGING ALL OUR ROUNDS!
IS THE ENEMY TANK AND DRIVER **REALLY** THAT GOOD?
HM?
MS. NISHIZUMI, THE FLAG TANK IS TAKING A LEFT AT THE INTER-SECTION!
GRKK
GRKK
GRKK
GRKK
HUH?
WAIT...
THEY'RE TAKING THE SAME TURNS.

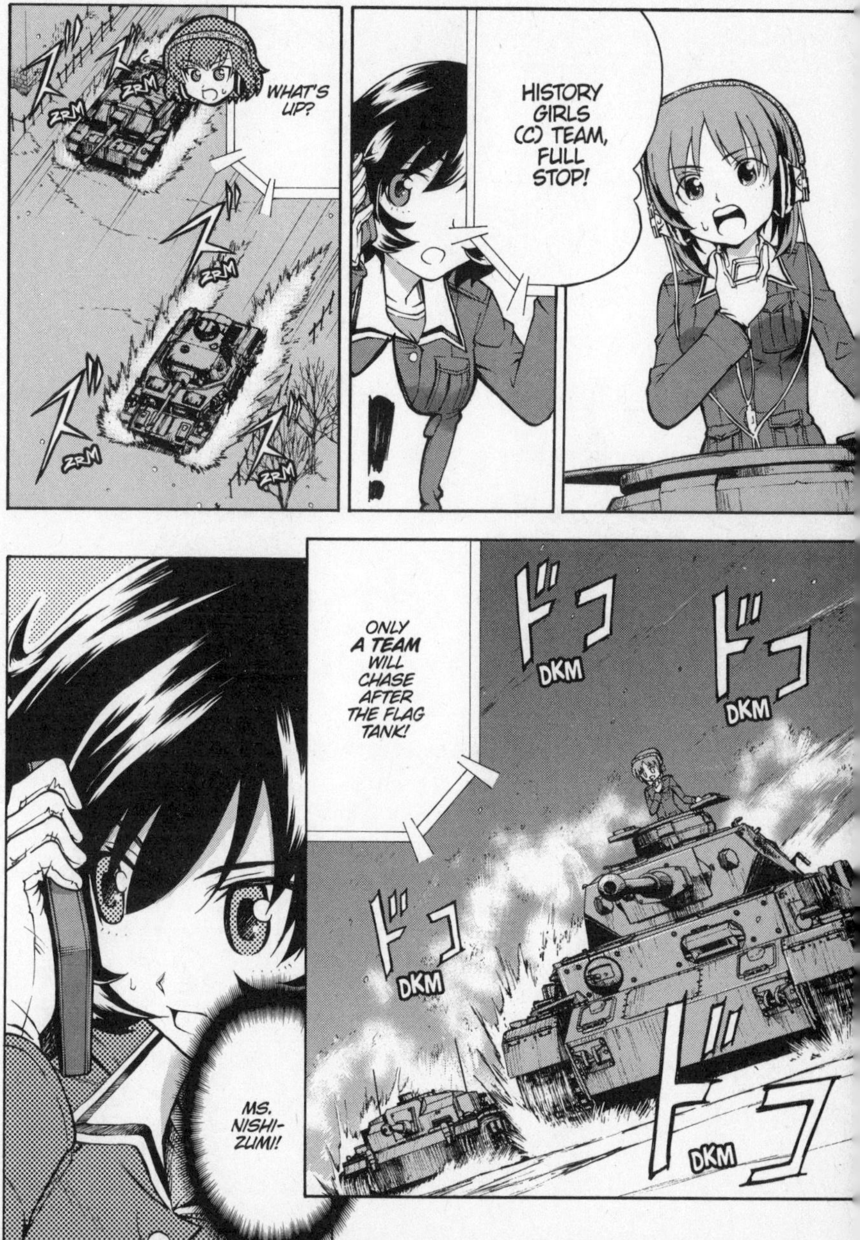
HISTORY GIRLS (C) TEAM, FULL STOP!
!
WHAT'S UP?
ZRM
ZRM
ZRM
ZRM
ZRM
ZRM
ドッ
DKM
ドッ
DKM
ONLY A TEAM WILL CHASE AFTER THE FLAG TANK!
ドッ
DKM
ドッ
DKM
MS. NISHI-ZUMI!

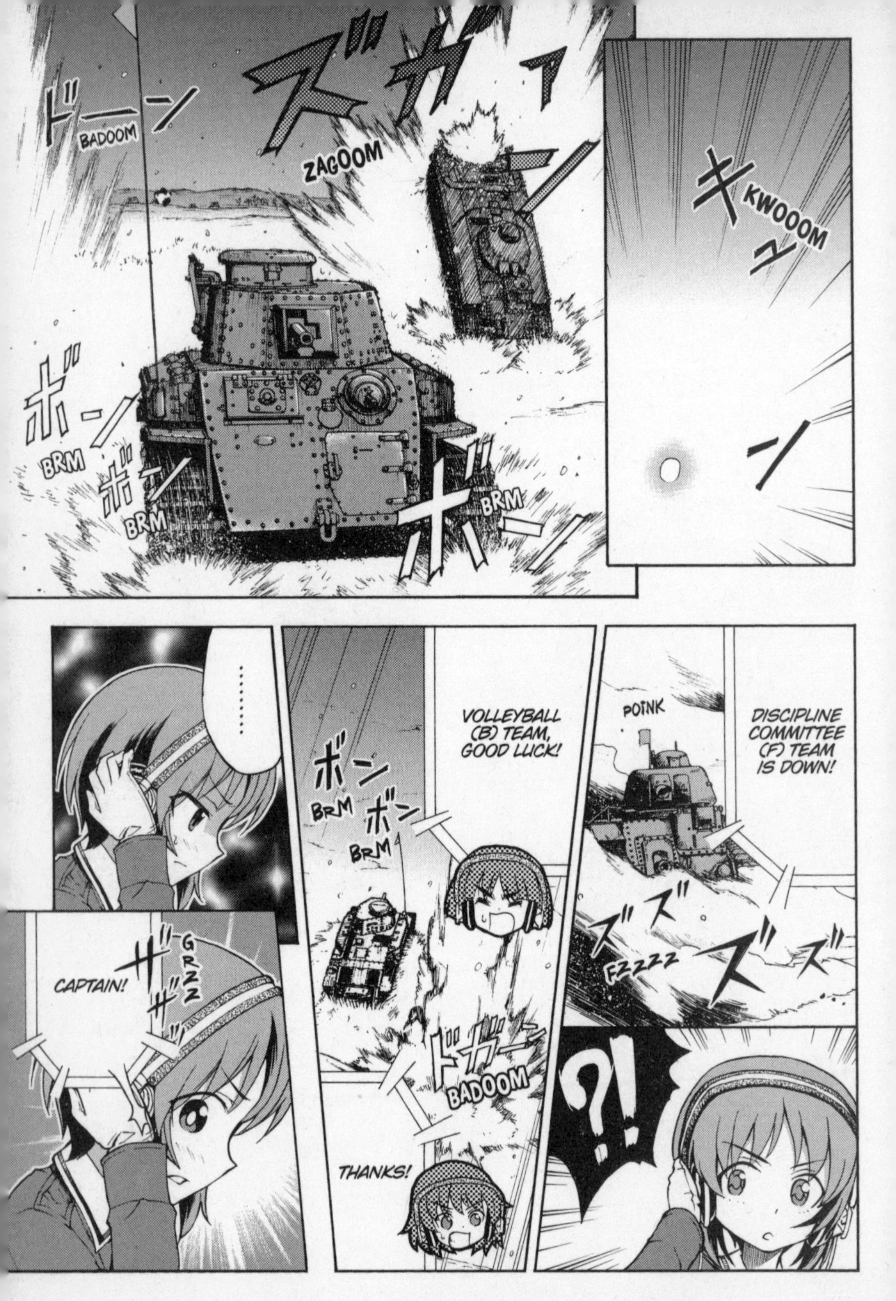

キーン
KWOOOM
ドーーン
BADOOM
ズガァ
ZAGOOM
ボーン
BRM
ボン
BRM
ボー
BRM
DISCIPLINE COMMITTEE (F) TEAM IS DOWN!
POINK
ズズズ
FZZZZ
?!
VOLLEYBALL (B) TEAM, GOOD LUCK!
ボン
BRM
ボン
BRM
ドガーン
BADOOM
THANKS!
......
CAPTAIN!
ザザ
GRZZ

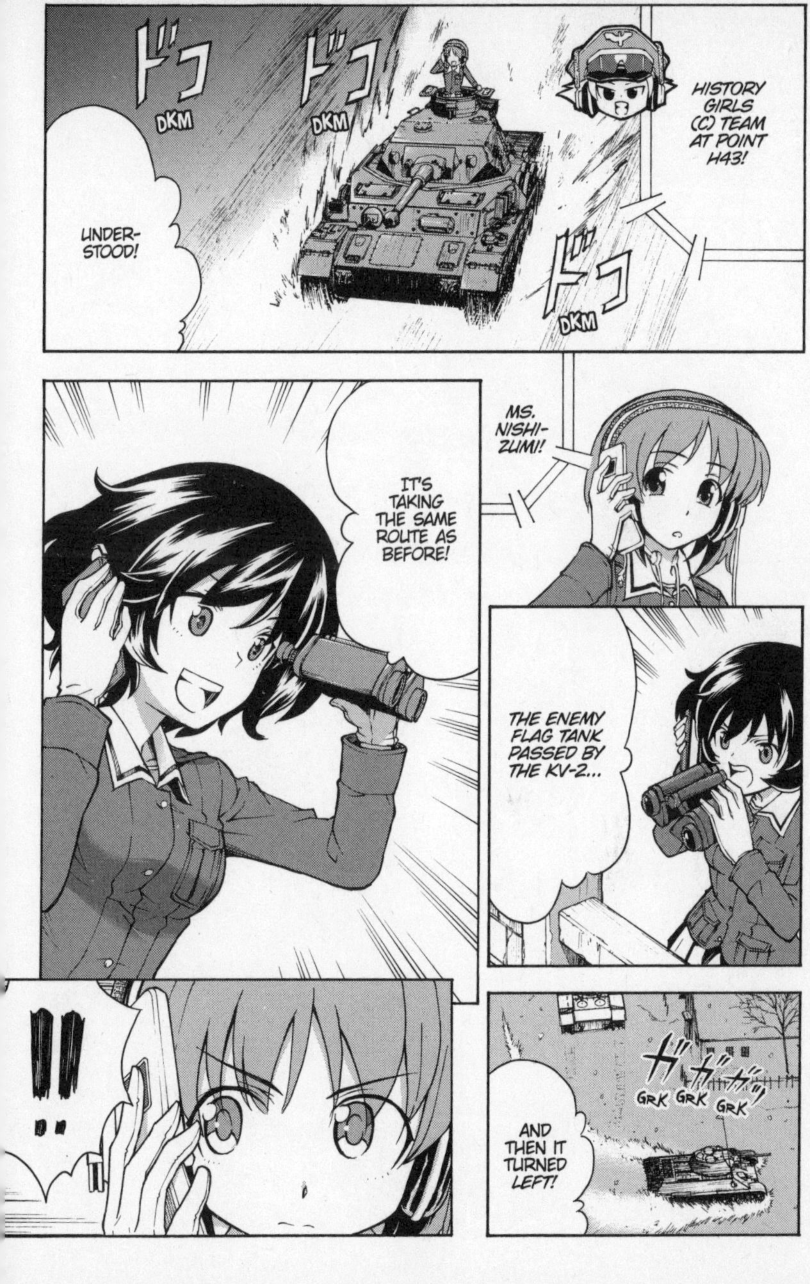
HISTORY GIRLS (C) TEAM AT POINT H43!
ドッ
DKM
ドッ
DKM
ドッ
DKM
UNDER-STOOD!
MS. NISHI-ZUMI!
THE ENEMY FLAG TANK PASSED BY THE KV-2...
IT'S TAKING THE SAME ROUTE AS BEFORE!
ガッ ガッ ガッ
GRK GRK GRK
AND THEN IT TURNED LEFT!
!!

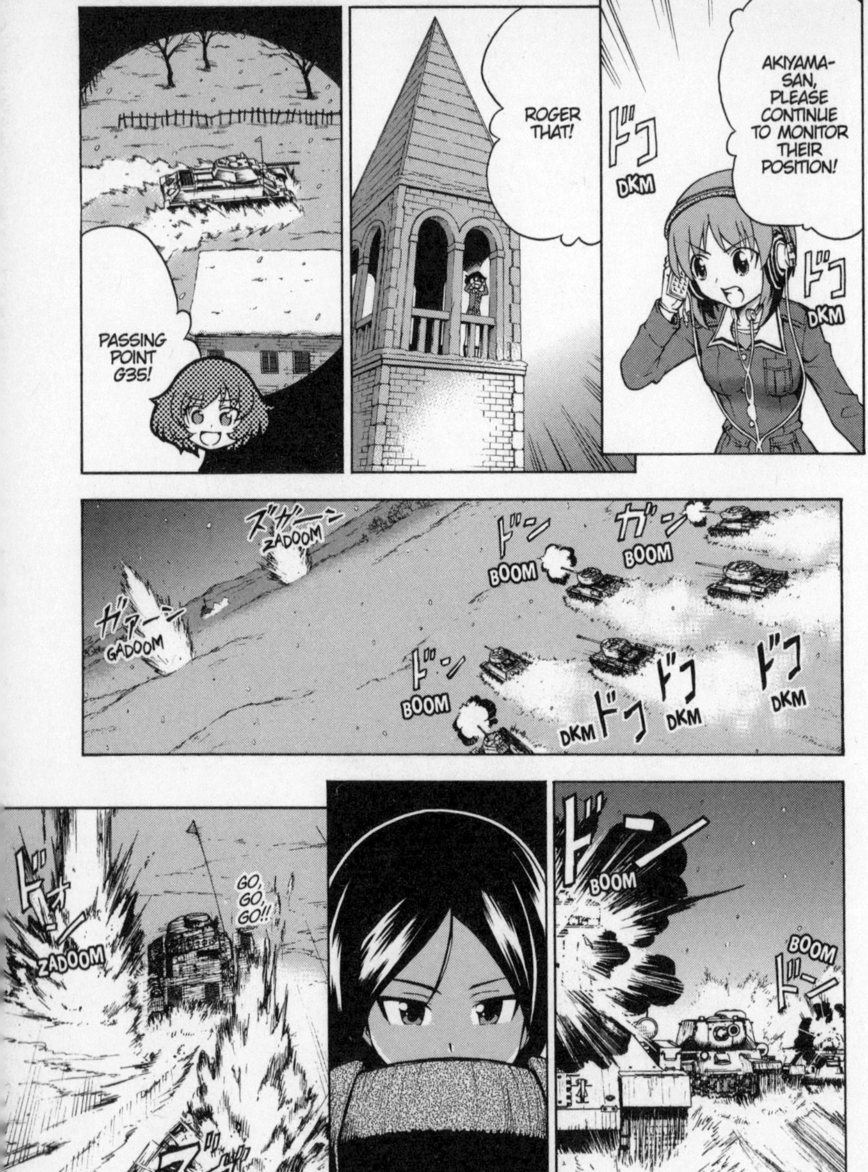
AKIYAMA-SAN, PLEASE CONTINUE TO MONITOR THEIR POSITION!
DKM
DKM
ROGER THAT!
PASSING POINT G35!
BOOM
BOOM
ZADOOM
BOOM
GADOOM
DKM
BOOM
DKM
DKM
BOOM
BOOM
GO, GO, GO!!
ZADOOM
ZADOOM

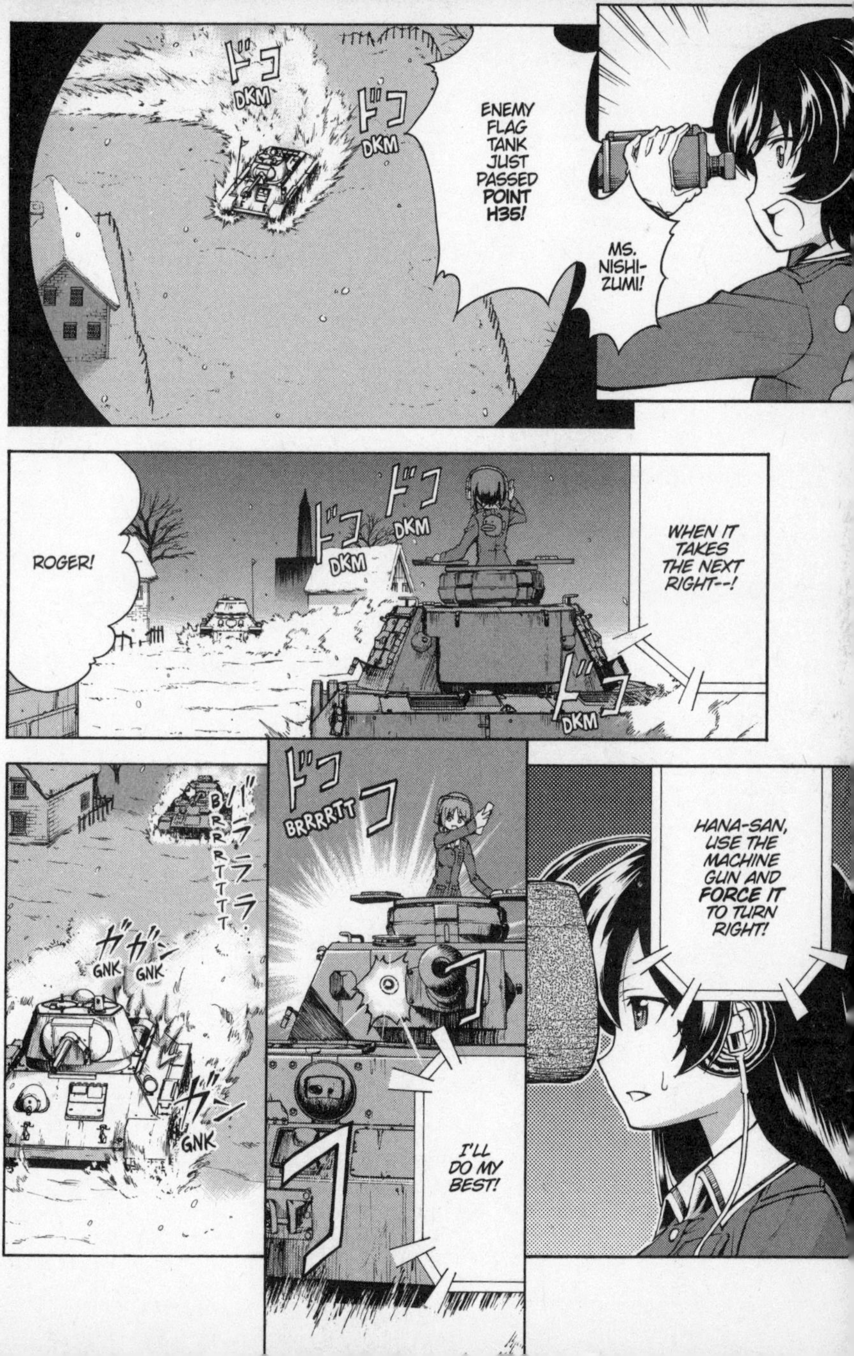

ENEMY FLAG TANK JUST PASSED POINT H35!
MS. NISHI-ZUMI!
ドコ
DKM
ドコ
DKM
WHEN IT TAKES THE NEXT RIGHT--!
ドコ
DKM
ドコ
DKM
ドコ
DKM
ROGER!
HANA-SAN, USE THE MACHINE GUN AND FORCE IT TO TURN RIGHT!
ドコ
BRRRRTT
I'LL DO MY BEST!
BRRRTTTT
GNK
GNK
GNK

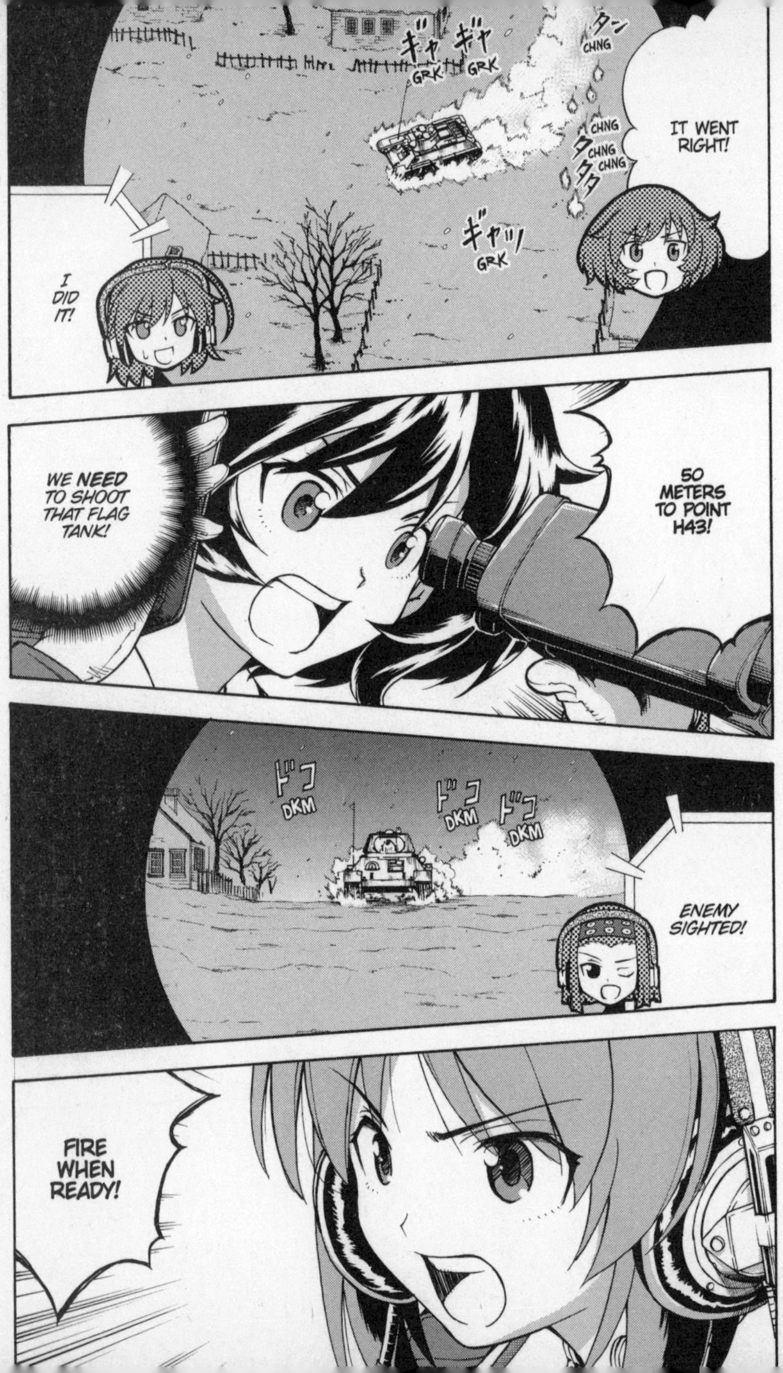
タン
CHNG
IT WENT RIGHT!
ギャ ギャ
GRK GRK
CHNG
タタタ
CHNG CHNG
ギャッ
GRK
I DID IT!
50 METERS TO POINT H43!
WE NEED TO SHOOT THAT FLAG TANK!
ドコ
DKM
ドコ
DKM
ドコ
DKM
ENEMY SIGHTED!
FIRE WHEN READY!

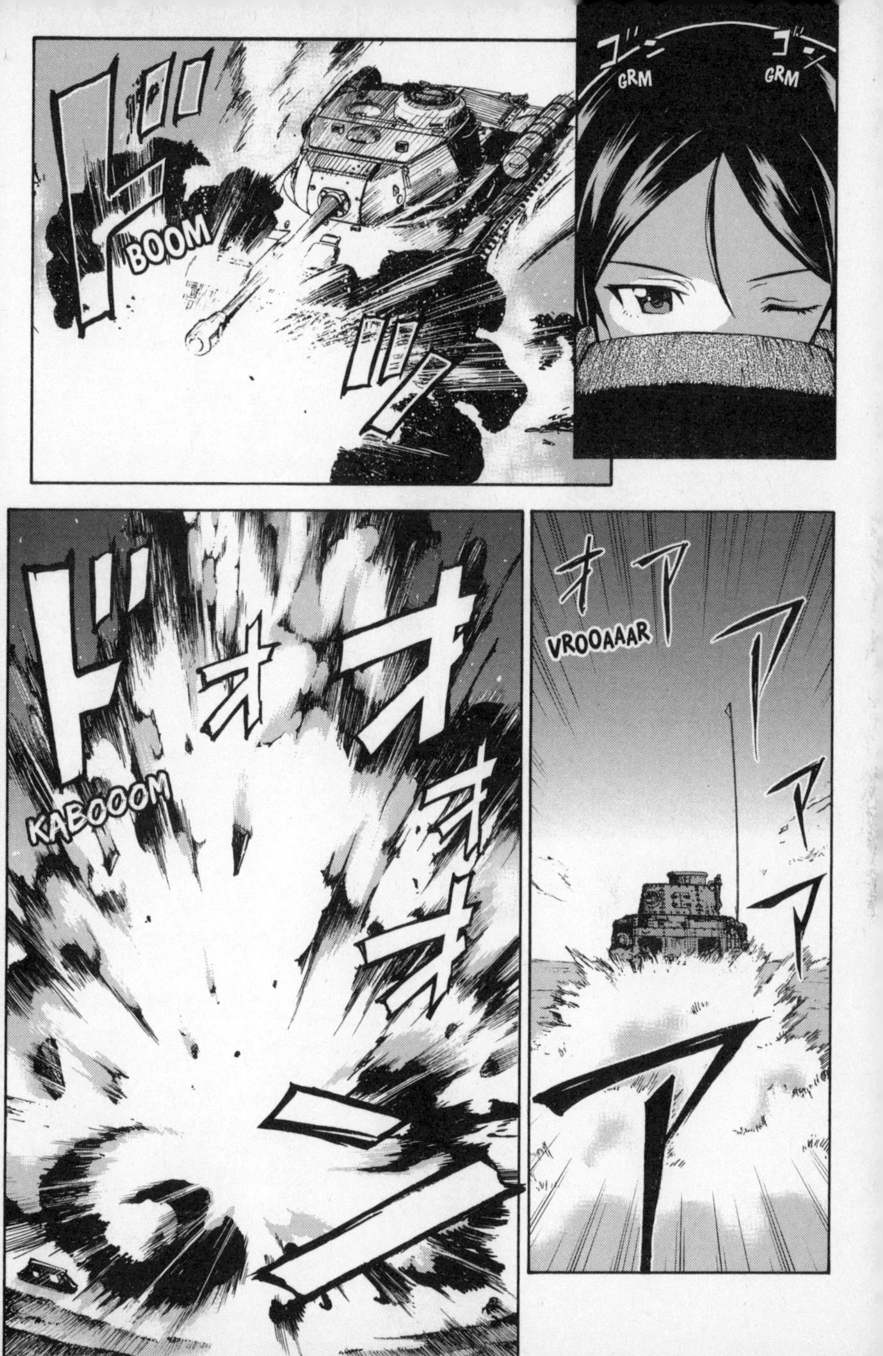
GRM
GRM
BOOM
VROOAAAR
KABOOOM

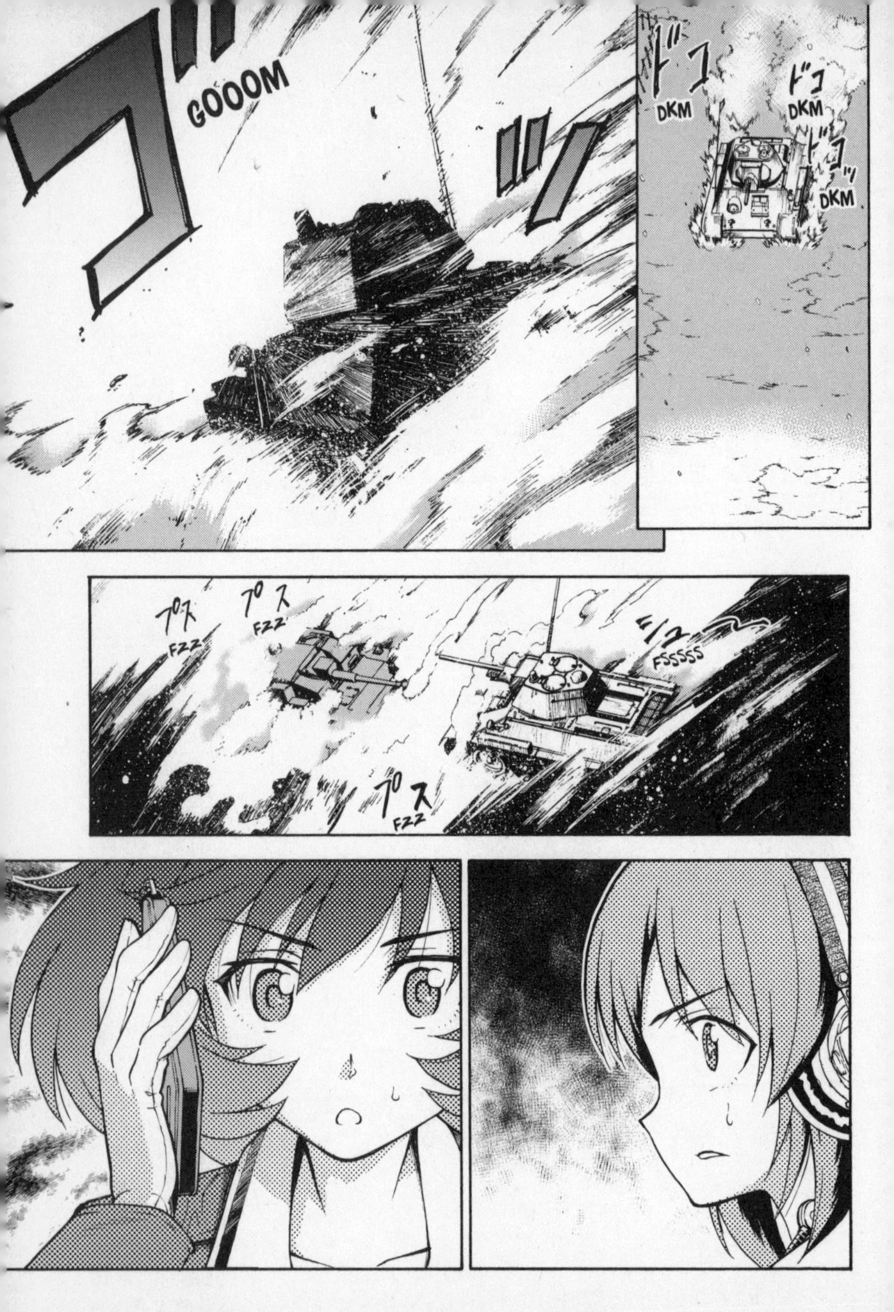

ドコ
DKM
ドコ
DKM
ドコッ
DKM
ゴゴ
GOOOM
シュ～
FSSSSS
プス
FZZ
プス
FZZ
プス
FZZ

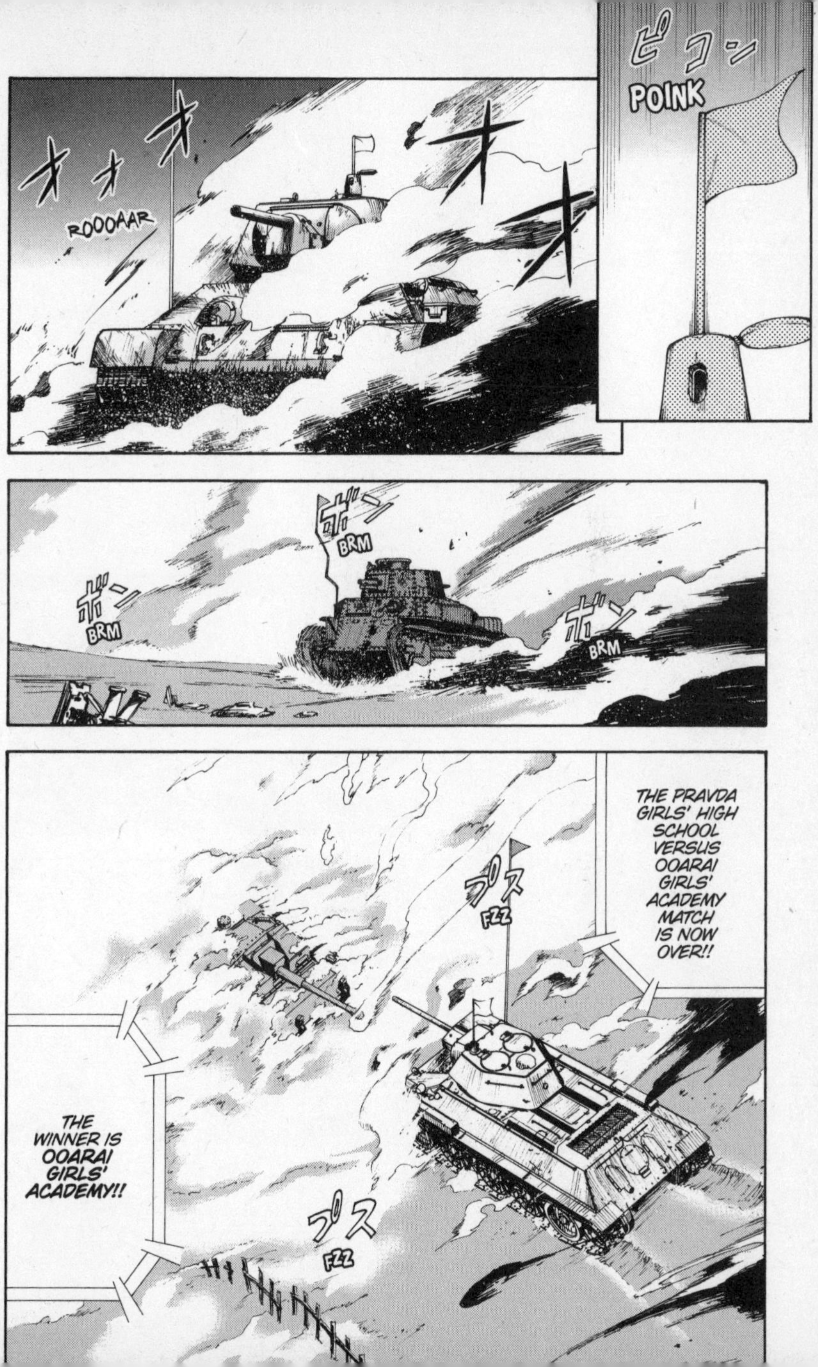
ピコン
POINK
オオオオ
ROOOAAR
ボン
BRM
ボン
BRM
ボン
BRM
THE PRAVDA GIRLS' HIGH SCHOOL VERSUS OOARAI GIRLS' ACADEMY MATCH IS NOW OVER!!
プス
FZZ
THE WINNER IS OOARAI GIRLS' ACADEMY!!
プス
FZZ

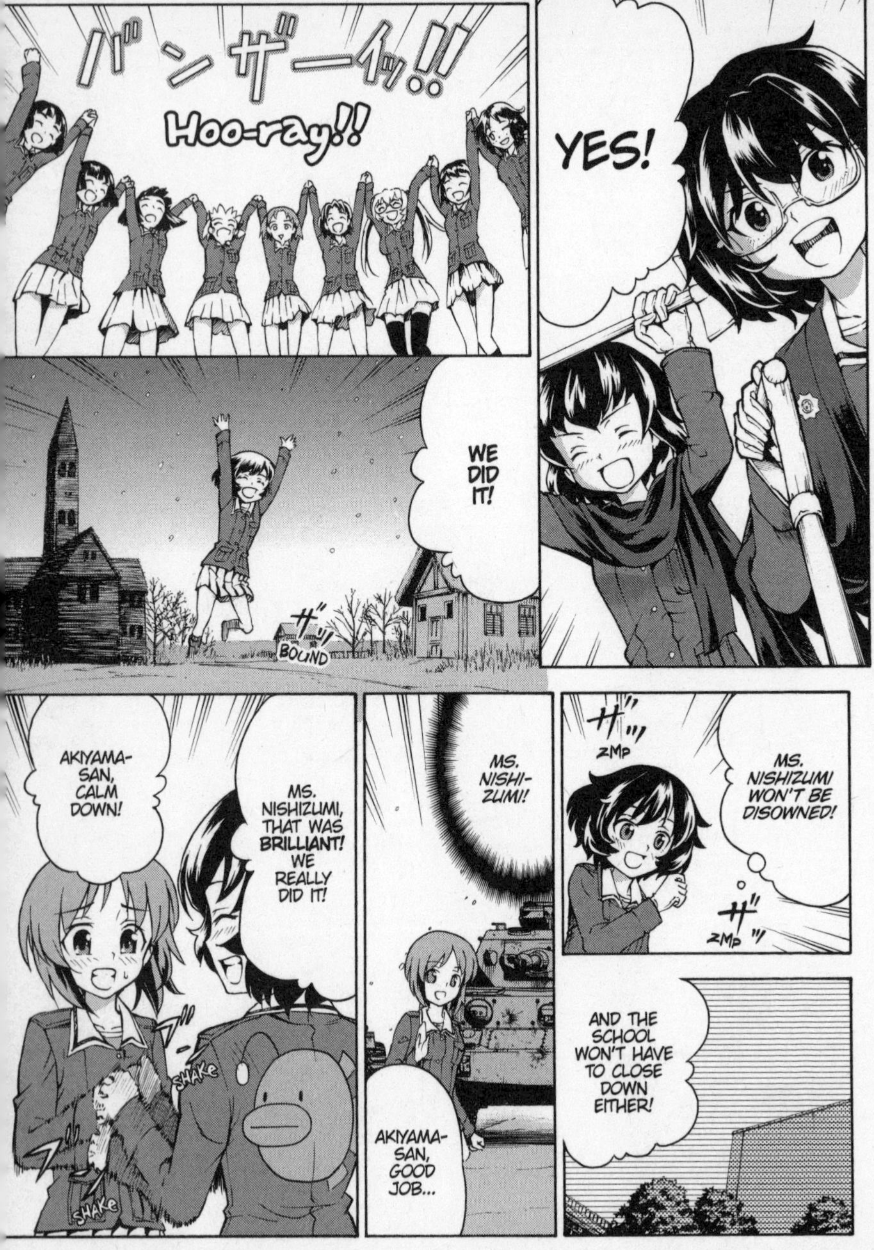
YES!
バンザーイッ!!
Hoo-ray!!
WE DID IT!
BOUND
MS. NISHIZUMI WON'T BE DISOWNED!
ZMP
ZMP
AND THE SCHOOL WON'T HAVE TO CLOSE DOWN EITHER!
MS. NISHIZUMI!
AKIYAMA-SAN, GOOD JOB...
MS. NISHIZUMI, THAT WAS BRILLIANT! WE REALLY DID IT!
AKIYAMA-SAN, CALM DOWN!
SHAKE
SHAKE

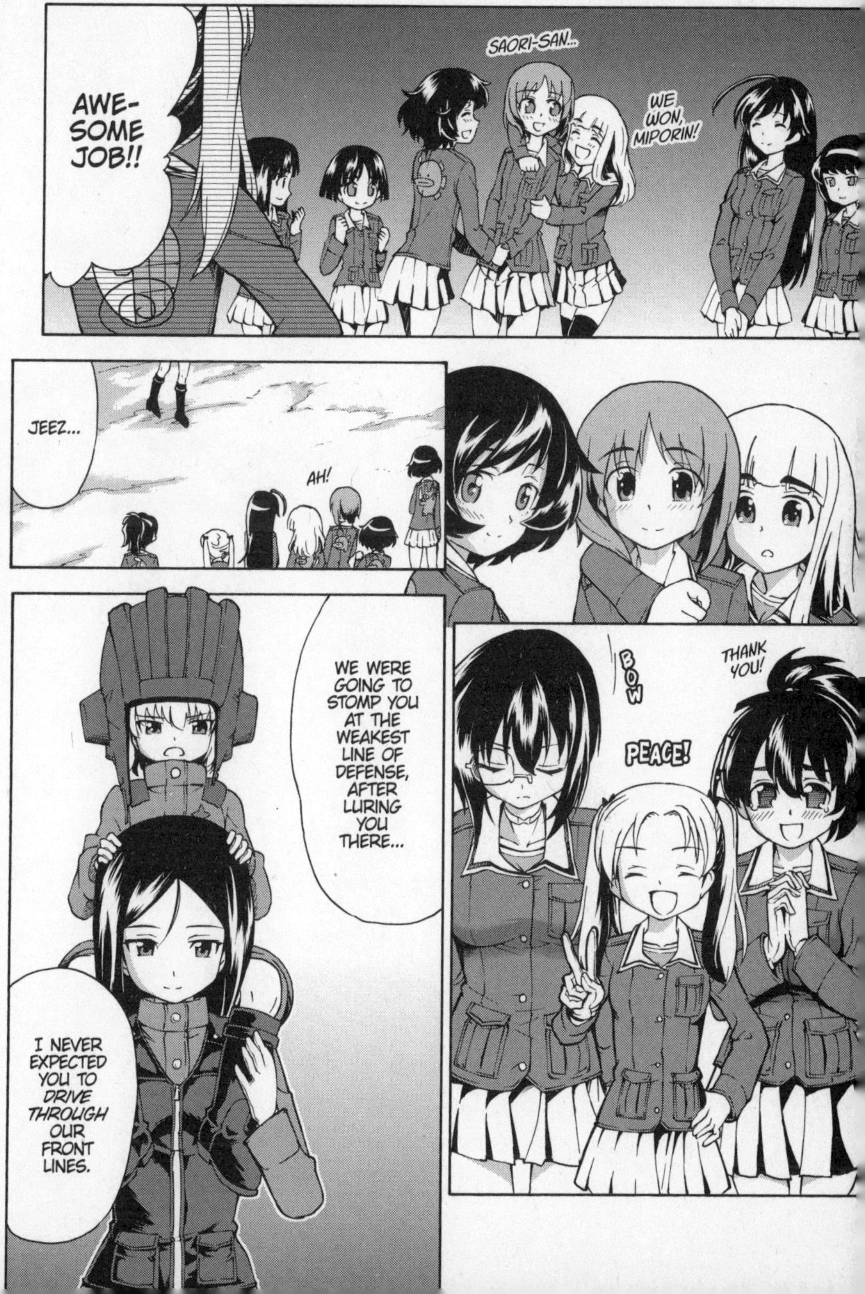
WE WON, MIPORIN!
SAORI-SAN...
AWE-SOME JOB!!
AH!
JEEZ...
THANK YOU!
BOW
PEACE!
WE WERE GOING TO STOMP YOU AT THE WEAKEST LINE OF DEFENSE, AFTER LURING YOU THERE...
I NEVER EXPECTED YOU TO *DRIVE THROUGH* OUR FRONT LINES.

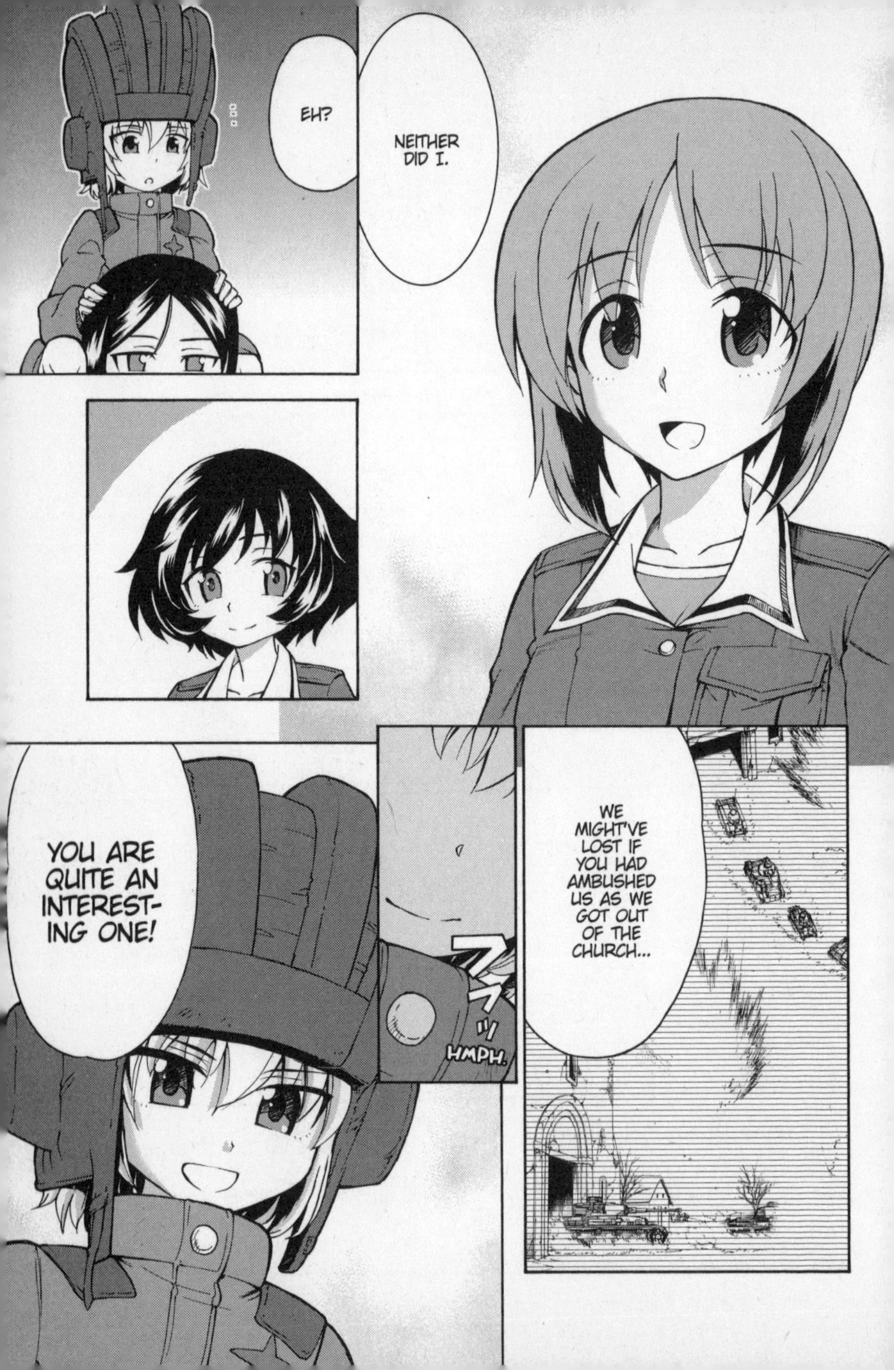
NEITHER DID I.
EH?
WE MIGHT'VE LOST IF YOU HAD AMBUSHED US AS WE GOT OUT OF THE CHURCH...
HMPH.
YOU ARE QUITE AN INTEREST-ING ONE!

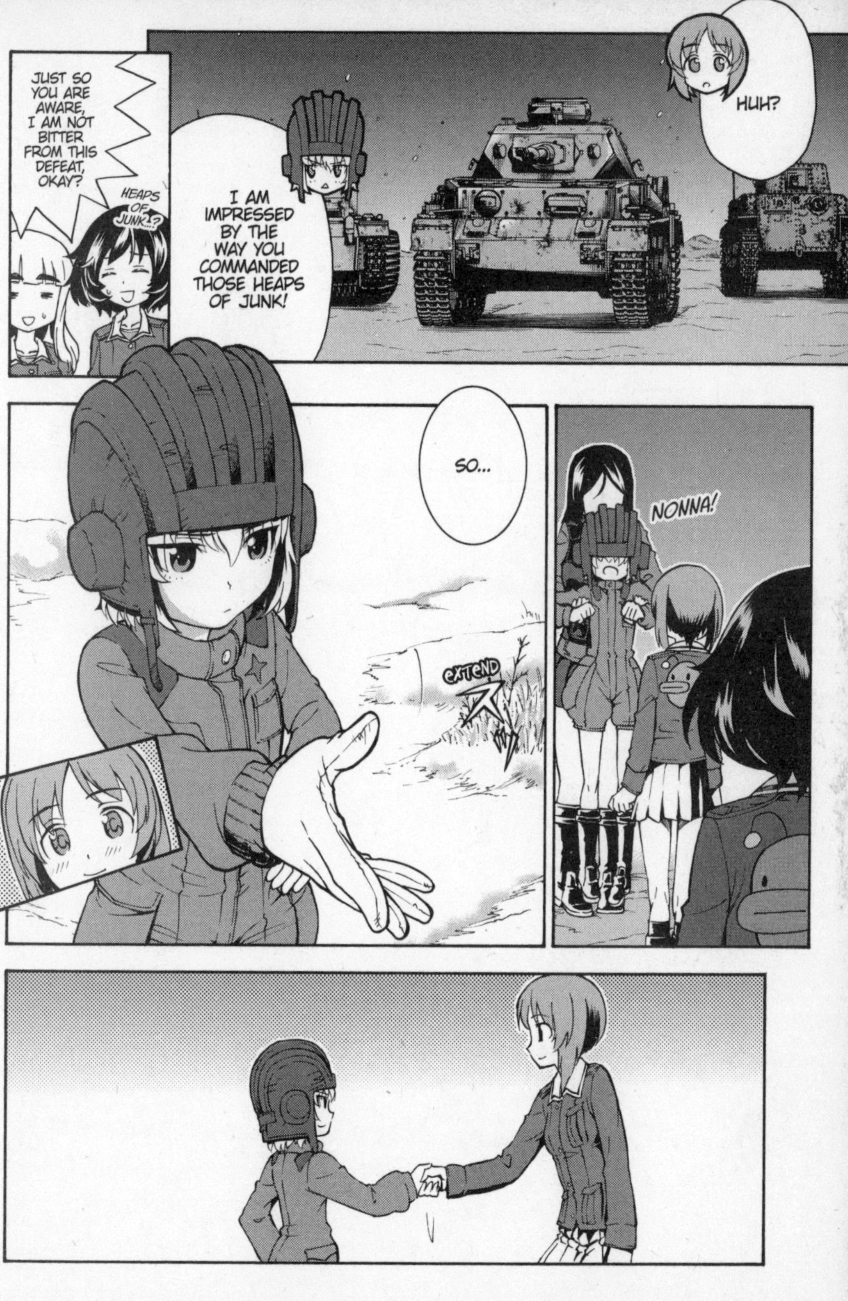
I AM IMPRESSED BY THE WAY YOU COMMANDED THOSE HEAPS OF JUNK!
HEAPS OF JUNK!?
JUST SO YOU ARE AWARE, I AM NOT BITTER FROM THIS DEFEAT, OKAY?
HUH?
NONNA!
SO...
EXTEND

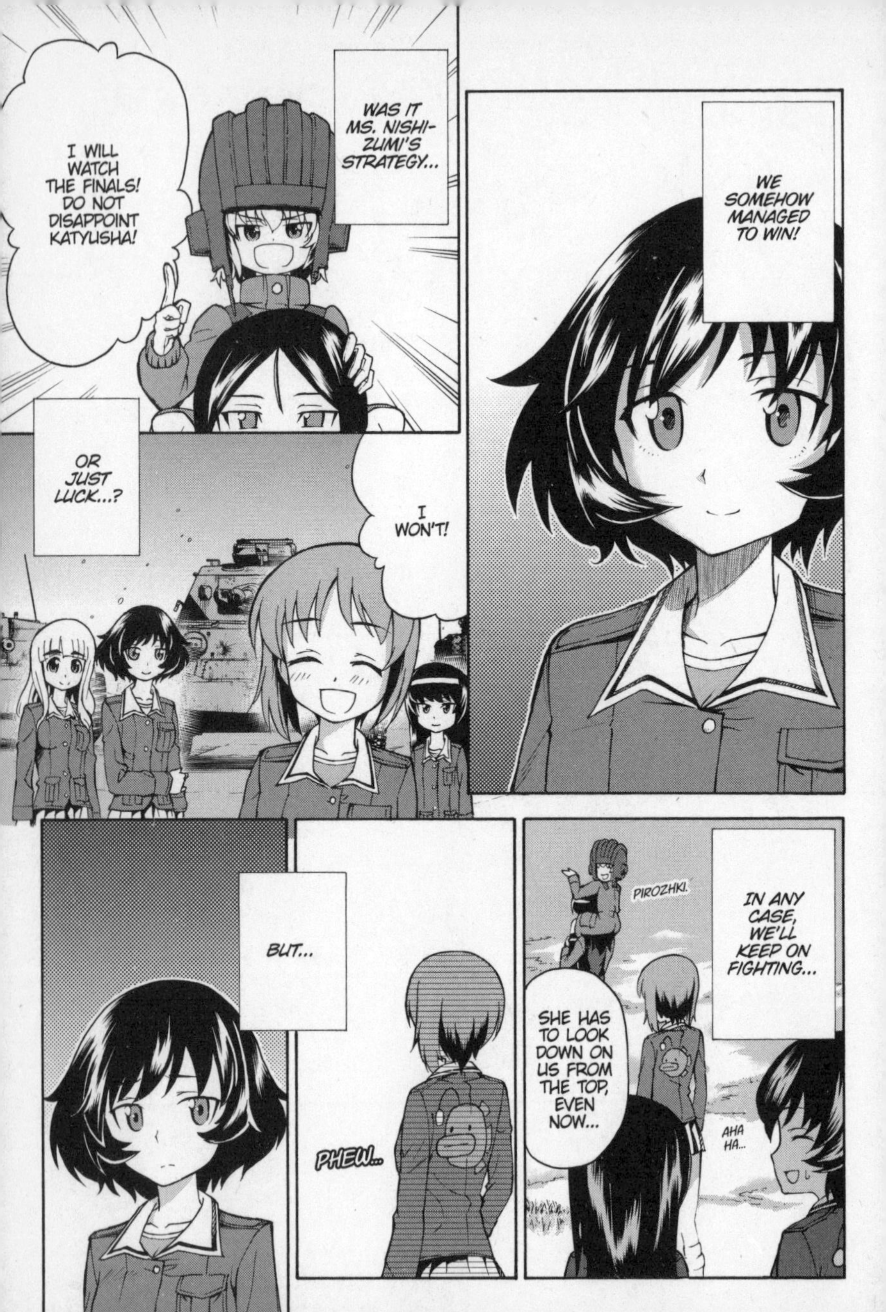
WE SOMEHOW MANAGED TO WIN!
WAS IT MS. NISHI-ZUMI'S STRATEGY...
I WILL WATCH THE FINALS! DO NOT DISAPPOINT KATYUSHA!
OR JUST LUCK...?
I WON'T!
IN ANY CASE, WE'LL KEEP ON FIGHTING...
PIROZHKI.
SHE HAS TO LOOK DOWN ON US FROM THE TOP, EVEN NOW...
AHA HA...
PHEW...
BUT...

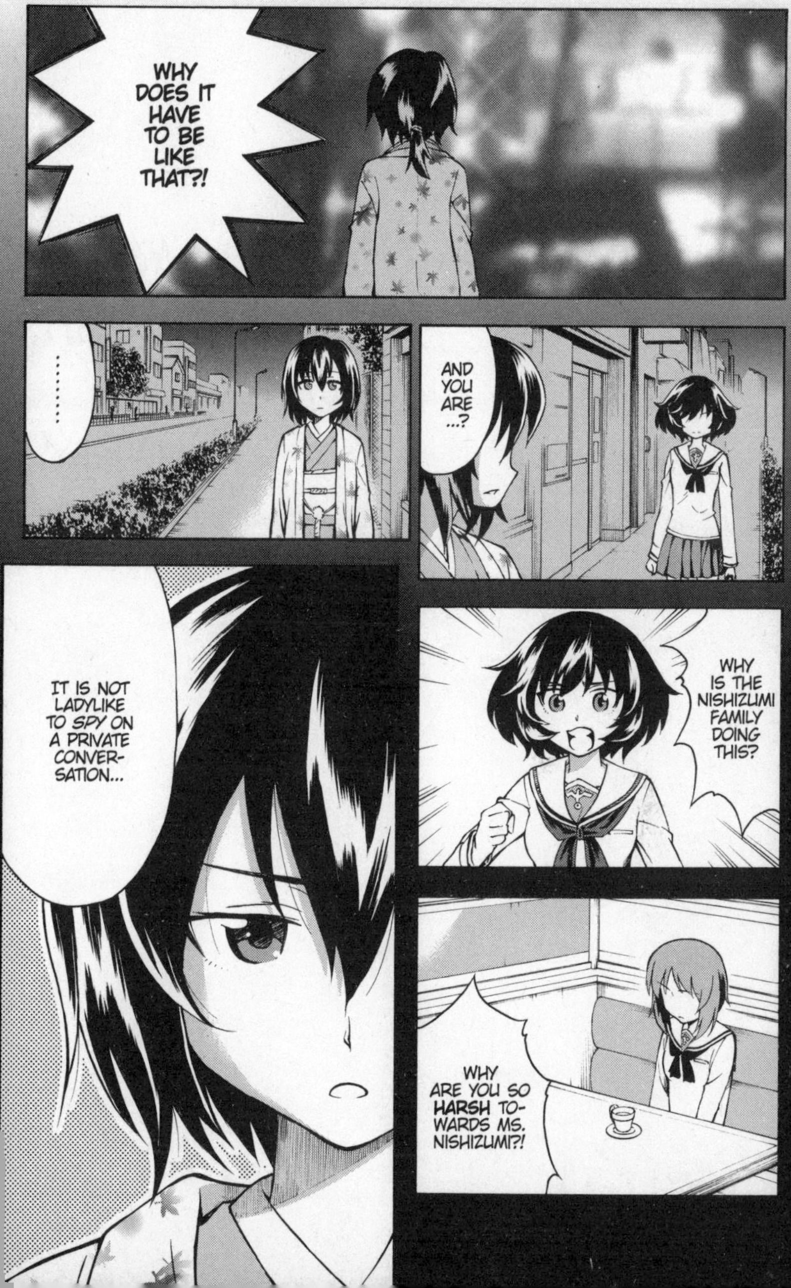
WHY DOES IT HAVE TO BE LIKE THAT?!
AND YOU ARE ...?
......
WHY IS THE NISHIZUMI FAMILY DOING THIS?
WHY ARE YOU SO HARSH TO-WARDS MS. NISHIZUMI?!
IT IS NOT LADYLIKE TO SPY ON A PRIVATE CONVER-SATION...

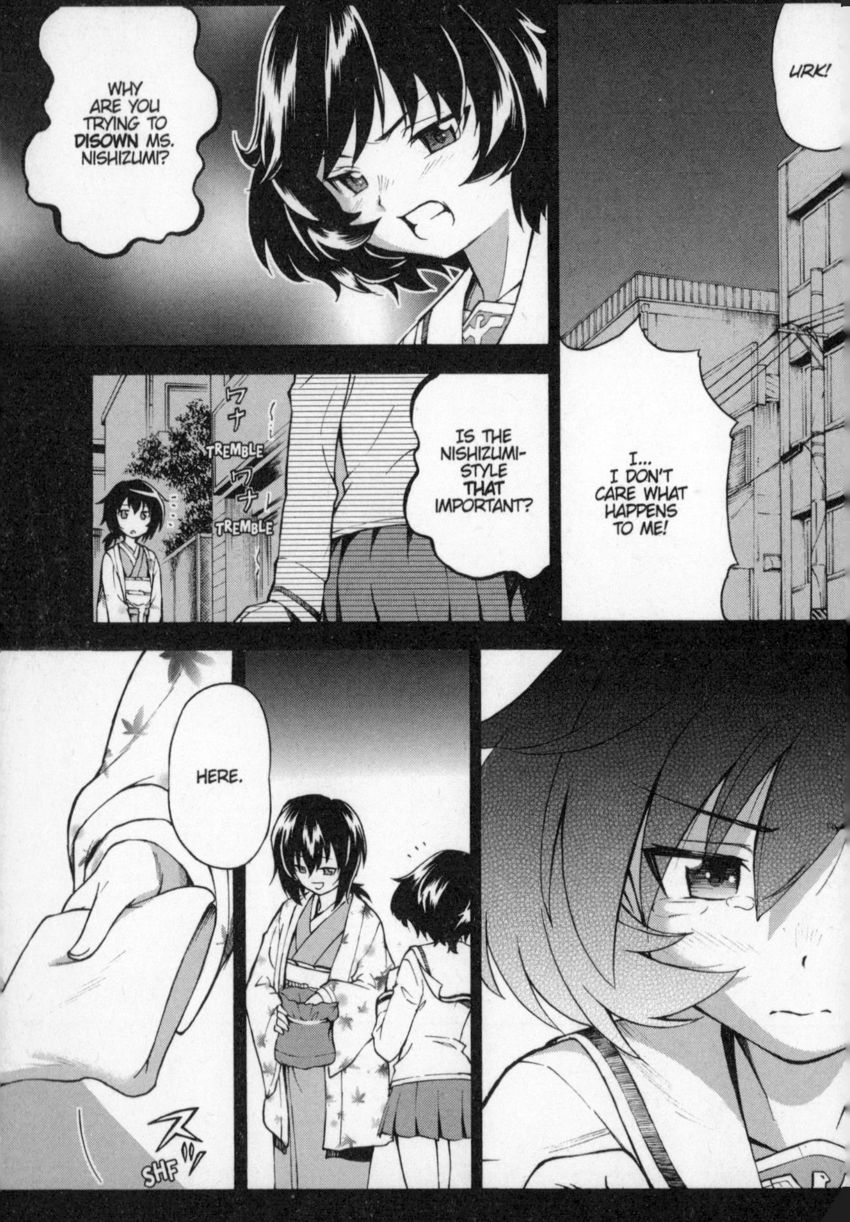
URK!
I... I DON'T CARE WHAT HAPPENS TO ME!
WHY ARE YOU TRYING TO DISOWN MS. NISHIZUMI?
IS THE NISHIZUMI-STYLE THAT IMPORTANT?
ワナ
TREMBLE
ワナ
TREMBLE
HERE.
ス
SHF

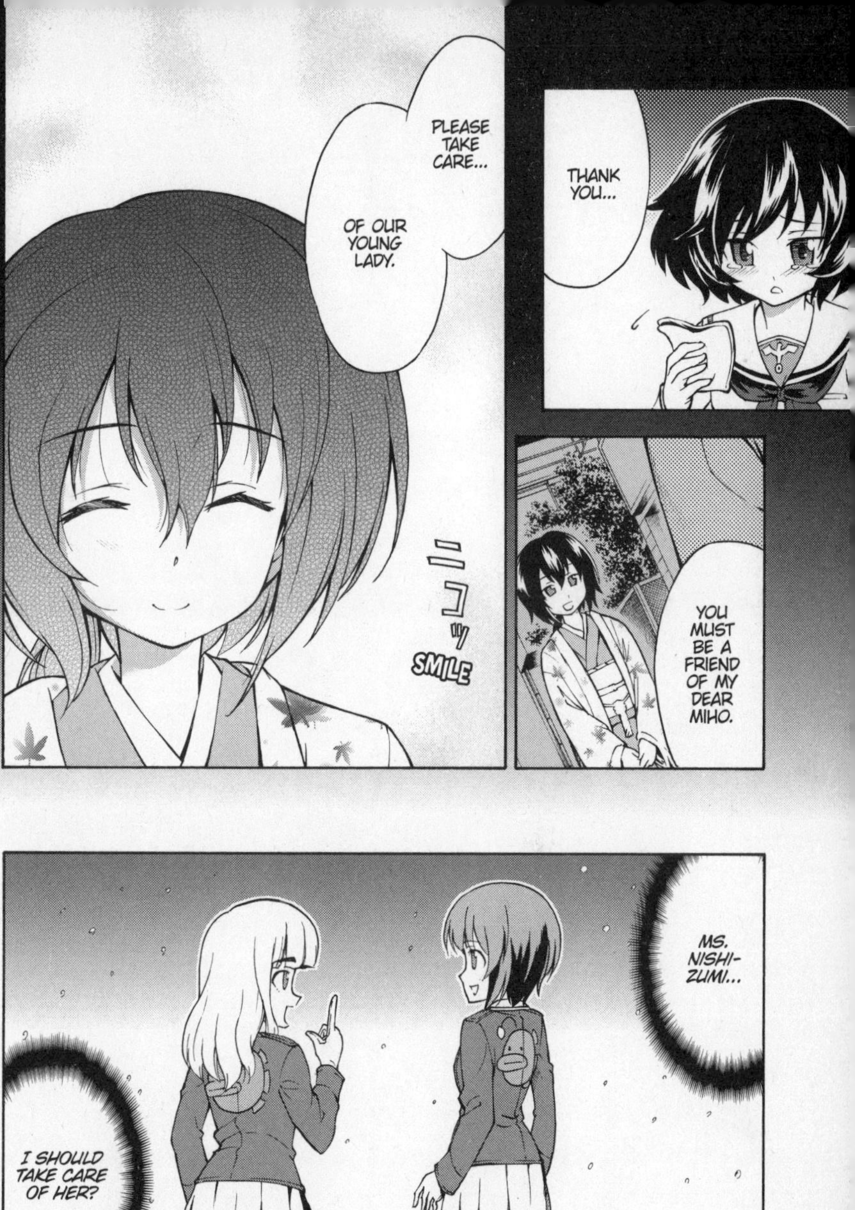
THANK YOU...
YOU MUST BE A FRIEND OF MY DEAR MIHO.
PLEASE TAKE CARE...
OF OUR YOUNG LADY.
ニコッ
SMILE
MS. NISHIZUMI...
I SHOULD TAKE CARE OF HER?

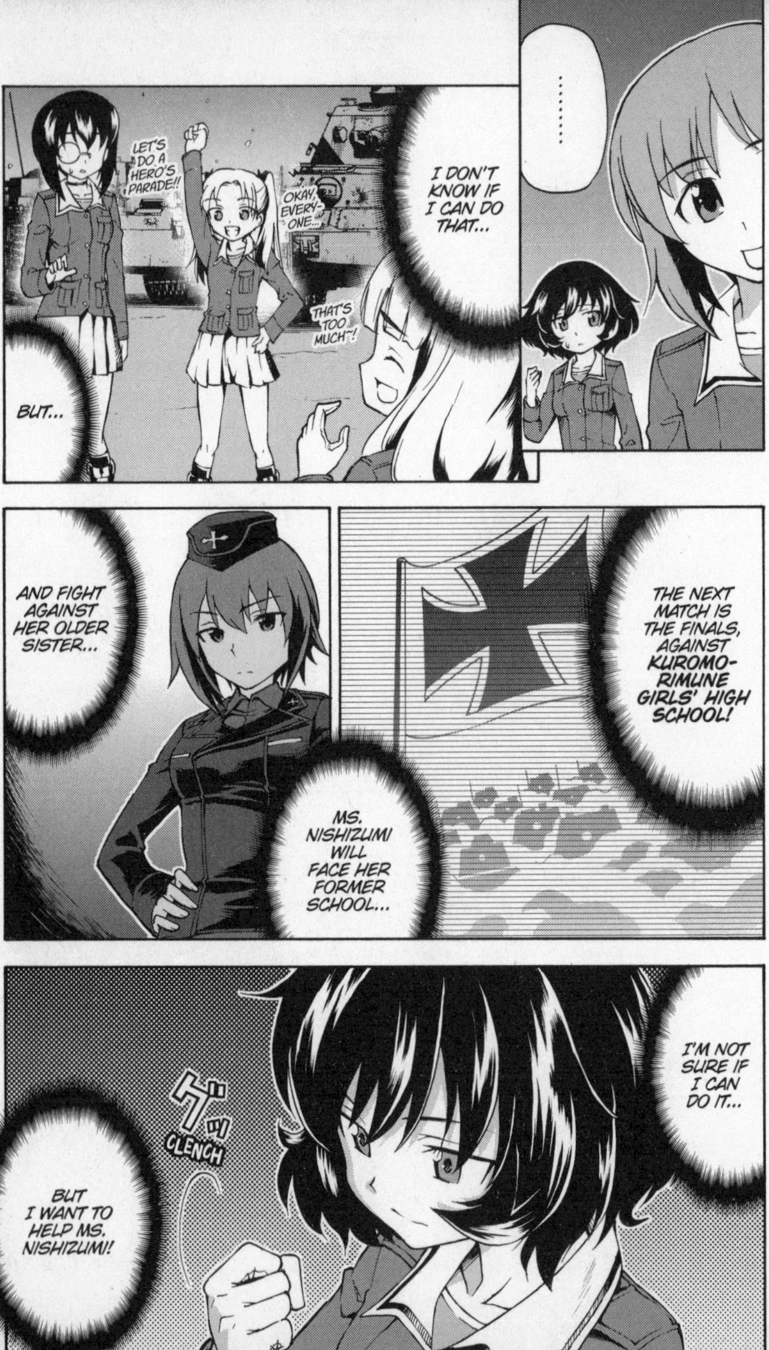
......
I DON'T KNOW IF I CAN DO THAT...
OKAY, EVERY-ONE...
LET'S DO A HERO'S PARADE!!
THAT'S TOO MUCH~!
BUT...
THE NEXT MATCH IS THE FINALS, AGAINST KUROMO-RIMUNE GIRLS' HIGH SCHOOL!
MS. NISHIZUMI WILL FACE HER FORMER SCHOOL...
AND FIGHT AGAINST HER OLDER SISTER...
I'M NOT SURE IF I CAN DO IT...
グッ
CLENCH
BUT I WANT TO HELP MS. NISHIZUMI!

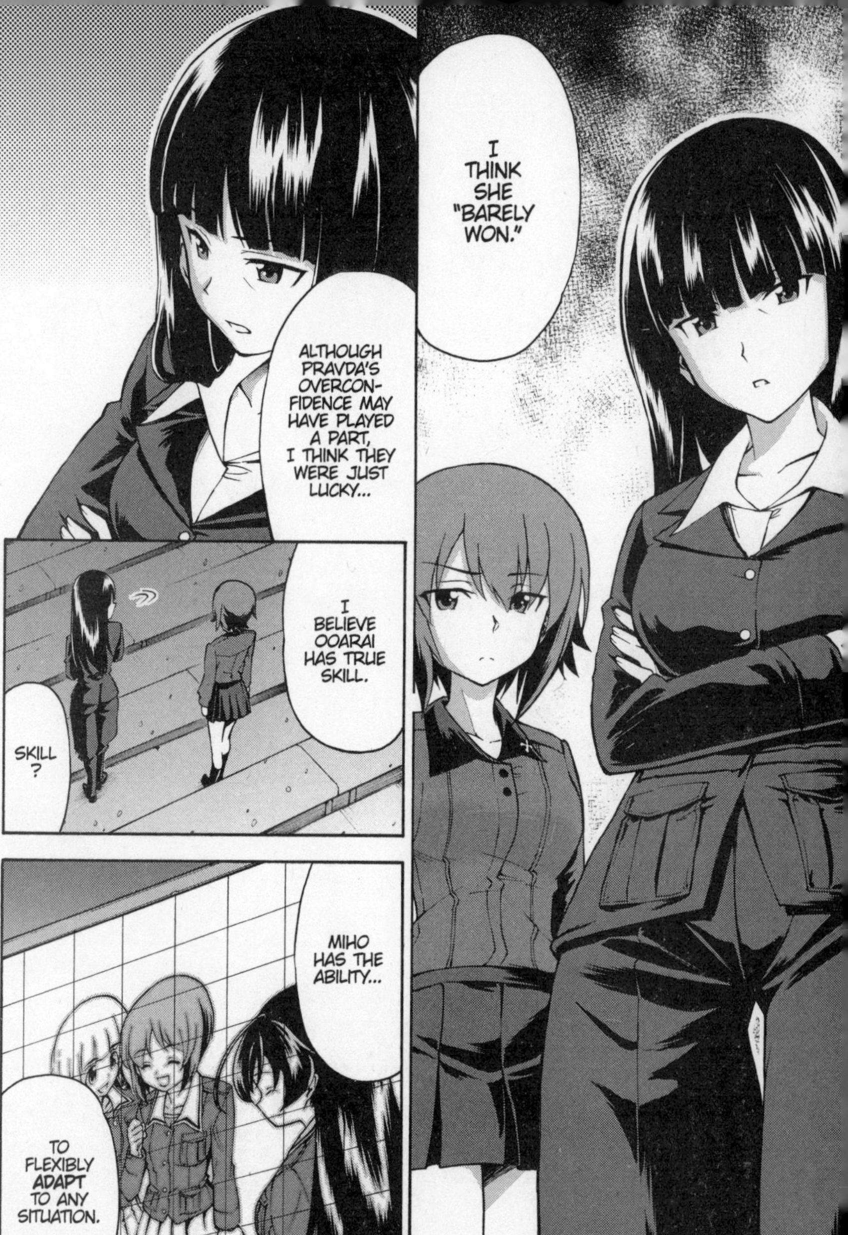
I THINK SHE "BARELY WON."
ALTHOUGH PRAVDA'S OVERCONFIDENCE MAY HAVE PLAYED A PART, I THINK THEY WERE JUST LUCKY...
I BELIEVE OOARAI HAS TRUE SKILL.
SKILL?
MIHO HAS THE ABILITY...
TO FLEXIBLY ADAPT TO ANY SITUATION.

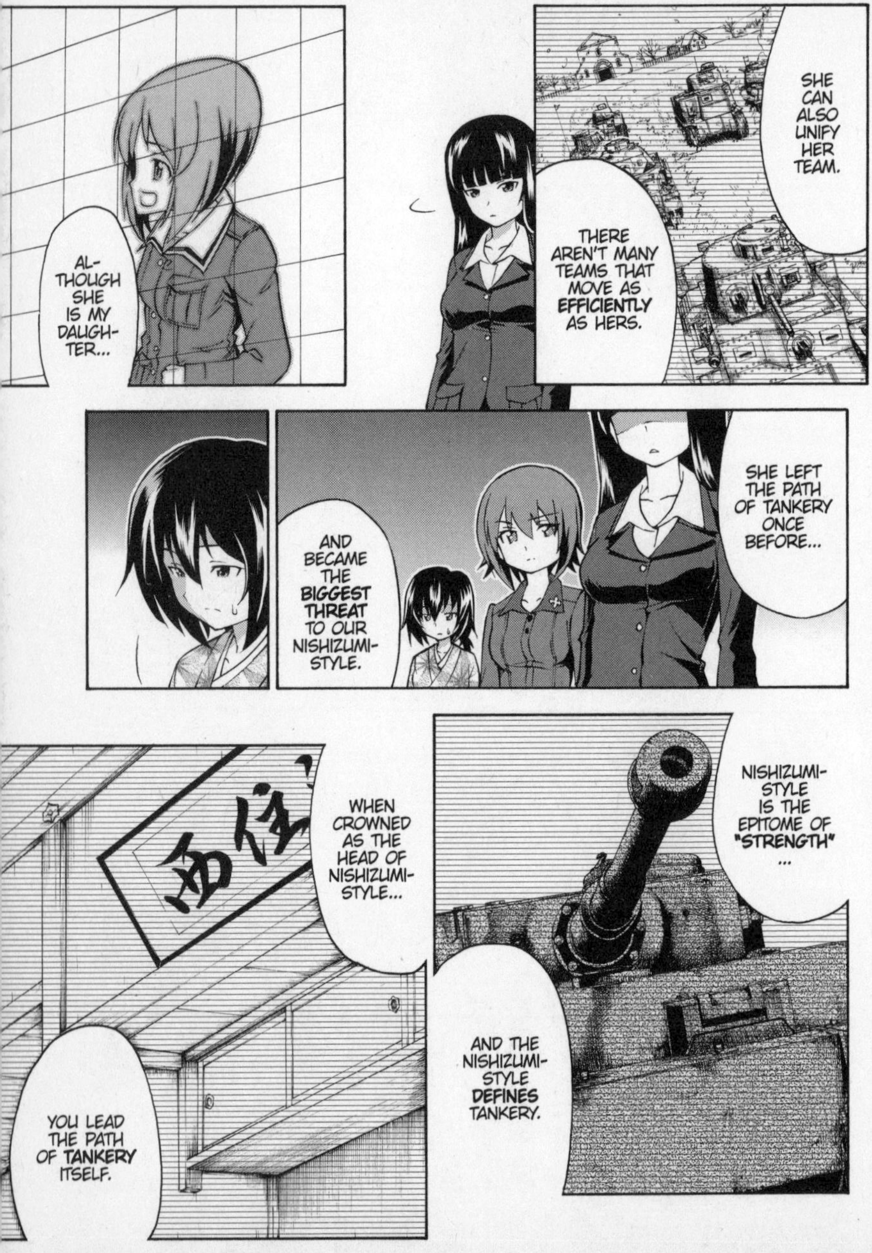
SHE CAN ALSO UNIFY HER TEAM.
THERE AREN'T MANY TEAMS THAT MOVE AS **EFFICIENTLY** AS HERS.
ALTHOUGH SHE IS MY DAUGHTER...
SHE LEFT THE PATH OF TANKERY ONCE BEFORE...
AND BECAME THE **BIGGEST THREAT** TO OUR NISHIZUMI-STYLE.
NISHIZUMI-STYLE IS THE EPITOME OF **"STRENGTH"** ...
AND THE NISHIZUMI-STYLE **DEFINES** TANKERY.
WHEN CROWNED AS THE HEAD OF NISHIZUMI-STYLE...
YOU LEAD THE PATH OF **TANKERY** ITSELF.

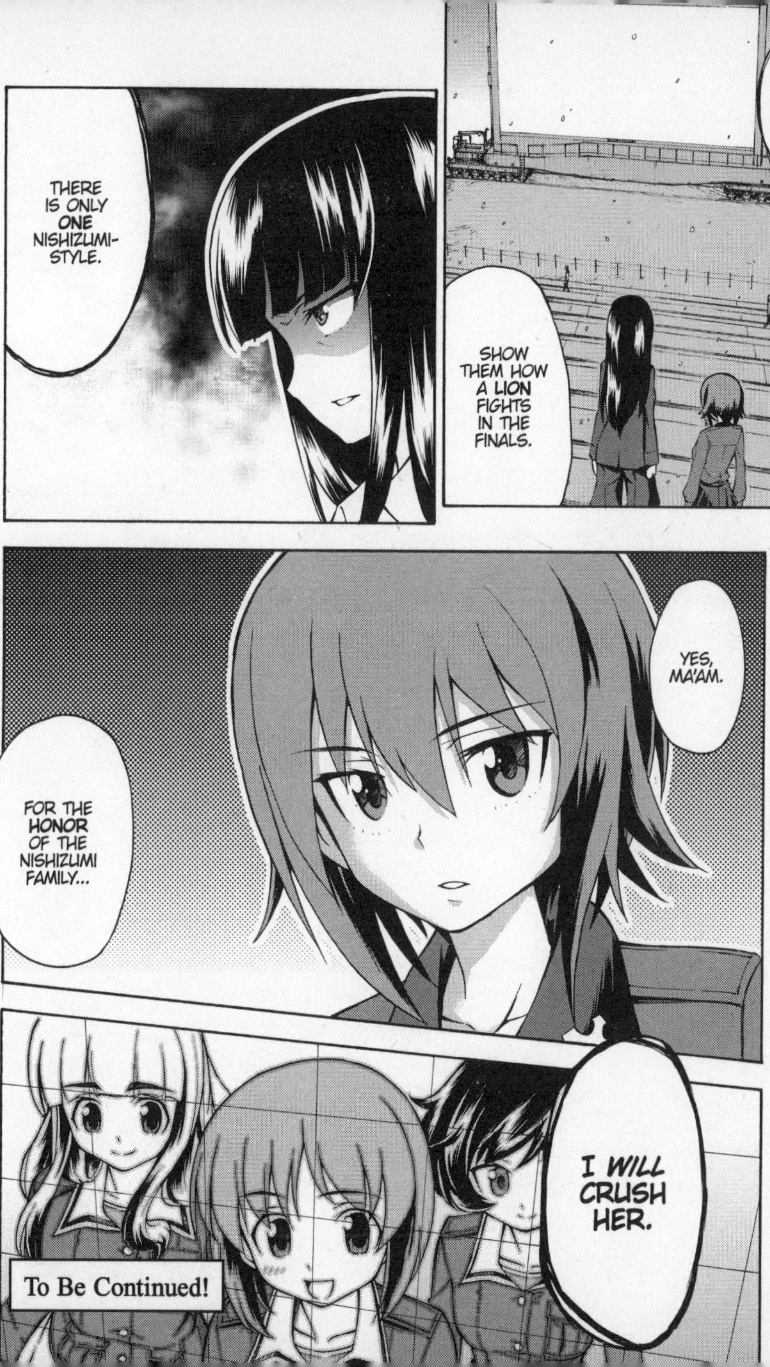
MAHO ...
SHOW THEM HOW A LION FIGHTS IN THE FINALS.
THERE IS ONLY ONE NISHIZUMI-STYLE.
YES, MA'AM.
FOR THE HONOR OF THE NISHIZUMI FAMILY...
I WILL CRUSH HER.
To Be Continued!

GIRLS und PANZER

▶▶▶ **3**

DRAWING STAFF

才谷屋龍一
RYOHICHI SAITANIYA

浅乃ミサキ
MISAKI ASANO

かわじ
KAWAZI

式神黒子
KUROKO SIKIGAMI

源大雅
TAIGA MINAMOTO

宮本正幸
MASAYUKI MIYAMOTO

With Who?

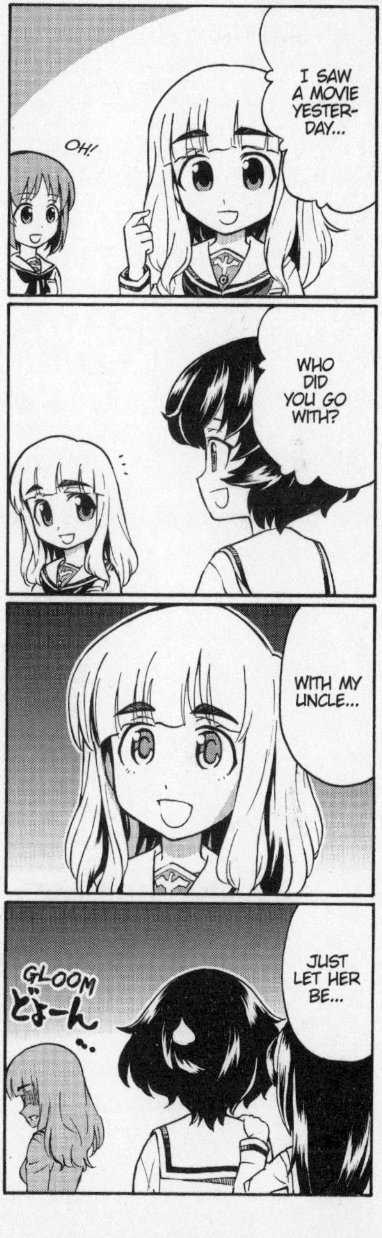
I SAW A MOVIE YESTER-DAY...
OH!
WHO DID YOU GO WITH?
WITH MY UNCLE...
JUST LET HER BE...
GLOOM
どよーん

Test Studies

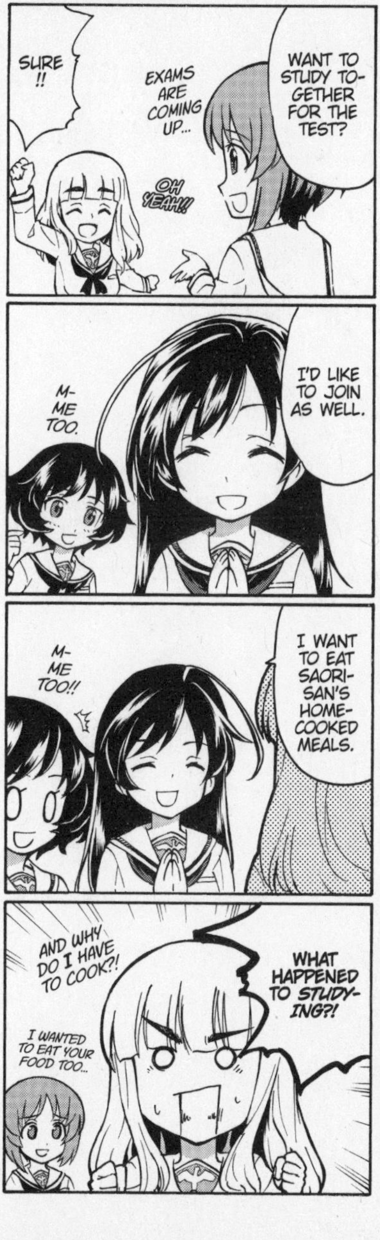
WANT TO STUDY TO-GETHER FOR THE TEST?
EXAMS ARE COMING UP...
SURE!!
OH YEAH!!
I'D LIKE TO JOIN AS WELL.
M-ME TOO.
I WANT TO EAT SAORI-SAN'S HOME-COOKED MEALS.
M-ME TOO!!
WHAT HAPPENED TO STUDYING?!
AND WHY DO I HAVE TO COOK?!
I WANTED TO EAT YOUR FOOD TOO...

AFTERWORD

● Nonna and Katyusha

Although this duo didn't have too many appearances in the manga, I really enjoyed drawing them. Katyusha was rather difficult to draw, because it was hard to draw the right size of helmet for her. In comparison, Nonna was fairly easy and quite fun to draw. Both characters' personalities were pretty much set in the anime version, so I tried to stay true to that and retain their attractive qualities.

I hope you will enjoy them as much as I did.

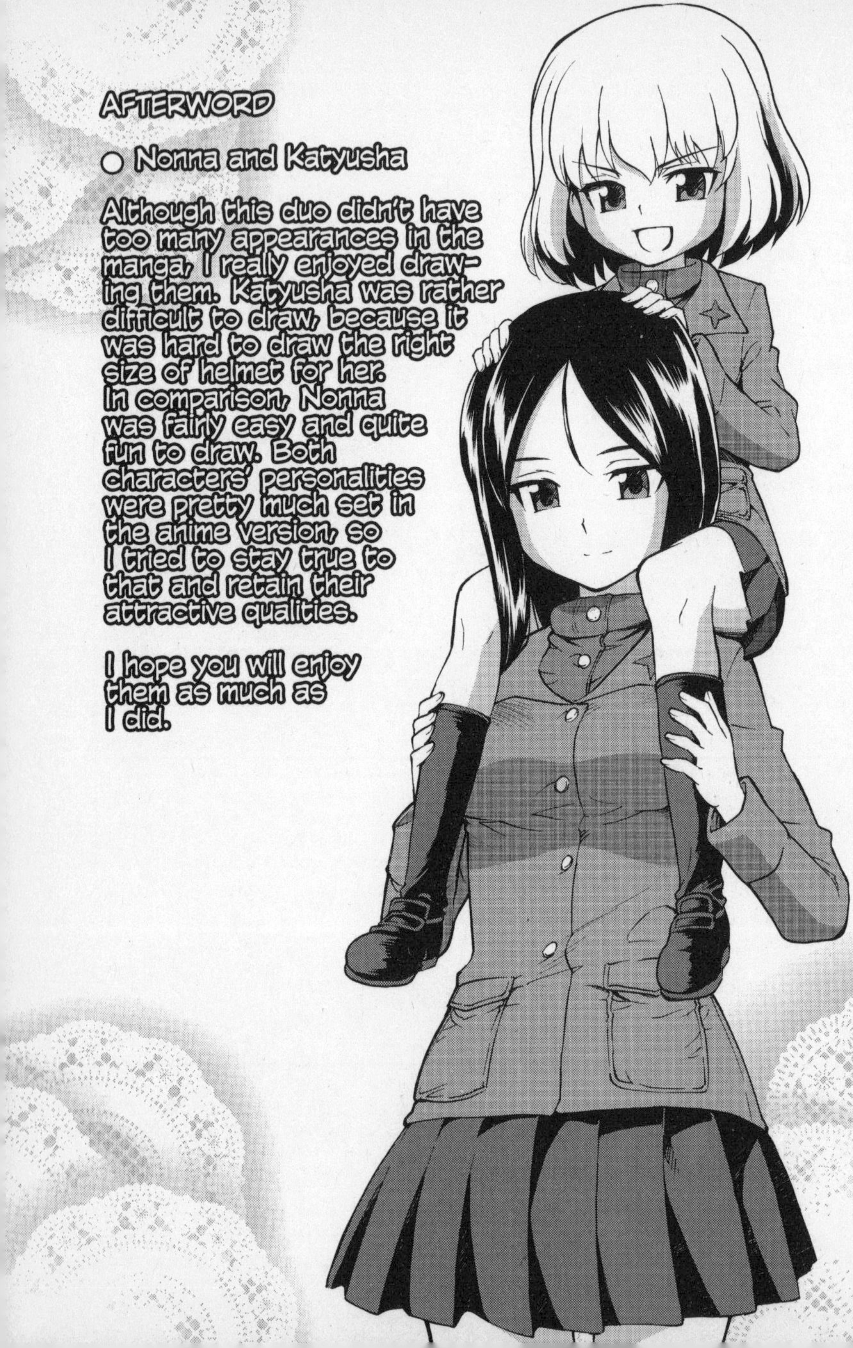

Introduced Tanks

1

T-34/76

An exceptional tank, developed by the Soviet Union, the T-34/76 was employed as a capable tank against the German Panzer III and Panzer IV tanks on the Eastern Front from the middle to the last stages of the war. With its thick, sloped armor, a diesel-powered engine that was less likely to catch fire when hit, and its powerful 76mm gun, the T-34/76 surprised the German armed forces so much that their encounter brought about what was later dubbed the "T-34 shock."

SPECIFICATIONS:

Nationality: Soviet Union
Manufacturer: No. 183 Kharkov Locomotive Factory, others.
Crew: Four
Engine: Model V-2-34 V12 water-cooled four-stroke diesel engine.
Weight: 30.9 tons
Length: 6.75 meters
Width: 3.00 meters
Height: 2.60 meters
Maximum speed: 55km/h road, 30km/h off-road
Maximum range: 300km road
Main armament: 76.2mm F-34 main gun (total ammunition 100 rounds)
Secondary armament: Two 7.62mm DT machineguns
Armor: 16~70mm
Total production: 35,467

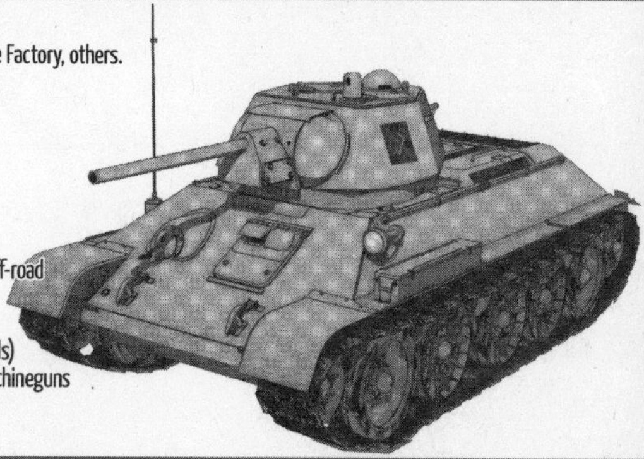

2

T-34/85

An enhanced variant of the T-34, where an enlarged turret equipped with a hard-hitting 85mm anti-air gun was coupled with the body of T-34. The larger space inside the new turret allowed three crew members to fit inside the fighting compartment, allowing the commander, gunner and loader enough space to focus on their respective duties. The wartime production of the T-34 tanks, including both the 76 and 85 variants, amounted to a total of 57,000. Postwar production continued in nations such as Poland and Czechoslovakia until 1958.

SPECIFICATIONS:

Nationality: Soviet Union
Manufacturer: No. 183 Ural Factory, others.
Crew: Five
Engine: Model V-2-34 water-cooled V12 four-stroke diesel engine.
Weight: 32 tons
Length: 8.10 meters
Width: 3.00 meters
Height: 2.72 meters
Maximum speed: 55km/h road, 30km/h off-road
Maximum range: 300km road
Main armament: 85mm ZiS-S-53 main gun (total ammunition 56 rounds)
Secondary armament: Two 7.62mm DT machineguns
Armor: 16~90mm
Total production: 25,899

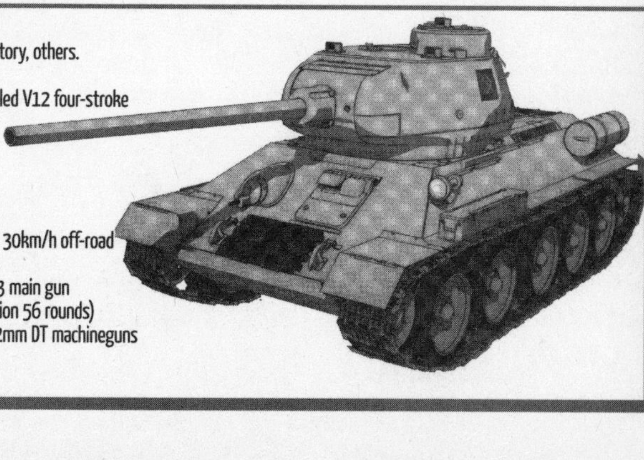

KV-2

A heavy tank developed by the Soviet Union during World War II. The KV-2 featured a large turret equipped with a huge 152mm main gun. This gun was, in fact, a howitzer, but it was so powerful that it could crack open the armor of enemy tanks. During the first stages of the war between Germany and the Soviet Union, a single KV-2 stood its ground in the fork of a road and frustrated all German attempts to continue their advance. This feat contributed to the KV-2 being called the "Road Monster." However, because its main gun was such a large caliber howitzer, the gun couldn't be reloaded quickly, as the projectile and propellant charges had to be inserted separately.

SPECIFICATIONS:

Nationality: Soviet Union
Manufacturer: No. 100 Kirov Factory
Crew: Six
Engine: Model V-2-K water-cooled V12 four-stroke diesel engine.
Weight: 52 tons
Length: 6.95 meters
Width: 3.32 meters
Height: 3.24 meters
Maximum speed: 34km/h road, 15km/h off-road
Maximum range: 250km road, 180km off-road
Main armament: 152mm M10 howitzer model 1938/40
　　　　　　　　(total ammunition 36 rounds)
Secondary armament: Three 7.62mm DT machineguns
Armor: 30~110mm
Total production: 202

IS-2

As the war on the Eastern Front continued, the Soviet Union's T-34 tank lacked power when faced against the newer Panther and Tiger I tanks being introduced by the Germans. Thus, Russian designers went about developing a new, more powerful heavy tank. The result was the IS series of tanks, and the IS-2 was notable for being equipped with a huge 122mm tank gun inside of a compact turret. Because the space inside the turret was cramped, the IS-2 could only be sent into the field with a limited number of rounds, but the 122mm gun was so powerful that not only could it penetrate the frontal armor of a German Tiger I tank with an armor-piercing round, but its high explosive rounds could also crack open a Tiger I's armor.

SPECIFICATIONS:

Nationality: Soviet Union
Manufacturer: No. 100 Kirov Factory, Chelyabinsk Tractor Plant, others.
Crew: Four
Engine: Model V-2-IS water-cooled V12 four-stroke diesel engine.
Weight: 46.08 tons
Length: 9.83 meters
Width: 3.07 meters
Height: 2.74 meters
Maximum speed: 37km/h road
Maximum range: 240km road
Main armament: 122mm D-25T tank gun
　　　　　　　　(total ammunition 28 rounds)
Secondary armament: One 12.7mm DShK heavy machinegun
　　　　　　　　Two 7.62mm DT machineguns
Armor: 20~120mm

GIRLS UND PANZER 3

Story: GIRLS und PANZER Projekt
Art: Ryohichi Saitaniya

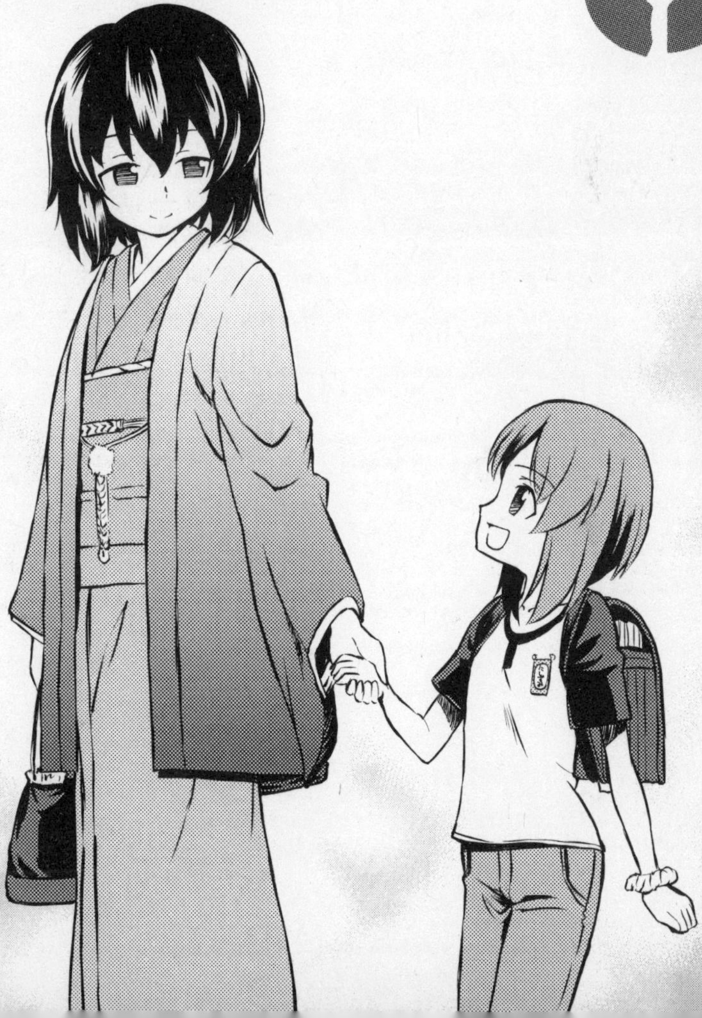

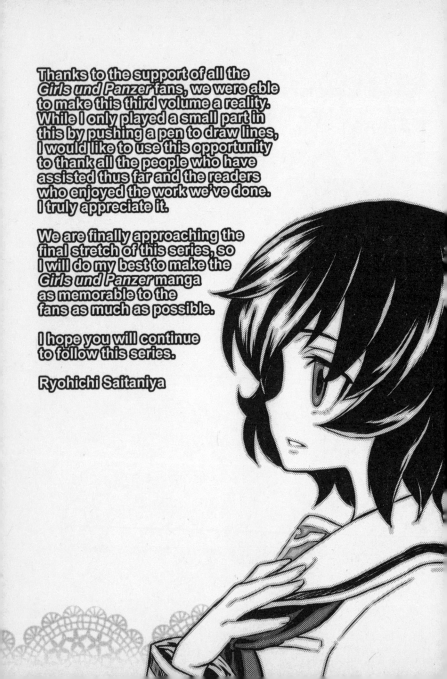

Thanks to the support of all the *Girls und Panzer* fans, we were able to make this third volume a reality. While I only played a small part in this by pushing a pen to draw lines, I would like to use this opportunity to thank all the people who have assisted thus far and the readers who enjoyed the work we've done. I truly appreciate it.

We are finally approaching the final stretch of this series, so I will do my best to make the *Girls und Panzer* manga as memorable to the fans as much as possible.

I hope you will continue to follow this series.

Ryohichi Saitaniya

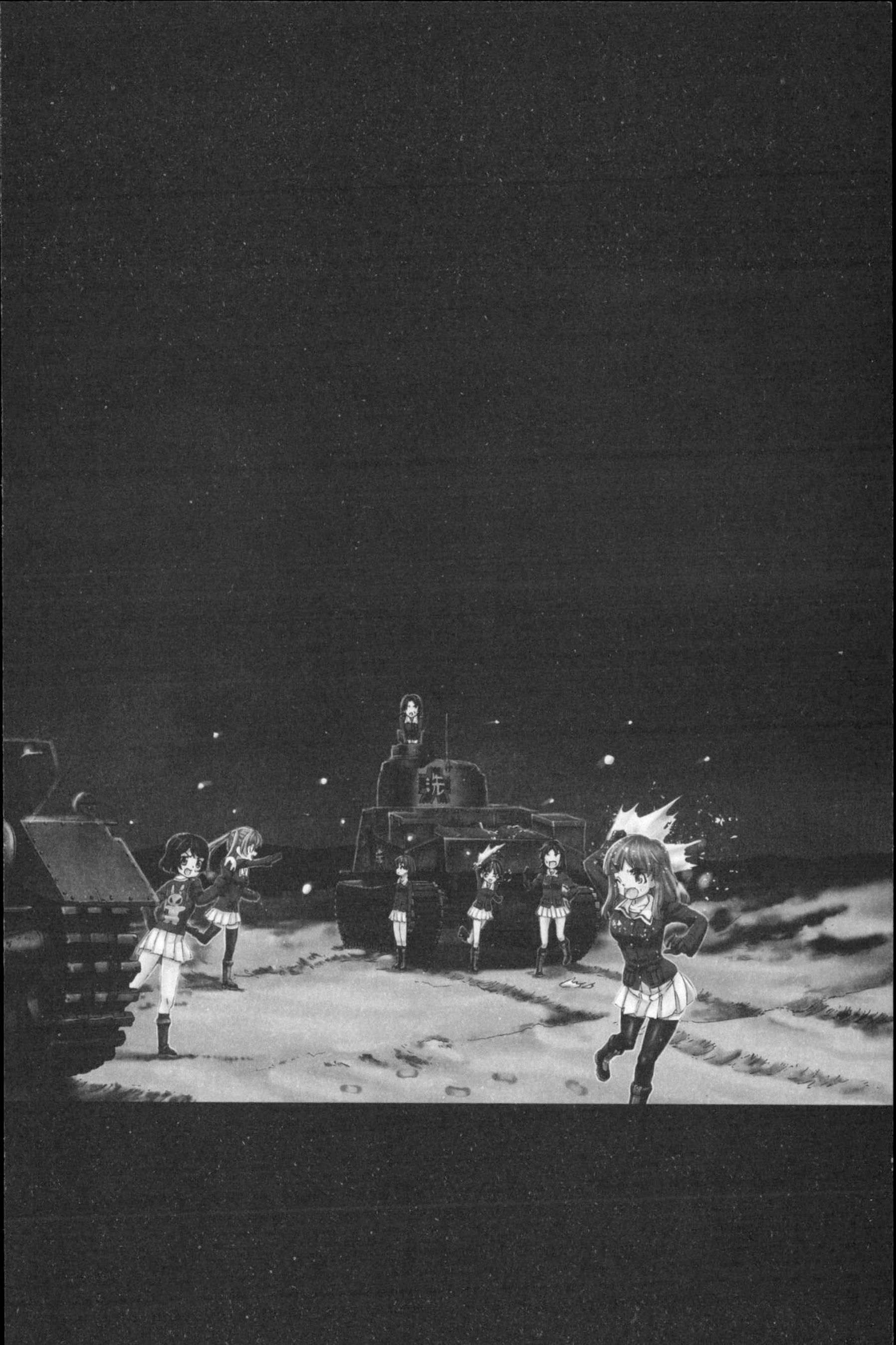

SEVEN SEAS ENTERTAINMENT PRESENTS

GIRLS & PANZER

story by GIRLS UND PANZER PROJEKT / art by RYOHICHI SAITANIYA   VOLUME 3

TRANSLATION
Anastasia Moreno

TECHNICAL CONSULTANT
Dan Kanemitsu

ADAPTATION
Janet Houck

LETTERING AND LAYOUT
Alexandra Gunawan

COVER DESIGN
Nicky Lim

PROOFREADER
Katherine Bell
Lee Otter

MANAGING EDITOR
Adam Arnold

PUBLISHER
Jason DeAngelis

GIRLS UND PANZER VOL. 3
© Ryohichi Saitaniya 2013, © GIRLS und PANZER Projekt 2013
Edited by MEDIA FACTORY.
First published in Japan in 2013 by KADOKAWA CORPORATION, Tokyo.
English translation rights reserved by Seven Seas Entertainment, LLC.
under the license from KADOKAWA CORPORATION, Tokyo.

Seven Seas books may be purchased in bulk for educational, business, or
promotional use. For information on bulk purchases, please contact Macmillan
Corporate & Premium Sales Department at 1-800-221-7945 (ext 5442)
or write specialmarkets@macmillan.com.

Seven Seas and the Seven Seas logo are trademarks of
Seven Seas Entertainment, LLC. All rights reserved.

ISBN: 978-1-626921-01-6

Printed in Canada

First Printing: January 2015

10 9 8 7 6 5 4 3 2 1

FOLLOW US ONLINE: *www.gomanga.com*

READING DIRECTIONS

This book reads from *right to left*, Japanese style.
If this is your first time reading manga, you start
reading from the top right panel on each page and
take it from there. If you get lost, just follow the
numbered diagram here. It may seem backwards at
first, but you'll get the hang of it! Have fun!!

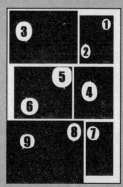

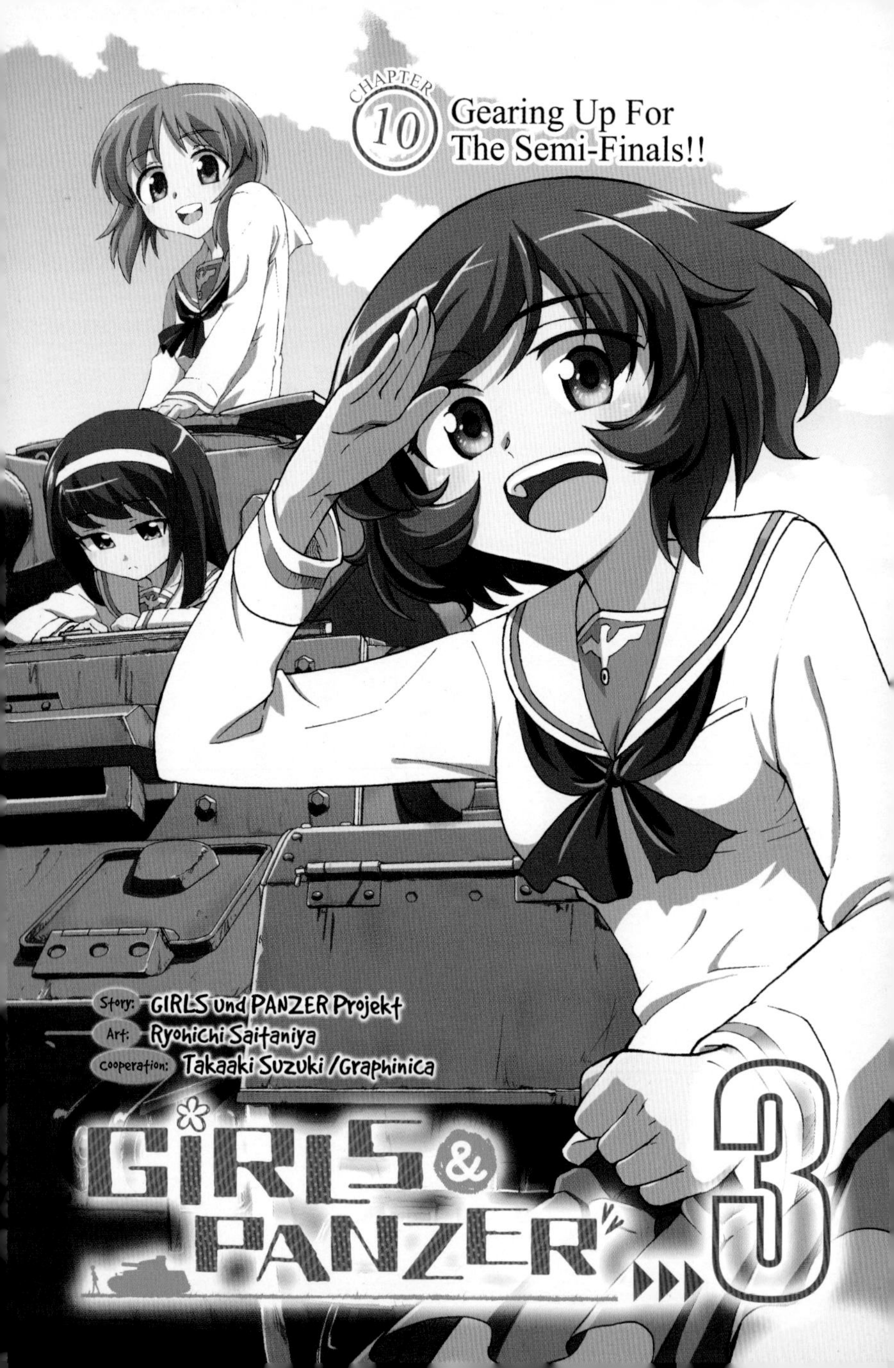
CHAPTER 10
Gearing Up For The Semi-Finals!!
Story: GIRLS und PANZER Projekt
Art: Ryohichi Saitaniya
cooperation: Takaaki Suzuki /Graphinica
GIRLS & PANZER 3

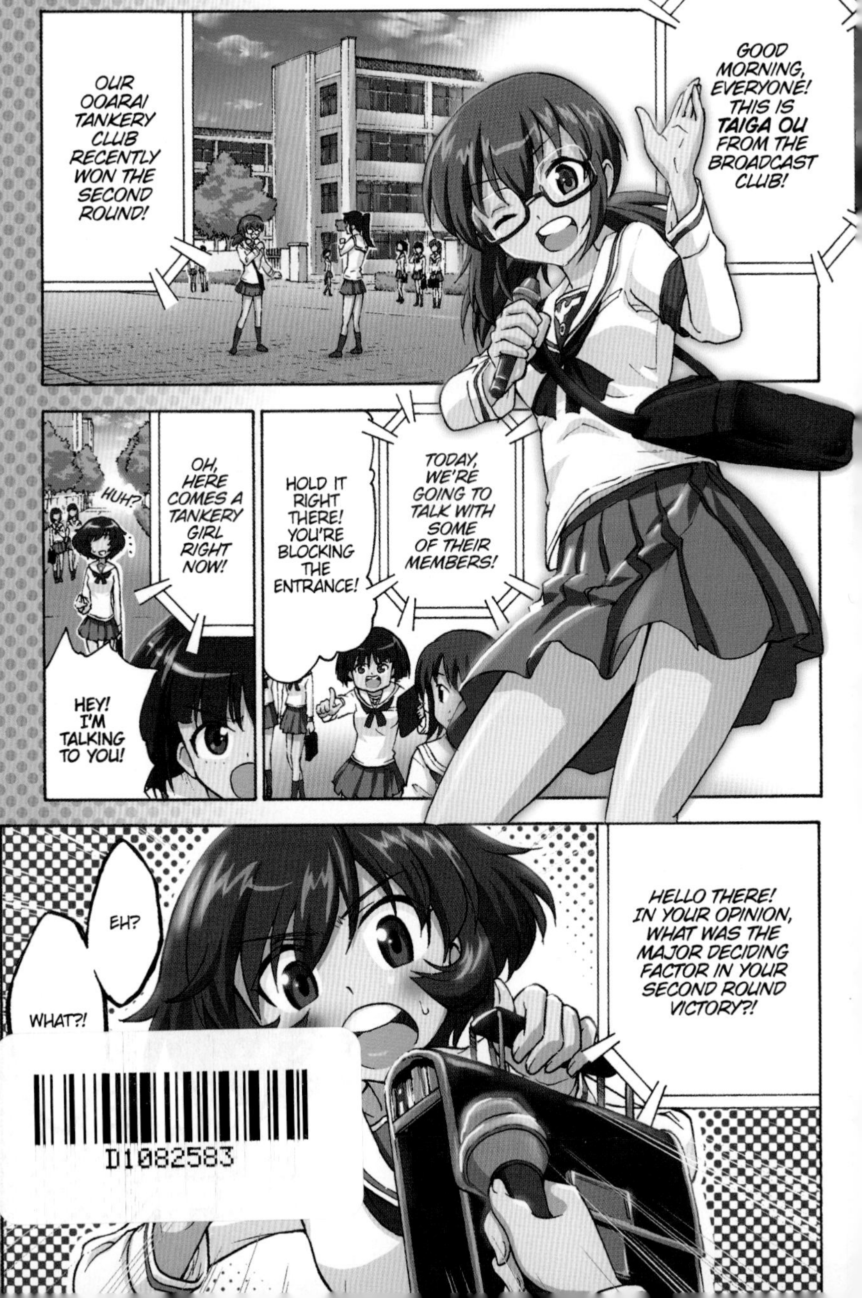
GOOD MORNING, EVERYONE! THIS IS TAIGA OU FROM THE BROADCAST CLUB!
TODAY, WE'RE GOING TO TALK WITH SOME OF THEIR MEMBERS!
OUR OOARAI TANKERY CLUB RECENTLY WON THE SECOND ROUND!
HOLD IT RIGHT THERE! YOU'RE BLOCKING THE ENTRANCE!
OH, HERE COMES A TANKERY GIRL RIGHT NOW!
HUH?
HEY! I'M TALKING TO YOU!
HELLO THERE! IN YOUR OPINION, WHAT WAS THE MAJOR DECIDING FACTOR IN YOUR SECOND ROUND VICTORY?!
EH?
WHAT?!